Sexual Deviance and the LAW

legal

regulation

of

human

sexuality

Scott R. Senjo, JD, Ph.D.

Kendall Hunt
publishing company

Kendall Hunt
publishing company

www.kendallhunt.com
Send all inquiries to:
4050 Westmark Drive
Dubuque, IA 52004-1840

Printed in the United States of America
10   9   8   7   6   5   4   3   2

Contents

Chapter Two

Illegal Consensual Sex: Fornication, Statutory Rape, Sodomy, Adultery, Seduction, Miscegeny 59

Chapter Three

Chapter Four

Sex Workers: Prostitution, Pimping, Strippers/Nudity, Sex Tourism 185

Chapter Five

The Law of Pornography: Possession, Distribution, and Production of Obscene and Child Porn

Chapter Six

Paraphilia and Legal Prohibitions: Necrophilia, Erotic Asphyxiation, Zoophilia, Sadomasochism

Chapter Seven

Digital Sex Crimes: Sexting, Cell Phone Porn, Computer Exhibitionism, Internet Enticement of Minors

Preface

The Criminal Justice System is serious when it comes to sex offending. Various forms of nudity, touching, pornography, and texting come under the scrutiny of the state for adherence to sexual propriety. When it comes to intimate contact with a partner, even greater regulation applies. Sex exchanged for a fee, done outdoors, with someone underage or under the influence, with nonconsenting adults, or done with violence can all be charged as criminal. Sentences are substantial and can come with a membership on the sex offender registry.

An explanation for the magnitude of importance applied to sex crime cases will have to be the subject of another book. For this book, because of the wide variety of laws and cases, it is necessary to draw together all categories of sex offenses into a single volume. *The Law of Sexual Deviancy: Legal Regulation of Human Sexuality* examines the array of legal prohibitions for nuisance sex crimes, crimes against morality and decency, "unspeakable" acts, offenses involving minors, violent sex offenses and Internet sex crimes. Historical analyses are used throughout to place the law into perspective when compared the social mores from earlier eras.

Intriguing and thought-provoking cases appear in each chapter to give the reader a chance to study a unique realm of sexual behaviors and gain an appreciation for the challenging task of the judicial branch when it comes to deciding controversial cases. The reader is left to speculate as to how a judge arrived at a particular decision when it comes to cases of inobvious touching, cyberprostitution, "obscene" imagery, mistake-of-age cases, or rulings on homosexual or miscegenous sex relations. By the end of the book, the reader will have a greater appreciation for the legal orientation to sexual deviancy and the role of the law in managing this group of offenses. Questions for Review and Key Terms appear at the end of each chapter.

The Law of Sexual Deviancy serves a variety of readerships. This title guides undergraduate students in understanding the historical pattern of government control of human sexuality in the United States. This book also challenges upper division and Masters students to understand the trends and conditions of human trafficking, paraphilias, police entrapment, and *res gestae* factors of criminal episodes. Ideal for law students, this book studies accessory liability, lesser included offenses, strict liability, and state and federal statutes. Lastly, this book is a desktop reference for police officers, prosecutors, judges, and other criminal justice system professionals as they work with lewdness, prostitution, child porn, and other persistent sex crimes cases.

Scott R. Senjo
ssenjo@weber.edu

About the Author

Scott R. Senjo, JD, Ph.D. is a former lawyer and presently a Professor of Criminal Justice in the Weber State University Department of Criminal Justice in Ogden, Utah. His research interests include deviant behavior, sex crimes, legal theory and research methods. He has worked and conducted research for 15 years in a sex offender treatment program, studying patterns of behavior and variables to criminal offending. Dr. Senjo is a widely published author and has published material in numerous journals, including the *Journal of Sexual Aggression, Sexual Addiction and Compulsivity, Sex Roles,* and *Journal of Human Sexuality.*

Chapter One

The Law of Sex in the Family:

Spousal Rape, Polygamy, Bigamy, Incest,

Domestic Partnerships

"The state has a legitimate interest in prohibiting incestuous relations and
in protecting the family unit and family relationships."

State v. Lowe
Ohio Court of Appeals
2005 Ohio 4274[1]

Legal Background

Regardless of the exact form it takes, the marital context is heavily regulated by the law and courts, including all sexual activity within the marriage. Marriage, sex, and familial status are pursued according to custom, tradition, and in modern times, individual autonomous choice, but are nevertheless bound by the edicts of the criminal law. Social norms in relation to the law of sex in the family today reflect historical patterns of sex and procreation. These deeply personal activities have been heavily influenced over time by many factors, in particular Christian religion and its historical embrace of patriarchy, heterosexuality, monogamy, and procreation.[2] In many cases, the Christian tradition in the United States and social desire for conformity are so deeply embedded in the social psyche, a married couple can go a lifetime without ever questioning why they got married, procreated, and raised a family. This chapter reflects the inobvious, yet undeniable role of the law when it comes to a variety of sexual expressions that take place within a family unit.

A breadth of a legal landscape shapes and supports the important traditions that are a part of marriage, sex, and family relations. Statutes and legislation promulgated by the fifty states and federal government outlaw various types of partnerships, living arrangements, or sexual

Figure 1   The law regulates numerous forms of sex inside and outside the family.

activities that do not comport with the deeply held convictions of traditional society, religion, and biological urges.

Legal provisions applied to the family are not all from an earlier era of morality. The law also takes an active role as it concerns contemporary morals and how one's sexuality may emerge from modern moral perspectives. Meaning, laws are designed from a historically conservative foundation and implement social, religious, and moral codes, but are also drafted to target activities that may be directly harmful to the parties involved, threaten the spread of STDs, or possibly cause an unwanted pregnancy. Today, the crimes selected for study in this chapter—spousal rape, polygamy, bigamy, incest, and same-sex marriage—all fall under the purview of the law and the courts and are regulated with a combination of traditional statutes and modern legal provisions.

Families and Sex in Historical Perspective.

The regulation of sex crimes in the family today reflects, to a degree, the regulation of familial structures in Ancient Egypt, Greece, and Rome.[3] These ancient legal regimes strongly influenced the familial make-up in Great Britain during the 300-year history of the British Empire (circa 1645–1945) and subsequently the American Colonies and United States. A look at sex in the family in ancient times provides a comparative example of how human sexual expression follows an ebb and flow of moral changes and is always more or less regulated by the criminal law.

In certain historical epochs, family-based behaviors not normally condoned in modern times were legitimized on the grounds of wealth, royalty, or superstition, but often only for a short time before being universally condemned on religious grounds. For example, incest was legal for royal families in ancient times because these families wanted to preserve their bloodlines.[4] The famous Egyptian Cleopatra VII was married to her younger brother, Ptolemy XIII. Her mother and father, Cleopatra V and Ptolemy XII, had also been brother and sister.

In Ancient Greece, gay military personnel were held in high esteem in their family and other social institutions. It was believed at the time that the power of male sexual relationships was a catalyst to bravery in the military and hence was condoned. A passage in Plato's Symposium reads:

> [H]e would prefer to die many deaths: while as for leaving the one he loves in a lurch, or not succoring him in peril, no man is such a craven that the influence of Love cannot inspire him with a courage that makes him equal to the bravest born.[5]

In Native Eskimo culture of Greenland and the Bering Sea, it was a matter of ritual to share one's wife sexually with an important visitor to the home. A man of wealth may participate in "ritual spouse exchange" with a shaman priest if he thought, for example, it would increase the chances for an abundant fall harvest. Wife sharing was also a custom in Ancient Greece around 500 BCE. Today, the law views "ritual wife exchange" as an adulterous practice. The crime of adultery is described more fully in chapter 2: Illegal Consensual Sex.

Orgiastic participation and nudity within or between families was thought to be a natural mechanism for the release of sexual energy in an older era. Aphrodite, Greek goddess of sex and love, was venerated as was Dionysus, god of wine and intoxication. Dionysian festivals in ancient Greece included festivals and parades with giant floats in the shape of a phallus (erect penis). Both gods were characteristic of the moral relativity and freedom of expression in Greece just before the time of Christ.[6] Toward the end of Greek preeminence and the fall of Rome, once the Roman Empire made Christianity it's official religion in 384 CE, the worship of Aphrodite and Dionysus was frowned on and made a criminal offense. We would almost certainly criminalize a Dionysian parade today if it included large floats in the shape of an erect penis. Such displays would violate a law pertaining to obscenity, indecency, or misdemeanor lewdness. In any event, as moral perspectives in Rome changed and sex was less acceptable, Rome and other European city-states found a great deal of harmony between the criminal law and Biblical scripture and used sexual acts such as incest and adultery to exemplify the soundness of this relationship. Very much today, the Bible is used as a guide for sexual relations generally, and sexual expression specifically within a family unit.

After the fall of the Roman Empire, much of Europe entered the Dark Ages where sexuality in the family would not change much.[7] What men and women were allowed to contemplate sexually was limited. A great deal of fear supported legal codes that permitted a narrow range of sex in the family. After the Dark Ages, Western culture developed throughout Europe, including during the Age of Enlightenment in Florence and Paris, and laws that came to prohibit certain family-based sex patterns, such as sodomy or incest, were grounded in religious precept and eventually adopted all over Europe, including the British Isles and England.[8]

It is important to consider the British perspective on sex in the family since the U.S. adopted the British model in 1776. In Britain, prior to the founding of the American Colonies, law and justice were carried out in roughly two systems. One was ecclesiastical (Roman Catholic Church–based) and the other was state-based, such as the kind we use today, i.e., police and court systems. Both systems supported each other and were compatible in implementing morality, rules, and civil order throughout the land. The Church would cover crimes such as adultery and the state would cover crimes such as theft. The Church-based legal system, naturally, was highly protective of marriage, children, procreation, and other inherently fundamental practices pertaining to domestication and family life. It has long been a primary duty of religious organizations to guide families when it comes to sexuality, procreation, and child rearing.[9]

The Church influenced the British Parliament and both the Church and Parliament shaped a legal culture that had roughly the same set of objectives: to protect the health, safety, and welfare of the greater society and to promote the values of family and procreation within a traditional, Christian-based family model. The Church and the State laid down many rules, for example, man and wife should never occupy any other sexual position other than the mission-ary position because it was thought that this position had the greatest chance of producing a male offspring. At the time, a woman who had sexual relations with a brother or father was not considered as evil as a woman who engaged in a nonsanctioned sex position.[10]

Understandable for the times, both the British ecclesiastical and state-based systems of criminal law enforcement were brutal when it came to adultery, sodomy, fornication, prostitu-tion, or other behavior that appeared to threaten the traditional notion of family or deviated from the norms of civil society. This is the legacy of the thirteen Colonies and also, to a lesser degree, of the United States' political, religious, and sexual mores today.

The European Renaissance started in the 1400s and was an emergence from the Dark Ages and feudalism into a period of human enlightenment. We might have expected more from the European Renaissance when it came to human sexuality, but the grip of religious control would not allow for it. The Renaissance in Europe between 1400 and 1700, which began in Florence, Italy, was a comeback in culture from the Dark Ages and represented a renewed interest in various art forms. In the Renaissance, the human body was once again celebrated (rather than shamed) and many artists took to creating beautiful art forms depicting the sensuousness of the body. The Renaissance exposed more of the human body to the masses than had been seen since Ancient Greece and Aphrodite and Dionysus. The Renaissance, however, never colluded with the sexual perspectives of Aphrodite or Dionysus. The celebration of the body in this unique era was mostly limited to the relationship between the body and God. Meaning, the body was depicted as a manifestation of the beauty and likeness of God, not the beauty of sexuality.[11] God was associated with the loveliness of the body, irrespective of the sexual function of the body. Sex was still considered evil.

Touching or passionately caressing one's husband or wife was not depicted in Renaissance art even though the artwork may certainly have compelled the desire to do so. Such thoughts were still considered unseemly for proper social morality. Sexuality has always been frighten-ing to social groups and it was equally so in Florence, even during a period of cultural rebirth such as with the Renaissance. Where the Renaissance did explore sex, it did so in the negative. For example, in the period of enthusiasm to become closer to God, many Renaissance think-ers pointed to sexual abstinence as a preferred and morally enlightened lifestyle. This way, distractions of emotions and unforeseeable romantic entanglements could give way to a more spiritual, enlightened manner of living where one could pray and know God more completely.

The Renaissance affected England the same way it did the European Continent and that is important, since England strongly influenced the United States. In England during the Renaissance, human sexuality was a subject to be dealt with expediently and without feeling. As the legislative body throughout the United Kingdom, Parliament reinforced long-standing premises of ancient European culture, ideology, and religion by supporting several powerful social and sexual mores: (1) sex is only allowed in a family; (2) a family consists of a marriage between one man and one woman; (3) husband and wife should not engage in sex frivolously or for recreation, and must use only the missionary position; and (4) sex by husband and wife is morally superior to all other forms of sex, thus other forms of sex should be shamed, criminalized, or somehow discouraged by the social order.[12] King Henry VIII passed the Buggery Act in 1533 that made sodomy a capital crime and he outlawed brothels in 1546. But these laws, as a general matter, would have an unceasing ebb and flow depending on the political current of the time.

The Roman Catholic Church in Britain embraced Renaissance ideals of artistic expression but nevertheless maintained tight control over many aspects of British social life, including sex-related matters. The hegemony of the Church, however, was too much for some English citizens and catalyzed certain forms of social protest. One protest and reform movement was the English Reformation, a period of social and political change in England during the early 1500s.

The English Reformation is credited with the establishment of Protestantism and the subsequent Puritan Movement. The Reformation was a social, political, and religious movement to create change with the hegemony of the Roman Catholic Church in Europe and Britain. During the English Reformation, King Henry VIII established the Church of England in 1534 and broke away from the Catholic Church.[13] Even though the new Church of England signified greater freedom for Great Britain, it was not good enough. Yet another reform movement called the Puritans developed in response to the Church of England. The Puritans separated from the Church of England because they felt England was still too allied with the Catholic Pope. The Puritans were so distraught, they sought refuge in the New World (North America) where they contributed, among other settlers, to the establishment of the thirteen British Colonies in America.[14]

The Puritans of the thirteen Colonies were exactly as their name implied: adherents of clean and "pure" living. This meant practicing a highly controlled and limited form of sexual expression. The Puritans did not trust sexual feelings and allowed sex for only limited reasons such as procreation between husband and wife.[15] For them, most other forms of sex were to be punished severely. Homosexuality, incest, bestiality, and sodomy all received the sentence of death in Colonial America; this was no place to experiment sexually. In fact, if experimentation were to occur, the Puritans would highly recommend celibacy and abstinence. In the U.S. today, some public schools across the country teach abstinence-only sex education and inculcate in students that they can only engage in sex after marriage. Hence, the influence of the Puritans is seen today in the United States.

Once away from Mother England and established along the eastern seaboard in North America, Puritan colonial life did not have a great need for specific legal regulation of sex because of the primitive social conditions. The colonial settlers left London and the commerce of European city-states and entered an unfamiliar and threatening wilderness in the New World.

The primary mode of security was inherent in the colonial village itself and the watchful eye of one's neighbor for external threats, especially from Native Indians. The watchful eye of the village, however, was not relegated to security and external threats but was also applied to sexual behavior. Social pressure to conform to basic standards of sexuality were as effective if not more effective than specific criminal laws.

Combined with social disapproval, the colonists also had the law to govern the sexual behavior of the colonies. At the founding of the United States in 1776, the early colonial pioneers adopted the law of the Puritans and the common law of England and copied it for use throughout the colonies and eventually the American states.[16] Through the time of the Founding Fathers and the Declaration of Independence, social and political reform did not center on sex in the family or at all on sex law reform. Early Americans found no problem with the adoption of the sexual and familial standards so durably developed over a thousand years in Europe.

Throughout much of U.S. history, European and British perspectives on sex in the family have strongly influenced the milieu of American family life.[17] The same principles from the European Renaissance, though developed long ago, still applied. Sexuality was limited to family life, and within the family, sexual expression was thoroughly regulated. It would be a long time before sex in the family or elsewhere was legitimized as a value in and of itself, independent of procreation. It would be even longer before law and morality would countenance the idea that two persons of the same gender could love each other.

While conservatism certainly marked the first 175 years of the U.S., since World War II, Elvis Presley, the Beatles, and the Civil Rights Movement, a surprising number of changes have occurred in the legal status of sex in the family in the U.S. and they are addressed in this chapter. The legalities surrounding the purchase and use of contraceptives, mixed race marriage and miscegeny, spousal rape and spousal sexual assault, and sodomy represent some of the most fundamental changes in consensual sexual relations in the family and the law of human sexuality for a very long time—well before the founding of the United States. While still controversial, the legal changes in the thirty-eight-year period between the Griswald decision in 1965[18] and the Lawrence decision in 2003[19] have distinctly tended to move human sexuality and family relations away from abstract theological restrictions and toward discretionary and reasonable individual autonomous choice. In many ways, the changes have been profound.

That said, legal changes do not always compel social changes. Today, as a general matter, sexual deviance in the family setting is consistently looked on with social disapprobation, even though the reason for the disapproval has changed from one era to the next. Today, the law entertains more, but certainly not all varieties of sex within the family, and consistently enforces and reinforces a relatively strict code of behavior.

Spousal Rape

T he history of the balance of power between a man and woman in a marital partnership is replete with instances of the male as the dominant party. Traditionally in a marriage, the woman was considered distinctly inferior to the man. The subordinate status of the female was usually conceptualized as the woman being the property of the man—chattel.[20] Hence, under such conditions, the man was free to do with her as he desired and she had no recourse in law. This arrangement often resulted in **spousal rape**.

In many cases, the female in a marriage was little more than a domestic servant and/or sex slave. The law supported these arrangements and considered a woman to be a piece of property of the man she married. Today one may ask why any woman would voluntarily subject herself to such a threatening arrangement. Such a query is important, but reflects how far we've come toward equalizing the balance of power between a man and a woman in a legal marriage. What we perceive as fundamentally wrong today was not so bad given the context of the times earlier in the history of the U.S. As an example, in the 1700s and 1800s, many women were directed by parents, peers, and local authorities (either governmental or religious) that their inherent value and worth depended on being married to a man. In addition, many women married because the prospects for surviving on one's own, without a husband, were bleak at the time.[21] Also, of course, many women married because of the desire to do so and for the love of their spouse and hope for having children. Many reasons explain why women entered into marital arrangements at a time when the criminal and civil law provided no support to them.

The U.S. adopted the Common Law of England and the Common Law supported sexism, patriarchy, and gender inequality within the legal framework of a marriage. This was illustrated clearly in the infamous Sir Matthew Hale's 1736 legal treatise *Historia Placitorum Coronae, History of the Pleas of the Crown.* In it, Hale wrote, "the wife hath given up herself in this kind unto her husband, which she cannot retract."[22]

The Common Law allowed for the lawful rape of one's spouse. The very concept of marital rape was treated as a legal impossibility. The legitimization of the Common Law rested on three justifications. First, the woman was chattel, and the property of the husband. Second, that women have no legal identity and cannot look for recourse in a court of law, and third, that upon marriage, a female is duty bound to have sexual intercourse with her husband.[23] The duty implies automatic consent and thus negates a central element to rape, which is a lack of consent.

With the Common Law as a foundation for American jurisprudence, it is not hard to imagine that many husband-and-wife arrangements in the early history of the United States resulted in the man demanding that the woman give him sex lest she be punished in some way. If she refused his advances, he could rape her and it was legal. In the 1857 case of *Commonwealth v. Fogerty,* two men were found guilty of raping a woman.[24] The Supreme Court of Massachusetts, in dictum, mentioned that the defendants were guilty, but if the victim were the wife of one of the men, it would be a different story. The court averred:

> Nor was it necessary to allege that the prosectrix was not the wife of the defendant. Such an averment has never been deemed essential in indictments for rape, either in this county or in England. The precedents contain no such allegation. A husband may be guilty at common law as principal in the second degree of a rape on his wife by assisting another man to commit a rape upon her; Lord Audley's case, 3 Howell's State Trials, 401; and under our statutes he would be liable to be punished in the same manner as the principal felon. Rev. Sts. c. 133, § 1. An indictment charging him as principal would therefore be valid. *Of course, it would always be competent for a party indicted to show, in defense of a charge of rape alleged to be actually committed by himself, that the woman on whom it was charged to have been committed was his wife.*[25] (italics added)

Tremendous change has taken place with the law of rape, including marital rape. For example, in 1991 England overturned Sir Matthew Hale's maxim in the case of R v. R.[26] While rejecting the accused's defense that the marriage contract was a legal imprimatur to sexually assault his wife, a legal summary of the case reads,

> the fiction of implied consent has no useful purpose to serve today in the law of rape and the marital rights exemption is a common law fiction which had never been a true rule of English law. R's appeal is accordingly dismissed and he is convicted of the rape of his wife.[27]

England joins many other nations today and the United Nations Assembly in outlawing marital rape and such a violation is today a Human Rights issue around the world. In 2006, the UN Secretary General found that marital rape may be prosecuted in at least 104 nations. Of these, 32 have made marital rape a specific criminal offence, while the remaining 74 do not exempt marital rape from general rape provisions. Four nations criminalize marital rape only when the spouses are judicially separated.

In the United States, the statistics on marital rape draw the attention of legal reformers. In all instances of rape, marital rape is the most frequently occurring type. Rape in a marriage is considered the most common yet most neglected area of sexual violence perpetrated. The forms of sexual violence are many and include coerced sexual contact, sexual harassment or sexual degradation of the victim in front of others, and forced penetration. Finkelhor estimated that 10 to 14 percent of all married American women have been or will be raped by their husbands.[28] Other studies seem to arrive easily at the empirical conclusion that the most common perpetrator of a rape is a husband, ex-husband, or partner.[29] In 2005, the Bureau of Justice Statistics reported that 17 percent of all rapes are committed by intimate partners.[30] Anecdotal data suggest that one woman is highly likely to have been subject to marital rape violence on more than a single occasion. Age should also be kept in mind and 16–24-year-old women appear most likely to be subject to intimate violence by a partner.[31]

The United States prohibits marital rape in all fifty states today. The first state to outlaw marital rape was South Dakota in 1975 and the last state to outlaw it was North Carolina in 1993. After 1993, a married woman was no longer considered the legal property of her husband in the U.S.

Definition of the Offense

Spousal rape or marital rape is nonconsensual sex in which the perpetrator is the victim's spouse.[32]

Elements of the Offense

The elements of the crime of spousal rape that must be proved beyond a reasonable doubt are:

1. sexual intercourse with a person who is the spouse of the perpetrator,
2. through force, the threat of force, or through guile,
3. without the lawful consent of the victim.[33]

Sample Statute

The state of Wyoming spousal rape statute reads as follows:

Wyo. Stat. § 6-2-307. Evidence of marriage as defense.

(a) The fact that the actor and the victim are married to each other is not by itself a defense to a violation of [rape statutes] W.S. 6-2-302(a)(i), (ii) or (iii) or 6-2-303(a) (i), (ii), (iii), (vi) or (vii).[34]

Arguments Made By The Prosecution

Any type of rape case is difficult to prosecute, especially a rape case where the parties are married. Marriage implies sexual contact and it is nearly guaranteed that the married parties had sex in the past that was not objected to by either party and possibly enjoyed. Hence, the state has to show that there was a situation where force was involved and that it was a different situation from the past where force was not involved.

Arguments Made By The Defense

The advantage is to the defense when it comes to rape cases. There is almost always an absence of witnesses, tape recordings, or video recordings. It is a "he said, she said" scenario and comes down to one person's word against the others. The defense is assisted even further if drugs or alcohol were somehow part of the crime context because this will suggest a degree of recklessness, lowered inhibitions, and possibly a case where the playing around merely got out of hand.

Variations of the Law of Spousal Rape

A. Equal Protection

In *Liberta v. Kelly,* the defendant Mario Liberta historically had engaged in violent behavior with his wife, Denise.[35] As a result of a pattern of domestic violence, the parties were legally separated and Liberta had restricted custody rights to their children. While exercising his custody rights one afternoon, the defendant visited with his young son and wife by having them over to the motel room where he was living. At the motel room, the defendant engaged in violent behavior, raped, and sodomized his wife in front of their young son.

The police were notified, Liberta was taken into custody and charged with rape and sodomy pursuant to the rape statute in the state of New York.[36] Section 130.35 of the New York Penal Law provides in relevant part that "[a] male is guilty of rape in the first degree when he engages in sexual intercourse with a female by forcible compulsion".[37] "Female," for purposes of the rape statute, was defined as "any female person who is not married to the actor."[38] Since the victim was married to the actor, Liberta appealed and sought to be exculpated from guilt. He essentially admitted to perpetrating the violence, but sought to use the law to "get off on a technicality."

In the court documents, Liberta made two arguments. First, he argued that the law of the state of New York contained a marital exemption whereby a man could have forcible sex with his spouse with impunity.[39] A marital exemption means that the rape of a spouse is a legal impossibility. Second, Liberta argued that the law he was convicted under is invalid and a violation of equal protection[40] since it does not apply equally to both men and women.

As for his first argument, Liberta was correct. The State of New York indeed had in Section 130.35 a marital exemption for rape. But Liberta's attempt to use it as a means to commit violence drew attention to the abhorrence of the existence of the law. The appeals court judge seemed so repulsed by Liberta's behavior, in a feat of rare judicial policymaking, the judge rescinded the marital exemption law with the stroke of a pen. The judge stated:

> We find that there is no rational basis for distinguishing between marital rape and non-marital rape. The various rationales which have been asserted in defense of the exemption are either based upon archaic notions about the consent and property rights incident to marriage or are simply unable to withstand even the slightest scrutiny. We therefore declare the marital exemption for rape in the New York statute to be unconstitutional.

Lord Hale's notion of an irrevocable implied consent by a married woman to sexual intercourse has been cited most frequently in support of the marital exemption. Any argument based on a supposed consent, however, is untenable. Rape is not simply a sexual act to which one party does not consent. Rather, it is a degrading, violent act which violates the bodily integrity of the victim and frequently causes severe, long-lasting physical and psychic harm. To ever imply consent to such an act is irrational and absurd. Other than in the context of rape statutes, marriage has never been viewed as giving a husband the right to coerced intercourse on demand. Certainly, then, a marriage license should not be viewed as a license for a husband to forcibly rape his wife with impunity. A married woman has the same right to control her own body as does an unmarried woman.[41]

As it concerns the gender-specific nature of the rape law in New York, the reviewing court rejected this argument as well, stating that the legislature could have constitutionally drawn the line that limited criminal liability to only males who commit [spousal] rapes.[42] The appellate court also noted that the equal protection clause of the Fourteenth Amendment does not demand that a statute necessarily apply equally to all persons or require things which are different in fact to be treated in law as though they were the same.[43]

B. Common Law

Days before their official divorce, the defendant Laverne "Sonny" Shunn showed-up at his soon-to-be ex-wife's home despite a mutual restraining order prohibited contact between Shunn and his wife. On March 8, 1986, Mrs. Shunn was confronted in her bedroom by Shunn where he began striking her with a wooden baton, drawing blood. After striking her with the baton, he sexually assaulted her with it. After that, he had sexual intercourse with her. After the violent episode, she called the police.

Shunn was charged and later found guilty of both sexual assault and aggravated assault. At trial, the district court sentenced Shunn to a five- to seven-year term of imprisonment for the sexual assault charge and a six- to eight-year term on the aggravated assault charge, which was suspended and reduced to probation on eventually serving the sexual assault term.[44]

On appeal, Shunn argued that the Common Law originally adopted in the state of Wyoming takes precedence and should be the applicable law in the case. Shunn argued for the application of the Common Law because the Common Law, an older code, allowed for a man to rape his wife. The appellate court disagreed and affirmed the conviction of the trial court. The reviewing court stated that the Common Law may have applied in the state of Wyoming at a time earlier in the state's history, but since then, the state had passed various laws and one of them was the law that removed the marital exemption to rape in the state's modern rape statute.[45] The ruling stated in summary:

> The adoption of Common Law by Wyoming was not an adoption of a set code of law. Nor was the adoption one of status or non changing law. To allow a spousal exception to rape would be inconsistent with the history of legislation in this state. When the legislature enacted Section 6-2-307 and repealed the statutory spousal exception allowed by the 1977 Statutes, it removed the Common Law spousal exception to rape in Wyoming.[46]

Statutory and societal changes have significantly affected the appropriateness of a marital rape exception. Today, Hale's theory is both unrealistic and unreasonable. We agree with the court's analysis in the case of People v. Liberta, 64 N.Y.2d 152, 485 N.Y.S.2d 207, 474 N.E.2d 567 (1984), that no rational basis exists for distinguishing between marital and nonmarital rape. The degree of violence is no less when the victim of a rape is the spouse of the actor. We therefore see no justification to reinstate the Common Law marital exception to sexual assault.[47]

C. Separated, But not Divorced

The rape of a stranger is an obvious violent felony offense. Additionally, contemporary law has done away with the marital exemption to rape. It logically follows that the rape of one's spouse cannot be defended due to a marital separation. In fact, the rape of one's spouse during a legal separation seems to enhance the severity of the offense, making it more akin to the depraved crime of a rape of a stranger.

In *State v. Smith*, the accused and his wife lived in different cities and had been legally separated for approximately one year, and married for seven years. One morning, Mr. Smith broke into his wife's apartment at 2:30 a.m., beat her, and forced her to have sex with him. Smith was charged with "atrocious assault and battery, private lewdness, impairing the morals of a minor, and rape."[48] Since the enactment in New Jersey of a new rape law, no person can claim that a sexual assault committed after September 1, 1979, is exempt from prosecution because the accused and victim were husband and wife. The Criminal Code in New Jersey expressly excludes marriage to the victim as a defense against a prosecution of sexual crimes.[49]

In court, Mr. Smith tried to argue that the legal separation meant that he and his wife were still legally married, which they were, and therefore, he was entitled to make sexual advances on his wife. The court cited legal precedent in the state and noted a ruling in a case titled Ellam v. Ellam:

Since the advent of the no-fault ground for divorce, any spouse may make a unilateral decision to end the marriage. By separating from her husband and living apart for 18 months, a wife is entitled to a divorce without further proof of proper grounds. The corollary of this right is that a wife can refuse sexual intercourse with her husband during the period of separation. If a wife has a right to refuse intercourse, or deny consent, then a husband's forceful carnal knowledge of his wife clearly includes all three essential elements of the crime of rape. He cannot defend by asserting that there was no lack of consent because he was still legally married to the victim.[50]

With this precedent, and the admittedly weak argument made by Mr. Smith, the court concluded,

The narrower question here is whether such a marital exemption, even if it existed, would have applied inflexibly for as long as a marriage continued to exist in the legal sense. We think not.[51]

If a wife had a right to live separately from her husband, it follows that she also had a right to refuse sexual intercourse with him at least while they were separated.[52]

Additional Court Cases: Spousal Rape

U.S. v. Streete

AFCCA 36757, US Air Force (2009)

CASE SUMMARY

PROCEDURAL POSTURE: Appellant technical sergeant appealed his conviction and sentence after being found guilty on two charges and two specifications of rape, one charge and specification of failure to obey a lawful order, and one charge and specification of failure to go, in violation of Unif. Code Mil. Justice, arts. 120, 92, 86, 10 U.S.C.S. §§ 920, 892, 886.

OVERVIEW: There was no impermissible spillover from trying the two rape charges together. The evidence was distinct and clearly defined and was compartmentalized. Any confusion was caused by appellant that resulted in additional questions in attempting to clarify his evasive testimony. Each rape charge was independently supported by overwhelming evidence. Nor was counsel ineffective for failing to move for severance, since if severance had been granted, they would likely have had to defend against two rape cases, where evidence of one could potentially have been used in the other case. Two separate trials would have given the government two bites at the apple and would have subjected appellant to double the potential sentence. The sentence was appropriately significant, given that appellant raped his wife, then six years later raped his fiancée, violating the trust expected in a marital or "engaged" relationship. He continued with his rapes despite both women protesting and telling him "no" more than once. He was a 20-year noncommissioned officer who not only committed two egregious rapes, he violated a direct no-contact order and failed to go to his commander's office twice.

OUTCOME: The convictions and sentence were affirmed.[53]

Polygamy

Early in American history, the federal government began expansion westward from the Mississippi River in hopes of settling areas of the Midwest plains and eventually the rugged lands out west. Manifest Destiny, an ideological and philosophical position that suggested a moral rightness in the assertive settlement of western lands, led settlers and homesteaders to venture into uncharted territory out west, conflict with Native Peoples, and establish their family-based value system in the western territories of North America.[54] Manifest Destiny settlers supported the federal government and fully embraced the traditional model of one husband and one wife.

Once out west and into the vast Utah Territories, the pioneers encountered Mormon Polygamist settlers.[55] These particular religious settlers practiced **polygamy** as a part of their religious belief system. Polygamy, among other things, was a practice of having plural wives. The practice of multiple wives—where no legal marriage certification is present—was different from what was normally practiced as it concerned marriage in the former colonies and the newly founded United States. In short, polygamous marriage was an affront to prevailing beliefs about what is decent, proper, and "normal" when it comes to familial status and sexual relations, at least those adopted in the U.S. from Britain and Europe in the 17th century.[56]

The notion of multiple wives and the grooming of teenage females to become polygamous brides and teenage boys to become head of a polygamous household was never a part of mainstream European culture, nor a part of the social life of British and Puritan settlers to the New World. Hence, polygamy did not square with the ideology of Manifest Destiny. As a result, as the federal government began expansion westward, it strongly objected to the practice of polygamy engaged in the Utah Territories.[57]

Polygamy is practiced today by Utah Mormons in Colorado City on the border between Utah and Arizona. Local entrepreneurs offer guided tours of the desolate but unique area.

A serious riff was in the making. The Mormon settlers had equally as strong objections to the thought of giving up their practice. Polygamy was a message from God and such orders were not to be taken lightly. The Mormon Church taught its followers that God required a polygamist lifestyle. The Church doctrine stressed that extraordinary eternal rewards for women can only be met through polygamous marriage and bearing children and also stressed that equally extraordinary eternal punishments await those women who refuse to enter into polygamous marriages. This direct conflict between the federal government and Utah Territory Mormons was a serious conflict. The federal government felt a need to take action to enforce the legal and moral code of the newly formed nation and it was one different from Utah polygamists.[58] In one of the first battles within the arena of sex law politics in the United States, the adherents of polygamy could not muster the arguments to convince the federal government of its legitimacy. The federal government took action and dictated to Mormon leaders that if they did not cease the sex crime of polygamy, the government would resettle the Mormons in the same manner that the government had resettled the Native Indians. The Polygamists "surrendered." According to Strassberg:

> In 1887, Congress abrogated the charter of the Church of Jesus Christ of Latter Day Saints, dissolved its corporate status, and confiscated most of its property. The [Mormon] Church renounced the practice of polygyny in 1890[59] and Utah was admitted into the Union in 1894.[60]

Polygamist's religious conviction tends to supercede adherence to secular laws and Mormon polygamy continues to be a small-scale religious practice in the United States and Canada today despite its illegality. Many people, however, believe polygamy should be off-limits to the criminal law.[61] If two men can have sex, why can't other "alternative" families engage in consensual sex? Although there is an absence of public interest in enforcing criminal polygamy statutes today, polygamists constantly face the threat of criminal prosecution.

Just as in 1887, a controversy swirls around the practice of polygamy. Some of the legal implications include welfare fraud, internecine domestic disputes, and neglected children. More serious, the practice of polygamy is also implicated in the felony offenses of statutory rape, incest, unlawful sexual conduct with a minor, child abuse, and cohabitant abuse. Polygamous heads of households are often older men who take teenage "brides" in a noncontractual spiritual marriage. These girls are often so young, they are not legally permitted to marry, let alone engage in consensual sexual relations.[62] The taking of young brides in this manner raises other legal issues pertaining to duress, seduction, consent, and legal marriage. In sum, plenty of legal bases exist to confront the practice of polygamy.[63]

Polygamy is still legal in the Islamic world, but illegal in all fifty states in the U.S. When polygamy involves one man and multiple wives, it is termed polygyny, and where the practice involves one woman and several husbands, it is called polyandry.

Definition of the Offense

Model Penal Code § 230.1 states that a person is guilty of a third-degree felony if he or she "marries or cohabits with more than one spouse at a time in purported exercise of the right of plural marriage."[64]

Elements of the Offense

The elements of the crime of polygamy that must be proven beyond a reasonable doubt are:

1. knowingly already having a husband or wife,
2. he or she intends to marry or marries another person.[65]

Sample Statute

Canadian Criminal Code § 293(1):

> Everyone who practices or enters into or in any manner agrees or consents to practice or enter into any form of polygamy, or any kind of conjugal union with more than one person at the same time, whether or not it is by law recognized as a binding form of marriage, or celebrates, assists or is a party to a rite, ceremony, contract or consent that purports to sanction (such) a relationship … is guilty of an indictable offence and liable to imprisonment for a term not exceeding five years.[66]

Arguments Made By The Prosecution

Historically in the United States, the state has asserted a public interest in the preservation of the "one man, one woman" model of familial relations. Polygamy clearly violates this tradition. The state is usually suspicious of marital and familial relationships (i.e., gay or lesbian partnerships) that stray from the dominant paradigm of one man, one woman. The prosecution is well

Mormon Church polygamy is illegal but prosecutorial efforts are modest nevertheless. Polygamy is still practiced in Mormon subculture.

aware that polygamy cases involve the inducement of a minor to join a pseudomarriage with an adult and engage in sexual relations with the adult or else be shamed, chastised, and possibly banished. The state will typically bring a case of sexual abuse of a minor, which is commonplace in a polygamous household.

Arguments Made By The Defense

"Celestial marriage" is the main defense used by the accused in polygamy cases. The polygamous head of household asserts that having multiple spouses (including spouses who are minors) is necessary to fulfill the will of God. The defense will argue that no harm is done, and to the contrary, everyone in the polygamous family benefits since the arrangement is pursuant to a divine purpose. A defense of polygamy will also compare the law prohibiting polygamy to laws in other nations that allow for the freedom to engage in premarital or extramarital sex, and argue that the same latitude should be applied to the practice of polygamy. Finally, polygamists correctly argue that if alternative forms of marriage, such as same-sex marriage, are legally permissible, their form of alternative lifestyle should be as well.

Variations of the Law of Polygamy

A. Rape as an Accomplice

Due to the unconventional lifestyle of the polygamist community, various criminal charges can be brought for alleged acts of sexual deviancy. In 2006 polygamist "prophet" Warren S. Jeffs became one of the FBI's Ten Most Wanted Felons for sex crimes perpetrated within a polygamous community.[67] When finally apprehended, Jeffs was charged with "accomplice rape of a child." Using his "prophet status" to influence and coerce, the accused induced a 14-year-old polygamous church member to enter into a nonlicensed spiritual marriage with a 19-year-old cousin whom the girl stated she did not like nor wanted to marry. The orchestration of the marriage under duress made Jeffs culpable even though he was not present when the eventual sexual contact ensued. Jeffs implicitly wanted the minor to engage in sexual acts with her cousin, but did not commit any overt act to be sure the adult male had sex with the nonconsenting female minor. Nevertheless, Jeffs was charged with rape as an accomplice and convicted by a jury in Washington County, Utah on November 20, 2007. He was sentenced to ten years to life in prison.[68]

The state convicted Jeffs under the state accomplice liability statute, which reads:

> Every person, acting with the mental state required for the commission of an offense who directly commits the offense, who solicits, requests, commands, encourages, or intentionally aids another person to engage in conduct which constitutes an offense shall be criminally liable as a party for such conduct.[69]

Religious leaders can be held criminally liable for encouraging family-based sexual interactions that violate the law.

Upon presenting the evidence that the accused induced and persuaded the minor to marry her cousin (and engage in sexual relations with him), the jury was persuaded that Jeffs was an accomplice. He refused to "release" the victim from her marriage to her cousin and counseled her to ""give herself to [her cousin], … mind, body and soul.""[70] Those instructions were enough to constitute acting as an accomplice under the law of the state of Utah. The trial court judge instructed the jury on accomplice liability as follows:

> To convict Warren Jeffs as an accomplice to the crime of rape, you must find from the evidence, beyond a reasonable doubt, all of the following elements of that crime:
>
> 1. That the defendant, Warren Jeffs:
>
>   a. intentionally, knowingly, or recklessly solicited, requested, commanded, or encouraged another:
>
>   i. to have sexual intercourse:
>
>   ii. with Elissa Wall without consent.

The theory of rape as an accomplice and the practice of "mix and match" with wives, husbands, cousins, and children in a polygamous environment is legally challenging. For example, when this case was appealed, the Utah Supreme Court overturned the conviction and ordered a new trial. The State Supreme Court considered it an injustice that the state showed Jeffs' influence in the incestuous marriage, but did not prove that Jeffs intentionally and knowingly arranged the marriage for the purpose of an adult engaging in nonconsensual sex with a minor. The State Supreme Court stated:

This [accomplice liability law] mandates that the defendant, in this case one who acts as an accomplice to rape, undertake his actions intentionally, knowingly, or recklessly. But intentionally, knowingly, or recklessly in regard to what?

In *State v. Comish,* we held that a security officer who purchased marijuana in a sting operation could not be considered an accomplice for testimonial purposes because ""[u]nder [the] statute and under the [generally accepted meaning of the term, ... "accomplice" ... does not include a person who ... merely provides an opportunity for one who is disposed to commit a crime."" 560 P.2d 1134, 1136 (Utah 1977).

To convict the defendant as an accomplice to rape, the State was required to establish that he, acting with the requisite mental intent, solicited, requested, commanded, encouraged or intentionally aided the husband in having nonconsensual sexual intercourse with the victim. Because defendant did not engage in sexual intercourse with the victim, it was erroneous for the jury instructions to equate the term ""actor"" with the term ""defendant"" in instructing the jury as to whether the State had met its burden of proving that the sexual intercourse was nonconsensual. Because the consent instructions told the jury that defendant's position of special trust and his enticement of the victim could give rise to a lack of consent, they were erroneous. Without defendant's proposed instruction as to intent, the jury could have convicted him if it found that he intentionally did some act, and such intentional act unintentionally aided the husband in having nonconsensual sexual intercourse with the victim.[71]

With his conviction overturned, the state is presently considering whether to retry Jeffs. That decision may be moot, however. In 2010, Jeffs was extradited from Utah to the state of Texas to face the charges of sexual abuse of a minor and bigamy for his involvement with a polygamous community in the state of Texas.

B. Racketeering

In 2010, U.S. Senate Majority Leader Harry Reid from Nevada, himself a member of the Mormon Church, called for a federal investigation into the practice of polygamy and suggested prosecution of polygamist leaders in any state under the RICO Act (Racketeer Influenced and Corrupt Organizations Act of 1970).[72] RICO was enacted by section 901(a) of the Organized Crime Control Act of 1970.[73]

Originally, RICO primarily targeted the American Mafia and that crime family's infiltration of legitimate business enterprises in the U.S. Since any law generally can take on a life of its own, RICO took on a life of its own. RICO has come to be used for a bevy of purposes and the original goal of disrupting illicit infiltration of legitimate businesses has been largely underrepresented in RICO prosecutions. RICO has been used more frequently as a means of attacking the members of racketeering organizations (organizations that chronically engage in illegal criminal activities), as well as the actual organizations themselves. Under RICO § 1962(c), by virtue of that provision's inclusion of "any person" who "conducts or participates, directly or indirectly, in the conduct of [a RICO] enterprise's affairs through a pattern of racketeering activity," it is possible to indict an unusually broad array of criminal masterminds. Admittedly, the RICO statute is a broad legal application.[74]

Racketeers, such as the Mafia, within an organized criminal syndicate are usually disciplined and come together for the purpose of participating in a centralized subsystem of illegal activities. Their criminal activities are organized and the organized crime family separates itself from democratically elected government, which it does not trust, and needs to shield itself from law enforcement investigations. Leaders within the organization usually use fear and intimidation to coerce compliance among members. The Hells Angels motorcycle club,[75] a Florida police department, the American Baseball League, and other organizations have faced RICO prosecution efforts. Some Catholic church dioceses have been targeted and RICO laws have been used to prosecute the authorities in the episcopacy for abuses committed by those under their authority. A Cleveland grand jury acquitted two bishops of racketeering charges, finding that their mishandling of sex abuse claims within their diocese did not amount to criminal racketeering.

Senator Reid wants RICO used in an effort to decrease the practice of polygamy in the U.S. Polygamist sects are alleged to be highly disciplined in that members come together based on their faiths and religious doctrines.[76] Their lifestyles and lives are dominated by religious orientation and prescription. To allow polygamy to survive, polygamist community leaders use a variety of coercive tactics that seek to maintain adherence to the religious orthodoxy and, hence, the group affiliation. For example, followers will be threatened with a type of excommunication for failure to dedicate oneself to the practices of the community. Shame and guilt are other more subtle, equally coercive strategies. Followers who ask questions or appear nonconformist are subject to painful ridicule and made to seem foolish for questioning the controversial acts of the leadership.[77]

Polygamous communities are thought to engage in racketeering since they systematically engage, if not come together for, an array of illegal activities.[78] Polygamists historically are alleged to systematically engage in crimes such as bigamy, child sexual abuse, statutory rape, welfare fraud, and income tax evasion among other crimes. As a result, they can be subject to the regulations of the RICO Act.

C. Sexual Assault of a Minor

In the 2009 case of *Texas v. Jessop*, polygamist Merrill Leroy Jessop, 31 years old at the time of the crime, was convicted by a Texas jury for the first degree felony sexual assault of a 15-year-old female.[79] Church elders in his polygamist church community in Texas had assigned the girl to him as one of his many wives. Jessop dutifully complied with the orders given to him, married the girl in an extralegal ceremony, and subsequently engaged in marriage-based sexual relations with her and his other wives. Jessop was charged with sexual assault of a minor, a crime that includes statutory rape activities. He was sentenced to seventy-five years in prison in 2010.[80]

Jessop and the victim had moved along with an entire polygamous community to El Dorado, Texas, a small, isolated town in the region of San Antonio in the southern part of the state. They moved there to privately pursue a religious faith that they did not want to be subject to interference from secular authorities. Upon relocating to El Dorado, the community leaders indicated that the ranch they had purchased, and where they were established, was a corporate hunting retreat. They said this to avoid harassment from the state or local government. In reality, the ranch was the YFZ Polygamous Ranch (Yearning for Zion). On this 1,700-acre property, the fundamentalists believed they could live their lifestyle without interference. A hope that never came true.

As part of the religious practice in El Dorado, young women were wed to older men for many reasons, including the perpetuation of the community. However, locals soon began sniffing around and that did not bode well for the polygamists. The state of Texas requires a county marriage license before it will recognize a marriage contract. At the YFZ Ranch, there were no marriage contracts in the marriages. Despite a lack of legal marriages, sexual touching occurred between the young girls and older men. In the state of Texas, the sexual touching of a woman who is under 17 and not the wife of the perpetrator constitutes the crime of sexual assault of a child regardless of any type of consent, spirituality, divine order, etc.[81]

One of the young women at the Ranch eventually called the authorities about the sexual touching and abuse. In response, Texas CPS (Child Protective Services) took action and the result was a highly publicized April 2008 raid on the ranch where an astonishing 533 woman and children were legally and forcibly seized and taken into protective custody by the state pursuant to state law.[82] CPS spokesperson Darrell Azar stated, "There was a systematic process going on to groom these young girls to become brides," and that the children could not be protected from possible future abuse on the ranch.[83] Interviews with the children "revealed that several underage girls were forced into 'spiritual marriage' with much older men as soon as they reached puberty and were then made pregnant.[84]

Merrill Leroy Jessop, an adult, engaged in sexual relations with a woman under 17 who was not his wife, and therefore was guilty of a sex crime at the ranch.[85] He was arrested and prosecuted in Tom Green County, Texas, the county the ranch was situated in. The resultant child born from the incident was further DNA proof of the sexual contact between the accused and the victim. Hence, the Tom Green County jury heard testimony for nine days before rendering a verdict of guilty. He was sentenced to seventy-five years in prison.[86]

Additional Court Cases: Polygamy

Reynolds v. U.S.

98 U.S. 145 (1879)

CASE SUMMARY

PROCEDURAL POSTURE: Defendant appealed his conviction for bigamy in the District Court for the Third Judicial District of the Territory of Utah.

OVERVIEW: Defendant married a second wife while his first wife was still living. Defendant was convicted of bigamy at a trial where questioned jurors had acknowledged forming some opinion on the case prior to trial, but indicated an ability to view the evidence impartially. Further, the prosecution admitted into evidence testimony of the second wife given at a different trial charging defendant with bigamy. The Court found the fifteen-person grand jury that indicted the defendant was proper because the statute governing territorial courts was applicable. The Court found the question of whether a juror was impartial to be an issue of fact that was reversible only for clear error. The Court determined that defendant had not met his burden of showing a juror's actual opinion raising the presumption of partiality. The Court decided that the introduction of the second wife's former testimony was proper because she was made unavailable by defendant.

OUTCOME: The Court affirmed defendant's conviction for bigamy because his indictment was proper under a fifteen-person grand jury, the jurors were not shown to be partial, and the introduction of former testimony by the second wife was proper when defendant made her unavailable for trial.[87]

Bigamy

Bigamy involves a second marriage prior to the dissolution of the first marriage. Somewhat more technically, it refers to any secondary legally recognized marriage that comes after the only, first, government-allowed, legally recognized marriage. Bigamy may be conceptualized as an anti-polygamy law but it has a greater breadth than that. In European history before the U.S. was founded, bigamists alerted both government and church authorities to the prospect of one man marrying two virgins. The threat was that a virgin would get married for the primary purpose of securing fidelity in exchange for her offering herself to her husband. In a bigamous arrangement, one virgin would be left in the lurch, without a monogamous husband, but having given herself to him. Bigamy was also a concern to spiritual leaders. The prohibition against bigamy sought to deter a single metaphysical union from being tainted by a second, carnal union.[88]

Bigamy does not have a religious tradition, per se, nor does it usually involve three or more (multiple) spouses; only one other spouse is typically involved. Bigamy also is nonviolent and does not usually involve a prepubescent minor or disturbing "paraphilic" behaviors. In fact, bigamy most often occurs by accident or neglect. For example, the accused and his or her spouse become estranged, move away from one another, and never see each other again. The accused then re-marries, but never gets around to legally terminating the first marriage. If the accused has a single secondary spouse, the government will use a single count of bigamy as the charge. But two or three or more secondary marriages will result in a multiple-count indictment against the accused. Upon conviction for the charge of bigamy, the first, valid, marriage becomes legally void and subject to annulment.

The most famous case of bigamy in American history is that between American President Andrew Jackson (7th U.S. President) and his spouse Rachel Robards Jackson. This high profile couple agreed to marry in the state of Tennessee, but Rachel had failed to obtain a legal divorce from her first husband. Andrew Jackson's political enemies discovered this innocent omission and exploited it to the fullest, causing much embarrassment and humiliation to both Andrew and Rachel. Rachel eventually obtained the proper divorce decree from her first marriage, and she and Andrew thereafter became husband and wife on safe legal footing. Political adversaries of the Jackson's continued to try and defame them with the incident, including during the presidential election of 1828. Even though Jackson won the election, Rachel died just after the inaugural ball; many think her death was a result of the attacks from her political opponents who continued to decry her bigamous past.[89]

Today, the act of bigamy remains a felony in most states, but obviously not a very serious social harm compared to some other family based sex crimes.

Definition of the Offense

According to **Russell on Crimes**, historically, and mostly based in canon law, "bigamy, in its proper signification, is said to mean only being twice married, and not having a plurality of wives at once."[90]

Elements of the Offense

The elements of the crime of bigamy that must be proven beyond a reasonable doubt are:

1. a prior marriage,
2. going through the form of a second marriage before the first marriage is dissolved.[91]

Sample Statute

The State of Oklahoma bigamy statute reads as follows:

21 Okla. Stat. § 881. Bigamy.

> Every person who having been married to another who remains living, marries any other person except in the cases specified in the next section is guilty of bigamy.[92]

The law regulates numerous contexts of sexual behavior within or between families.

Distinguishing Polygamy and Bigamy. From the descriptions above, the main legal distinctions between polygamy and bigamy concerns the number of spouses; plural spouses apply to cases of polygamy, and only one other spouse applies to cases of bigamy. A polygamy case may be prosecuted as the crime of bigamy since, as a practical matter, polygamy involves a type of second marriage before the dissolution of the first marriage. However, a case of bigamy may not constitute the offense of polygamy since multiple spouses are not the subject of bigamy cases. Factors relating to age (i.e., minors) or gender are irrelevant to the crime of bigamy, but involve other crimes.

Both parties can be charged and convicted, and "good faith" is no defense to either polygamy or bigamy. Meaning, if a woman marries a man and later finds out he has another wife (either with an undissolved contract, or, as part of his practice of plural marriage), she, too, is guilty of either crime. The only solid defense available to an unsuspecting victim is to demonstrate in court that all prior marriages were dissolved by death, divorce, or annulment.[93]

Variations of the Law of Bigamy

A. Statute of Limitations

Under certain statutes it is not considered bigamous for an individual to remarry if a certain number of years have passed. After three or more years, the law of bigamy entertains the prospect that the former spouse is permanently missing or dead. Remarriage before the statutory period, however, constitutes bigamy since the first marriage is still regarded as valid.

In *Scoggins v. State* from 1877, the defendant and his first wife parted ways, she joining with another man and he with another woman.[94] Scoggins never annulled his first marriage before contracting for his second marriage and hence was charged and convicted of the crime of bigamy. On appeal he argued that since three years had passed, the issue was no longer relevant, but the court disagreed and upheld his conviction. The court did not place much emphasis on the three years' time passed, but reinforced the importance of the single contractual arrangement:

> The crime, in the language of our act, was completed, when any person now married, or who shall be hereafter married, doth take to himself or herself another husband or wife, while his or her former wife or husband is still alive. There can be no question but that this is done, when the parties, before the authorized minister, declare that they there take each other for man and wife. Marriage, or the relation of husband and wife, is in law complete, when parties, able to contract and willing to contract, actually have contracted to be man and wife in the forms and with the solemnities required by law.[95]

B. Invalidity of Original Marriage Ceremony

If the accused in a bigamy case can demonstrate there was no first marriage, then there can be no crime of bigamy. Said differently, a person who is unmarried cannot legally be a bigamist. As one judge noted, "It will be observed that one having no husband or wife could not, by marrying, be guilty of bigamy as defined, although punishable for an unnamed crime."[96] To exculpate oneself from guilt, many defendants charged with bigamy will try to argue that their alleged first marriage was invalid in some way.

In *State v. Martinez*, the accused was convicted of bigamy pursuant to the state of Idaho bigamy statute which read: Bigamy consists in having two wives, or two husbands, at one and the same time, knowing that the former husband or wife is still alive.[97] Martinez was found guilty of legally marrying someone in May of 1923 and someone else in October in 1923. It appeared he was married to two persons at the same time and hence guilty of the crime of bigamy.

Martinez appealed, arguing that his purported first marriage was invalid. He argued that no proof existed that the justice of the peace in the first ceremony was legally authorized to perform a marriage ceremony and, therefore, the first marriage was invalid, and hence he cannot be guilty of bigamy.[98] Taken from the court transcript: "We will refer to the alleged marriage to Hazel Butler at Spokane as the 'first' marriage, and to the marriage to Mary G. Prosper at Coeur d'Alene as the 'second' marriage. Appellant specifies as error insufficiency of the evidence to establish that the defendant 'was the groom' in the first marriage."

The court noted that in a bigamy case, the two marriage ceremonies had to be legally recognizable from the point of view of the state in order for guilt to be maintained. The court stated, "Consent to and subsequent consummation of marriage may be manifested in any form, and may be proved under the same general rules of evidence as facts in other cases."

The appeals court analysis came down to the ability of the accused to establish the legal authority of the justice of the peace in the first marriage to perform a valid marriage. The court held that the justice of the peace was indeed legally authorized to perform the first marriage and, absent of any proof that there was no such legal authorization, the first marriage was valid.[99]

> Appellant argues that there was no proof that a justice of the peace could perform a lawful marriage ceremony in the state of Washington. While there is some conflict in the decisions of other courts, some holding that in a prosecution for bigamy the state must not only prove a marriage in fact, but a marriage valid under the law of the state in which it took place, the better rule is that the validity of a ceremonial marriage will be presumed in the absence of evidence tending to show that it was not regular and in accordance with law, and that the presumption applicable to civil actions, that the law of a foreign state, not being shown, will be presumed to be the same as the law of this state, is applicable in a matter where, especially with relation to marriages, the right of parties capable of marriage, being a common right, valid by common law prevailing throughout Christendom, we cannot presume that there is a law of a foreign state prohibiting a marriage which, when shown, would be valid in this state.[100]

C. Marriage Contract from a Different State

Cases arise where someone is accused of a bigamous marriage when one of the two marriages was performed in a state different from the one where the defendant was charged with bigamy. In the U.S., the laws of marriage and bigamy may conflict slightly from state to state. In such cases, if a marriage takes place in one state, but that marriage ceremony is not recognized in another state, is it a legally recognizable marriage for purposes of a bigamy conviction?

In the case of *Dale v. State*, the accused had assumed two identities, traveled and lived in several states in the U.S., and married at least two persons, apparently being legally married to two people simultaneously.[101] He was eventually discovered and charged and convicted of the crime of bigamy.

The court transcript read

> Dale … did lawfully marry Emma T. Horton and had her to his lawful wife, and afterwards, whilst he was so lawfully married to her, in December, 1884, in Paulding county, Georgia, he did knowingly marry and take to wife Effie Smith, said Emma T. being then alive and his lawful wife, of which fact he had full knowledge; that his real name was and is J. O. H. Nutall; that he came to Paulding county under the assumed name of W. R. Dale, and under such assumed name was married to Effie Smith.[102]

On appeal from his conviction, Dale argued that the laws of the state in which his first marriage took place (North Carolina) are invalid in the state where he was charged and convicted (Georgia). An additional part of the court transcript reads, "One of the grounds mainly relied upon was the fourth, which complains that the evidence was insufficient to show a marriage valid under the laws of North Carolina."[103]

The grounds for the appeal did not seem to present a great deal of difficulty for the appellate court. The court ruled on the question of reconciling different laws from different states when it comes to marriage and bigamy by stating:

> In a trial for bigamy, the first marriage may be established by proof of a marriage in fact celebrated in another State of the Union, followed by cohabitation in that State and the birth of children. These facts will authorize the jury to infer the validity of the marriage even though the marriage laws of that State be not affirmatively proved, there being nothing in the evidence tending to show that the marriage was not regular and conformable to law.[104]

Additional Court Cases: Bigamy
State v. Ezeonu
588 N.Y.S.2d 116 (1992)

CASE SUMMARY

PROCEDURAL POSTURE: Defendant was indicted for the crime of rape in the first and second degrees and moved in limine seeking to raise the defense of marriage pursuant to N.Y. Penal Law § 130.30.

OVERVIEW: Defendant was indicted for the crimes of rape in the first degree and rape in the second degree. Defendant moved in limine seeking to raise as a defense that at the time of the alleged crimes the complainant was his junior wife, given to him by her parents in Nigeria, pursuant to the laws and tribal customs of that country. The court found that defendant stipulated that he was legally married in New York and Nigeria at the time when he purportedly married complainant. Further, while Nigerian law and custom permitted a junior wife, New York did not recognize that status. Therefore, defendant's marriage to complainant was absolutely void. Accordingly, defendant was not entitled raise the marriage defense.

OUTCOME: Defendant could not raise his purported marriage to complainant, as a defense to the charge of rape in the second degree because defendant was married to his living wife and his "marriage" to complainant was absolutely void.[105]

Incest

Cleopatra and her brother, Ptolemy, may have been married, but any legitimization of incestuous relations probably stopped with them. For example, in the famous case of Oedipus in Sophocles's 428 BCE play, Oedipus engages in sexual relations with his mother, Jocasta. As a result, Jocasta commits suicide, Oedipus went blind, and he eventually entered self-imposed exile from society, thus implying the serious negative consequences of the act. Most moral codes from Egypt and Greece onward viewed incest as odd, an inexplicable attraction and anomie-like orientation to personal boundaries and social and familial roles. Aside from superstition and speculation, numerous practical reasons exist to criminalize incest within a family.[106]

First, **incest** victims are often nonconsenting parties. They may not explicitly tell their transgressor "no," but in most cases do not say "yes." Most incest victims are controlled and manipulated into the act by unscrupulous authority figures such as biological parents, foster parents, or adoptive parents. The offender is often an intimidating, uncompromising, seductive, or predatory deviant. Many transgressors of incest who would do such a thing are skilled in the art of predation and subjugation.[107]

Upon engaging in incestuous relations, the psychological and emotional injury suffered by the incest victim can be severe. This damage is not limited to physical touching but also includes injuries due to latent and covert sexual leering or fantasies. Teasing and jokes about sex, sexuality, or sexual body parts can encroach on the illegality of incest or sexual abuse of a child if the victim is a minor. Incest victims may never fully recover from the confused family roles and subsequent psychosexual trauma. In addition, they will have to endure their own future sex life with aberrant compulsions and inconsistencies as a result of being a victim of incestuous relations. This fact is even more serious when considering that most incest victims are minors.[108]

On a more practical level, the early settlers needed an expansion of the family, not a cognitively and emotionally contracted one. Meaning, it was more beneficial for the family to enter into a union with another entirely separate family for purposes of defense and security. There was safety in numbers and incest-based relationships ran counter to the goals of familial self-preservation. A bigger family sustained from relations with the outside world also supported the commercial success of the family. As the family got bigger, more persons became available to assist with building sheds and farmhouses, planting and harvesting fields, delivering goods to market, and cooking and cleaning for the clan.

Families typically seek to enjoy domestic peace and solitude. But incest can easily provoke domestic feuding. The prohibition of incest is based on the promotion of solidarity and peace within the family and the prevention of sex rivalries and jealousies among family members.[109] Scientific evidence also suggests that inbreeding often results in defective offspring due to recessive gene combinations between blood relatives. In early times, a deformed baby was thought to serve as proof that the copulation that produced the baby was somehow unlawful and sinfully incestuous.

Lastly, issues of inheritance and contracts are blurred when relationships become confused. Although this issue is a less serious aspect of incest, and only pertains to cousins, it forms another basis for legal regulation. Bienen notes:

> Marriage was the mainstay of [this] social system, defining all other relationships. Marrying your wife's cousin by marriage is prohibited not because it would be inbreeding, but because it would confuse an existing, rigidly structured, kinship relationship with your wife's family. Marriage and the legitimacy of children had and continue to have significant consequences for the ownership of property and title to land. Wealth and stature in the community was based upon ownership of land. The marriage of in-laws would confuse the lines of inheritance and ownership and land and had to be prohibited.[110]

In sum, incest has a dramatic history, but as a practical matter, goes against the grain of family preservation. Most importantly, incest can rank very high as an irreparably damaging act, especially if the victim is a minor child who is incapable of consenting. The law of incest seeks to protect potential victims, but also has an interest in protecting traditional notions of marriage and family. As noted on the first page of this chapter, the judge in the case of State v. Lowe stated, the law "has a legitimate interest in prohibiting incestuous relations and in protecting the family unit and family relationships."[111]

Table 1 Two Main Types of Family Relatives.

Type of Relationship		Example
1. Consanguinity	(blood relative)	Brother and Sister
2. Affinity	(marriage relative)	Stepfather and Stepdaughter

The crime of incest may exist depending on the type of relationship in the family. Statutes differ from state to state as to the exact degree of relationship required for the offense to take place, but are very similar when it comes to sexual relations between consanguineous parties, for example, father and daughter, mother and son, brother and sister, uncle and niece, and aunt and nephew.

With the shifting nature of family relations in the United States today, numerous marriages occur where one or both spouses bring their respective children to the new marriage creating adopted children, stepchildren, and stepparents. Hence, the law of incest applies equally to newly formed affinity relationships between stepfather and stepdaughter, stepmother and stepson and brother-in-law and sister-in-law.

Numerous variations of incest may occur and all will come to fall under the purview of legal regulation and sanction. The least serious forms of incest may be so innocent, only by accident do they qualify as illegal. For example, if an extended family meets for summer vacation every year and on one occasion, two of the curious younger children reveal their genitals to one another with nothing more involved, the act is incest depending on the relationship between the two involved. Of course, the effort to prosecute such a case, if it were incest, would be minimal.

Where a systematic or continual pattern occurs, the seriousness of the offense does as well. A more-than-one-time scenario will require an investment in secrecy and the secrecy will create inner conflict, confusion, and shame for both parties. Hence, the law hopes to deter any pattern of incest, however "innocent" it may seem and will do so for the mental wellness and sexual health of the parties concerned.

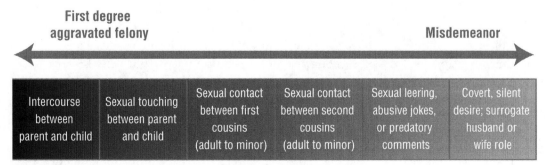

Figure 2 Continuum of Seriousness: Incestuous Familial Relationships.

Any incestuous activity between adult and minor family member is an immediate concern for the law. Where the minor is 17 and the adult is 19, for example, the penalty will be less severe. Where the age range increases, the seriousness and penalty does as well. Where there is an obvious age disparity between the adult and minor, the "one time" context becomes irrelevant to the seriousness of the offense. For example, the law will not entertain a defense to a 30-year-old male uncle who convinces a 16-year-old cousin to have sexual contact.

Definition of the Offense

Incest can be defined generally as sexual contact among family members or marriage among family members. The family members can be blood relatives (consanguinity) or related by marriage (affinity).[112]

Elements of the Offense

The elements of the crime of incest that must be proven beyond a reasonable doubt are:

1. marriage or sexual intercourse,
2. between persons within the degree of relationship proscribed by law.[113]

Sample Statute

The State of Alabama incest statute reads as follows:

(a) A person commits incest if he marries or engages in sexual intercourse with a person he knows to be, either legitimately or illegitimately:

(1) His ancestor or descendant by blood or adoption, or

(2) His brother or sister of the whole or half-blood or by adoption; or

(3) His stepchild or stepparent, while the marriage creating the relationship exists; or

(4) His aunt, uncle, nephew, or niece of the whole or half blood.[114]

Arguments Made By The Prosecution

The state will seek to find a pattern of sexual contact between the two (or more) parties. A one-time incident weakens the prospects for conviction and is susceptible to claims of an accidental touching. Not only will the prosecution look for a pattern of activity, it will also seek to see an obviously sexual interaction (i.e., intercourse) rather than mere touching, which could be mistaken for basic gestures of affection (e.g., putting one's arm over the shoulders of someone).

Arguments Made By The Defense

In many cases of sexual touching, the defense will argue the concept of consent and that the actors involved were mature, loving adults. Painting this picture always reduces the intensity of the allegation. Since consent is irrelevant to the crime of incest, the defense's best strategy is to argue that the relationship that existed between the parties that had sex was not either consanguineous or one based in affinity—hence, one not proscribed by law. Instead, the defense will argue that both persons came together as strangers and took time to develop their relationship.

Variations of the Law of Incest

A. Death of a Spouse

In the absence of a specific statute, allegations of incest may be legally impossible on the death of a certain family member. For example, in *Wilson v. State,* the defendant was accused of incest when it was discovered that he had fathered a baby with his wife's sister.[115] The defendant was charged with the crime of incest pursuant to Tennessee statute 6767 which reads: "If any person shall be guilty of begetting an illegitimate child on the body of his wife's sister, he is guilty of a felony."[116]

After his conviction, the offender appealed, arguing the exact wording of the statute and claiming that he cannot be guilty due to the death of his wife. The court agreed. After a careful examination of various dates and timelines, the court held that the defendant's wife had died before he ever had sexual relations with his deceased wife's sister (his sister-in-law). The court stated that once the defendant's wife died, the defendant and his wife's sister "were strangers" for purposes of the crime of incest.[116] "The begetting of an illegitimate child on the body of the sister of a deceased wife is not within Code section 6767, making it a felony for any person to beget an illegitimate child on the body of 'his wife's sister.'" Therefore, the two of them were not related by the requisite blood or affinity ties and the defendant was acquitted by the appeals court of the charge of incest. The ruling by the court may seem inconsistent since the sister would still seem to be a relative of the accused. However, part of the policy justification for incest is to promote domestic peace.[118] Therefore, the deceased wife's absence would decrease the chances of jealousy, rivalry, or family feuding as a result of the relationship between the two parties. The court stated:

> The offense created by this statute, and made the subject of punishment, is that of begetting a child upon the body of the sister of a living wife. This is the literalism of the statute, and the spirit is not broader than the letter. It recognizes an existing relation of husband and wife, out of which the relationship by affinity has grown. The person whom it seeks to protect against the approaches of the husband is the sister of his wife then alive. By marriage, the husband becomes the brother, by affinity, of that sister, and the purpose of this legislation was to preserve the purity of this intimate relationship. But this relationship is terminated by the death of the wife. Thereafter the surviving

husband and the surviving sister of the deceased wife, in contemplation of the law, are again strangers, and the statute in question has ceased to operate so far as they are concerned.[119]

B. Adult Status of Daughter-Victim

The law is unequivocal when the incest victim is a minor, but in a consanguineous relationship, what if the victim is an adult, fully capable of consenting to the act? In *People v. Scott,* the accused was the biological father of his 18-year-old daughter. Upon engaging in a consensual sexual relationship with her, he was charged with the crime of incest pursuant to California incest statute, Penal Code 285.[120]

The state incest statute applied to persons related by consanguinity and who are of the opposite sex. Thus, § 285 served the state's legitimate interest in protecting against inbreeding, as well as its legitimate interests in protecting the integrity of the family unit and protecting persons who may not be in a position to freely consent to a sexual relationship. Section 285 reads: "Persons being within the degrees of consanguinity within which marriages are declared by law to be incestuous and void, who intermarry with each other, or who being 14 years of age or older, commit fornication or adultery with each other, are punishable by imprisonment in the state prison."[121]

After his conviction at trial, Scott appealed and used the federal Constitution as a basis. He argued that he had a lawful liberty interest and was constitutionally protected to engage in consensual relations with another consenting adult pursuant to the due process clause of the Fourteenth Amendment.[122]

Scott's argument was somewhat weak. Just because the victim turns 18 or 19 does not all of a sudden make her any less exploitable or vulnerable to a predatory parent. As a result, the appellate court ruled against Scott and upheld the state of California's incest law. The court reasoned that even though the victim was a mature, consenting adult, the father nevertheless maintained a substantial degree of power and influence over his daughter.[123] The court relied on the more basic intents of incest law and many other sex crime statutes in advancing the goal of protecting vulnerable parties. The court stated:

> [We need to protect] persons who might be injured or coerced or who are situated in relationships where consent might not easily be refused. Even adult daughters are typically in positions of vulnerability vis-a-vis their older, and thus more authoritative fathers, in matters pertaining to sex.[124] The state has a legitimate interest in maintaining the integrity of the family unit ... The incest statute serves this purpose. Thus, defendant's conviction did not violate his due process rights.[125]

C. Concealment of Relationship

Under most circumstances, the unlawful incidence of incestuous relations is no secret to the two parties involved. Both know who each other is and are aware of the degree of familial attachment between them. This knowledge is what often contributes to the confusion and pain of the victim. In some situations, however, the offending party will attempt to conceal the existence of the familial relationship to the victim party in the hope that such deceit will aid in the advancement of the offender's plans.

In *Morgan v. State*, the accused never married the mother of his daughter and did not have contact with either his daughter or daughter's mother for an extended time.[126] Hence, the time lapse between contacts made the accused appear to be more like a stranger than a parent. When the accused did have contact with his daughter and her mother, he concealed the fact that he was his daughter's father and neither did the mother make the disclosure. Thus, when the father visited the daughter, the daughter thought he was a stranger. The father made advances on his daughter, engaged in sexual intercourse with her, and was charged and convicted of the crime of incest. The charging document read:

> being then and there the father of one Sarah Morgan, and within the degree of consanguinity within which marriages are by law declared to be incestuous, and void, and then and there knowing the said Sarah Morgan to be his daughter, did then and there live with said Sarah Morgan, in a state of adultery.[127]

On appeal, the accused argued that the lack of knowledge on the part of the victim (his daughter) negated the crime. The court ruled that the lack of knowledge on the part of the victim does not relieve the perpetrator from guilt. The court also stated that it did not want to reward the offender with the ignorance of the victim. Finally, the court held that knowledge of the familial relationship by both parties is not required so long as one of the parties has such knowledge. The court stated:

> The crime with which the admission is connected, is so revolting to natural propriety and decency, that it would seem almost incredible, and for this reason, if no other, a mere confession of the relationship ought not to produce a conviction. But we do not understand that this was all the evidence before the jury on this subject. The charge is, that the admissions were competent, and we are not prepared to say, they were otherwise. We can see no error in the record. Judgment affirmed.[128]

Additional Court Cases: Incest

Sutton v. Commonwealth

324 S.E.2d 665 (1985)

CASE SUMMARY

PROCEDURAL POSTURE: Defendant uncle and defendant aunt appealed from the judgments of the Circuit Court of the City of Newport News (Virginia), which convicted the uncle of the rape of his niece as a principal in the first degree and convicted the aunt of rape as a principal in the second degree. The court found that sexual intercourse between the uncle and the niece was the result of intimidation by both defendants in violation of Va. Code Ann. § 18.2-61 (1982).

OVERVIEW: The 15-year-old niece testified that she had intercourse on multiple occasions with the uncle out of fear of violence from him and out of fear of being returned to her abusive father. On appeal, the court found that an amendment to Va. Code Ann. 18.2-61 (1982) expanded the definition of rape from intercourse by force to include intercourse by force, threat, or intimidation. The court held that intimidation could occur without threats and meant putting a victim in fear of bodily harm by exercising such domination and control of her as to overcome her mind and overbear her will, and that intimidation could be caused by the imposition of psychological pressure on one who, under the circumstances, was vulnerable and susceptible to such pressure. The court held that the fact that the aunt could not be a principal in the first degree did not prevent her conviction as a principal in the second degree. The court found the aunt's actions in persuading the niece to submit and in fostering the atmosphere of intimidation supported a finding of constructive presence on the specific occasion that she was not physically present during the intercourse.

OUTCOME: The court affirmed the conviction of the uncle of rape as a principal in the first degree and the court affirmed the conviction of the aunt of rape as a principal in the second degree.[129]

Domestic Partnerships

The law of sex in the family can be relatively straightforward. For example, marital rape is prohibited by law and if the aggrieved party can prove their case, the accused will be convicted. Other criminal law issues were also fairly clear-cut in this chapter. Few Americans support polygamy, bigamy, or incest. The subject of **domestic partnerships** (same-sex marriage), however, is a more complicated issue legally, socially, and politically. The legal landscape of domestic partnerships is strewn with legal landmines.

Domestic partnership concerns the criminal law because of the historical prohibition on sodomy-related same-sex sexual contact. Historically, many societies considered sex between same-sex partners on a par with having sex with a beast. Indeed, in many parts of the world and in European history, homosexuals or suspected homosexuals (absent any evidence of sexual contact) have been castrated, torched by fire between the legs, burned at the stake, and subject to capital execution. In some parts of the world, this is still the case and this includes bisexual and transgendered persons.

Although in the Legal Background portion of this chapter, we examined a brief epoch where homosexuality in the Greek military was found to be desirable, in most other eras of history it is difficult to come to grips with the fury that manifests over homosexuality.[130] It is difficult to comprehend why such hatred could manifest over the private sexual desires of others. The hatred is so severe, an unusual number of atrocities and deaths are directly related to the hatred of gay persons. Sadly, there is every reason to believe such violence is exists today.

Many nations, including the United States, have had to enact hate crime laws that create a sentence enhancement for any convicted criminal who is motivated by homophobia to perpetrate a crime. In the U.S., the Hate Crime law that pertains to sexual orientation is called the Matthew Shepard Act.[131] This act was passed by Congress on October 22, 2009 and signed into law by President Barack Obama on October 28, 2009. The law expands the 1969 U.S. Hate Crime law to include crimes motivated by a victim's actual or perceived gender, sexual orientation, or gender identity. The 2009 law is the first federal law in the history of the U.S. to extend any type of legal protection to transgendered persons.

In sum, same sex partnerships imply homosexual sexual relations and such activity has historically been regulated and outlawed by state criminal codes until very recently with the *Lawrence v. Texas*[132] U.S. Supreme Court decision (see chapter 3).

Despite the untold controversy with homosexuality, same-sex marriages have occurred legally and even ritualistically throughout human history. In the southern Chinese province of Fujian, through the Ming dynasty period, females would bind themselves in contracts to younger females in elaborate ceremonies. As for men, an example of male domestic partnerships may be found from the Zhou Dynasty period of China and recorded in the story of Pan Zhang and Wang Zhongxian. This same-sex marriage was approved by the wider community and

Gay couples face a formidable legal challenge to have rights equal to those of married couples.

was similar to a heterosexual marriage. Same-sex marriages also occurred during the Roman Empire in Europe from 342 and after.[133]

While same-sex marriages have occurred throughout history, since the founding of the United States in 1776, the idea of a homosexual union has not been well received. When Emperor Constantine made Christianity the state religion of the Roman Empire, the rest of Europe followed suit and laws and codes prohibiting homosexual practices were in force in Europe from the 4th to the 20th centuries. The British Empire certainly was vehemently opposed to gay couples, as were the Puritans and other American colonists. Nazi Germany included gays as targets during the Holocaust from 1940–1945. Today, at its most basic level, most Americans oppose sexual contact between persons of the same gender, despite the existence of consent. In addition to a discomfort over the "oddity" of having sex with someone of the same gender, domestic partnership is severely threatening to social mores, customs, tradition, and culture.[134]

In the U.S., a gay marriage is often considered antagonistic to Biblical accords concerning one man and one woman, the legacy of Patriarchy, Divine credence for procreation, and the subordinate status of the female species. All of these cherished cultural traditions are directly challenged with same-sex marriages. Thus, to say that gay marriage flies in the face of tradition is an understatement. In fact, in 2004 thirteen states went out of their way to enact a state constitutional amendment expressly and directly banning same-sex marriage.[135] It is difficult to find analogous social movements that assertively seek to deny rights to others, although easy to find examples of groups seeking to provide rights to others.

Obviously, the salience of the social issue of same-sex marriage has caused a social and political backlash.[136] For example, Alaska law states: "A same-sex relationship may not be recognized by the state as being entitled to the benefits of marriage."[137] Today, several countries in Africa will execute anyone found guilty of engaging in a homosexual marriage.

California and the Law of Same-Sex Marriage.

The playing field for the heated political competition to advance, and to restrict, the legal rights on behalf of sexual orientation and marriage could find no better example than the state of California in 2008. For some time, California used a statutory provision in its Civil Code that read: "Marriage is a personal relation arising out of a civil contract between a man and a woman."[138] Even though this was state law, the municipal and county jurisdiction of San Francisco ignored the law and in 2004 began issuing marriage licenses to same-sex couples who wanted to get married. This act by the politically formidable coalition of gay activists in San Francisco was certainly a renegade act and one that easily fanned the flames of anti-gay sentiment throughout the populous state.

Offended by such boldness as well as the openness of same-sex marriage, the Campaign for California Families sued the City of San Francisco to stay the issuance of the same-sex marriage licenses there. The suit was filed in San Francisco Superior Court, and the Superior Court refused to grant the stay, rather predictably. Undeterred, the plaintiffs next used the California Attorney General Office and filed the suit someplace other than in San Francisco, such as the State Supreme Court located in Sacramento. There, the petitioners had better luck. The State Supreme Court upheld the state statute restricting marriage to male and female only and asserted that the City's actions were unlawful and warranted [the court's] immediate intervention."

As the showdown continued, on March 11, 2004, the California Supreme Court ordered government officials of San Francisco "to enforce the existing marriage statutes and to refrain from issuing marriage licenses not authorized by such provisions." The ball was in San Francisco's court and they took the ball and ran with it. The City and County of San Francisco, in response to their loss in the State Supreme Court, sued to enjoin enforcement of the existing law restricting marriage to a man and a woman. The case was filed once again with the State Supreme Court. The issue finally came to a head in the case of *In Re Marriage*. In the case, the State Supreme Court invalidated the traditional law and held on behalf of the effort behind same-sex marriage. The court stated:

> The existing Family Code laws were unconstitutional insofar as their provisions drew a distinction between opposite-sex couples and same-sex couples and excluded the latter from access to the designation of marriage. The right to marry, as embodied in California Constitution Article 1, Sections 1 and 7 guaranteed same-sex couples the same substantive constitutional rights as opposite-sex couples, including the right to choose one's life partner. The statutes posed a serious risk of denying the official family relationship of same-sex couples equal dignity and respect, a core element of the fundamental right to marry.[139]

Despite the clarity of the Court's ruling, all was not settled in California.[140] After the California Supreme Court ruled that the state constitution required that same-sex couples be allowed to marry, in response, voters throughout the state approved a ballot measure for the next election called Proposition 8 (the California Marriage Protection Act). Prop 8 amended the state constitution to ban same-sex marriage.[141] Proposition 8 was one of the most expensive ballot measures in the history of the United States and it was passed by the voters on November 4, 2008. Prop 8 specifically states that "only marriage between a man and a woman is valid or recognized in California." Prop 8 overturned the State Supreme Court decision in *In Re Marriages*.

Whose ball is it now? In response, numerous lawsuits were filed in the State Supreme Court challenging the legality of Prop 8.[142] The legality of the proposition soon found itself in the State Supreme Court. The Court upheld the constitutionality of the popularly supported proposition. When the State High Court upheld Prop 8, the various backers of same-sex marriage filed suit in federal district court rather than in the State Supreme Court—and won. Same-sex marriage was back. In the case of *Perry v. Schwarzenegger,* federal District Court judge Vaughn R. Walker overturned Prop 8 on August 4, 2010 even though it was passed by the people in a democratic election. In response—of course—opponents of gay marriage (those who initiated Prop 8 to begin with) appealed. Their appeal went to the Ninth Circuit Court of federal appeals that hears federal appellate court cases from most of the western states in the U.S. The Ninth Circuit upheld the decision of the District Court and continued the stay of Prop 8, keeping Judge Walker's ruling on hold pending another appeal.[143]

The voters in the State of California were not legally permitted to deny gay persons the right to marry, despite their successful political activism. The turn of events in California as it concerns the law of domestic partnerships is truly remarkable.

Despite the radical orientation of domestic partnerships, and the controversy and degree of political backlash, recent law has nevertheless evolved to create more permissions for this type of union, as surprising as it may seem. In the United States today, approximately five jurisdictions permit same-sex marriage. Even so, in no jurisdiction in the U.S. are the legal rights of these unions nearly as expansive as the rights conferred under a traditional marriage contract (see Table 1 below). It is thought that over one thousand legal benefits accrue from a traditional marriage contract while not nearly as many derive from a domestic partnership arrangement. Some of these rights include the inheritance of the spouse's property and the receipt of a spouse's uncollected wages on death. In addition, although a few jurisdictions allow for it, each is different with different sets of rights, duties, and obligations. Domestic partnerships are riddled with legalities.

Table 2 Legal Rights Afforded to Traditionally Married Couples.

- Life or death health care decision making and information access
- Inheritance rights when the spouse passes away
- A spouse may bring a wrongful death action based on the death of the other spouse
- Community property rules apply to a marriage
- Dissolution laws apply to a marriage
- Domestic violence statutes apply to a marriage
- Certain property transfers in a marriage are not taxed
- State veterans benefits apply to a marriage
- The right to use sick leave to care for a spouse apply

- The right to wages and benefits when a spouse is injured, and to unpaid wages on the death of a spouse

- The right to unemployment and disability insurance benefits

- The right to workers' compensation coverage

- Insurance rights, including rights under group policies, and policy rights after the death of a spouse

- Rights related to adoption, child custody, and child support all apply in a marriage

- Business succession rights apply in a marriage

Definition of the Offense

Unlawful cohabitation of two persons of the same sex.[144]

Elements of the Offense

The elements of the crime of domestic cohabitation that must be proven beyond a reasonable doubt are:

1. the living together of a man and a man or a woman and a woman,

2. in a long-term relationship that resembles a marriage and includes sexual relations.[145]

Sample Statute

In the state of Oregon, a 2004 constitutional amendment bans same-sex marriage from being recognized or performed in the state. State of Oregon Constitution Section 5a(2) reads:

> Policy regarding marriage. It is the policy of Oregon, and its political subdivisions, that only a marriage between one man and one woman shall be valid or legally recognized as a marriage.[146]

Arguments Made By The Prosecution

The complicated legalities of domestic partnerships will require the prosecutor to be adept with newer, local legal provisions. Everything depends on what city, county, and state the case derives from. As a general matter, the prosecution may argue that no such law exists which allows for the marriage of two gay people, and therefore, an unlawful cohabitation exists.

Arguments Made By The Defense

The task for the defense in a case of same sex marriage is similarly challenging as with the prosecution. If the parties seek to take advantage of the benefits and opportunities that are typically afforded to heterosexual married couples, the defense must show that some type of law exists to provide such benefits. In the absence of a law that allows for a legal union to be either of two men or two women, the defense has very little to go on.

Variations of the Law of Domestic Partnerships

A. Civil Rights

In the state of Colorado and other states, many municipalities have passed antidiscrimination ordinances that prohibit discrimination based on race, religion, gender, etc., in areas of housing, employment, education, public accommodations, health and welfare services, etc. Some municipalities in the state of Colorado went further and included sexual orientation in their list of protected classifications.

This trend in Colorado was threatening to traditional interests and caused a political backlash in the state in the early 1990s. Similar to the situation in California mentioned earlier, voters throughout the state went on the offensive to curtail the trend toward rights based on sexual orientation. Voters engaged in political activism, gathered signatures, and were able to place a measure on the ballot in a general election called Amendment 2.[147]

Amendment 2 was a proposal to modify the Colorado state constitution that would have prevented any city, town, or county in the state from taking any legislative, executive, or judicial action to recognize gay and lesbian citizens as a protected class. Voters went to the polls and Amendment 2 passed in 1992 by a narrow margin of 54 percent to 47 percent of the vote.[148]

When legal provisions and regulatory mechanisms do not appear to provide for any tangible health or safety features, they will come under strict scrutiny in the courts. As applied to Amendment 2, immediately after Amendment 2 was passed, several organizations successfully sued to enjoin and prevent the enforcement of the law because it did not appear to further the betterment of society. The trial court granted the stay of Amendment 2 and stated that "the amendment was not necessary to support any compelling state interest and was not narrowly tailored to meet such an interest."[149] The injunction was affirmed by the State Supreme Court on appeal.[150] The case eventually wound its way all the way to the nation's highest court, the U.S. Supreme Court, in the form of *Romer v. Evans.*[151]

Romer v. Evans was significant since it would provide a national, rather than statewide, barometer on the subject of same-sex marriage. In the case, the U.S. Supreme Court struck down Amendment 2, ruling that blatant discrimination against homosexuals[152] based on nothing more than "moral disapproval" of gays, lesbians, and bisexuals is unconstitutional and a civil rights violation.[153] Writing for the majority, Justice Kennedy stated:

> Amendment 2 classifies homosexuals not to further a proper legislative end but to make them unequal to everyone else. This Colorado cannot do. A State cannot so deem a class of persons a stranger to its laws. Amendment 2 violates the Equal Protection Clause.[154]

In a dissent, Justice Scalia stated:

> The people of Colorado have adopted an entirely reasonable provision which does not even disfavor homosexuals in any substantive sense, but merely denies them preferential treatment. Amendment 2 is designed to prevent piecemeal deterioration of the sexual morality favored by a majority of Coloradans, and is not only an appropriate means to that legitimate end, but a means that Americans have employed before. Striking it down is an act, not of judicial judgment, but of political will.[155]

B. Indiscriminate Imposition of Inequalities

The U.S. Supreme Court has allowed restrictions on certain groups from participating in government-protected activities so long as such restrictions are rationally related to a legitimate government objective.[156] Public policies may be deemed legitimate even though they impose incidental disadvantages to certain groups.[157] For example, disallowing convicted felons the right to vote is permissible based on the deterrence of those who may contemplate felonious behavior.[158] Legislation that meets the legal "rational basis test" is not invalid because it fails to embrace everyone but instead is limited, for example, to persons or subjects that the legislation is applied to or evils or abuses to be corrected. Equal protection is not achieved through indiscriminate imposition of inequalities. However, a slight discrimination effect is not the test of a denial of equal protection of the law. A discrimination that is merely technical or accidental does not render a statute void.

That said, however, the disqualification of a particular group on the basis of a single trait (i.e., homosexuality), the rights and opportunities that everyone else enjoys, raises constitutional objections, as seen in this section of the chapter. Regardless of its specific applications, the equal protection clause applies to "any person," and its lofty purpose, while often unachievable, is to secure equality of treatment to all.

In one case of the indiscriminate imposition of inequality, the U.S. Supreme Court stated, "discriminations of an unusual character especially suggest careful consideration to determine whether they are obnoxious to the constitutional provision [of equal protection for all]".[159]

C. Equal Employment Opportunity

An employee, coincidentally of the federal court system, applied to her agency's benefits manager for her wife to receive health care benefits pursuant to a standard benefits policy of that government unit. The benefits manager denied the plaintiff, Ms. Golinski, any benefits for her wife. The denial occurred when the director of the administrative office of the United States

Courts refused to certify Golinski's identification of her spouse as family, because he believed that such an identification was barred by the federal Defense of Marriage Act (DOMA).[160]

DOMA was passed in response to the threat of gay marriage and provides that, when interpreting federal law, the term "marriage" means only a legal union between one man and one woman, and the word "spouse" refers only to a person of the opposite sex who is a husband or a wife. According to the judge in *In re Golinski*, "Whether DOMA's sweeping classification has a proper legislative end, or whether it reflects no more than an invidious design to stigmatize and disadvantage same-sex couples, is a hard question."[161]

Golinski brought suit, claiming she was denied a benefit of employment on the basis of sexual orientation, a violation of the EEO (Equal Employment Opportunity) Plan that covers her workplace.[162] The stage was set, once again, for a legal battle over the rights of domestic partnership.

In the case, the court made note of the curious distinction based on sexual orientation, identifying that Golinski had been denied health insurance benefits for her spouse, while similarly situated heterosexual employees received health insurance benefits for their spouses, the only difference being gender and sexual orientation. The case highlighted unequal treatment on account of sexual orientation, namely the gender of Golinski's wife. The court also noted that the availability of health insurance for oneself and one's family is a valuable benefit of employment. The court therefore ruled that the denial of such a benefit on account of gender and sexual orientation violates the terms of the EEO plan that covers Golinski. The court ruled:

> The Director of the Administrative Office of the United States Courts is therefore ordered to submit Karen Golinski's Health Benefits Election form 2809, which she signed and submitted on September 2, 2008, to the appropriate health insurance carrier. Any future health benefit forms are also to be processed without regard to the sex of a listed spouse.[163]

Additional Court Cases: Domestic Partnerships

Varnum v. State

763 N.W.2d 862 (2009)

CASE SUMMARY

PROCEDURAL POSTURE: Defendant county appealed summary judgment granted by the Iowa District Court for Polk County in favor of plaintiffs, six same-sex couples, challenging the district court's holding that Iowa Code § 595.2 (2009), which prohibited same-sex marriages, was unconstitutional because it violated the equal protection clause of the Iowa Constitution, Iowa Const. art. I, § 6.

OVERVIEW: Six same-sex couples filed suit challenging the constitutionality of Iowa Code § 595.2(1) (2009). The parties moved for summary judgment, and the district court granted summary judgment in favor of the couples, ruling that Iowa Code § 595.2 violated Iowa Const. art. I, § 6. On review of the district court ruling that the statute violated equal protection rights, the court concluded that excluding gay and lesbian people from civil marriage was not substantially related to any important governmental objective. A strict scrutiny analysis applied because the history of discrimination against gay and lesbian people suggested that any legislative burdens placed on them as a class were more likely than others to reflect deep-seated prejudice rather than legislative rationality in pursuit of some legitimate objective. The court had a constitutional duty to ensure equal protection of the law; faithfulness to that duty required a conclusion that Iowa Code § 595.2 violated the Iowa Constitution; if gay and lesbian people were required to submit to different treatment without an exceedingly persuasive justification, they were deprived of the benefits of the principle of equal protection.

OUTCOME: The judgment of the district court was affirmed. The language in Iowa Code § 595.2(1) that limited civil marriage to a man and a woman was to be stricken from the statute, and the remaining statutory language was to be interpreted and applied in a manner allowing gay and lesbian people full access to the institution of civil marriage.[164]

Chapter One Summary

The family unit is a highly protected entity in law and society. Throughout history, different forms of sexual relations have been allowed and practiced in families, such as incest or spouse-sharing. However, over time, these practices fall under the scrutiny of the law, are deemed suspicious and appear threatening to the preservation of the traditional family unit. In the history of Western Europe, the American Colonies, and the present day U.S., only certain forms of sexual relations have been allowed within the family and other practices such as having multiple wives is against the law. Many reasons exist for these legal regulations and they may be moral, practical, or legal and constitutional.

Table 3   Chapter One Offenses—Primary Legal Objections.

	Multiple Spouses	Two Spouses	Intrafamilial Sexual Contact	Sex with Spouse with Use of Force	Homosexual Sex
Polygamy	X				
Bigamy		X			
Incest			X		
Spousal Rape				X	
Gay Marriage					X

Religious-based Christian influences adopted early on in U.S. history criminalize forms of sex that stray from the one man, one woman model embraced by the majority in the Western world. As an example of the strong influence of Christian codes of sexual morality, polygamy is against the law, even though the polygamist arrangement of multiple wives is based in the dedication to religious principles. In the case of *State v. Jessop,* Jessop was sentenced to seventy-five years in prison for, what he considered, the practice of his faith.[165] The court record indicates he was convicted of the sexual assault of a minor. Different types of family-based sexual practices may emerge from time to time and will be measured morally against the traditional family model. Spousal rape was once legal, then became illegal; gay marriage was once illegal, but has become legal in some states.

The one husband and one wife form of sexual relations is legally permissible so long as both parties consent. A lack of consent may lead to the violent felony offense of spousal rape. Surprisingly, as recent as 1993 it was legal for a man to brutalize his wife sexually. The old, outdated legal tradition in the United States not only commanded a one man, one woman model, it also used to compel a structurally uneven relationship between them. Earlier in history, the woman was considered the property of the man and he could do whatever he wanted to her. The New York Appellate Court case of *People v. Liberta* rescinded the marital exemption to rape and set a precedent for other courts to use.[166] In outlawing spousal rape, the judge in the Liberta case stated, "Other than in the context of rape statutes, marriage has never been viewed as giving a husband the right to coerced intercourse on demand." Today, the law has worked to create equality within the one man, one woman model and spousal rape is against the law in all fifty states.

Polygamous arrangements similarly violate equality between one man and one woman marriages. Defined as a practice of having multiple wives, polygamy is a serious affront to traditional marriage and, as a legal matter, is implicated in numerous criminal offenses, the most serious being rape of a child. Polygamy was identified by federal authorities in the late 1800s and seen as too deviant to tolerate.[167] The federal government forced polygamists who were living in the western Utah Territories to declare polygamy illegal or face an abrogation of the legal status of the state of Utah. Polygamy can become so systematically lawless that a U.S. Senate Majority Leader suggested prosecuting polygamists leaders as racketeers under the federal RICO law. However, that may not be necessary. The manner in which local criminal justice systems prosecute polygamists may make the application of RICO irrelevant—one polygamous leader, Merrill Jessop was sentenced by a jury to seventy-five years in prison for sexual abuse of a child in 2009 in Tom Greene County, Texas. He was not the only polygamist in the local polygamist community to receive a long prison sentence for crimes related to the practice of polygamy.

The heightened concern over polygamous practices is not over. In 2006 a polygamous community leader named Warren Jeffs found himself on the FBI's Ten Most Wanted list, a short catalogue usually reserved for violent offenders. Jeffs was also subject to a novel legal theory when he faced prosecution: accomplice to rape.[168] The state tried to convict him of aiding and abetting a rape even though he was only guilty of arranging a marriage. His conviction in Utah was overturned, but he was extradited to the Texas criminal justice system that will be next in line to demonstrate its disapproval of polygamy.

Bigamy—going through a second marriage ceremony before the first one is terminated—was originally crafted as a statute to protect two virgins who married the same man. Modern concerns are more centered on the potential for civil unrest and resentful parties. Both spouses in a bigamous arrangement can feel betrayed and develop feelings of anger and resentment. If the brothers and uncles of the victims use self-help to seek revenge, a ripple effect of violence can occur. Hence, the law has traditionally regulated bigamous relationships on behalf of civil peace, as well as to support the dominant paradigm of one man, one woman. Many defendants in a bigamy prosecution will allege the invalidity of the first marriage contract, thereby terminating the allegation they were married twice simultaneously.[169]

More injurious to the victim than in cases of polygamy or bigamy, incestuous relations in a family are classified as felony offenses in most states and can result in severe penalties for perpetrators when minors are involved.[170] Whether in consanguineous or affinity structures, sexual contact between family members is widely objected to on the grounds of sexual health, intrafamily rivalries, and the exploitation of vulnerable family members such as minors. Consent, whether actual or constructive, is often absent in cases of incest. Incestuous relations by consanguinity are more serious cases than those pertaining to episodes of sex between affinity-related family members.

In all the sex crimes in the family discussed in this chapter, rarely if ever is there much political support for legal reform in favor of, for example, more spousal abuse, polygamy, bigamy, or incest. These offenses are characterized as deviant because the population of persons who subscribe to the practices is relatively small and the harm is distinct and sometimes severe. However, the law is not so clear-cut when it comes to gay marriage.

The populations of people who support gay marriage are not only relatively large, but they are also well organized and vocal when it comes to legal reform. Equally large and vocal, however, are the populations that oppose gay marriage. As a result, same-sex marriage has been an astonishing legal battleground that has crystallized the moral sentiment for both traditional marriage and gay marriage. A prime example of the legal wrangling over gay marriage is the litigation surrounding California's Proposition 8. After a mind-boggling legal journey, Proposition 8—a law that banned same-sex marriage—was stayed by the Ninth Circuit Court of Appeals.[171] As a result, domestic partnerships can derive legal status in jurisdictions that choose to confer such legal status in the state of California.

At stake in a marriage are numerous legal rights such as the right of inheritance and property transfer. These rights flow naturally to a marriage of one man, one woman, but are often denied to gay couples for no other reason than sexual orientation. As a result of this "indiscriminate imposition of inequalities," the courts have had to address many cases of allegations of opposition to gay marriage. In *Romer v. Evans,* the U.S. Supreme Court banned a democratically approved law in the State of Colorado that prohibited gay marriage.[172] Writing for the majority opinion, Justice Kennedy stated, "Amendment 2 classifies homosexuals not to further a proper legislative end but to make them unequal to everyone else."[173] Writing for the minority, Justice Scalia stated, "Amendment 2 is designed to prevent piecemeal deterioration of the sexual morality favored by a majority of Coloradans."[174] Today, gay marriage is legal in five states in the U.S., but the legal landscape is in no way settled on this aspect of sex in the family.

Key Terms

Spousal Rape 00

Polygamy 00

Organized Crime 00

RICO 00

Statute of Limitations 00

Bigamy 00

Incest 00

Affinity 00

Consanguinity 00

Colorado Amendment 2 00

Domestic Partnerships 00

Marriage Benefits 00

Concepts & Principles

One Man One Woman 00

Common Law 00

Christian Religion 00

Chattel 00

Legal Rape 00

Rape as an Accomplice 00

Racketeering 00

Sexual Mores 00

Spiritual Marriage 00

Internecine Dispute 00

Discrimination 00

Indiscriminate Imposition of Inequalities 00

Chapter One Select Court Cases	
Case	**Point of Law**
Liberta v. Kelly (p. 00)	A legal marriage does not serve to justify a rape
Shaun v. State (p. 00)	Older common law provisions do not take precedence over modern statutes
State v. Smith (p. 00)	A legal marital separation serves as no justification for rape
Texas v. Jessop (p. 21)	Polygamous practice charged as unlawful sexual contact with a minor
State v. Ezeonu (p. 00)	Nigerian practice of having a "junior wife" not valid in the State of New York
Dale v. State (p. 00)	A foreign marriage contract does not apply where a U.S.-based charge of bigamy in concerned
Wilson v. State (p. 00)	Sister-in-law status legally ceases upon death of spouse
People v. Scott (p. 00)	Adult status of consenting parties does not make incest legal
Morgan v. State (p. 00)	A lack of awareness of familial tie does not make incest legal
Romer v. Evans (p. 00)	Colorado Amendment 2 ruled unconstitutional as it serves no compelling state interest

Questions for Review

1. What was the legal justification that allowed for a husband to rape his wife?

2. Approximately what year did the law make spousal rape a crime in the U.S.?

3. Even though spousal rape is illegal, what makes these cases challenging for either party to prevail in court?

4. What makes polygamy illegal?? Aren't all religious practices legal?

5. What is the difference between polygamy and bigamy?

6. How is it possible to be found guilty as an accomplice to rape?

7. Does the law treat some forms of incest more severely than others? Please provide an example.

8. What is the difference between a marriage and a domestic partnership? Should there be a difference?

9. Does every state in the U.S. have a law permitting domestic partnerships?

10. What is the main argument against the legality of domestic partnerships?

1 State v. Lowe, Stark App. No. 2004CA00292, 2005-Ohio-4274.

2 DON S. BROWNING, *MODERN LAW AND CHRISTIAN JURISPRUDENCE ON MARRIAGE AND FAMILY*, 58 Emory L.J. 31 (2008).

3 JOCELYN HO, *INCEST AND SEX OFFERDER REGISTRATION: WHO IS REGISTRATION HELPING AND WHO IS IT HURTING?*, 14 CARDOZO J. L. & GENDER 429 (2008).

4 *Id.*

5 *Id.* at 41.

6 JOHN D'EMILIO & ESTELLE B. FREEDMAN, INTIMATE MATTERS: A HISTORY OF SEXUALITY IN AMERICA (University of Chicago Press)(1988).

7 JOHN SCHIED, AN INTRODUCTION TO ROMAN RELIGION (JANET LLOYD TRANS., 2003).

8 HENRY DE BRACTON, ON THE LAWS AND CUSTOMS OF ENGLAND (SAMUEL E. THORNE TRANS., 1968).

9 BRONISLAW MALINOWSKI, SEX, CULTURE, AND MYTH (1962).

10 *Id.*

11 WAYNE MORRISON, JURISPRUDENCE: FROM THE GREEKS TO POST-MODERNISM (1997).

12 Note, *INBRED OBSCURITY: IMPROVING INCEST LAWS IN THE SHADOW OF THE 'SEXUAL FAMILY'*, 119 Harv. L. Rev. 2464.

13 JUSTO L. GONZALEZ, THE STORY OF CHRISTIANITY (1985).

14 *Id.*

15 E. BROOKS HOLIFIELD, THEOLOGY IN AMERICA: CHRISTIAN THOUGHT FROM THE AGE OF THE PURITANS TO THE CIVIL WAR (2003).

16 DON S. BROWNING, *MODERN LAW AND CHRISTIAN JURISPRUDENCE ON MARRIAGE AND FAMILY*, 58 EMORY L.J. 31, 34 (2008).

17 JOHN D'EMILIO & ESTELLE B. FREEDMAN, INTIMATE MATTERS: A HISTORY OF SEXUALITY IN AMERICA (University of Chicago Press)(1988).

18 Griswold v. Connecticut, 381 U.S. 479 (1965).

19 Lawrence v. Texas, U.S. 539 U.S. 558 (2003).

20 ANNA CLARK, WOMEN'S SILENCE MEN'S VIOLENCE: SEXUAL ASSAULT IN ENGLAND 1770–1845 (1987).

21 *Id.*

22 SIR MATTHEW HALE, THE HISTORY OF THE PLEAS OF THE CROWN 635 (London Professional Books 1971). Hale was the Chief Justice of the Court of King's Bench in England. This treatise was first published in 1736 and has been significant in the development of American law.

23 SUSAN ESTRICH, RAPE, 95 Yale L. J. 1087 (1986).

24 Commonwealth v. Fogerty, 74 Mass. 489 (Mass. 1857).

25 *Id.*

26 R v. R, [1992], 1 A.C. 599 (H.L.) (appeal taken from Eng.).

27 *Id.*

28 DAVID FINKELHOR & KERSTI YLLÖ, LICENSE TO RAPE (Free Press 1985) (1985).

29 U.S. DEPARTMENT OF STATE, 2008 COUNTRY REPORTS ON HUMAN RIGHTS PRACTICES (2008).

30 BUREAU OF JUSTICE STATISTICS, U.S. DEPARTMENT OF JUSTICE, CRIMINAL VICTIMIZATIONS 2004 (2005).

31 STEPHEN T. HOLMES & RONALD M. HOLMES, SEX CRIMES: PATTERNS AND BEHAVIORS 233 (3d ed. 2009) (citing VIRGINIA SEXUAL AND DOMESTIC VIOLENCE ACTION ALLIANCE, VIOLENCE ON CAMPUS: OVERVIEW *available at* http://theredflagcampaign.com:8000/docs/Violence_on_Campus_fact_sheet.pdf).

32 WYO STAT. ANN. § 6-2-307 (2010).

33 *Id.*

34 *Id.*

[35] People v. Liberta, 474 N.E.2d 567 (N.Y. 1984).

[36] *Id.*

[37] N.Y. Penal Law § 130.35 (McKinney 1992).

[38] *Id.*

[39] *Id.*

[40] U.S. Const. amend. XIV.

[41] People v. Liberta, 474 N.E.2d 567 (N.Y. 1984).

[42] People v. Liberta, 839 F.2d 77 (2d. Cir. 1988).

[43] *Id.*

[44] Shunn v. State, 742 P.2d 775 (Wyo. 1987).

[45] *Id.* at 777.

[46] *Id.* at 778.

[47] *Id.*

[48] State v. Smith, 426 A.2d 38 (N.J. 1981).

[49] N.J. STAT. ANN. § 2C:14-5(b) (West 1978).

[50] Ellam v. Ellam, 333 A.2d 577 (N.J. Super. Ct. Ch. Div. 1975).

[51] State v. Smith, 426 A.2d 38 (N.J. 1981).

[52] *Id.*

[53] U.S. v. Streete, AFCCA 36757, US Air Force (2009).

[54] BAUER, W. J., NATIVE AMERICAN, DISCOVERED AND CONQUERED: THOMAS JEFFERSON, LEWIS AND CLARK, AND MANIFEST DESTINY. HISTORY: REVIEWS OF NEW BOOKS, 36(2), 49-52 (2008).

[55] JESSIE L. EMBRY, MORMON POLYGAMOUS FAMILIES: LIFE IN THE PRINCIPLE (1987).

[56] *Id.*

[57] MAURA J. STRASSBERG. THE CRIME OF POLYGAMY, 12 TEMP. POL. & CIV. RTS. L. REV. 353, 355 (2003).

[58] *Id.* at 360-361.

[59] UTAH CONST. art. XXIV, § 2 ("All laws of the Territory of Utah now in force, not repugnant to this Constitution, shall remain in force until they expire by their own limitations, or are altered or repealed by the Legislature. The act of the Governor and Legislative Assembly of the Territory of Utah, entitled, 'An Act to punish polygamy and other kindred offenses,' approved February 4th, A.D. 1892, in so far as the same defines and imposes penalties for polygamy, is hereby declared to be in force in the State of Utah.").

[60] Strassberg, *supra* note 57 at 355.

[61] SAMANTHA SLARK, ARE ANTI-POLYGAMY LAWS AN UNCONSTITUTIONAL NFRINGEMENT ON THE LIBERTY INTERESTS OF CONSENTING ADULTS?, 6 J.L. & Fam. Stud. 451 (2004).

[62] Catherine Blake, *The Sexual Victimization of Teenage Girls in Utah: Polygamous Marriages Versus Internet Sex Predators,* 7 J.L. & Fam. Stud. 289 (2005).

[63] Shayna M. Sigman, *Everything Lawyers Know About Polygamy Is Wrong,* 16 Cornell J.L. & Pub. Pol'y 101 (2006).

[64] MODEL PENAL CODE § 230.1 (1985).

[65] Canada Criminal Code, R.S.C. 1985, c. C-46 s. 293(1).

[66] *Id.*

67 Edwards, C., *Is Hell Illegal? The Implications of the Warren Jeffs Decision.* Free Inquiry, 30(3), 52-53 (2010).

68 State v. Jeffs, 2010 UT 49, 243 P.3d 1250.

69 Utah Code Ann. § 76-2-202 (1973).

70 State v. Jeffs, 2010 UT 49, 243 P.3d 1250.

71 *Id.*

72 *Reid Presents Bill Aimed at Polygamy.* Las Vegas Review Journal. Feb. 11, 2010. http://www.lvrj.com/news/25845989.html (Last visited August 9, 2010).

73 Organized Crime Control Act of 1970, Pub. L. No. 91-452, 84 Stat. 922 (1970) (codified as amended at 18 U.S.C. §§ 1961–1968 (2006)).

74 *Id.*

75 United States v. Barger, 454 U.S. 817 (1981).

76 *Regulating Polygamy: Intimacy, Default Rules, and Bargaining for Equality,* 110 Colum. L. Rev. 8 (2010).

77 Irwin Altman & Joseph Ginat, Polygamous Families in Contemporary Society (1996).

78 *Id.*

79 *FLDS TRIAL: Jury Finds Jessop Guilty: Man Faces Life Sentence in Sex Assault.* San Angelo Standard Times, March 17, 2010, 12:16 pm. http://www.gosanangelo.com/news/2010/mar/17/jessop-case-goes-to-jury/.

80 Trish Choate, *FLDS Trial: Jessop Guilty of Sexual Assault,* Go San Angelo StandardTimes, Nov. 5, 2009, http://www.gosanangelo.com/news/2009/nov/05/jury-in-jessop-trial-will-hear-closing-arguments/. Jessop was convicted of sexual assault of a child, a second-degree felony.

81 Tex. Penal Code § 22.011 (2003).

82 Tex. Fam. Code Ann. § 262.201(b) (Vernon Supp. 2009).

83 Affidavit in Support of Original Petition for Protection of Children in an Emergency and for Conservatorship in Suit Affecting the Parent-Child Relationship at 2-3, *In re A Child,* No. 2902 (51st Dist. Ct., Schleicher County, Tex. Apr. 7, 2008).

84 *Id.*

85 Tex. Penal Code § 22.011 (2003).

86 *Jessop Sentenced to 75 Years.* San Angelo Standard Times, March 19, 2010, 2:56 pm. http://www.gosanangelo.com/news/2010/mar/19/breaking-news-jessop-sentenced-to-75-years/.

87 Reynolds v. United States, 98 U.S. 145 (1879).

88 Ariela Dubler, *Wifely Behavior: A Legal History of Acting Married,* 100 Colum. L. Rev. 957 (2000).

89 Basch, N., *Marriage, Morals, and Politics in the Election of 1828.* 80 J. American History 3, 890-918 (1993).

90 Russell William Odnall, Russell on Crime (12th ed. 1964).

91 Okla. Stat. tit. 21, § 881 (1997).

92 Okla. Stat. tit. 21, § 881 (1997).

93 John Klotter, Criminal Law 373-375 (7th ed. 2004).

94 Scoggins v. State, 401 S.E.2d 13 (Ga. 1990).

95 *Id.* at 19.

96 State v. Martinez, 250 P. 239, 242 (1daho 1926).

97 Idaho Rev. Stat. § 6805 (1887).

98 State v. Martinez, 250 P. 239 (Idaho 1926).

[99] *Id.*

[100] *Id.* at 249.

[101] Dale v. State, 15 S.E. 287 (1892).

[102] *Id.* at 291.

[103] *Id.* at 295.

[104] *Id.* at 299.

[105] People v. Ezeonu, 588 N.Y.S.2d 116 (N.Y. Sup. Ct. 1992).

[106] Connolly, B., *Every Family Become a School of Abominable Impurity: Incest and Theology in the Early Republic.* 30 Journal of the Early Republic 3, 413-442 (2010).

[107] Ashley Morgan, *Full Circle,* 11 J. L. & Fam. Stud. 541 (2009); 2009 Utah L. Rev. 589.

[108] *Id.* at J. L. & Fam. Stud. 549.

[109] Signs v. State, 250 P. 938, 940 (Okla. Crim. App. 1926).

[110] Leslie Bienen, *Defining Incest,* 92 Nw. U. L. Rev. 1501, 1531 (1998).

[111] State v. Lowe, Stark App. No. 2004CA00292, 2005-Ohio-4274.

[112] Del. Code Ann. tit. 11, § 766 (2005).

[113] Iowa Code § 709.3 (2007) (defining sex with a victim under age 12 as a Class B felony); *id.* § 726.2 (defining incest as a Class D felony); id. § 902.9 (providing that Class B felonies carry a maximum twenty-five-year sentence, while Class D felonies carry a maximum five-year sentence).

[114] Ala. Code § 13A-13-3 (defining incest); see also § 13A-5-6 (providing mandatory sentences). Alabama's incest provision does not include any limitations on the basis of age, so it can apply to sexual contact between a parent and young child or between two consenting adults.

[115] Wilson v. State, 46 S.W. 451, 455 (Tenn. 1898).

[116] Tenn. Code § 6767 (1890).

[117] Wilson v. State, 46 S.W. 451 (Tenn. 1898).

[118] Signs v. State, 250 P. 938, 940 (Okla. Crim. App. 1926).

[119] *Wilson,* 46 S.W. at 459.

[120] Cal. Penal Code § 285 (West 2006).

[121] *Id.*

[122] People v. Scott, 54 Cal. Rptr.3d 674 (Cal Ct. App. 2007).

[123] *Id.* at 678.

[124] *Id.* at 680.

[125] *Id.* at 683.

[126] Morgan v. State, 11 Ala. 289 (Ala. 1847).

[127] *Id.*

[128] *Id.*

[129] Sutton v. Commonwealth, 324 S.E.2d 665 (1985).

[130] Scott Senjo, Book Review, Electronic J. Hum. Sexuality, Vol. 13, Jan. 23, 2010 http://www.ejhs.org/volume13/Bookreview%2013-2.htm (reviewing Homophobia: An Australian History (Shirleene Robinson ed., 2008)).

131 Matthew Shepard and James Byrd, Jr. Hate Crimes Prevention Act, Pub. L. No. 111-84, §§4701-13, 123 Stat. 2190, 2835-44 (2009); Matthew Shepard Act § 4704(a)(1) (2009).

132 Lawrence v. Texas, 539 U.S. 558 (2003).

133 Novkov, J., *The Miscegenation/Same-Sex Marriage Analogy: What Can We Learn from Legal History?* 33 Law & Social Inquiry 2, 345-386 (2008).

134 Eric Lobsinger, *A National Model for Reconciling Equal Protection for Same-sex Couples with State Marriage Amendments:* Alaska Civil Liberties Union Ex Rel. Carter v. Alaska. 23 Alaska L. Rev. 117 (2006).

135 *Id.* at 125.

136 *Id.* at 133.

137 Alaska Stat. § 25.05.013(b) (2004).

138 Cal. Fam. Code, § 300(a) (West 1977).

139 In re Marriage Cases, 183 P.3d 384 (Cal. 2008).

140 *Equal Protection—Same-Sex Marriage—California Supreme Court Classifies Proposition 8 as "Amendment" Rather than "Revision."—Strauss v. Horton,* 207 P.3d 48 (Cal. 2009). 123 Har. L. Rev. 6, 1516-1523 (2010).

141 Cal. Const. art. I, § 7.5 (2009).

142 Strauss v. Horton, 207 P.3d 48 (Cal. 2009).

143 *Equal Protection—Same-Sex Marriage—California Supreme Court Classifies Proposition 8 as "Amendment" Rather than "Revision."—Strauss v. Horton,* 207 P.3d 48 (Cal. 2009). 123 Har. L. Rev. 6, 1516-1523 (2010).

144 Miss. Code Ann. § 97-29-1 (1972).

145 *Id.*

146 Or. Const. § 5a(2).

147 Dailey, J., & Farley, P., *Colorado's Amendment 2: A Result in Search of a Reason.* 20 Har. J. L. & Pub. Pol. 1 (1996).

148 *Id.* at 13.

149 Evans v. Romer, 882 P.2d 1335 (Colo. 1994).

150 *Id.*

151 Romer v. Evans, 517 U.S. 620 (1996).

152 Colo. Const. art. II, § 30b.

153 U.S. Const. amend. XIV.

154 Romer v. Evans, 517 U.S. 620, 638 (1996).

155 *Id.* at 643.

156 Kadrmas v. Dickinson Pub. Sch., 487 U.S. 450 (1988).

157 Heller v. Doe, 509 U.S. 312 (1993).

158 Davis v. Beason, 133 U.S. 333 (1890).

159 Louisville Gas & Elec. Co. v. Coleman, 277 U.S. 32, 37–38 (1928).

160 1 U.S.C. § 7 (1996).

161 In re Golinski, 587 F.3d 901, 909 (2009).

162 *Id.* at 913.

163 *Id.* at 917.

164 Varnum v. State, 763 N.W.2d 862 (2009).

[165] *Jessop Sentenced to 75 Years.* SAN ANGELO STANDARD TIMES, March 19, 2010, 2:56 pm. http://www.gosanangelo.com/news/2010/mar/19/breaking-news-jessop-sentenced-to-75-years/.

[166] People v. Liberta, 474 N.E.2d 567 (N.Y. 1984).

[167] Catherine Blake, *The Sexual Victimization of Teenage Girls in Utah: Polygamous Marriages Versus Internet Sex Predators,* 7 J.L. & FAM. STUD. 289 (2005).

[168] State v. Jeffs, 2010 UT 49, 243 P.3d 1250.

[169] Scoggins v. State, 401 S.E.2d 13 (Ga. 1990).

[170] Leslie Bienen, *Defining Incest,* 92 Nw. U. L. Rev. 1501, 1531 (1998).

[171] *Equal Protection—Same-Sex Marriage—California Supreme Court Classifies Proposition 8 as "Amendment" Rather than "Revision."—Strauss v. Horton,* 207 P.3d 48 (Cal. 2009). 123 HAR. L. REV. 6, 1516-1523 (2010).

[172] Romer v. Evans, 517 U.S. 620 (1996).

[173] *Id.* at 638.

[174] *Id.* at 643.

Chapter Two

Illegal Consensual Sex: Fornication,

Statutory Rape, Sodomy, Adultery,

Seduction, Miscegeny

"Prescriptions against sodomy have very ancient roots."

Bowers v. Hardwick
United States Supreme Court
478 U.S. 186 (1986)[1]

Legal Background

T he legal foundation for regulating consensual sexual activities stems from a variety of social, religious, and political factors. These factors wove a fabric of public sentiment that defined the culture of the time during the 17th century. Toss in a little superstition, fear, and rigid morality, and there's little wonder why consensual sex between mature adults was prohibited in many ways during the start of the American republic.

There's no better place to start than Jamestown in 1662. Here, the settlers faced the formidable task of clearing away the rugged wilderness for farming and agriculture and surviving in a strange, new environment. "Modern" contemplation of new standards of morality was the furthest thing in the minds of the hard-working settlers. To the contrary, with the threat of conflict with Indians, foreign colonists, and the Mother Country of England, the stresses of early American living may have caused the public to rail even more so against "deviant" acts such as adultery and sodomy as a means of gaining perceived control over the hostile world they lived in. In short, there would be no legal reform of the criminal law as it pertained to consensual sex in Colonial America. The colonists had other things to worry about.

Even though Colonial living was harsh and humorless, the survival-based living, without more, does not adequately explain the impermissiveness applied to sexual mores at the time. Religion, of course, shaped the concern over sexual deviancy outside of marriage, consensual or otherwise. Prevailing theological sentiment, largely influenced by the Roman Catholic Church and the principles of Saint Augustine from the 4th Century, held on to time-worn beliefs about marriage and sex: Sex was dangerous, sinful, and when used for procreation within a marriage, should not be enjoyed.[2] King Henry VIII and the Protestant Reformation from 1550 to 1600 gave marital sex a degree of permission beyond procreation, but did so quite discreetly. In sum, from 400 to 1600, a form of superstitious negativity cast a pall over consensual sexual expression in Europe and eventually the Thirteen Colonies.[3]

As the Colonies were established, the legal regime was influenced by religious leaders and religious leaders were influenced by the legal regime; they were one and the same. It was simply too risky to pull the lid off any sexual desire, especially for women. There were prostitutes and servants use for sex, but it was very hush-hush. Obedience and compliance with social mores meant frowning on sexual expression of any type. Church attendance in Colonial America was required by law and local communities assigned lookouts to police congregations for anyone absent from church. It should go without saying that the talk given by the minister, such as Puritan leader Cotton Mather, on Sunday did not speak about sex with much affection. Mather and other leaders belabored congregations to avoid sexual stimulation and to suppress their desires. They emphasized marriage as the only suitable outlet for sexual expression, and condemned masturbation and fornication. Entire communities were trained to think of sex as "disgusting." In his book *Colonial Crimes and Punishments,* Cox states:

> In the Puritan north a religious message leaps out from almost every page of the early criminal codes. Sin, of course, existed in the eyes of the beholders, and the eyes were everywhere—as you might expect in small, inbred communities. Consider the scrutiny given to observance of the Sabbath. The law usually required churchgoing, and someone was always checking attendance. In early Virginia, every minister was entitled to appoint four men in his fort or settlement to inform on religious scofflaws.[4]

As Cox implies, behavior (moral and otherwise) was strictly regulated and communities conducted inquisitions of themselves, looking out for the slightest sign of a moral transgression. The Salem Witchcraft Trials in 1692 reflect the communal anxiety over behavior that was not somehow explicable or in conformity with local comfort levels, especially sexual behavior. As painfully demonstrated during the Witchcraft Trials, women especially had to be careful. Chastity was put forth as a young woman's most treasured asset, one to be guarded with all due care, especially in the face of smooth-talking, newly arrived immigrants.

The early Americans used shame as a deterrent to deviancy and appeared to dole it out in large quantities. Convicted offenders, whether for sex crimes or not, could be branded, pilloried, or somehow put on notorious display for all to see. Nathaniel Hawthorne's 1850 novel *The Scarlet Letter* tells the story of sin, law, and shame in 1600s Puritan Boston and the shameful letter "A" required to be worn in public by convicted adultress Hester Prynne.[5] Hester was a type of public enemy for engaging in consensual sex with a mature adult. Public flogging and whippings were distinct forms of criminal sentences and were often served in the middle of the town square for all to see and, hence, ridicule. Public displays of shame for a convicted criminal furthermore sent a message to onlookers about the fate in store for them should they get caught committing a sex crime or other crime. Today's Sex Offender Registry may be seen as a 21st century form of public humiliation and ridicule. A convicted sex offender is legally required to be placed on the Registry in the digital town square for all to see and admonish.

While acts such as adultery and fornication were seen as deviant as well as shameful, law and morality combined with mythological superstition when it came to the deviance of sodomy. Prescriptions against sodomy have ancient roots. The first codified ban on sodomy in the U.S. came immediately after the Revolution in 1776. For example, after the Revolution, the Northwest Territories adopted the English buggery law with a 1795 Northwest Territory ordinance, thus making sodomy a capital offense for males only. Sodomites got the death penalty; consent was legally irrelevant. Lawmakers in the 1800s were so caught up in despising sodomy, they couldn't bring themselves to define it. Sodomy remained the "infamous crime against nature," an act so horrible, it was "not fit to be named."[6] We know of few parallels in law where a crime is so bad, we don't know what to call it. No wonder sodomy has suffered through numerous tortured definitions over time.

Such was the social, moral, and legal climate for the criminality of consensual sex for the first part of American history up until the Age of Industrialization in the late 1800s.[7] It would not be until the Jazz Era of the 1920s that consensual sex would first be conceptualized as a private, rather than a moral and community matter, and hence, less of an evil than it was heretofore.

Landmark legal cases barely dotted the landscape for consensual sex offenses in the 1800s, save for Supreme Court case of *Pace v. Alabama* in 1883.[8] This case steadfastly maintained the prevailing orthodoxy about sex, and sex and race relations. The Pace court ruled that laws prohibiting black and white consensual couples were legal and constitutional. Change would be inspired, however, from industrial invention and progress in the time of Henry Ford and J. P. Morgan. Immigrants were needed for the new economic machine, young and old began a pattern of urban mobility, and curiosity was given a greater stage upon which to animate the mind, and also the body.

Change, however, is historically threatening and the threat was imminent. Immigration and urbanization gave rise to the ubiquitous dance hall saloon and red light district in cities and mining camps across the Transcontinental Railway from Chicago to Los Angeles with Las Vegas in between. Technological improvements in the printing press, such as the creation of the steam powered rotary printing press in 1843 allowed millions of copies of a page in a single day. Rustic pornographers were quick to use the new technology and take advantage of the disposable income provided to masses of workers during the Industrial Revolution.

These developments, however, may have been too much, too fast for a nation that only fifty years before made decisions about the sex lives of others on a local community level. As one reaction, public moralist Anthony Comstock unilaterally took up the task of combating sex in print, art, and personal correspondence. After a year of lobbying the state and federal legislatures to tighten anti-obscenity laws, the U.S. Congress passed "An Act for the Suppression of Trade in, and Circulation of Obscene Literature and Articles of Immoral Use"[9] (the Comstock Act) in 1873 without debate.[10] In addition, The Mann Act (also known as The White Slave Traffic Act) was passed in 1910 to address prostitution-related activities.[11]

The forces for change were nevertheless too far set in motion; there was no turning back. The early 1900s manifested more wealth than had ever been seen before in the U.S. World War I was a somber time, but after that, the "Roaring Twenties" were in full swing. Coming from the Gilded Age of the late 1800s, the 1920s after the war meant unprecedented advancements in the areas of education, science, and technology. Automobiles, moving pictures, and the radio catapulted social and cultural mannerisms into an entirely new realm of experimentation.

Relatively greater standards of living created space for the contemplation of leisure pursuits such as the arts, romance, travel, human expression, justice, and equality. Communities no longer policed each other and immigrants landed ashore with more liberalized ideas about romance than existed in the bashful, relatively young nation. A population boom created a new generation who would grow up and witness a bit of social undressing in balls, banquets, and cocktail parties. Although their parents would always be Victorian Moralists, the new generation would be catapulted into a new world of opportunity derived from industrial invention, personal profit, and the new sound of jazz music. The new generation would see little reason to return to the Augustinian viewpoint that sex was awful.

Freud aided in the amorphous, tentative boundaries surrounding sex at the time. An influential neurologist who began work in Austria in the 1930s, Freud demonstrated that the human mind had a unique ability to repress thoughts and feelings that were threatening or uncomfortable.[12] Whether such repression is mentally healthy is beyond the scope of this discussion. Freud's contributions were that sex is far too prominent in the human experience to keep it repressed. Uncovering sexual desire thus became worthy of consideration, if for no other reason than to halt the working against one's natural impulses.

The Gilded Age wealth and leisure, Sigmund Freud, and an influx of massive immigration from Europe, and the United States was infused with change that would move in both directions. Freud's theories considered the idea of sexual repression, but that did not mean unrepressed sex would be tolerated by the criminal justice system. At the time of Freud, due to advances in science and medicine, sexual aberrations were now to be viewed through the lens of psychopathy. In 1938, due to the urbanization of Chicago and commensurate levels of sex crimes, Illinois was the first state to pass a Sexual Psychopath Law, legislation that demonized, criminalized, and institutionalized sexual deviants. Challenged as an old school form of *The Scarlet Letter,* the laws were upheld as legal and constitutional.[13] Anyone found to be exhibiting an undefined "mental disorder" and who had "criminal propensities to the commission of sex crimes" was considered a sexual psychopath. This umbrella label, however, tended to miss the mark and cast a net too wide over persons who were more appropriately termed hypersexual and were actually not psychopathic.[14]

A second world war in the 1940s resulted in the expansion of cities as industries there assisted in the war effort. Jazz music flourished, especially in large southern cities such as Atlanta, New Orleans, and Dallas and the music paved the way for a liberalization of social mores and eventually the likes of Elvis Presley and Johnny Cash. The Beatles followed Elvis and,ef combined with a gladness for the war to be over, American society appeared ready for a sexual revolution.

The Roaring Twenties combined wealth with new ideas from European immigrants about love, sex, and morality.

By the end of World War II, it was not only a transformation of consciousness that created change. In addition, social science data were used to provide concrete conclusions about considerations that were heretofore merely speculations. American zoologist Alfred Kinsey embarked on an unprecedented study of human sexual behavior, asking detailed research questions about personal sexual practices of a cross-section sample of subjects. In one of his publications, the 1948 *Sexual Behavior in the Human Male,* Kinsey conveyed for all to see that numerous populations of males enjoy premarital sex, masturbation, same-sex relations, and other forms of sex.[15] Kinsey's findings were so startling, his follow-up publication *Sexual Behavior in the Human Female* was censored for fear of what truth and details might emerge from it. The American public can only take so much truth when it comes to human sexual desire.

By the time the Baby Boom generation was being conceived, there was little anyone could do to stem the tide of the sexual revolution. In 1965 the U.S. Supreme Court made it legal for a married couple to purchase, possess, and use birth control devices, and that any law restricting this freedom was an infringement on the "marital right of privacy."[16] The Griswold decision overturned an 1879 state law that prohibited the use of "any drug, medicinal article or instrument for the purpose of preventing conception."[17] As an indication of the need to break new ground in the area of consensual sex, the High Court had to craft a right to privacy out of the Constitution since no such right was ever built in by the Founding Fathers. One justice saw a right of privacy in the Fourteenth Amendment, and another justice found the right in the Ninth Amendment. This newly crafted Ninth Amendment right to privacy was used to uphold a women's right to choose in the 1973 *Roe v. Wade* Supreme Court decision. The Court's ruling in Griswold was the first-ever ruling in the U.S. that gave constructive permission to married couples to engage in consensual sex independent of procreation.

The 1967 *Loving v. Virginia* case was handed down two years later.[18] In this case, the Supreme Court gave an imprimatur to sexual relations between a mixed-race married couple, thus furthering the legitimacy of consensual sex between safe and supportive married couples. The *Loving* decision reversed the *Pace* decision of 1883 and invalidated the Racial Integrity Act of 1924. In 1969, *Stanley v. Georgia* further nudged the legal apparatus in the direction of autonomous choice by holding that pornography that is otherwise illegal may be possessed and consumed in the privacy of one's home.[19]

From the time of the Stanley decision in 1969 until 2000, the trend toward legalization of private morality and sexual expression was stilled. The centerpiece legal ruling in this era was the Supreme Court case of *Bowers v. Hardwick* in 1986.[20] The ruling may have been a backlash from the sexual revolution of the 1960s, or it may have been a reaffirmation of the safety and stability of marriage, marital sex, and the one man, one woman relationship which has been the dominant paradigm throughout the history of the U.S. In 1996 Congress passed the DOMA (Defense of Marriage Act),[21] and also in 1996, the Supreme Court upheld the military's Don't Ask, Don't Tell ban on disclosures of one's gay sexual orientation while serving in the military.

In 2003, the pinnacle decision of sexual choice and personal freedom in sexual matters was handed down in the case of *Lawrence v. Texas.*[22] In the Lawrence decision, the Supreme Court invalidated the Bowers ruling and held that two consenting adults cannot be subject to the criminal law for sharing sexually and safely in the privacy of their own home. No other legal ruling has given such wide scope to autonomous sexual expression in the history of the United States. What does the Lawrence decision actually stand for? Have other decisions supported Lawrence? These are challenging questions. The answers remain to be seen.

The legal background of consensual sex reflects that, in some cases, the legal prohibitions on consensual sex crimes were repealed, such as with some adultery and fornication statutes at mid century. At mid century, some sodomy statutes were also repealed. In other cases, enforcement of certain sex crime laws dropped off completely, leaving them as almost (but not completely) dead letters. Finally, in yet other situations, new justifications have arisen for the resurrection of old laws, such as in the case of disease control (HIV/AIDS) as a justification for the regulation of prostitution. The periodic enforcement of these laws has been shifted somewhat to reflect those new concerns.

Fornication

C ommonly known as consensual sexual intercourse between an unmarried man and an unmarried woman, **fornication**[23] offends traditional and conservative principles of morality, family, religion, and the chastity of a woman. It was long thought that a proper and just society was enhanced and maintained through the fulfillment of traditional familial roles and remnants of this idea are still true today. Premarital sex is still considered taboo to a minor degree and several derogatory euphemisms may apply such as "shacking-up," "living in sin," "just using each other," or "having sex out of wedlock."[24]

The Common Law in England was used to regulate this offense and the Colonies adopted the Common Law of fornication. In one county in Colonial America, there were a recorded 210 convictions for the crime of fornication and a total of 40 convictions for all other crimes combined.[25] Biblical standards foster the ideals of proper consensual relations and lend themselves to standards of a "good" social order. Social stability is thought to manifest through the maintenance of family roles such as mother and father, husband and wife. These roles are defined with various duties and responsibilities and chief among them are the focus inward toward the family unit, dedication to the family, and the love and support of one's spouse. Fornication arguably defies these long-standing roles and creates a degree of chaos and uncertainty; social stability is threatened, hence, the legal prohibition.

Approximately 16 states codified the Common Law into formal statutes to legally criminalize fornication. These statutes are rarely enforced and many have been repealed or struck down by the courts. The litigation is ongoing today as competing moral perspectives duel one another in the court system.

The changing legal landscape for fornication may have begun in 1972 with the U.S. Supreme Court ruling in *Eisenstadt v. Baird.*[26] This case struck down a Massachusetts law that prohibited the possession of contraceptive devices by unmarried persons. Formerly, only legally married persons were allowed to use contraception—their use by unmarried persons would signal an approval for fornication and premarital sex. The ruling in Eisenstadt was the first in the history of the U.S. to recognize the rights of single people to procreate *vel non* (or not) on the same basis as married couples. Eisenstadt may have come before its time as many states retained their fornication laws. In addition, in 1986, the U.S. Supreme Court ruled that single people could not have sex, at least if the two were both male.

In 1989, the ACLU initiated a lawsuit against the state of Utah, attempting to declare the state's fornication and heterosexual sodomy laws a violation of the constitutional right to privacy. Under the title of *Oliverson v. West Valley City,* when the case came before a federal magistrate in 1994, the judge dismissed the case reviewing it as a case of adultery and sidestepping a ruling on the legality of fornication.[27] In 1998, the Georgia Supreme Court struck down the state's antifornication law that was first drafted in 1833. The State Supreme Court held that the Georgia constitution provided protection for sexual acts that occurred without force in a private home between persons legally capable of consenting to the acts.[28] In a minority of states today, fornication is a class B misdemeanor offense punishable by fine and possible short-term incarceration.

Anti-fornication laws, however, may have become universally obsolete as a result of the Lawrence decision. The 2003 ruling in *Lawrence v. Texas* invalidated sodomy laws nationwide and presumably invalidated laws against fornication in the process, although the decision did not articulate as much.[29] *Lawrence* supports the right to private, consensual, noncommercial intimate relations between unrelated adults. Even without *Lawrence,* social stability is maintained by civility, respect, and rational self-interest. The social structure does not appear to face much of a threat if two unmarried, consenting adults engage in sexual contact. Concern today over fornication is not so much about religion, family, duty, and society but more about unwanted pregnancy, STDs (sexually transmitted diseases), and the HIV virus.

Definition of the Offense

Fornication is typically defined as the consensual, voluntary sexual intercourse between two unmarried adults.[30]

Elements of the Offense

The elements of the crime of fornication that must be proven beyond a reasonable doubt are:

1. voluntary sexual intercourse and
2. the parties involved were unmarried at the time the sexual intercourse occurred.[31]

Sample Statute

The State of Utah fornication statute reads as follows:

Title 76, Chapter 7, Crimes Against the Family, § 104. Fornication (76-7-104).

(1) Any unmarried person who shall have voluntary sexual intercourse with another is guilty of fornication.

(2) Fornication is a class B misdemeanor.[32]

Arguments Made By The Prosecution

Not a lot of variation exists to prove the crime of fornication. The state will demonstrate that intercourse occurred and that the parties were unmarried. That will constitute the bulk of the evidence for the state.

The emergence of other types of evidence will suggest a more serious case, and a more serious penalty. For example, if one of the parties is a minor, or was somehow coerced or forced into the intercourse, the accused will instead face a type of rape charge instead of fornication.

Arguments Made By The Defense

Strategies and theories are in relatively short supply for an offender who faces the charge of fornication. Remote possibilities include that there was only partial penetration of the vagina by the penis, or that there may have been penetration but there was no ejaculation.

Variations of the Law of Fornication

A. Fornication as a Predicate Offense

Some crimes are a constituent offense to a more serious infraction. For example, fornication is a predicate act to crimes such as adultery and seduction. It is not possible for the crime of adultery to occur without the crime of fornication to occur simultaneously. Under such circumstances, fornication would be considered a lesser included offense (LIO) to the crime of adultery. With the occurrence of multiple offenses in a single criminal episode, how does the state prosecute the accused?

The prosecution has the discretion to proceed in a number of ways. Since there is a proliferation of constituent offenses, the U.S. Supreme Court has provided the government with wide latitude to fragment charges and bring multiple prosecutions based on a single criminal event. The prosecutor may be lenient with a first-time offender who has ties to the community (e.g., employment, marriage, family ties) or may be stricter with a repeat offender, a violent offender, or someone who is a risk to flee the jurisdiction. Politics will also play a role in the decision of the prosecutor. The public may want more or less attention paid to certain offenses and public sentiment is a factor in the type of charge that is brought by the state.

Whatever the state decides, the decision needs to be made at one point in time and cannot legally be made in the form of multiple indictments. For example, if someone commits the crime of incest and engages in fornication, the prosecutor will have to charge the accused with incest, or fornication, or both in the same indictment. The state cannot legally begin with an indictment for incest, and later, return another separate indictment for fornication. Doing so would subject the accused to two trials for a single act and such a procedure is prohibited pursuant to the law that governs double jeopardy.

The Fifth Amendment to the United States Constitution provides in part that "no person shall be placed twice in jeopardy of life or limb."[33] The need for double jeopardy protection is due to the existence of multiple criminal provisions that address the same conduct. Meaning, a single crime can be addressed by several statutes, depending on the crime. Legislatures have not taken responsibility for creating a less duplicative code of criminal law and the use of double jeopardy prohibitions attest to this. Since there is no constitutional limitation on the number of offenses the legislature can define in a state code, criminal laws have developed without adequate concern for coherence or coordination. The proliferation of crimes is driven by political forces that encourage legislators to add to prosecutors' arsenals and that discourage the repeal of criminal laws. Legislatures respond to newsworthy events with new criminal provisions that often overlap with existing provisions.

In the case of *Commonwealth v. Arner*, Arner was accused of a crime, charged, and went to trial. He was convicted on a rape charge for having sexual contact with a 16-year-old minor.[34] He was also charged in a separate indictment for "fornication and bastardy," the lesser included, constituent offenses to rape. Arner appealed, arguing that he correctly entered a plea to the first prosecution ("not guilty, once in jeopardy"), and that when faced with the second prosecution, he was subject to double jeopardy for a single act.[35] He argued that the second prosecution for "fornication and bastardy" must be dismissed. The state Supreme Court of Pennsylvania agreed with him and stated:

> Fornication is a misdemeanor, for which an indictment lies, and a fine not exceeding $100 may be imposed. It is also a constituent of incest, adultery, seduction under promise of marriage, and rape. On the trial of an indictment for either of the offences which include

it, the defendant may be convicted or acquitted generally, or he may be acquitted of the major and convicted of the minor offence. In either case the verdict is a bar to a prosecution for the included misdemeanor. One acquitted or convicted of an offence, which necessarily includes a lesser one, cannot afterwards be convicted of the latter offence: Am. & Eng. Ency. of Law, vol. 11, p. 941, and cases cited: Dinkey v. Commonwealth, 17 Pa. 126; Com. v. Heikes, 26 Pa. 513. It is no objection to the application of this principle, that the major offence is a felony, and the minor one a misdemeanor.

A verdict of acquittal or conviction on an indictment for the minor offence, is a bar to a trial on an indictment for a crime which includes it. On this point the rule is thus stated in Am. & Eng. Ency. of Law, vol. 11, p. 939: "Where a greater offence includes a lesser one, being placed in jeopardy under an indictment for the included offence only, constitutes a bar to a prosecution for the greater offence." When the appellant was required to plead to the indictment for rape, he was in jeopardy, under the indictment for fornication, and, pending the deliberations of the jury in that case, he could not be lawfully subjected to a second trial for the same act.[36]

B. Liberty Interest

All citizens are afforded a liberty interest that is part of the Due Process Clause of the Fourteenth Amendment to the Constitution. Liberty interests include the participation in activities such as travel, education, property ownership, and similar activities related to basic freedoms. The Constitution protects these interests and considers them an inherent right. Sexual activity, so long as it is confined to a realm of privacy and is consensual, is another liberty interest that the Constitution protects.[37] Criminalizing fornication can constitute a violation of the liberty interest.

In *Martin v. Ziherl*, the Virginia Supreme Court addressed the liberty interest at stake in the act of fornication.[38] Martin and Ziherl were an unmarried couple and sexual contact was part of their relationship. They testified that they had been in a sexually active relationship for approximately two years. In June 2003, Martin was diagnosed with herpes. She was distraught about having contracted the condition and sued Ziherl, claiming that he had known all along he had herpes and failed to disclose the information to her. Martin made legal claims of negligence, intentional battery, and the intentional infliction of emotional distress and sought compensatory and punitive damages.

To defend himself, Ziherl answered the allegations by stating that fornication was illegal pursuant to Virginia statute 18.2-344. Hence, since he and Martin were engaged in an illegal activity, she could not legally state a claim. His argument is similar to a drug dealer who sues a customer for failing to pay him on time. The illegal context of the transaction is a bar to suit as a matter of law. The court, therefore, had to squarely address the question as to whether or not the statute in Virginia that makes fornication illegal is a violation of liberty interests protected by the federal Constitution.

The court noted that just because the majority of a community believes a particular practice is immoral does not mean the government can criminalize that practice.[39] Allowing the majority of a community to define liberty interests is what maintained the practice of slavery in the Antebellum South and is a means to produce a "tyranny of the majority."

In deciding the case, the Virginia Supreme Court referred to the 2003 U.S. Supreme Court decision of *Lawrence v. Texas,* a fundamental case for the law of sexual relations. Citing *Lawrence,* the Virginia Supreme Court ruled that engaging in a close, personal relationship and engaging in fornication is "within the liberty of persons to choose without being punished as criminals."[40]

The court explained that the Constitution protects such liberty interests of people when they have a personal relationship that is conducted "'in the confines of their homes and [involves] their own private lives'" and that an element of that relationship that is protected is its "overt expression in intimate conduct."[41]

According to the court in *Lawrence:*

> individual decisions by married persons, concerning the intimacies of their physical relationship, even when not intended to produce offspring, are a form of 'liberty' protected by the Due Process Clause of the Fourteenth Amendment. Moreover, this protection extends to intimate choices by unmarried as well as married persons.[42]

According to the court in this case, *Martin v. Ziherl:*

> Therefore, applying the reasoning of *Lawrence* as Martin asks us to do, leads us to conclude that Code § 18.2-344 is unconstitutional because by subjecting certain private sexual conduct between two consenting adults to criminal penalties it infringes on the rights of adults to "engage in the private conduct in the exercise of their liberty under the Due Process Clause of the Fourteenth Amendment to the Constitution."

> It is important to note that this case does not involve minors, non-consensual activity, prostitution, or public activity. The *Lawrence* court indicated that state regulation

of that type of activity might support a different result. Our holding, like that of the Supreme Court in *Lawrence,* addresses only private, consensual conduct between adults and the respective statutes' impact on such conduct. Our holding does not affect the Commonwealth's [of Virginia] police power regarding regulation of public fornication, prostitution, or other such crimes.[43]

C. Right of Privacy

The Constitution is, among other things, a protection against undue government interference and defines the relationship between the state and the people. Certain activity, such as private sex, may be off limits to government regulation as we have seen in *Lawrence* or the *Ziherl* case above. "Privacy" is not explicit in the Constitution but has been recognized in the First Amendment and other amendments to the Constitution. A privacy right regarding sexual expression was, in many ways, first recognized in the *Griswold v. Connecticut* case, which indicated that the purchase and use of contraceptives during sexual relations is a privacy right. According to the U.S. Supreme Court in Griswold:

> Various guarantees create zones of privacy. The right of association contained in the penumbra of the First Amendment is one, as we have seen. The Third Amendment in its prohibition against the quartering of soldiers 'in any house' in time of peace without the consent of the owner is another facet of that privacy. The Fourth Amendment explicitly affirms the 'right of the people to be secure in their persons, houses, papers, and effects, against unreasonable searches and seizures.' The Fifth Amendment in its Self-Incrimination Clause enables its citizen to create a zone of privacy which government may not force him to surrender to his detriment. The Ninth Amendment provides: 'The enumeration in the Constitution of certain rights, shall not be construed to deny or disparage others retained by the people.'[44]

In the case of *State v. Saunders,* two men and two women rendezvoused in the early morning hours to smoke marijuana and socialize in a single vehicle parked in a parkland setting in the region of Newark, New Jersey.[45] Sexual contact ensued by each of the two couples, respectively. A day after the incident, one of the women alleged that she was raped, but her background of prostitution raised suspicions as to the veracity of her claim. The state of New Jersey eventually took the case and decided to charge one of the men with fornication, rather than rape. As the case went to trial, in charging the jury with instructions, the judge defined that crime of fornication as "an act of illicit sexual intercourse by a man, married or single, with an unmarried woman." The case eventually called into question N.J.S.A. (New Jersey Statute Annotated) 2A:110-1 the law of fornication in the state of New Jersey.

The defendant was convicted at trial of fornication and the case was appealed to the state supreme court. The New Jersey Supreme Court held for the accused and overturned the state law that prohibited fornication between two consenting adults. The court reasoned that the law of fornication punishes couples for making a "fundamental personal choice" which was beyond the realm of government to regulate and sanction. The court held that fornication was part of a "zone of privacy for matters on intimate personal concern"[46] and stated that fornication involves the same type of privacy as does the decision to bear children. If the decision to have children is constitutionally protected, so should the decision to have sex that leads to bearing children. According to the court:

> [We underscore] the inherently private nature of a person's decision to bear or beget children. It would be rather anomalous if such a decision could be constitutionally protected while the more fundamental decision as to whether to engage in the conduct which is a necessary prerequisite to child-bearing could be constitutionally prohibited.

If this unmarried couple has sex, should they be arrested?

Surely, such a choice involves considerations which are at least as intimate and personal as those which are involved in choosing whether to use contraceptives. We therefore join with other courts which have held that such sexual activities between adults are protected by the right of privacy.[47]

The holding by the state supreme court also noted various governmental interests, such as preventing STDs, supporting the model of husband and wife relations (marriage), and the maintenance of high standards of public morality did not justify the state's infringement on the right to privacy inherent in the Constitution.[48]

Additional Court Cases: Fornication

State v. Poe

252 S.E.2d 843 (1978)

CASE SUMMARY

PROCEDURAL POSTURE: Defendant challenged the judgment of conviction, entered by the Superior Court of Durham County (North Carolina), for a crime against nature, which is prohibited under N.C. Gen. Stat. § 14-177. Defendant's conviction was based on evidence that he engaged in a consensual fellatio with an adult female.

OVERVIEW: On appeal, defendant argued that § 14-177 did not include the act of a consensual fellatio between an adult male and an adult female. The court rejected this argument, noting that force was not an essential element of the offense. The court also rejected defendant's argument that his right to privacy, under the Fourteenth Amendment, prevented him from being prosecuted under § 14-177. In so ruling, the court distinguished a prior case where the court extended the reach of the Equal Protection Clause to unmarried couples because the statute was not aimed at prohibiting certain sexual behavior, but was designed to prevent unmarried people from using contraception. Here, the court found, the statute prohibited certain sexual actions. Moreover, the court noted that it did not violate the Fourteenth Amendment to classify unmarried persons so as to prohibit them from engaging in a certain sexual act without placing the same prohibition on married persons. Finally, the court ruled that § 14-177 was not unconstitutionally vague. The court found that a person of ordinary intelligence would have concluded that a fellatio between a man and a woman was a criminal act under § 14-177.

OUTCOME: The court affirmed the superior court's judgment of conviction for a crime against nature.[49]

Statutory Rape

Statutory rape may be defined as sexual intercourse, whether consensual or not, with a person under the age of consent, as specified by state statute.[50] Table 1 below indicates the minimum age for consent and also the minimum age required to be legally married. As a general matter, the law has a heightened concern for vulnerable populations such as children and youths as well as other vulnerable groups, such as senior citizens, the mentally ill, etc. When it comes to the offense of statutory rape, the law has a heightened concern that a minor is vulnerable to being taken advantage of sexually and provides a penalty to those who would seek to exploit this vulnerability even if the minor consents to the act. The minor's consent is not an issue and neither is the perpetrator's mistaken belief that the victim was an adult; sexual intercourse with a minor is illegal and statutory rape is a strict liability offense where few defenses are available.

Table 1 Age of Consent for Sexual Activity and Minimum Age for Marriage.

State	Age of Consent	Minimum Marriageable Age	Minimum Marriageable Age With Parental Consent	Minimum Marriageable Age With Court Approval
Alabama	16	18	16	na
Alaska	16	18	16	na
Arizona	18	Parental consent or court approval if under 18	16	No minimum
Arkansas	16	18	16 females; 17 males	na
California	18	Parental consent or court approval if under 18	No minimum	No minimum
Colorado	17	18	16	No minimum
Connecticut	16	18	16	na
D.C.	16	18	16	na
Delaware	18	18	16 females; 17 males	na
Florida	18	18	16	na
Georgia	16	18; 16 if pregnant	15	na
Hawaii	16	18	15	na
Idaho	18	18	16	na
Illinois	17	18	16	na
Indiana	16	18	17; 15 if pregnant	15 if pregnant with parental consent
Iowa	16	18	16	na
Kansas	16	18	16	na

continued ...

Kansas	16	18	16	na
Kentucky	16	18	16	na
Louisiana	17	18	16	na
Maine	16	18	16	na
Maryland	16	18	16	
Massachusetts	16	18	12 females; 14 males	12 female; 14 male with parental consent
Michigan	16	18	16	15 with parental consent
Minnesota	16	18	16	na
Mississippi	16	21	15 females; 17 males	na
Missouri	17	18	15	na
Montana	16	18	16	na
Nebraska	17	19	17	na
Nevada	16	18	16	na
New Hampshire	16	18	13 females; 14 males	No minimum for "special cause" with parental consent
New Jersey	16	18; 16 if pregnant	16	na
New Mexico	17	18	16	na
New York	17	18	16	14 with parental consent
North Carolina	16	18	16; no minimum if pregnant	na
North Dakota	18	18	16	na
Ohio	16	16 females; 18 males	No minimum	na
Oklahoma	16	18	16	na
Oregon	18	18	17	na
Pennsylvania	16	18	16	14 if pregnant
Rhode Island	16	18	16	na

continued …

South Carolina	16	18	16	na
South Dakota	16	18	16	na
Tennessee	18	18	16	na
Texas	17	18	16	14
Utah	18	18	16	na
Vermont	16	18	16	na
Virginia	18	18	16	na
Washington	16	18	17	No minimum
West Virginia	16	18	16	No minimum
Wisconsin	18	18	16	na
Wyoming	18	18	16	na

In earlier times in Europe, then in Colonial America, this act was not a crime and conversely was encouraged. At Common Law, it was lawful for a male to have sexual intercourse with a female minor if she [and her family] consented, regardless of age. Parliament later criminalized the act in 1275 and provided that females under the age of 12 were incapable of consent.[51] Hence, sex with a female under 12 was rape, even though there was consent. In Colonial America the age of consent was 10 (and younger) at which a youth was thought to be incapable of engaging in mature sexual expression.

The reason sex with a minor was long ago a lawful act was because women were most fertile at a young age and older men would impregnate them to add more members to the clan for purposes of survival, defense against Indians, and clearing the land for the growing of food. It was not until modern times with corresponding increased life spans and decreased infant mortality that the law was needed to protect minor females from overtly exploitive older males. Today in the U.S., impressionable young women are "off-limits" sexually and despite an otherwise natural attraction, some segments of society consider sex with a minor female to be a perversion or pathology. This perspective would seem inexplicable since American culture is obsessed with youth and promotes youth culture and sexuality. Pop culture icons Brooke Shields, Britney Spears, and Miley Cyrus are good examples of teenage sex starlets adored by thousands of fans. These pop culture starlets successfully use overt sexuality as a means for self-promotion.

The Common Law was adopted in all jurisdictions in the U.S. and codified in their respective criminal codes, hence the term "statutory" in the name for this sex crime. It should be noted that the law is conflicting when it comes to the age of consent. Meaning, in most of the world, the age of consent is legally 14. In the U.S., the federal age of consent is 18. In most states in the U.S. the age of consent is legally 16. However, legal adult status in the U.S. is set at 18. Caution is advised, therefore, when viewing minors as unable to engage in sex since the age of consent is usually 16. Minors are legally able to engage in sex (in those states where consent is at 16). A final point, the age at which the line is drawn is, of course, an artificial and superficial guide necessary for regulatory purposes.

Today, statutory rape laws can be gender neutral, depending on the jurisdiction, to protect both male and female minors. A small minority of states will allow a reasonable mistake of age defense that implies a degree of legal leniency where the parties are close in age. Lastly, contemporary legal applications of these laws are also designed to prevent unwanted pregnancies and the transmission of STDs.[52]

Definition of the Offense

Statutory rape is defined as unlawful sexual intercourse accomplished with a female not the wife of the perpetrator, where the female is under the age of 18 years.[53] Case law has addressed certain other features of this law and is described below.

Elements of the Offense

The elements of the offense of statutory rape that must be proved beyond a reasonable doubt are:

1. Sexual intercourse with a female not his wife;
   (a) the female is less than 18 years old.[54]

Sample Statute

The State of Kentucky Statutory Rape statute reads as follows:

Kentucky Revised Statute § 510.060 (2009). A person is guilty of rape in the third degree (statutory rape) when:

(a) He engages in sexual intercourse with another person who is incapable of consent because he is mentally retarded;

(b) Being twenty-one (21) years old or more, he engages in sexual intercourse with another person less than sixteen (16) years old; or

(c) Being twenty-one (21) years old or more, he engages in sexual intercourse with another person less than eighteen (18) years old and for whom he provides a foster family home as defined in KRS 600.020.

(2) Rape in the third degree is a Class D felony.[55]

Arguments Made By The Prosecution

Since statutory rape is a strict liability offense, the prosecution has a relatively easy task. The state need only show that the victim was a minor, and depending on the specific statute, that intercourse occurred. The issue of consent is irrelevant. Of course, if the case involves force and a lack of consent, the case would be tried as a rape case, rather than a case of statutory rape.

The victim will likely have to come forward to testify and will need to be a credible witness. In rare instances, adults are "framed" for this crime merely by the false accusation of the victim. The case can come down to a "he said she said" exchange where there is little evidence and no witnesses. It is one person's word against the others. In State v. Roberts, four African-American male high school students accused their female teacher of statutory rape. It is alleged that the accusations were in retaliation for the teacher taking academic disciplinary action against the students.

Arguments Made By The Defense

Similarly, strict liability crimes limit the number of defenses available. In the absence of specific defenses, the defense may use certain other strategies such as cross-examination of the witness and impeachment of witness testimony for the purpose of creating reasonable doubt. If sexual contact did not occur, the defense may argue that the parties may have spent time alone together, but no crime occurred.

Variations of the Law of Statutory Rape

A. Consensual Sex Between Two Minors

As a general matter, any sexual activity that involves a minor is regulated by the state. As noted in Table 1 above, a researcher must be cognizant of age distinctions for consent, marriage, statutory rape, possession of pornography, etc. Some sex-related activities by a minor are more regulated than others. For example, pornography-related cases or adult–minor relations are felony crimes in most states. Minor to minor consensual sexual activity does not reach the same level of criminal scrutiny or sanction. Some states do not criminalize sex between two minors so long as both consent to the act.[56] Other states consider such an act to be two separate cases of statutory rape; both minors will be charged. The degree of criminality between two minors will also vary such as felony or misdemeanor. Extensive regulation of the sexual activity of minors is due to the policy of the law that is to protect minors from engaging in sexual activity when they may not be ready psychologically or emotionally. In the case of *B.B. v. State,* the State of Florida Supreme Court ruled that since the law of statutory rape was to protect a minor from being exploited by an adult, two teenagers' right to privacy precluded any prosecution of them for statutory rape.[57]

A 16 year-old male, B.B., engaged in sexual intercourse with a consenting 16-year-old female and both were charged and convicted pursuant to Florida statute 794.05. The law read, "Any person who has unlawful carnal intercourse with any unmarried person, of previous chaste character, who at the time of such intercourse is under the age of 18 years, shall be guilty of a felony of the second degree, punishable as provided in section 775.082, section 775.083, or section 775.084."

The State Supreme Court did not indicate that it condones underage sex or that it is seeking to change the age of consent in the state of Florida. Rather, by way of the law of privacy, the court modified the law that made it a felony crime for a minor to have consensual sex with another minor. The State of Florida Supreme Court stated:

> The issue here, however, is whether a minor who engages in "unlawful" carnal intercourse with an unmarried minor of previous chaste character can be adjudicated delinquent of a felony of the second degree in light of the minor's right to privacy guaranteed by the Florida Constitution.

> Carnal intercourse is by express definition an intimate act. In *Shevin v. Byron, Harless, Schaffer, Reid and Associates, Inc.,* 379 So. 2d 633, 636 (Fla. 1980), we recognized that various intimate personal activities such as marriage, procreation, contraception, and family relationships fall within the privacy interest recognized by the Federal Constitution.

> While we do recognize that Florida does have an obligation and a compelling interest in protecting children from sexual activity before their minds and bodies have sufficiently matured to make it appropriate, safe, and healthy for them and that this interest pertains to one minor engaging in carnal intercourse with another, the crux of the State's interest in an adult-minor situation is the prevention of exploitation of the minor by the adult. Whereas in this minor-minor situation, the crux of the State's interest is in protecting the minor from the sexual activity itself for reasons of health and quality of life. Having distinguished between the State's interest in the adult-minor situation and in the minor-minor situation, we conclude that the State has failed to demonstrate in this minor-minor situation that the adjudication of B.B. as a delinquent through the application of section 794.05 is the least intrusive means of furthering what we have determined to be the State's compelling interest.[58]

B. Statutory Sentence Enhancement

The vagaries inherent in consensual sexual relationships require the law to grade offenses proportionate to the harm done. For example, a case of consensual sex between two 17-year-olds commands the attention of the law differently than a case of nonconsensual sex between two 17-year-olds, or, as we see in the following case, consensual sex between an 11-year-old and a 29-year-old.[59]

Defendant, William Beith, was a 29-year-old high school principal at Liberty Baptist Bible Academy in Indiana where he met one of his students, 11-year-old sixth-grader "G.M." While at school, G.M. confided in Beith concerning some family problems of G.M. and the two developed a type of friendship and became "close." According to the court transcripts, G.M. would arrive late to class often because of talking to Beith at length in his principal's office. Faculty at the school became concerned about the relationship between G.M. and Beith.[60]

The interactions between the two became physical, involving physical touching and Beith began having G.M. over to his house. On one occasion, G.M. and a friend visited his home and Beith videotaped G.M. as she changed clothes; the camera was focused on her genitals. A few weeks later, at a church-sponsored retreat, Beith and G.M. spent time in bed together sharing sexually (obviously a crime). G.M. told a friend about her relationship with Beith and her friend was shocked. The friend told G.M.'s parents and her parents informed the police. Beith and G.M. found out and before the police could arrest Beith, Beith and G.M. ran away together and drove from Indiana to Las Vegas. In Las Vegas, Beith was arrested by the Las Vegas police and the case was turned over to the FBI.[61]

Beith was returned to Indiana where the United States Attorney's Office for the Northern District of Indiana returned a one-count information against Beith, charging him with transporting a child under the age of 18 across state lines with the intent to engage in prohibited sexual contact. The charged commenced pursuant to 18 U.S.C. § 2423(b), a transporting a minor ... statute. A presentence report (PSR) was prepared and referenced the 2001 edition of the United States Sentencing Guidelines (USSG). The presentence report recommended to the trial court to apply a base offense level of "27" for the violation of 18 U.S.C. § 2423(b) pursuant to U.S.S.G. (United States Sentencing Guidelines) § 2A3.1.[62]

By way of the criminal sexual assault cross reference, U.S.S.G. § 2A3.2(c)(1) is triggered when the victim is under the age of 12. The PSR also recommended a 4-level sentence enhancement pursuant to § 2A3.1(b)(2)(A), applicable where the victim has not attained the age of 12 years; a 2-level enhancement pursuant to U.S.S.G. § 2A3.1(b)(3), applicable where the victim was in the custody, care, or supervisory control of the defendant; a 4-level enhancement pursuant to U.S.S.G. § 2A3.1(b)(5), applicable where the victim was abducted; and a 2-level enhancement pursuant to U.S.S.G. § 3A1.1(b)(1), applicable where the victim was unusually vulnerable. Altogether, the PSR recommended a total offense level of "39." Altogether, the Sentencing Guidelines provided a sentencing range of 188 to 235 months imprisonment for the defendant. However, the statutory maximum sentence for his crime was 180 months; therefore, the court sentenced him to the statutory maximum term of 180 months.[63]

On appeal, Beith argued that he was not guilty of abduction, "inveigling and grooming" of G.M. because her participation was voluntary and fully consensual. If Beith could avoid the abduction offense, his sentence stood to be decreased. He even accused G.M. of being the initiator of the relationship. The appeals court sided with Beith on this issue and stated

> [W]e find that the evidence could not support a finding of "abduction by inveigling." Recall that it was G.M. who called to warn Beith of the police's intent to interview and possibly arrest him. The factual findings suggest that Beith's reprehensible actions were not so much concentrated toward imposing his will over G.M. in absconding to Las Vegas as they were motivated toward cultivating a sincere—albeit perverse and illegal—relationship. Indeed, he made no false promises to her, and his overtures, while undeniably vile, were cloaked in neither deceit nor trickery. At most, the findings upon which the district court based the abduction enhancement suggest that Beith endeavored to develop G.M.'s trust—a trust that he would ultimately abuse. This behavior also merits punishment, and for it the district court has already obliged by enhancing his sentence pursuant to U.S.S.G. § 2A3.1(b)(3).[64]

Beith also argued that he should not be subject to a sentence enhancement for having sex with someone under 12 because such a sentence would be tantamount to "double counting," something akin to the injustice of double jeopardy. The appeals court denied this appeal, stating:

> We reject appellant's argument for several reasons. First, the plain language of the Guidelines expressly directs this result. Second, the application of § 2A3.1 (base offense level of 27) over § 2A3.2 (base offense level of 24) does not amount to an "increase" or enhancement, as the Guidelines must be applied as a whole. Finally, the bar on double counting is not implicated because the Sentencing Commission in setting the base offense level for § 2A3.1 did not account for the victim's age.
>
> Double counting is permissible unless the guidelines expressly provide otherwise or a compelling basis exists for implying such a prohibition. *United States v. Harris,* 41 F.3d 1121, 1123 (7th Cir. 1994). According to the plain language of the Guidelines, as discussed above, a defendant must be sentenced pursuant to § 2A3.1 if the victim of his sexual abuse is under 12 years of age and then subsequently enhanced four points based on the same element. U.S.S.G. § 2A3.1(b)(2)(A).[65]

C. Mistake-of-Age Defense

The contexts of romantic relationships are numerous. Statutory rape cases by definition will involve at least one minor and the situations of mistake of age and statutory rape can be subtle. Oftentimes, both parties are "just dating" and do not necessarily inquire about DOBs (date of birth) and could not imagine why they would have to. When sexual contact ensues, it is unlikely that DOBs are asked about. Statutory rape law seeks to deter predatory adults from taking advantage of a vulnerable minor. But many times neither party is a predator and neither is particularly more vulnerable to the other.

In an innocent case where two people are in a bona fide relationship and it is an actual scenario of illegal consensual sex, should mistake of age be allowed as a valid defense to the criminal charge of statutory rape? In *State v. Yanez,* the Rhode Island Supreme Court ruled on the mistake of age defense. In the case, the adult defendant, Alejandro Yanez was 18 years old when he had sexual contact with a 13-year-old minor female. The accused was surprised and immediately told the police he was unaware that his friend was a minor and that had he known, he would not have engaged in sex with her. Apparently, the girl was physically developed for her age and did not appear to be a minor. The court noted, "the victim told him that she was of the age of consent, an appearance supported by her physical development and demeanor."[66] The accused was arrested and indicted on one count of first-degree child molestation sexual assault in violation of Rhode Island state law § 11-37-8.1. (1956).[67] The trial court convicted the accused and the state intermediate appellate court affirmed the conviction. Neither court allowed for the mistake of age defense. The accused appealed to the state Supreme Court, still hoping to prevail on the mistake defense.[68]

In its ruling, the state Supreme Court outlined the legal parameters to a strict liability offense. Statutory rape is a strict liability crime. In a strict liability crime, few if any defenses are available. Once the act is completed, the crime is satisfied. A strict liability offense does not include an intent element. Hence, even in cases of mistake, the criminal's state of mind and lack of criminal intent are not taken into consideration for a conviction. In cases of statutory rape, in addition to not having an intent requirement, there is no knowledge requirement. Meaning, the state does not have to prove the defendant had knowledge that the victim was a minor to convict the defendant. Strict liability offenses are easier cases for the state, relative to cases where the state must prove the accused acted with intent, and had full knowledge of what he or she was doing. The court record reads: The [trial] court interpreted the legislative history of the state's criminal statutes governing sexual assault and concluded that the legislature, in enacting § 11-37-8.1, intentionally omitted any requirement concerning defendant's state of mind, knowledge, or belief, thus making the crime of statutory rape a strict liability offense.[69] The Supreme Court affirmed the ruling of the lower courts. Part of the lower court transcript includes the judge's instruction to the jury:

Now under the terms of this law, the State need not prove that the act of sexual intercourse was committed against the wishes of the victim. Thus, in order for you to return a verdict of guilty, the State is required to prove, number one, that this defendant, Alejandro Yanez; two, on or about July 15, 1993, at West Warwick; three, did in fact engage in sexual intercourse with [Allison]; and four, that at the time, if you are satisfied he did engage in sexual intercourse with [Allison], at the time she was under the age of 14 years. The law also states when conduct is made criminal because the victim is a minor, and in Rhode Island [in the context of this case] that age being 14, it is no defense that the defendant was ignorant of or mistaken as to the victim's age. And it matters not that his mistaken belief was reasonable.[70]

Additional Court Cases: Statutory Rape

Michael M. v. Superior Court of Sonoma County

450 U.S. 464 (1980)

CASE SUMMARY

PROCEDURAL POSTURE: On certiorari, defendant challenged a judgment of the Supreme Court of California that denied his petition to set aside a criminal indictment charging him with violating Cal. Penal Code § 261.5. Defendant claimed that § 261.5, the statutory rape law, unlawfully discriminated on the basis of gender in violation of the Equal Protection Clause of the Fourteenth Amendment.

OVERVIEW: When defendant was just over 17 years old, he was charged in a criminal complaint in state court with violating Cal. Penal Code § 261.5 for having unlawful sexual intercourse with a female under the age of 18. Section 261.5 made men alone criminally liable for the act of sexual intercourse. Contending that the statute unlawfully discriminated against men, defendant filed a motion to set aside the information and complaint. The state courts denied the motion. On certiorari, the U.S. Supreme Court rejected defendant's contention that § 261.5 violated the Equal Protection Clause of the Fourteenth Amendment. Specifically, the Court ruled that the State had a strong, legitimate interest in preventing illegitimate pregnancies because of the social and economic problems such pregnancies caused it and the woman to suffer. The Court further held that the statute was sufficiently related to that state interest to pass constitutional muster. Moreover, the statute was not overbroad in its application to prepubescent females who could not become pregnant. The statute did not impermissibly discriminate between the genders by punishing only the male when both parties were under the age of 18.

> **OUTCOME:** The Court affirmed the judgment. The statutory rape law did not violate the Equal Protection Clause because it was sufficiently related to the State's strong interest in preventing teenage pregnancy, it was not overbroad, and its application only to men when both parties were minors did not render it invalid.[71]

Sodomy

Sodomy laws are a good example for the legal regulation of sexual behavior because sodomy may occur between mature, married consenting adults in the privacy of their own home and still be illegal. Sodomy has a long history of unusual lore and cryptic understanding and, hence, has been subject to many definitions. Typically defined as oral or anal sex, it has also been defined as sex with animals or with a corpse.[72] An additional haphazard definition has been any act of intercourse between husband and wife that is not strictly the missionary position. How sodomy has taken on such a diffuse set of behaviors is hard to understand. Complicating matters, since anal and oral sex are predominant forms of expression in the gay community, sodomy is laden with the history of social hysteria and homophobia as well. The famous U.S. Supreme Court case of *Bowers v. Hardwick* is often criticized as an opinion "obsessed with homosexuality."[73] The most accurate definition of sodomy is anal intercourse. Hence, the strong attachment of sodomy to homosexual sexual relations.

Beginning in Europe long ago, Roman Catholic Church authorities outlawed sodomy and those initial prohibitions carried over to Colonial America and the present day United States. Numerous traditional justifications exist for the use of sodomy laws such as the preservation of the family, following the "Will of God," doing "the right thing," being "normal," being "decent," and being "natural." All of these rationales tend to be ambiguous and could be used to legally outlaw any activity that is misunderstood and held in contempt.[74]

Today's sodomy laws tend to be outdated and various states began decriminalizing sodomy as far back as 1965. The rationale for the removal of sodomy laws from the books does not pertain to a new morality of human sexuality, but more so to the oddity and embarrassment of outlawing sexual expression that a loving married couple may prefer in the safe and supportive environment of a marriage or partnership.[75] Approximately 15 states have sodomy laws for all adults and five have sodomy laws that only apply specifically to same-sex couples, either male or female.[76]

These laws are referred to by unusual terms and have variegated legal definitions. Some terms include Crimes Against Nature (Arizona),[77] Sexual Psychopaths (Washington, D.C.),[78] Unnatural or Perverted Sexual Practices (Maryland),[79] and Sexual Perversion (Wisconsin),[80] to name a few. Some states use one definition and other states use a different one. The same is true for the courts. One court referred to sodomy as so "vile and degrading,"[81] a human being was incapable of talking about it. Another court stated it was unspeakable and "a crime not fit to be named,"[82] another stated that sodomy was "contrary to the order of nature,"[83] and yet another stated it was "abominable and detestable."[84] Whatever the specifics concerning sodomy, one thing is for sure, it has triggered serious fear in judges and legislators when it comes to regulating human sexuality.

© CREATISTA, 2011. Used under license from Shutterstock, Inc

Prior to Lawrence v. Texas, laws that prohibited intercourse between two men were constitutional.

The U.S. Supreme Court is traditional and conservative, but even it could not sustain the inexplicable disapprobation that surrounds sodomy. In 2003 the Court punctured the myths surrounding alternative forms of sexual expression in the case of *Lawrence v. Texas*.[85] While striking down a state antisodomy law, the Court provided a degree of permission for Americans to accept their own unique interpretation of their personal sexual feelings and sexual expression, free of the odd social restrictions of the past. The *Lawrence* decision calls into question any law that prohibits sex between consenting adults such as fornication, cohabitation, and same-sex relations.[86]

Writing for the majority, Justice Kennedy stated, "At the heart of liberty is the right to define one's own concept of existence, of meaning, of the universe, and of the mystery of human life."[87] Implicit in the Court's opinion is the protection of liberties concerning one's thoughts on marriage, procreation, family relationships, and education. The *Lawrence* decision respects forms of sexual expression that are safe, healthy, and supportive of marriage and partnership.

Definition of the Offense

The broadest definition of sodomy is: "Carnal copulation by human beings with each other against nature, or with a beast."[88] This definition includes the acts of bestiality, buggery, cunnilingus, and fellatio.[89] A more narrow definition is: "Carnal copulation between two human beings per anus or by a human being in any manner with a beast."[90]

Elements of the Offense

The elements of the crime of sodomy that must be proven beyond a reasonable doubt are:

1. any contact,
2. between any part of the genitals of one person and the mouth or anus of another person.[91]

Sample Statute

The State of Virginia Sodomy statute reads as follows:

State of Virginia Statute § 18.2-361 Crimes against nature.

A. If any person carnally knows in any manner any brute animal, or carnally knows any male or female person by the anus or by or with the mouth, or voluntarily submits to such carnal knowledge, he or she shall be guilty of a Class 6 felony.[92]

Arguments Made By The Prosecution

Assuming that the alleged act of sodomy does not involve any of the threshold factors (duress, age, prostitution, or intoxication), the state will surely take an alleged act of sodomy, even though the *Lawrence* decision makes sodomy legal. A substantial amount of symbolism is part of prosecutorial discretion and the state will seek to appease the public by taking these cases. In addition, the prosecutor is an elected official and will appeal to a broad base of voters by getting tough on sexual deviants.

Arguments Made By The Defense

Defending an allegation of sodomy can involve several strategies. Obviously, the defense can take the *Lawrence* ruling and argue that the law used to criminalize the act is invalid and unconstitutional. Another angle can include the argument that the two parties were together, in the bedroom, but were not engaged in sex but rather affectionate touching (which did not involve genitals). Lastly, even if the parties were expressing sexually, they can argue that none of the acts involved sodomy, e.g., no oral or anal sex was involved.

Variations of the Law of Sodomy

A. Lawrence v. Texas

One of the most significant sex law court cases in American history, *Lawrence v. Texas* declared that any law prohibiting sex between consenting adults, married or not, gay or straight, black or white, is unconstitutional and a violation of the due process clause of the Fourteenth Amendment. This case is a profound ruling when it comes to the rights of individual sexual expression.[93]

John Lawrence, age 55, and his friend, Tyron Garner, 31, were in the privacy of Lawrence's apartment in Houston, Texas around 11:00 p.m. Responding to a claim of a "weapons disturbance," a sheriff's deputy entered the unlocked apartment, found Lawrence and Garner engaged in the act of anal sex, and arrested them pursuant to the Texas anti-sodomy law.[94]

Lawrence, a single gay male, appealed his conviction and took his arrest all the way to the Supreme Court and won.[95] In a 6-3 decision, the court held that the prohibition of sodomy was a violation of one's right to due process and is unconstitutional. The decision in this case overturned the prevailing law on sodomy, *Bowers v. Hardwick,* which had formerly supported the prohibition on sodomy.[96] In overturning the Bowers decision, the Lawrence court stated: "*Bowers* was not correct when it was decided, and it is not correct today. It ought not to remain binding precedent. *Bowers v. Hardwick* should be and now is overruled."[97] The majority wrote:

> The convictions under the Texas statute violated the two men's vital interests in liberty and privacy protected by the due process clause, for among other reasons, (a) the statute, although purporting to do no more than prohibit a particular sexual act, sought to control a personal relationship that was within the liberty of persons to choose without being punished as criminals; (b) the stigma that the statute imposed was not trivial; and (c) the statute furthered no legitimate state interest which could justify the statute's intrusion into the personal and private life of the individual.

One of the three dissents in Lawrence was that of Antonin Scalia. Justice Scalia stated that with the decision, "The Court has largely signed on to the so-called homosexual agenda."[98] Justice Scalia stated:

> Liberty finds no refuge in a jurisprudence of doubt. *Planned Parenthood of Southeastern Pa. v. Casey,* 505 U.S. 833 (1992). That was the Court's sententious response, barely more than a decade ago, to those seeking to overrule *Roe v. Wade,* 410 U.S. 113 (1973). The Court's response today, to those who have engaged in a 17-year crusade to overrule *Bowers v. Hardwick,* 478 U.S. 186 (1986), is very different. The need for stability and certainty presents no barrier.
>
> Most of the rest of today's opinion has no relevance to its actual holding—that the Texas statute 'furthers no legitimate state interest which can justify' its application to petitioners under rational-basis review. ... nowhere does the Court's opinion declare that homosexual sodomy is a 'fundamental right' under the Due Process Clause; nor

does it subject the Texas law to the standard of review that would be appropriate (strict scrutiny) if homosexual sodomy *were* a 'fundamental right.' Thus, while overruling the *outcome* of *Bowers,* the Court leaves strangely untouched its central legal conclusion: 'Respondent would have us announce … a fundamental right to engage in homosexual sodomy. This we are quite unwilling to do.' Instead the Court simply describes petitioners' conduct as 'an exercise of their liberty'—which it undoubtedly is—and proceeds to apply an unheard-of form of rational-basis review that will have far-reaching implications beyond this case.[99]

B. Moral Outrage

It is by no means certain that the Lawrence decision will remain the law of private, consensual sodomy for long. While it may appear that the Lawrence decision is a predictable next step from the previous court decisions of *Griswold* and *Loving,* just as important court decisions such as *Miller* and *Bowers* moved in the opposite direction. In short, many people disagree with the *Lawrence* decision—prescriptions against sodomy have very ancient roots.[100] At the least, the religious community is not comfortable with homosexual behavior being provided a stamp of approval by the highest court in the land.

In *C.V. Kelly v. The People of the State of Illinois,* an adult male and a minor male allegedly had engaged in the act of fellatio, first one on the other, and then switching positions on one another.[101] The adult was reported by the minor and subsequently charged pursuant to Illinois Code Chapter 38, Section 47, Crimes Against Nature.[102] No witnesses were present and no evidence could corroborate the claim except for the allegations made by the complainant (the minor). The defendant denied that the sexual contact ever took place and, as a legal matter, pointed to an insufficiency of the evidence to sustain his conviction. The cards seemed stacked against the accused/adult from the outset and he was convicted. In upholding the conviction, the appellate court "felt the need again to express moral outrage over fellatio before making its decision.' [S]uch a crime cannot be described without shocking the moral sensibilities."[103] The court opined:

> We did not say the definition of the crime was 'generic,' but did hold that because of the abominable nature of the crime it was not necessary to set forth in detail the manner in which it was committed; and also that under our Criminal Code and the repeated decisions of this court it was sufficient to allege the crime in the language of the statute, or so plainly that its nature might be easily understood by the jury. The manner of committing the offense being too indecent to be set forth in the indictment itself, we are at

a loss to perceive how it could be consistently incorporated in a bill of particulars. It is only when it is made to appear that the defendant cannot properly prepare his defense without a bill of particulars, that the court will require the prosecuting attorney to furnish it. In this case the indictment informed the defendant that he was charged with the crime against nature with and upon Lyle Patterson, and that was sufficient. In short, we think counsel for plaintiff in error, throughout his argument, disregards the principal grounds upon which the indictment in the *Honselman* case was held sufficient,—that is, the fact that such a crime cannot be described without shocking the moral sensibilities.

Blackstone says, speaking of this crime: 'I will not act so disagreeable a part to my readers as well as myself as to dwell any longer upon a subject the very mention of which is a disgrace to human nature. It will be more eligible to imitate the delicacy of our English law, which treats it, in its very indictments, as a crime not to be named.' (Vol. 4, p. 215.)[104]

C. Sodomy in the Military—Don't Ask, Don't Tell

Up until recently, sodomy between male soldiers was a violation of federal law because homosexuality was prohibited in the military.[105] But can a military person merely admit that s/he is gay, even though they do not engage in any homosexual act? Until recently, the answer was no—in the U.S. military, the admission that one is gay was a violation of federal law and would result in a military discharge pursuant to the 1993 federal Don't Ask, Don't Tell policy.[106] From 1993–2010, thousands of service personnel have been discharged under Don't Ask, Don't Tell.[107]

This policy came about in 1993 when U.S. President Bill Clinton engaged in a series of debates with the four-star generals who commanded his armed forces. The debate regarded the eligibility of gay service personnel. President Clinton introduced Don't Ask, Don't Tell concerning the service of gay soldiers and the policy was codified in Section 571 of the National Defense Authorization Act of 1994.[108] Under the policy, gays can serve, but once they admit they are gay, they would be discharged. They were required to keep their sexual orientation to themselves.

In 1996, a Navy Lieutenant named Paul Thomasson sought to test the waters of Don't Ask, Don't Tell and wrote a letter to his commanders stating "I am gay" in order to challenge the policy and assert his First Amendment right to free speech. As a result of admitting he was gay, Thomasson was discharged pursuant to Don't Ask, Don't Tell. On being discharged, Thomasson sued, seeking to enjoin enforcement of the policy and to retrieve his service position in the

Navy. The case made its way to the Fourth Circuit Court of Appeals. In the case, the court ruled against Thomasson, upholding the policy and Thomasson's discharge. The court stated:

> Congress declared that military life is fundamentally different from civilian life, 10 U.S.C. § 654(a)(8), and that success in combat requires military units that are characterized by high morale, good order and discipline, and unit cohesion, 10 U.S.C. § 654(a)(6). Thus acknowledging that the demands of military life are distinctive, Congress further determined that the prohibition against homosexual conduct is a long-standing element of military law that continues to be necessary in the unique circumstances of military service. 10 U.S.C. § 654(a)(13). It also found that service members who demonstrate a propensity or intent to engage in homosexual acts create an unacceptable risk to the high standards of morale, good order and discipline, and unit cohesion that are the essence of military capability. 10 U.S.C. § 654(a)(15)[109]

Thomasson was not the only one who sued to enjoin enforcement of Don't Ask, Don't Tell. In 2004, the Log Cabin Republicans, a gay-rights organization challenged the law, just as Thomasson had done, and sued to overturn it. This time, the plaintiffs were successful. Federal trial court judge Virginia Phillips ruled that the law needlessly intrudes on service members' private lives and reduces military effectiveness by excluding skilled personnel who may not enlist due to feeling unwelcome. The judge stated that the policy also aggravates troop shortages and in her ruling banned all further discharges based on sexual orientation.

The Obama Administration appealed (even though President Obama has lobbied the Congress to repeal Don't Ask, Don't Tell), and in 2010, a federal appeals court judge enacted a stay on the ruling by Judge Phillips. A stay on Judge Phillips' order would have likely remained in effect throughout the appeals period. The appellate court sought to ensure a thoughtful process due to the magnitude of the proposed change and the sensitive situation of the U.S. military around the world. The case might have gone to the U.S. Supreme Court.

However, due to the relative unpopularity of Don't Ask, Don't Tell, it was repealed in December 2010. The Don't Ask, Don't Tell Repeal Act of 2010 repealed the policy,[110] but not necessarily with the stroke of a pen. According to the Congressional Research Service, the act

> provides for repeal of the current Department of Defense (DOD) policy concerning homosexuality in the Armed Forces, to be effective 60 days after the Secretary of Defense has received DOD's comprehensive review on the implementation of such repeal, and the President, Secretary, and Chairman of the Joint Chiefs of Staff (JCS) certify to the

congressional defense committees that they have considered the report and proposed plan of action, that DOD has prepared the necessary policies and regulations to exercise the discretion provided by such repeal, and that implementation of such policies and regulations is consistent with the standards of military readiness and effectiveness, unit cohesion, and military recruiting and retention.[111]

It was noted earlier in this book that in Ancient Greece, gay military personnel were highly prized as soldiers. Plato wrote that a soldier would fight more ferociously if the soldier's lover was also in the battle unit. The ancient Greeks did not debate the subject of gays in the military, except in the affirmative. Perspectives on sexuality are always reflective of social conditioning and today, gay military personnel are not necessarily considered poor soldiers in comparison to other soldiers, but are not lauded as they were in ancient Greece. Moral sentiments change over time, and from 1994 to 2010, it was illegal to admit one is gay and serve in the U.S. military.[112]

Additional Court Cases: Sodomy

Bowers v. Hardwick

478 U.S. 186 (1986)

CASE SUMMARY

PROCEDURAL POSTURE: On certiorari, the state challenged a decision from the United States Court of Appeals for the Eleventh Circuit, that ruled that Ga. Code Ann. § 16-6-2 unconstitutionally violated respondent's fundamental rights under the due process clause, U.S. Const. amend. XVI, in that it criminalized consensual sodomy.

OVERVIEW: Respondent was charged with violating O.G.C.A. § 16-6-2 (1984), which criminalized sodomy. Respondent allegedly engaged in sodomy with another adult male in the bedroom of his home. After the district attorney decided not to present the matter to the grand jury unless further evidence developed, respondent brought suit in federal district court, challenging the constitutionality of the statute insofar as it criminalized consensual sodomy. The court of appeals held that § 16-6-2 violated respondent's fundamental rights because his homosexual activity was a private and intimate association that was beyond the reach of state regulation by reason of U.S. Const. amends. XI and XIV. Reversing that judgment, the Court held that the Due Process Clause of U.S. Const. amend. XIV did not confer any fundamental right on homosexuals to engage in acts of consensual sodomy, even if the conduct occurred in the privacy of their own homes.

OUTCOME: The Court reversed the court of appeals' decision.[113]

Sodomy and Related Offenses

Table 2 Sodomy and Related Offenses

Sodomy	With Factual Change	Becomes a More Serious Charge
Sodomy	with force	becomes Rape
Sodomy	with force and Insertion of an object	becomes Object Rape
Sodomy	with a minor	becomes Sexual Assault upon a child
Sodomy	with an unmarried partner	becomes Unlawful Cohabitation
Sodomy	with a consanguinous relative	becomes Incest

Adultery

Some sex offenses are tinged with religious overtures more than others and adultery may be a good example. Adultery fleshes out the relationship between the law and the Bible. The Puritans of Colonial America equated sin with crime and handed down the sentence of death to anyone caught in the act of adultery.[114] The role of scripture concerning the immorality of adultery is codified in the Ten Commandments as "Thou shalt not commit adultery." Early Americans took ecclesiastical principles intensely seriously and had traditional beliefs about the roles of men and women. Women were not on the same legal footing as men when it came to this and other sex crimes. For example, originally only a woman could be charged and sentenced for adultery; the exact same behavior by a male was not considered criminal. In some foreign nations today, such as Nigeria and Pakistan, a woman who is raped by a stranger could stand trial for adultery. In general, a sentence for an adultery conviction can be severe. The criminal law in Zamfara, a state in Nigeria states:

> Whoever, being a man or a woman fully responsible, has sexual intercourse through the genital of a person over whom he has no sexual rights and in circumstances in which no doubt exists as to the illegality of the act, is guilty of the offence of *zina*.
>
> Whoever commits the offence of *zina* shall be punished with caning of one hundred lashes if unmarried, and shall also be liable to imprisonment for a term of one year; or if married, with stoning to death.[115]

Famous cases exist in history where a king or queen carried on with a concubine for years in an adulterous status, thereby adding a form of intrigue to adultery. In the overwhelming majority of cases, however, having sexual relations with someone behind the back of a trusted partner is a form of deceit, can instantly result in a relationship termination, and is a legal grounds for divorce. Famous athletes (Tiger Woods, Kobe Bryant), politicians (Bill Clinton), church ministers (Ted Haggard), and television figures (David Letterman, Eddie Murphy) have suffered significant consequences for engaging in adulterous sexual activity that later became public.[116] Adultery involves serious questions of sexual impropriety, but also equally serious questions of trust, loyalty, and personal integrity. In addition, adultery can lead to sexually transmitted disease, the birth of unexpected children, and the payment of state child support to single parents. In a case that upheld an 1887 state law prohibiting adultery, the judge stated:

> The results can be tragic and the social costs may impact innocent children and relatives. The fact that adultery may occur with some frequency is no justification for a constitutional restriction on the criminalization of adultery any more than on embezzlement or numerous other violations of trust which frequently occur. Extramarital sexual relations are not within the privacy rights spelled out by the Constitution. Other courts have ruled that extramarital sexual activity such as polygamy, child sexual abuse and homosexual sodomy are not protected by the right to privacy. Neither is adultery.[117]

The harm done to a relationship by definition is largely a matter of the values brought to the relationship. Some partnerships are less sensitive to marital infidelity.[118] As a legal matter, the seriousness of the offense of adultery has waned with the growth of contemporary social standards, urban living in large metropolitan cities, and different family compositions such as single-parent families. Thus once a serious violation of religious codes and defined as "sexual intercourse with another's wife," today adultery is not as alarming as it once was and is often referred to as "being unfaithful" or practicing "infidelity" and goes largely unprosecuted in the criminal justice system.[119]

The United States inherited the English Common Law that made adultery, as well as fornication (sex between unmarried people) and sodomy (anal sex), a punishable crime. In the mid and late 19th centuries, when various states wrote their criminal codes, they incorporated these Common Law sex crimes.[120] Twenty-six states continue to

© Galina Barskaya, 2011. Used under license from Shutterstock, Inc.

The criminalization of adultery seeks to deter the devastating effects of adultery on a marriage.

Figure 1 Contextual variations of adultery. Adultery may be conceptualized as sexual relations with someone whom the actor could not have contracted a valid marriage with.

Adultery/ Polygamy	Adultery/ Incest	Adultery/ Prostitution	Adultery/ Sodomy	Adultery/ Bestiality	Adultery/ Rape

have anti-adultery laws on the books today. These laws vary considerably from state to state. Some define adultery as any intercourse outside marriage. According to others, it occurs when a married person merely lives or cohabits with someone other than his or her spouse. In West Virginia[121] and North Carolina,[122] simply "to lewdly and lasciviously associate" with anyone other than one's spouse is to be an adulterous entanglement.[123]

A single person in an adulterous relationship can be found guilty of adultery, not just the married party. All but seven states that criminalize adultery punish both parties. Colorado, Georgia, Nebraska, North Dakota, and Utah only punish the married person. In the District of Columbia and in Michigan, when a married man sleeps with an unmarried woman, only the man is guilty, but when a married woman sleeps with an unmarried man, they are both guilty. Most laws make no exceptions for couples that are separated or in the process of obtaining a divorce. Punishments also vary from state to state. Adultery is a felony in Massachusetts, Michigan, Oklahoma, and Idaho, and a misdemeanor everywhere else it is against the law.[124] While it is an obvious threat to the stability of a marriage or partnership, a very small percentage of marriage partners actually consent to one or both partners having an occasional extramarital affair.[125] Indeed, in most marriages, adultery is viewed as harmful, but in a small number of others, it is considered helpful to various perspectives of the partnership.

Definition of the Offense

Adultery is typically defined as voluntary sexual intercourse between persons, one of whom is lawfully married to another, both parties being guilty.[126]

Elements of the Offense

For the crime of adultery, the elements that must be proven beyond a reasonable doubt are:

1. voluntary sexual intercourse, and
2. the parties involved were unmarried at the time the sexual intercourse occurred, and
3. at least one of the parties being married to someone else.[127]

Sample Statute

State of Georgia statute § 16-6-8 (1997). Adultery. A married person commits the offense of adultery when he voluntarily has sexual intercourse with a person other than his spouse and, upon conviction thereof, shall be punished as for a misdemeanor.[128]

Arguments Made By The Prosecution

Seldom prosecuted, the red flag in an adultery case is not so much the sexual contact, but that one of the parties is married to someone other than the person they are in an affair with. Once the state can establish that sexual contact occurred, the remaining task is to prove the legality of the marriage of one, or both, of the participants. After proving sex and marital status, the state has a relatively open-and-shut case.

Arguments Made By The Defense

Defense attorneys always have a few strategies to work with when it comes to any criminal case and that is true for adultery cases as well. The strategies and theories may not work, but typically, there is no harm in trying them, and working to create doubt is part of what a defense attorney's job is all about.

The first line of reasoning defending an adultery case is to show that no sex occurred, or if it did, it did not take the form of intercourse, but rather mere touching. In the majority of cases, neither party wants to get caught and if asked, they may very well both deny that intercourse occurred; they were not exactly honest to begin with by having an affair and stand to avoid a criminal conviction with one more episode of dishonesty. The two may say that touching occurred, but not intercourse. Hence, they cannot be convicted of adultery, although they will be morally responsible for the relationship otherwise.

Of course, the other theory for the defense is to somehow prove that neither party was married at the time, thereby negating the second crucial element. The defense may try to argue that the marriage ceremony took place in a foreign nation or under such circumstances that the marriage contract is invalid and unenforceable in a court of law.

Variations of the Law of Adultery

A. Payment of Alimony as Punishment for Adultery

Adultery is a breach of the marriage contract and many marriages have ended in divorce as a result of an episode of adultery. Some marriages tolerate extramarital activity, allow it, or even in rare cases encourage it, but these scenarios are the exception to the fundamental bases for a marital accord. In most states, if a marriage is contested on the basis of an adulterous affair, the judge in a divorce proceeding is legally allowed to take into consideration the adulterous act when determining the amount of alimony to be paid. For example, in the state of Florida, Florida Revised Statute 61.08 provides that "the court may consider the adultery of a spouse and the circumstances thereof in determining whether alimony shall be awarded to such spouse and the amount of alimony.[129]

In *Escobar v. Escobar,* the aggrieved partner, Mrs. Escobar, was betrayed and angered to the point of filing for divorce.[130] In the divorce case, the wife asked the court for custody of their two children and to consider her husband's adulterous acts when considering the amount of alimony he should pay her on the consummation of the divorce. Typically, a divorce court relies on two primary factors when determining alimony: (1) demonstrated need, and (2) ability to pay. At the divorce trial, the judge considered the marriage irretrievably broken and therefore did not see a need to allow evidence pertaining to the adultery. The judge assumed the marriage would come to an end eventually, regardless of the adultery. The wife appealed.

The appeals court affirmed the custody of the two children to Mrs. Escobar.[131] When it came to the consideration of the adultery episode in the determination of alimony, the court insinuated that it had the legal authority by statute to consider the ex-husband's adulterous acts pursuant to Florida statute section 61.08, which provides: "The court may consider the adultery of a spouse and the circumstances thereof in determining whether alimony shall be awarded to such spouse and the amount of alimony." Despite the existence of the law, the court refused to use the law and did not consider the adulterous act. Conversely, the court stated that it would assess the husband's adultery if he were seeking alimony (if as though he might be punished for the adultery). But since it was the wife who was asking for alimony, the court did not assess the husband's adulterous acts. The court stated

> We hold that the court cannot preclude a party to a dissolution action from raising the issue of adultery as a *mitigating defense* to the awarding of alimony and the amount thereof. Here the wife hoped to obtain alimony by showing her husband's adultery. Since any alimony must be based upon the wife's demonstrated need and the husband's ability to pay no error appears [by precluding information about the husband's adultery].[132]

B. Marital Consent Vitiated After Adultery

In most cases, husband and wife sexual contact occurs after both parties ascertain a genuine degree of trust, commitment, and mutual support. Typically, only until such time can the parties feel secure enough to expose themselves to their sexual vulnerability. The exposure of one's sexual self is often highly selective and made after a series of careful considerations. In many cases of infidelity, the unfaithful party does not disclose the affair and keeps it a secret and returns to sexual relations with the spouse as if no affair exists. This type of scenario is highly disturbing to the victimized party; the sense of betrayal can be quite profound.[133]

In *Neal v. Neal,* the husband Mr. Neal engaged in a marital affair and did not disclose it to the wife, but nevertheless returned home and resumed regular sexual contact with her.[134] On discovering the affair, Mrs. Neal was outraged and sued for "civil battery," claiming that the affair constituted a "tortious interference" with her marriage contract. She claimed that had she known of the affair, she would never have consented to the subsequent episodes of sexual contact with her unfaithful husband. Her argument is that she did not consent since she was deceived; deceit cannot produce actual or constructive consent. On hearing her novel argument, the trial court was not persuaded and dismissed her complaint finding no legal basis for it. She appealed.

On appeal, the Idaho Supreme Court examined three legal questions: (1) whether Idaho law recognizes a cause of action for criminal conversation based on an alleged right to an exclusive sexual relationship with a spouse; (2) whether a party may recover for mental anguish resulting from the fear of contracting a sexually transmitted disease where there is no allegation of exposure to such disease; and (3) whether the facts alleged are sufficient to state a prima facie claim of civil battery.[135]

The court threw out the first two questions and addressed them in the negative. In leading up to the main issue, the court briefly addressed the old law of conversion in dicta, stating "[the laws pertaining to adulterous partners] has its genesis in the proposition that a husband has a property right in his wife and her services." This property interest in one's spouse could be "stolen" by a third party through adultery. Since a wife was her husband's property and servant, her consent to the adultery was no defense to her husband's suit against her paramour.

As it concerns the plaintiff's cause of action for possibly contracting an STD from her husband's affair, the court also dismissed this claim and stated:

> Damages are recoverable for emotional distress claims resulting from the present fear of developing a future disease only if the mental injury alleged is shown to be sufficiently genuine and the fear reasonable. We hold that there can be no reasonable fear of contracting such a disease absent proof of actual exposure. *See Carroll v. Sisters of St. Francis Health Services,* 1993 WL 532592 (Tenn.) (in order to recover emotional damages based on the fear of contracting AIDS, the plaintiff must prove, at a minimum, actual exposure to AIDS); *Burk v. Sage Products, Inc.,* 747 F. Supp. 285 (E.D. Pa. 1990).[136]

However, when it came to the issue of consent, the court reversed the decision of the lower court and held for the aggrieved wife, allowing her to sue for damages in civil court. The ruling was not specifically in regard to the adultery. As the case concerns the infidelity, the court stated: "Mary Neal contends that the obligation of fidelity imposed by I.C. § 32-901 provides the basis for an actionable claim for damages for the invasion of her exclusive sexual relationship with her husband. We disagree."[137] The court stated that the remedy for infidelity lies in the divorce law and in an action for divorce. What the court did allow, however, as it concerns the adultery, was a civil suit for battery based on lack of consent.

The court began by defining civil battery. "Civil battery consists of an intentional, unpermitted contact upon the person of another which is either unlawful, harmful or offensive." The court continued:

> [L]ack of consent is also an essential element of battery. W. Prosser & W. Keeton, The Law of Torts § 9 at 41 and § 18 at 112 (5th ed. 1984). Consent obtained by fraud or misrepresentation vitiates the consent and can render the offending party liable for a battery. W. Prosser & W. Keeton, The Law of Torts § 18 at 119; Bowman v. Home Life Insurance Co. of America, 243 F.2d 331, 333 (3d Cir. 1957).[138]

C. Failure to Disclose Adulterous STD

It is one thing to engage in adultery. It is another to fail to disclose the transgression. Worse yet, it is yet another thing to contract an STD from an adulterous affair and fail to disclose it to one's partner, thereby transmitting the adulterous STD to one's partner (and/or others). Many legal ramifications come into play under such circumstances.

In *Maharam v. Maharam,* a husband and wife had been married for thirty-one years. In a long-term marriage, it is reasonable to assume that both parties rely on one another to make certain disclosures for the overall good of the partnership. These disclosures concern matters pertaining to the marriage such as financial, familial, medical, and other practical and important information.

Mr. Maharam had an adulterous affair and contracted the STD of genital herpes.[139] Mr. Maharam ascertained his condition from a medical examination, but thereafter, did not disclose the condition to his wife and she subsequently caught the same STD from him (she was monogamous and did not have sex outside of the marriage). On discovering that she had been infected with an STD, she became distraught and sued for divorce. She also sued for the wrongful transmission of genital herpes under the theory of fraud and negligence, alleging that her husband was "grossly negligent" for his failure to disclose his condition, especially based on their thirty-one years of marriage.[140]

In the legal documents, the husband countered with a proximate cause argument, stating that "it will be virtually impossible as a matter of law for [his] wife to establish definitively that he transmitted the disease to her and to rule out conclusively any and all other possible means by which she may have contracted the disease."[141]

The New York Appellate Court held for the wife, first addressing the husband's proximate cause defense. The court stated, "this contention [of proximate cause] misapprehends the applicable burden of proof. In order to withstand the motion for summary judgment dismissing the tort cause of action for legal insufficiency, the wife was not required to prove causation to a mathematical certainty."[142] By this, the court insinuated that the burden of proof was on the wife to show that she contracted herpes from her husband with a reasonable degree of certainty and did not require proof beyond the capacity of science to comprehend. This ruling allowed the case to proceed to a trial and avoid a dismissal of the suit.

With the legal claims still intact, the case then turned on the wife's claim about her husband's failure to disclose. The applicable law for this part of the case was New York Public Health Law, Section 2307. Section 2307 states, "Any person who, knowing himself or herself to be infected with an infectious venereal disease, has sexual intercourse with another shall be guilty of a misdemeanor."[143] On studying the facts and the law, the court reinstated the wife's claim of injury and allowed the case to go to trial. The court noted, "the allegation in the third cause of action that the husband contracted genital herpes from third parties suffices to apprise him of the circumstances which give rise to the wife's personal injury claims."[144] The court stated,

> By order entered March 18, 1986, Special Term granted the motion for an order directing the husband to appear for a physical examination and denied the cross motion for summary judgment, finding that the third and fourth causes of action were viable. The court reasoned that the allegations that the husband had a legal duty to disclose his condition to his wife of 31 years, breached that duty, and that he caused injury were sufficient to state a negligence claim under *Palsgraf v. Long Is. R. R. Co.* (248 NY 339 [1928]). As to the fraud claim, the court noted that there is a duty to speak, and in some circumstances the failure to do so is equivalent to fraudulent concealment. Liberally construing the pleadings, in view of the 31-year marriage between the parties, the court held that the wife at 'a minimum' stated a claim for constructive fraud.[145]

Additional Court Cases: Adultery

In re Blanchflower[146]

834 A.2d 1012 (N.H. 2003)

CASE SUMMARY

PROCEDURAL POSTURE: Petitioner, a husband, sought a divorce from respondent, his wife, on grounds of adultery under N.H. Rev. Stat. Ann. § 458:7(II) (Supp. 2002). Co-respondent, the wife's alleged female lover, moved to dismiss the action. The Lebanon Family Division (New Hampshire) denied the motion to dismiss, and the lover appealed. The state supreme court accepted this matter as an interlocutory appeal under N.H. Sup. Ct. 8.

OVERVIEW: The lover argued that a homosexual relationship between two people, one of whom was married, did not constitute adultery under N.H. Rev. Stat. Ann. § 458:7(II) (Supp. 2002). The state supreme court found that the statute did not define adultery. The plain and ordinary meaning of adultery was voluntary sexual intercourse between a married man and someone other than his wife or between a married woman and someone other than her husband. The plain and ordinary meaning of sexual intercourse was defined to required insertion of the penis in the vagina, which clearly could only take place between persons of the opposite gender. The state supreme court found that the New Hampshire's criminal adultery statutes also required intercourse for a finding of adultery. Therefore, the state supreme court held that N.H. Rev. Stat. Ann. § 458:7(II) (Supp. 2002) did not include homosexual relationships in the definition of adultery. The state supreme court rejected the husband's argument that an interpretation of adultery that excluded homosexual conduct subjected homosexuals and heterosexuals to unequal treatment.

OUTCOME: The judgment was reversed and remanded.[147]

Seduction

Obtaining property fraudulently or by deceit has historically come under the purview of the law. The outdated law of romantic and sexual **seduction** is analogous to the law of obtaining property by false pretenses. In the context of seduction, the actor (usually male) enters the "contract" with the object of his desire in bad faith, seeking to take from the arrangement certain goods by means of false promises. The victim (usually female) enters the scenario interested in the prospect of a stable marriage or committed partnership. She gives of herself sexually as part of the exchange where commitment and faithfulness may be provided in return.[148]

Hence, seduction is a manner of becoming involved sexually, which is proscribed to protect the victim of such deceit. In an older era, a woman's inherent value centered on her virginity. A successful seduction irreparably harmed a victim since she no longer had that which was considered her most prized possession. Biblical myths gave rise to the threat of a skilled seduction, such as Eve's seduction of Adam in the Garden and the Serpent's seduction of Eve, also in the Garden. Greek mythology pertaining to Dionysus (God of Seduction) and even the modern celebration of James Bond both add luster to and make one wary of the art of seduction.

The law of seduction is less used today as a means to protect the chastity of a woman. In the modern era, a woman's virginity is not necessarily any more elevated in status than a man's virginity. A female's worth is inherently multifaceted and no longer exclusively centered on her sexuality. In an era where private, autonomous sexual expression is a value given the backing of Supreme Court decisions, many contemporary women do not consider virgin status as the treasured asset it once was. Indeed, today, some women may feel incomplete during their adult years if they have never engaged in some form of sexual expression. While the law sanctions deceit, in the case of seduction today, the law is also concerned with the safety and wholeness of the victim.

English Common Law defined the crime of seduction as a felony committed "when a male person induced an unmarried female of previously chaste character to engage in an act of sexual intercourse on a promise of marriage." The father of the victim had the right to maintain an action against the offender for the seduction of his daughter since this deprived him of family honor, the value of the daughter to the family, and the loss which comes with expanding the family without the hoped-for marriage.[149]

A famous case of relatively recent origin was that of entertainment personality Frank Sinatra. Sinatra was charged in the state of New Jersey in 1938 with seduction, having enticed a woman "of good repute to engage in sexual intercourse with him upon his promise of marriage." The charges were dropped when it was discovered that the woman was already married. Alternatively, both Sinatra and the woman could have been charged with adultery pursuant to state statute.[150]

In short, seduction statutes seek to deter a woman from losing her virginity to a dishonest suitor by means of enticement, persuasion, solicitations, bribes, promises, or other means without the use of force or threats. Under most of the remaining statutes, consent of the woman is no defense nor is a consummated marriage and legal marriage contract; the offender may still be found guilty. In most cases, a conviction for the crime of seduction requires the woman to have been unmarried and previously chaste.[151] Seduction is distinguished from adultery because the chastity of the victim previous to the alleged seduction is necessary for the offender to be found guilty.

Definition of the Offense

English Common Law defined the crime of seduction as a felony committed "when a male person induced an unmarried female of previously chaste character to engage in an act of sexual intercourse on a promise of marriage." A father had the right to maintain an action for the seduction of his daughter (or the enticement of a son who left home), since this deprived him of services or earnings.[152]

Elements of the Offense

For the crime of seduction, the elements that must be proven beyond a reasonable doubt are:

1. Inducement and persuasion to overcome the female's resistance,
2. unlawful sexual intercourse (sex outside of marriage),
3. the use of fraud and deceit to betray confidences and accomplish one's goal.[153]

Sample Statute

According to the Criminal Code of the state of Mississippi: Seduction. Chastity of woman. Code 1891, § 1298. Under Code 1892, § 1298, it is a crime to seduce a woman over sixteen years of age by virtue of any reigned or pretended marriage or false promise of marriage, the previous chaste character of the woman is an essential element of the crime.[154]

Arguments Made By The Prosecution

In the unlikely event of a prosecution for seduction, the state will have a challenging case when it comes to the element of deceit. As for the first two elements, the state will show that the victim was an unmarried female and, pursuant to her own admission that she engaged in sexual intercourse with the defendant. The final element, that she only had sex in exchange for a promise to marry, will involve a lot of contradictory claims and assertions by both sides. It will be helpful if the state can show the victim's previously chaste character, and that the perpetrator has somehow terminated his involvement with the victim. An absentee offender will be circumstantial evidence to suggest he really did not want to be in a relationship with the woman after all and hence lied about his commitment to gain sexual favors from her.

Arguments Made By The Defense

The defense can create doubt by simply painting a picture of an offender who merely wanted to spend romantic time with the victim and had no plans of marriage in mind. Doing so will implicate the victim in her own consent and negate the element of "promise to marry." The defense can try to portray the victim as bitter and seeking revenge through a criminal prosecution.

Of course, a speedy end to the case will result if the defense happens to show the woman was already married (thereby nullifying any claim to previously chaste character), or that she had been with other men. A long-term pattern of sexual contact between the victim and offender will also create doubt that the woman was a victim of seduction.

Variations of the Law of Seduction

A. Previous Chaste Character

The crime of seduction is not exclusively centered on deterring the deceit of the offender, but also concerns protecting the chastity of the victim. In *Norton v. State*, the accused was charged with seduction pursuant to state statute. The statute read:

> Seduction of females over age of sixteen, by frauds, etc.—If any person shall obtain carnal knowledge of any woman or female child over the age of sixteen years, by virtue of any feigned or pretended marriage, or any false or feigned promise of marriage, he shall, upon conviction, be imprisoned in the penitentiary not more than five years; but the testimony of the female seduced alone shall not be sufficient to warrant a conviction.[155]

The accused argued that the victim was already seeing another man (including having sexual contact with him), and in fact was engaged to be married to him. Therefore, she could not possibly be invested in the defendant's advances as a matter of law. The court did not find the proffered defense plausible and stated:

> It is no defense to the indictment that Miss Katie Douglass was engaged to another man, or had illicit connection with another man. If you believe from the evidence that the defendant obtained illicit connection with her by a false or feigned promise of marriage, he is guilty as charged.[156]

The case turned on the element of chastity. The court wrangled over whether or not proof of previous chaste character was required for a conviction for the crime of seduction. The court decided it was and stated:

> We have found, after careful examination, but two statutes identical with ours, and those are the statutes of Arkansas and Texas; and, in the case of *Polk v. State*, 40 Ark. 482, a case strikingly like this in its facts, speaking of testimony offered by defendant to show previous unchaste character, which had been excluded by the court below, the court says: 'In every prosecution for seduction, the character of the seduced female is involved in the issue ... It is not, indeed, expressed in our statute, as it is in the

statute of New York and of some of the other states, that the woman should have been of previous chaste character, but it is plainly implied.'

The Alabama statute originally did not have the words 'of previous chaste character' in it, but, by amendment, had them when this opinion was delivered. But the opinion on the point of what seduction is, is directly relevant. It is abundantly settled that a woman who has fallen and has really reformed, is chaste, as Chief Justice Brickell says, within the meaning of all these statutes; for she is then chaste when the second time seduced by the reigned promise. 3 Lawyers' Anno. Rep., 529; 29 Ohio St. 545; 33 Mich. 117. She, thus restored, is protected, because chaste then; but the prostitute who is such at the time of the promise, cannot then be seduced; she is already at the time without chastity.

The word 'seduce,' as found in the statute [one on this subject], imports not only illicit sexual intercourse, but it imports also a surrender of chastity. The statute is for the protection of the chastity of unmarried women, and the existence of the virtue at the time of the intercourse is a necessary ingredient of the offense; for, as has been often said, the prostitute may be the victim of rape, but is not the subject, of seduction.[157]

B. The Defense of Victim Disappointment

In a typical seduction case, the female is drawn into the episode by, among other things, a promise to marry. The premise that underlies the law of seduction is the enticement of the marriage proposal. The female party trusts her partner and gives herself to him with the expectation that he is a committed partner. In *Boyce* v. *State*, the offender sought to engage in sexual relations with the victim and promised to marry her if she would consent.[158] She consented and subsequently became pregnant but no marriage ever ensued. He was, however, with her throughout the entire pregnancy. A criminal action for unlawful seduction under promise of marriage was brought against defendant. The lower court convicted the defendant as charged, holding that his conduct violated N.Y. Penal Code § 111 (1848). The defendant appealed and, according to the court transcript:

The prisoner's counsel asked the court to charge in substance that, if the promise to marry was not an existing one, but an inchoate proposition depending upon the result of illicit intercourse as furnishing evidence of virtue to complete the mutuality of the contract, the case was not within the statute.[159]

On appeal, the convicted offender argued that the case had been wrongfully turned around. The offender initially wanted to marry the victim and engaged in sex solely for the purpose of verifying her status as a virgin. The record indicates that "The prosecutrix also testified that the accused, to induce her to consent to his proposal, stated in substance that he never would marry a girl unless he was satisfied she was a virgin, which he could ascertain only by her assenting to his proposition."[160] As far as the defendant was concerned, the case, therefore, was not about seduction for the purpose of obtaining sex, but rather, sex as a test to determine marriageability.

Regardless of the offender's motive for having sex with the victim, the female began to have serious reservations about him. After having sex with him, she experienced a lack of trust and did not feel a sense of security with him. The record states "and the fact that, after consenting, she endeavored to persuade him to desist, and at a time when it was too late to withdraw without his permission, she besought him to leave her, promising never to ask him to marry her if he would do so."[161]

The court was not persuaded by either argument. The defendant's motive did not persuade, nor did the fact that the victim didn't want to be married to the offender. The court ruled solely according to the facts and the law. The facts showed a promise of marriage in exchange for sex and when no marriage resulted, the law of seduction was made-out. The court ruled:

> The court declined so to charge. *Held* (Church, Ch. J., and Rapallo, J., dissenting), no error, as there was no just foundation in the evidence to claim that the promise was to marry only in case the accused should be satisfied that the prosecutrix was a virgin; that it was to the promise and not to any test of virginity that she gave her consent.

> Seduction is accomplished under promise of marriage, within the act to punish seduction as a crime (chap. 111, Laws of 1848), when it is effected by a conditional promise that, if the female will submit to an illicit connection, the offender will marry her; and the fact that, after consenting, she endeavored to persuade him to desist … is no excuse or palliation of the offence.[162]

C. Multiple Episodes Obviate Seduction Element

What if a previously chaste woman consented to sex in exchange for a promise to marry, but somehow carried on with a series of romantic meetings with the same man, each time believing that the romantic encounter would lead to marriage? Does the law of seduction apply in a long-term relationship? Or is the offense limited to a single act of sex? In *People* v. *Clark*, the initial facts of the case took on all the flavor of a seduction offense.[163] There was a promise to marry and there was sexual contact. However, the two parties continuously and without interruption kept meeting for sex and never got around to the marriage part of the agreement. After some time went by, the female put a stop to everything and had the man charged with the crime of seduction. The court stated:

> Illicit intercourse alone would not constitute the offense charged [a promise is also required]. In addition to this the complainant, relying upon some sufficient promise or inducement, and without which she would not have yielded, must have been drawn aside from the path of virtue she was honestly pursuing at the time the offense charged was committed. Now, from her own testimony it would seem that the parties had illicit intercourse as opportunity offered. Such is the force and ungovernable nature of this passion, and so likely is its indulgence to be continued between the same parties, when once yielded to, that the constitution of the human mind must be entirely changed before any man's judgment can resist the conclusion that where parties thus indulge their criminal desires it shows a willingness upon her part that a person of chaste character would not be guilty of, and that although a promise of marriage may have been made at each time as an inducement, it would be but a mere matter of form, and could not alone safely be relied upon to establish the fact that she would not have yielded had such a promise not been made.[164]

The ruling by the court indicated that multiple episodes of romantic encounters runs counter to the purposes of a seduction statute. Multiple meetings suggest, by circumstantial evidence, that the female is not tying her willingness to meet to a marriage proposal. If that were true, according to the logic of the appeals court, she would cease meeting her partner until such time as a marriage could be consummated. The fact that she kept meeting him tended to suggest she was not yielding for purposes of marriage, but for reasons unrelated to marriage. If the sexual interludes are not tied to a marriage contract, the law of seduction fails to apply. The appellate court dismissed the case.[165]

Additional Court Cases: Seduction

Kenyon v. People

26 N.Y. 203 (1863)

CASE SUMMARY

PROCEDURAL POSTURE: Plaintiff in error prisoner filed a writ of error from a judgment of a supreme court (New York), which affirmed the prisoner's conviction for seducing and having illicit connection with the prosecutrix under the promise of marriage.

OVERVIEW: The prisoner was indicted under 1848 N.Y. Laws 111, which was enacted to punish seduction as a crime. The prisoner offered to prove on the trial that the character for chastity of the witness and prosecutrix was, by general reputation among her neighbors, bad. In affirming, the court held that the character evidence for chastity of the prosecutrix was properly excluded. The supreme court properly charged to the jury that if they found that the prisoner promised to marry the prosecutrix if she would have carnal connection with him and that the prosecutrix believed and confided in such promise and intending to accept the offer of marriage did have such carnal connection, such a promise was sufficient under 1848 N.Y. Laws 111. Chapter 111 did not contemplate that the female had to be supported or corroborated on every material fact alleged. The prosecutrix's chastity did not have to be proved. General reputation evidence that the prosecutrix's mother's house was a house of ill fame was clearly incompetent.

OUTCOME: The court affirmed the judgment.[166]

Miscegeny

Miscegeny is marriage or sexual relations between two people of different races. Slavery in America implied a contempt for African-Americans and early on in the United States, a miscegenous couple was in trouble with the law. The law in early America and into the 20th century considered both blacks, and females, to be in a socially subordinate status. In a miscegenous case of a black male and a white female, there could not be a more offensive pairing when it came to social and legal perspectives at the time.[167] These racist and sexist sentiments blossomed in England and were imported to North America with the founding of the U.S.[168] Early American leaders, even Founding Fathers Madison, Hamilton, and Jefferson were influenced by European scholars such as Johann Friedrich Blumenbach, a German physiologist and anthropologist who wrote:

Almighty God created the races white, black, yellow, malay and red, and he placed them on separate continents. And but for the interference with his arrangement there would be no cause for such marriages. The fact that he separated the races shows that he did not intend for the races to mix.[169]

Antimiscegenation statutes found a great deal of durability, outlasting slavery, the Civil War, Jim Crow laws, and the 1964 Civil Rights Act. Although the term "miscegenation" was not coined until 1864, the first antimiscegenation statutes were enacted by the Colonial Authorities in 1662 (Virginia) and 1663 (Maryland), applying prohibitions to marriages between free white persons and slaves.[170]

It is important to note how antimiscegeny laws lasted for so long. As the laws that required blacks and whites to use separate facilities (Jim Crow laws) began to be defeated in the 1950s and 1960s, including the requirements that blacks ride in the back of public buses, the courts nevertheless allowed for the existence of antimiscegenation laws. The courts distinguished antimiscegenation statutes from the Jim Crow provisions by asserting the "equal application" theory, which held that antimiscegenation laws were not discriminatory because both whites and blacks were equally prevented from intermarrying; no one was actually being singled out for disparate treatment. This rationale was used in the 1883 Supreme Court case of *Pace v. Alabama*[171] and was consistent with the *Brown v. Board of Education*[172] and similar cases.

The courts argued that, even after enacting the Fourteenth Amendment Equal Protection Clause, the drafters of the clause probably intended to allow states to continue to ban interracial marriages since no one was actually being targeted for unfair treatment. Such strategically deployed legal arguments allowed defenders of these statutes to effectively prevent consensual interracial unions, despite successful constitutional challenges to other forms of Jim Crow discrimination (e.g., school and public facility segregation).

These statutes were around for approximately 300 years before being invalidated in 1967 by the U.S. Supreme Court in *Loving v. Virginia* (see below).[173] At the time of the Loving decision, sixteen states still had antimiscegenation laws in effect. Some states will consider themselves separate republics and, hence, refuse to follow precedent set by the highest court in the land. As an example, Alabama kept an antimiscegeny law on the books until 2000 when it was repealed by the state legislature.[174]

Today, substantial social progress has taken place from early times. Advances have been made in civil rights for racial minorities and law and justice has achieved greater equality between the genders. Socially, the United States has more single adults and single-parent families than ever before, suggesting an opening-up of moral and social codes of relationship and family development. Laws and social standards have made room for the exercise of individual preference when it comes to marriage and sexual expression.[175] Today, miscegenistic partnerships constitute a lawful marriage and sexual practice, so long as the parties are adults, consenting, not from the same family, and not married simultaneously to someone else.

Definition of the Offense

Miscegeny is the mixing of different racial groups through marriage, cohabitation, sexual relations, and procreation.[176]

Elements of the Offense

For the former crime of miscegeny, the elements that must be proved beyond a reasonable doubt are:

1. voluntary marriage, cohabitation, or sexual relations
2. with someone of a different race or ethnicity.[177]

Sample Statute

State of Virginia Anti-Miscegeny statute § 20-59. Punishment for marriage. If any white person intermarry with a colored person, or any colored person intermarry with a white person, he shall be guilty of a felony and shall be punished by confinement in the penitentiary for not less than one nor more than five years.[178]

Arguments Made By The Prosecution

Like with many older prohibitions based on race, the case for the state was relatively easy. The prosecution only needed to show that one of the parties was nonwhite, even to the slightest biological degree. No harm needs to be shown, no intent, and no pattern of behavior, only the slightest medical certainty of racial composition. The state would then show that the other party was white and both are guilty of the crime of miscegeny.

Arguments Made By The Defense

The cards were stacked defending a miscegeny case. If one of the parties is white and the other nonwhite, the defense had no options and time may be better spent on arguing for a light sentence instead of a not guilty verdict. The defense, of course, would verify the race of the parties since that is what the case hinges on.

Variations of the Law of Miscegeny

A. Sexual Deviance, not Race, Is the Issue

When miscegeny was illegal, both racism and a fear of sex were competing to see which of the two could cause Americans the most anxiety. Since sex was probably the greater of the two evils at the time, early miscegeny cases were turned around to be an issue of sexual deviance rather than about race relations.

In the highly relevant case of *Pace v. Alabama,* Tony Pace, an African-American male, and Mary Cox, a Caucasion female, were in a committed love relationship in the state of Alabama in 1881.[179] When the police were informed of their relationship, they were arrested and charged with a black person and a white person living together "in a state of adultery or fornication" and hence in violation of the state's antimiscegenation statute. Both were convicted and sentenced. Section 4184 of the Code of Alabama provides that

> if any man and woman live together in adultery or fornication, each of them must, on the first conviction of the offence, be fined not less than one hundred dollars, and may also be imprisoned in the county jail or sentenced to hard labor for the county for not more than six months.[180]

Section 4189 of the same code declares that

> if any white person and any negro, or the descendant of any negro to the third genera-tion, inclusive, though one ancestor of each generation was a white person, intermarry or live in adultery or fornication with each other, each of them must, on conviction, be imprisoned in the penitentiary or sentenced to hard labor for the county for not less than two nor more than seven years.[181]

Pace appealed his conviction in the case all the way to the U.S. Supreme Court, stating that the law violated his constitutional rights to equality of the laws and equal protection before the law. The U.S. Supreme Court acknowledged the equal protection argument by stating:

> The counsel is undoubtedly correct in his view of the purpose of the [equal protection] clause of the amendment in question, that it was to prevent hostile and discriminating State legislation against any person or class of persons. Equality of protection under the laws implies not only accessibility by each one, whatever his race, on the same terms with others to the courts of the country for the security of his person and property, but that in the administration of criminal justice he shall not be subjected, for the same of-fence, to any greater or different punishment.[182]

The Supreme Court did not see any violation of equal protection since no group or race was being singled out. In this case, both blacks and whites were subject to the law equally. The court stated,

> The defect in the argument of counsel consists in his assumption that any discrimination is made by the laws of Alabama in the punishment provided for the offence for which the plaintiff in error was indicted when committed by a person of the African race and when committed by a white person. The two sections of the code cited are entirely consistent. The one prescribes, generally, a punishment for an offence committed between persons of different sexes; the other prescribes a punishment for an offence which can only be committed where the two sexes are of different races. There is in neither section any discrimination against either race. Sect. 4184 equally includes the offence when the persons of the two sexes are both white and when they are both black. Sect. 4189 applies the same punishment to both offenders, the white and the black.[183]

Pace lost his appeal. The court stated, "Whatever discrimination is made in the punishment prescribed in the two sections [of the Alabama statute] is directed against the offense designated and not against the person of any particular color or race."[184]

B. Invalidation of a Will

As noted in chapter 1, a legal marriage comes with many benefits and protections that are not afforded to couples not lawfully married. Conversely, proof of an invalid marriage vitiates those same benefits. Hence, a showing of legal marriage has many important practical ramifications.

Allan Monks and Marie Antoinette were married for twenty-one years before Allan Monks passed away.[185] Upon his death, it was discovered unexpectedly that he wrote two wills bequeathing the same estate to two different people. In one, he left everything to his wife, but in the other he left everything to a good friend named Ida Lee. Both heirs were confused and contacted their respective attorneys.

Lee's attorneys used an aggressive strategy. They proffered evidence that their competition, Marie, was one-eighth African-American. By showing that Marie, Allan's wife, was African-American, their marriage could be ruled as miscegenous and therefore, illegal. If the thirty-one-year marriage between Allan and Antoinette was illegal, the will to Marie was invalid, and Ida would inherit the estate. The only remaining valid will would be the one that named Ida Lee as beneficiary.[186]

When the case was provided a court date, the court merely accepted the evidence of the miscegenous marriage between Allan and Antoinette to declare their marriage invalid pursuant to the California antimiscegeny law at the time.[187] The California antimiscegeny law read as follows: "The marriage of persons of Caucasian blood, or their descendants, with Negroes, Mongolians or Indians, and their descendants shall be null and void."[188] As a result of the invalidity of the marriage, the will to Marie was also invalid and unenforceable. From the court transcript:

> The appellant vigorously assails the finding of the trial court that she was of Negro descent, but contends that even if such finding is supported by credible evidence, nevertheless the Arizona miscegenation statute is unconstitutional as imposing an absolute prohibition against marriage upon any person of mixed Negro and Caucasian blood. As to the first of these points little need be said. At the trial one Malcolm J. Rogers, an anthropologist, testified that in his opinion appellant "was at least one-eighth Negroid." Dr. James C. Anbers, a physician who had had much experience in the southern states and in Africa in his profession, gave as his opinion that appellant had, as near as he could determine, one-eighth Negro blood.
>
> The court predicated its refusal to admit the so-called Giraudo will of August 4, 1928, to probate on two grounds, namely, fraud and undue influence. The fraud alleged and found consisted of false and fraudulent representations by appellant to decedent that appellant was a member of the Caucasian race, of pure French descent and ancestry; that she was not a descendant of a member of the Negro race; that such representations were false, fraudulent and untrue, and that they were known by the appellant at the time they were made to be false, fraudulent and untrue. It was further found that in reliance upon the representations so made, decedent became affianced to appellant prior to August 4, 1928, in the belief that a valid marriage could and would be consummated, and that in further reliance upon the representations the will was executed.[189]

C. Due Process and Equal Protection

The landmark Supreme Court case that overturned the Pace decision above and ruled as unconstitutional any antimiscegeny law was *Loving v. Virginia* in 1967.[190] Mildred Delores Jeter, a woman of African and Rappahannock American Indian descent (1939–2008) and Richard Perry Loving, a white man (1933–1975) were residents of the state of Virginia but married in the District of Columbia. At the time, interracial marriage was illegal in Virginia pursuant to various provisions of the Racial Integrity Act of that state.[191] This act was a law banning marriages between any white person and any nonwhite person. After marrying in Washington, D.C., they returned to Virginia and were arrested and charged pursuant to the Racial Integrity Act. Specifically, they were caught sleeping together in their bedroom by the police who had conducted a brief surveillance of them.

Figure 5 Prior to Loving v. Virginia, mixed race couples were illegal.

The act was codified as Section 20-58 of the Virginia Code, which prohibited interracial couples from being married out of state and then returning to Virginia, and Section 20-59, which classified miscegenation as a felony, punishable by a prison sentence of between one and five years. On January 6, 1959, the Lovings pleaded guilty and were sentenced to one year in prison, with the sentence suspended for 25 years on condition that the couple leave the state of Virginia. The Lovings took their case all the way to the U.S. Supreme Court.[192]

The Supreme Court sided with the Lovings and ruled in their favor and also invalidated the Racial Integrity Act. The Court invalidated the statute and found it to be a violation of the constitutional rights to due process and equal protection. In addition, the Court found an additional glaring problem with antimiscegeny laws. The Court concluded that antimiscegenation laws were racist and had been enacted to perpetuate white supremacy. The court stated:

> There is patently no legitimate overriding purpose independent of invidious racial discrimination which justifies this classification. The fact that Virginia prohibits only interracial marriages involving white persons demonstrates that the racial classifications must stand on their own justification, as measures designed to maintain White Supremacy.[193]

In 2007, before she died, Mildred Loving issued a rare public statement, which commented on same-sex marriage, prepared for delivery on the fortieth anniversary of the *Loving v. Virginia* decision:

> Surrounded as I am now by wonderful children and grandchildren, not a day goes by that I don't think of Richard and our love, our right to marry, and how much it meant to me to have that freedom to marry the person precious to me, even if others thought he was the "wrong kind of person" for me to marry. I believe all Americans, no matter their race, no matter their sex, no matter their sexual orientation, should have that same

freedom to marry. Government has no business imposing some people's religious beliefs over others. Especially if it denies people's civil rights.

I am still not a political person, but I am proud that Richard's and my name is on a court case that can help reinforce the love, the commitment, the fairness, and the family that so many people, black or white, young or old, gay or straight seek in life. I support the freedom to marry for all. That's what Loving, and loving, are all about.[194]

Additional Court Cases: Miscegeny

Naim v. Naim

87 S.E.2d 749 (1955)

CASE SUMMARY

PROCEDURAL POSTURE: Appellee husband filed suit against appellant wife, seeking to annul their marriage under the state's miscegenation statute, Va. Code Ann. § 20-54. The Circuit Court of the city of Portsmouth (Virginia) entered a decree, which held that the marriage was void under § 20-54. The wife sought review.

OVERVIEW: The husband was Chinese and the wife was Caucasian. The couple was married in North Carolina for the purpose of evading the Virginia miscegenation law, § 20-54, which forbade their marriage. After the marriage, they immediately returned to Virginia, where they lived as husband and wife. The wife argued that the miscegenation statute was beyond the power of the state to enact under the Due Process and Equal Protection Clauses of U.S. Const. amend. XIV. The court found that (1) the Fourteenth Amendment did not prohibit the state from enacting legislation to preserve the racial integrity of its citizens; (2) the prevention of miscegenetic marriages was a proper governmental objective, and within the competency of the state to effect; and (3) the classification of races under § 20-54 to effect the preservation of racial integrity was not arbitrary or unreasonable.

OUTCOME: The decree appealed from was affirmed.[195]

Chapter Two Summary

U pon initial thought, consensual sexual contact would seem to be legally permissible since the parties involved voluntarily agree to engage in the activity. However, as this chapter explains, nothing could be further from the truth. Numerous examples—from fornication to miscegeny—exist that the law seeks to regulate (or used to regulate) for a variety of reasons. Consent will always make an episode of sexual relations less serious compared to a case involving force, violence, or intimidation, but does not automatically make sex legal.

Numerous reasons justify the use of the criminal law when it comes to the regulation of consensual sexual activity. In cases of fornication, the state seeks to downplay the freedom of sexual expression and instead, support marriage-based intimacy. An outdated cloud of negativity casts a shadow on premarital sex and certain stigmatizing terms are still used to refer to fornication such as "living in sin" or having sex "out of wedlock." Although the landmark Supreme Court decision in *Lawrence v. Texas*[196] in 2003 calls into question the constitutionality of fornication statutes, many states still prohibit sexual relations outside of marriage. It is highly likely that these laws will decrease, rather than increase in the next twenty-five years.[197]

Statutory rape cases are also consensual but a little easier to comprehend when it comes to the justification behind the legal prohibition. Statutory rape cases occur behind a veil of consent, but in cases where the minor involved in sexually immature, legal consent becomes an impossibility; minors are thought to be incapable of forming actual consent due to their age, and emotional and intellectual development. The law behind this form of "rape" correctly seeks to protect minors from an activity that may be detrimental to the emotional and psychological well-being of a minor. As Figure 1 below shows, the younger the minor, the more serious the case. Many states increase the penalty as the age of the victim decreases.

Figure 1 Severity of Offense and Age Inverse Correlation.

Adults 18 and over have to recognize the vulnerability of minors and seek to protect them from the exposure to sexual stimulation when they are not yet prepared for it. Statutory rape is a strict liability offense and all adults are held criminally liable for the sexual touching of a minor in any manner. A very small number of states, however, will allow for a reasonable mistake of age defense for cases where one or both of the parties had every reason to believe the other person was of the age of consent.[198] It will be exceptionally helpful in such a defense for the accused to demonstrate that he or she made a good faith effort to discover the age of the person they engaged with. The precise age of consent varies state by state. In most states, the age of consent is 16. It is interesting to note that the age of consent allows for a youth to legally have sex even though they are not yet an adult. Hence, in many states, minors may legally engage in sexual activity.[199] Hopefully, parental guidance will be used to the fullest extent possible.

The illegality behind fornication and statutory rape laws has logical bases. The promotion of marriage and the accompanying domestic stability is important for fornication laws and the protection of minors an obvious concern for statutory rape cases. When it comes to sodomy, fear is mixed in with the obvious concerns just mentioned. Meaning, a phobic type of fear permeates thoughts of consensual sodomy between homosexuals. Homosexuality in general, even without any sexual touching, stirs anger and fury in many Americans. The weight of religious and moral disapproval for certain types of sexual relations is seriously pronounced in cases of same-sex sexual activity.[200]

Historically, sodomy was not mentioned, but only prohibited. In such cases, the participants faced the threat of criminal prosecution for doing something they couldn't know for sure was illegal. Sodomy has been subject to many tortured definitions, but is probably best explained as anal intercourse. Sodomy is an obvious sexual act in the gay male community, thus inciting further disapprobation for the act.

Despite the intensity of the disapproval, the unusual logic behind homophobia has not been able to withstand public or scientific scrutiny. The question "What is so wrong with homosexuality?" has not yet been scientifically addressed, Biblical precepts notwithstanding. As a result, social disapproval, to a degree, has given way to tolerance and acceptance of a variety of relationships, such as black and white and man to man/woman to woman. The present-day tolerance and acceptance of consensual sodomy was validated in the 2003 Supreme Court decision in *Lawrence v. Texas*. In the Lawrence decision, the U.S. Supreme Court held that a law that prohibits consensual sodomy between adults is unconstitutional and a violation of due process.[201] The Lawrence decision overturned the 1986 *Bowers v. Hardwick* decision.[202]

Adultery cases, on the other hand, have not received public approval. The courts continue to uphold laws banning adulterous sexual activity. In these cases, which are also consensual, the potential for injury to someone other than the two participants is great and the law seeks to protect the devastation that can result to a spouse whose partner is unfaithful and engages in sex outside of the committed relationship. Adultery paves the way for fault-based divorce cases and may give rise to civil liability lawsuits if the unfaithful party transmits an adulterous STD to a marriage partner. Dependent children will also suffer substantial emotional injury when a parent is involved with a third party. Despite the high level of publicity that accompanies adulterers such as President Bill Clinton, golfer Tiger Woods, or evangelicals such as Jimmy Swaggart and Jim Bakker, the police typically do not enforce adultery laws. In addition, high-profile public figures are adept at deflecting the already short attention span of the public and usually go on to lead normal lives after the transgression.

This chapter ended with an interesting look at older seduction and miscegeny cases. A skilled seductor calls into question the consent given by the victim and most courts rule that no consent is possible if obtained by fraud and deceit. In an earlier era, the laws of seduction sought to protect a woman's virtue and chastity. The law also had it's sights on the sanction for a male who selfishly engaged in intimacy solely for purposes of sexual gratification, knowing the woman wanted to be married, and exploited the vulnerability of the woman. A seduction conviction requires the victim party to be unmarried and chaste at the time of the sexual activity.

Miscegency laws, arguably, were the most curious of all of the laws covered in this chapter. Anti-miscegeny laws applied where two people were not allowed to marry because of their skin color. Sometimes, the skin color looked identical between the two parties, but a court-ordered medical test could show an otherwise imperceptible racial difference between the two parties. It seems like this outdated racial prejudice tended to cease with the advancements of civil rights in the 1960s, and the increase in the variety of family composition. However, at least one state still had an antimiscegeny law as recently as 2000. Here in the 21st century, none of the fifty states has a law prohibiting miscegenous relationships. The *Loving v. Virginia* Supreme Court ruling in 1967 struck down all state anti-miscegeny laws as a violation of the equal protection clause.[203]

Key Terms

Illegal Consent 00

Fornication 00

Statutory Rape 00

Sodomy 00

Adultery 00

Seduction 00

Miscegeny 00

Promise of Marriage 00

Mistake of Age 00

Privacy Interest 00

Concepts & Principles

Scarlet Letter 00

Infamous Crime Against Nature 00

Moral Outrage 00

Don't Ask, Don't Tell 00

Marital Infidelity 00

Miscegenetic Marriage 00

Adulterous STD 00

Previously Chaste Character 00

Equal Protection 00

Liberty and Autonomy 00

Chapter Two Select Court Cases	
Case	**Point of Law**
Martin v. Ziherl 00	Fornication involves a liberty interest
B.B. v. State 00	Consensual sex between minors is legal
Bieth v. State 00	A sentence enhancement applies if the victim is under 12
State v. Yanez 00	Mistake of age is no defense (in this case)
Lawrence v. Texas 00	Sodomy is part of due process protections
C.V. Kelly v. Illinois 00	Sodomy may still be a crime against nature
Thomasson v. Perry 00	Don't Ask, Don't Tell is legal
Bowers v. Hardwick 00	Antisodomy laws are legal and constitutional
Escobar v. Escobar 00	An adultery conviction may affect alimony
Neal v. Neal 00	Adultery may result in a suit for civil battery
Norton v. State 00	Loss of chastity is required for a seduction conviction
People v. Clark 00	A long-term relationship cannot constitute seduction
Kenyon v. People 00	Promiscuous past is no defense to seduction
Pace v. Alabama 00	Mixed race couple implies automatic sexual deviancy
Loving v. Virginia 00	Antimiscegeny laws are unconstitutional and constitute a violation of equal protection

Questions for Review

1. Why are some forms of sexual activity illegal if both parties consent?

2. How rigorously are fornication laws enforced by the criminal justice system?

3. What is the legal distinction between fornication and adultery?

4. What is the legal difference between fornication and statutory rape?

5. Is statutory rape a consensual sexual act?

6. What is the historical justification for the criminalization of adultery?

7. What makes the Lawrence v. Texas decision historically significant?

8. What are the legal elements of the crime of seduction?

9. What harm is caused by the crime of seduction?

10. What is miscegeny?

1 Bowers v. Hardwick, 478 U.S. 186 (1986).

2 Don S. Browning, *Modern Law and Christian Jurisprudence on Marriage and Family,* 58 Emory L.J. 31 (2008).

3 John D'Emilio & Estelle B. Freedman, Intimate Matters: A History of Sexuality in America (University of Chicago Press)(1988).

4 James A. Cox, *Bilboes, Brands, and Branks: Colonial Crimes and Punishments,* Colonial Williamsburg J. (April 6, 2010), http://www.history.org/Foundation/journal/spring03/branks.cfm.

5 Nathaniel Hawthorne, The Scarlet Letter (1850).

6 2 William Blackstone, Commentaries *216.

7 Nancy F. Cott, Passionlessness: An Interpretation of Victorian Sexual Ideology, 1790–1850, in A Heritage of Her Own (Nancy F. Cott & Elizabeth H. Pleck, eds.) (1979).

8 Pace v. Alabama, 106 U.S. 583 (1883).

9 Passed on March 3, 1873, ch. 258, § 2, 17 Stat. 599.

10 Codified as The Comstock Act, 39 U.S.C.A. § 3001. The Comstock Law of 1873 also made it a crime to sell or distribute materials that could be used for contraception or abortion.

11 18 U.S.C.A. § 2421 *et seq.*

12 Sigmund freud, The Complete Introductory Lectures on Psychoanalysis (Norton Books) (1966).

13 People v. Simms, 47 N.E.2d 703 (Ill. 1943).

14 De Silva, W.P. *ABC of Sexual Health: Sexual Variations.* 318 British Medical Journal 7184, pps. 654-656. Found in Hickey, E. (Ed.) Sex Crimes and Paraphilia (Prentice Hall) (1999).

15 Alfred Kinsey, Sexual Behavior in the Human Male (Indiana University Press) (1948).

16 Griswold v. Connecticut, 381 U.S. 479 (1965).

17 *Id.*

18 Loving v. Virginia 38 U.S. 1 (1967).

19 Stanley v. Georgia, 394 U.S. 557 (1969).

20 Bowers v. Hardwick, 478 U.S. 186 (1986).

21 Defense of Marriage Act, Pub. L. No. 104-199, § 7, 110 Stat. 2419 (1996) (codified as amended in 1 U.S.C. § 7 and 28 U.S.C. § 1738C (2006).

22 Lawrence v. Texas, 539 U.S. 558 (2003).

23 Fornication is a term derived from the Latin word *fornix,* which means "archway" or "vault." *Fornix* became a euphemism for a brothel because in Rome, prostitutes could be hired under the vaults of the city. *Fornicatio* means "sex in the archway" and refers to prostitution activity under the vaults.

24 Deana A. Pollard, *Sex Torts,* 91 Minn. L. Rev. 769, 821-24 (2007). Most Americans are far from sexually promiscuous and engage in sexual behavior consistent with traditional norms. The most current data available indicates that over 80% of Americans ages 18 to 59 had zero or one sexual partner in the preceding year; 16% had between two and four partners; and only 3% had more than five partners.

25 William E. Nelson, *Emerging Notions of Modern Criminal Law in the Revolutionary Era,* in Crime, Law, and Society 73 (Abraham S. Goldstein and Joseph Goldstein eds., 1971).

26 Eisenstadt v. Baird, 405 U.S. 438 (1975).

27 Oliverson v. West Valley City, 875 F. Supp. 1465 (Dist. Court, D. Utah 1995).

28 Powell v. State, 510 S.E.2d 18 (Ga. 1989).

29 Lawrence v. Texas, 539 U.S. 558 (2003).

30 Oliverson v. West Valley City, 875 F. Supp. 1465 (Dist. Court, D. Utah 1995).

31   Uᴛᴀʜ Cᴏᴅᴇ Aɴɴ. § 76-7-104 (West 1973).

32   *Id.*

33   U.S. Cᴏɴsᴛ. amend. V

34   Commonwealth v. Arner, 24 A. 83 (Pa. 1892).

35   *Id.*

36   *Id.*

37   Legal sexual contact implies that the sexual encounter is noncommercial, does not involve a minor, and occurs between unrelated parties.

38   Martin v. Ziherl, 607 S.E.2d 367 (Va. 2005).

39   Lawrence v. Texas, 539 U.S. 558, 577–578 (2003).

40   Martin v. Ziherl, 607 S.E.2d at 369 (Va. 2005) (citing *Lawrence,* 539 U.S. at 567 (2003)).

41   *Id.*

42   *Lawrence,* 539 U.S. at 577–578 (2003).

43   Martin v. Ziherl, 607 S.E.2d at 369 (Va. 2005) (citing *Lawrence,* 539 U.S. at 567 (2003)).

44   Griswold v. Connecticut, 381 U.S. 479 (1965).

45   State v. Saunders, 381 A.2d 333 (N.J. 1977).

46   *Id.*

47   *Id.* at 340.

48   State v. Saunders, 381 A.2d 333 (N.J. 1977).

49   State v. Poe, 252 S.E.2d 843 (N.C. Ct. App. 1979).

50   F. Sᴄʜᴍᴀʟʟᴇɢᴇʀ, Cʀɪᴍɪɴᴀʟ Lᴀᴡ Tᴏᴅᴀʏ 239 (3d ed. 2006).

51   Wilson v. Commonwealth, 160 S.W.2d 649 (Ky. 1942).

52   Michael M. v. Super. Ct. of Sonoma Cnty., 450 U.S. 464, 471–72 (1981).

53   *Id.*

54   Kʏ. Rᴇᴠ. Sᴛᴀᴛ. Aɴɴ. §§ 510.000-510.150 (West 2009).

55   *Id.*

56   *Id.* An individual is deemed incapable of consent when he or she is less than 16 years of age. Individuals are exempt from prosecution for [statutory] rape (a felony) under the following circumstances: If the victim is less than 14 years of age and the defendant is less than 18 years of age, and, if the victim is between 14 and 16 years of age and the defendant is less than 21 years. However, it is a misdemeanor to engage in sexual intercourse or deviate sexual intercourse with someone under 16 years of age regardless of the age of the defendant.

57   B.B. v. State, 659 So.2d 256 (Fla. 1995).

58   *Id.*

59   U.S. v. Beith, 407 F.3d 881 (2005).

60   *Id.*

61   *Id.* at 887.

62   *Id.*

63   *Id.* at 898.

64   *Id.* at 899.

65   *Id.*

66   State v. Yanez, 716 A.2d 759, 760 (R.I. 1998).

67   R.I. Gen. Laws § 11-37-8.1 (1956).

68   State v. Yanez, 716 A.2d 759 (R.I. 1998).

69   *Id.* at 760.

70   *Id.* at 769.

71   Michael M. v. Super. Ct. of Sonoma Cnty., 450 U.S. 464 (1980).

72   "A person commits the offense of sodomy when he or she performs or submits to any sexual act involving the sex organs of one person and the mouth or anus of another." Ga. Code Ann. § 16-6-2 (1981).

73   Bowers v. Hardwick, 478 U.S. 186 (1986).

74   James A. Cox, *Bilboes, Brands, and Branks: Colonial Crimes and Punishments,* Colonial Williamsburg J. (April 6, 2010), http://www.history.org/Foundation/journal/spring03/branks.cfm.

75   DAVID GARLAND, THE CULTURE OF CONTROL: CRIME AND SOCIAL ORDER IN CONTEMPORARY SOCIETY (2001).

76   Daniel Allender, Note, *Applying Lawrence: Teenagers and the Crime Against Nature,* 58 Duke L.J. 1825 (2009).

77   Ariz. Rev. Stat. § 13-1411 (1987).

78   D.C. Code Ann. § 22-3502 (1946).

79   Md. Code Ann. § 27-554 (19991).

80   Wis. Stat. Ann. Ch. 384, § 6 (1984).

81   State v. Stokes, 161 S.E.2d 53 (N.C. Ct. App. 1968).

82   2 William Blackstone, Commentaries *216.

83   State v. Whittemore, 122 S.E.2d 396 (N.C. 1961).

84   R.I. Gen. Laws § 11-10-1 (2010).

85   Lawrence v. Texas, 539 U.S. 558 (2003).

86   In re Kandu, 315 B.R. 123, 148 (Bankr. W.D. Wash. 2004) ("Basing legislation on moral disapproval of same-sex couples may be questionable in light of Lawrence.").

87   *Id.*

88   81 C.J.S. *Sodomy* § 1 (1985).

89   *Id.*

90   Pruett v. State, 463 S.W.2d 191 (Tex. Crim. App. 1971).

91   Donoho v. State, 628 S.W.2d 483, 485 (Tex. App. 1982).

92   Va. Code Ann. § 18.2-361 (1950).

93   Lawrence v. Texas, 539 U.S. 558 (2003).

94   Tex. Penal Code Ann. § 21.06 (West 1972).

95   Lawrence v. Texas, 539 U.S. 558 (2003).

96   Bowers v. Hardwick, 478 U.S. 186 (1986).

97   *Lawrence,* 539 U.S. at 566.

98   *Id.* at 571.

99   Lawrence v. Texas, 539 U.S. 558 (2003).

[100] *Bowers,* 478 U.S. 186 (1986).

[101] Kelly v. People, 61 N.E. 425 (Ill. 1901).

[102] 38 ILL. REV. STAT. § 47 (1901).

[103] *Id.* at 431.

[104] *Id.* at 439.

[105] National Defense Authorization Act of 1994 § 571, 10 U.S.C. § 654 (1994).

[106] *Id.*

[107] SERVICEMEMBERS LEGAL DEFENSE NETWORK. Found at http://www.sldn.org/. Last visited September 22, 2010.

[108] *Id.*

[109] Thomasson v. Perry, 80 F.3d 915 (4th Cir. 1996).

[110] Don't Ask, Don't Tell Repeal Act of 2010 (H.R. 2965, S. 4023) (2010).

[111] Congressional Research Service, Congressional Research Service Home Page, January 6, 2011. www.congress.gov.

[112] National Defense Authorization Act § 571.

[113] Bowers v. Hardwick, 478 U.S. 186 (1986).

[114] LAWRENCE M. FRIEDMAN, CRIME AND PUNISHMENT IN AMERICAN HISTORY (1993).

[115] NIGERIAN STATE OF ZAMFARA SHARI'AH PENAL CODE LAW, Chapter 8, § 126 (1978).

[116] In 2003, there was one divorce for every two marriages. National Vital Statistics Reports: Births, Marriages, Divorces, and Deaths: Provisional Data for 2003, Centers for Disease Control and Prevention (United States Department of Health and Human Services), June 10, 2004, available at http://www.cdc.gov/nchs/data/nvsr/nvsr52/nvsr52_22.pdf.

[117] Oliverson v. City of W. Valley, 875 F. Supp. 1465 (D. Utah 1995).

[118] In re Marriage of J.T., 891 P.2d 729 (Wash. Ct. App. 1995) (stating that marital relationship is not a "special" relationship creating a duty of sexual fidelity or a duty to disclose third-party sexual relations).

[119] DAVID ROSEN, SEX SCANDAL AMERICA: POLITICS & THE RITUAL OF PUBLIC SHAMING (2008).

[120] LAWRENCE M. FRIEDMAN, CRIME AND PUNISHMENT IN AMERICAN HISTORY (1993).

[121] W. VA. CODE ANN. § 61-8-4 (Michie 2000).

[122] N.C. GEN. STAT. 14-184 (2003) (providing that "if any man and woman, not being married to each other, shall lewdly and lasciviously associate, bed and cohabit together, they shall be guilty of a Class 2 misdemeanor ... .").

[123] Katherine Shaw Spaht, *Covenant Marriage Seven Years Later: Its As Yet Unfulfilled Promise* 65 LA. L. REV. 605 (2005).

[124] Evan Buxbaum & Edmund DeMarche, NEW HAMPSHIRE EYES REPEALING LAW ON ADULTERY, CNN.com, Jan. 13, 2010, http://www.cnn.com/2010/CRIME/01/12/adultery.vote/index.html.

[125] In re Marriage of J.T., 891 P.2d 729 (Wash. Ct. App. 1995) (stating that marital relationship is not a "special" relationship creating a duty of sexual fidelity or a duty to disclose third-party sexual relations).

[126] Marvin M. Moore, *The Diverse Definitions of Criminal Adultery,* 30 U. KAN. CITY L. REV. 219 (1962).

[127] GA. CODE ANN. § 16-6-8 (West 2010).

[128] *Id.*

[129] FLA. STAT. § 61.08. Alimony. (2010).

[130] Escobar v. Escobar, 300 So. 2d 702 (Fla. Dist. Ct. App. 1974).

[131] *Id.* at 710.

[132] *Id.* at 714.

133 Laura W. Morgan, *What Constitutes Adultery?*, Fam. L. Consulting, Dec. 2003, http://www.famlawconsult.com/archive/reader200312.html ("No married person thinks that his or her spouse is adhering to the marriage vows when he or she engages in intimate sexual acts such as oral or anal sex with another person.").

134 Neal v. Neal, 873 P.2d 871 (Idaho 1994).

135 *Id.* at 875.

136 *Id.*

137 *Id.* at 878.

138 *Id.* at 879.

139 Maharam v. Maharam, 510 N.Y.S.2d 104 (N.Y. App. Div. 1986).

140 *Id.*

141 *Id.*

142 *Id.* at 107–108.

143 N.Y. Pub. Health Law § 2307 (McKinney 2010).

144 *Maharam*, 123 A.D.2d at 177.

145 *Maharam*, 123 A.D.2d at 183.

146 Bethany Catron, Case Note, *If You Don't Think This is Adultery, Go Ask Your Spouse: The New Hampshire Supreme Court's Faulty Interpretation of Adultery in In Re Blanchflower, 834 A.2d 1010 (2003)—Grounds for a Fault Based Divorce*, 30 U. Dayton L. Rev. 339 (2005).

147 In Re Blanchflower, 834 A.2d 1010 (2003).

148 Edward O. Laumann et al., The Social Organization of Sexuality (1994).

149 Mary Coombs, *Agency and Partnership: A Study of Breach of Promise Plaintiffs*, 2 Yale J.L. & Feminism 1, 9-11 (1989). Fathers were considered victims of their daughters' seduction starting in the mid seventeenth century, since the father could have trouble marketing "damaged" (nonvirgin) goods in the marriage marketplace. They thus suffered economic losses as a result of their daughters' dependence on them, and loss of services as well if pregnancy resulted.

150 Irvin, M. (1998, December 9). "F.B.I. Releases Its Sinatra File, With Tidbits Old and New." *New York Times*. p. 21.

151 Geoffrey Rose, *Sick Individuals and Sick Populations*, 14 Int'l J. Epidemiology 427 (2001). Presumably a far greater percentage of Americans have been emotionally harmed by deception perpetrated by a romantic partner than are inflicted with a sexually transmitted disease.

152 *Seduction*, Wikipedia, http://en.wikipedia.org/wiki/Seduction (last visited April 15, 2010).

153 John Klotter, Criminal Law 164 (7th ed. 2004).

154 Miss. Code Ann. § 1298 (1891).

155 Norton v. State, 16 So. 264, 269 (Miss. 1894).

156 *Id.* at 272.

157 *Id.* at 275.

158 Boyce v. People, 55 N.Y. 644, 649 (N.Y. 1873).

159 *Id.* at 651.

160 *Id.*

161 *Id.* at 655.

162 *Id.* at 657.

163 People v. Clark, 33 Mich. 112 (1876).

164 *Id.*

165 *Id.* at 119.

166 Kenyon v. People, 26 N.Y. 203 (N.Y. 1863).

167 Novkov, J., *The Miscegenation/Same-Sex Marriage Analogy: What Can We Learn from Legal History?.* 33 Law & Social Inquiry 2, 345-386 (2008).

168 Keenan Malik, The Meaning of Race (1996) ("Eighteenth century Europe was the cradle of modern racism" because "racism has its foundations" in the Enlightenment "preoccupation with a rational universe, nature and aesthetics.").

169 Johann Friedrich Blumenbach, The Anthropological Treatises of Johann Friedrich Blumenbach (Thomas Bendyshe trans. & ed., 1865).

170 James A. Cox, *Bilboes, Brands, and Branks: Colonial Crimes and Punishments,* Colonial Williamsburg J. (April 6, 2010), http://www.history.org/Foundation/journal/spring03/branks.cfm.

171 Pace v. Alabama, 106 U.S. 583 (1883).

172 Brown v. Board of Education, 347 U.S. 483 (1954).

173 Loving v. Virginia, 388, U.S. 1 (1967).

174 Somini Sengupta, *November 5-11; Marry at Will,* N.Y. Times November 12, 2000 *available at* http://www.nytimes.com/2000/11/12/weekinreview/november-5-11-marry-at-will.html (last visited Feb. 9, 2011) ("The margin by which the measure passed was itself a statement. A clear majority, 60 percent, voted to remove the miscegenation statute from the state constitution, but 40 percent of Alabamans—nearly 526,000 people—voted to keep it.").

175 Novkov, J., *The Miscegenation/Same-Sex Marriage Analogy: What Can We Learn from Legal History?.* 33 Law & Social Inquiry 2, 345-386 (2008).

176 John D'Emilio & Estelle B. Freedman, Intimate Matters: A History of Sexuality in America (University of Chicago Press)(1988).

177 Pace v. Alabama, 106 U.S. 583 (1883).

178 Va. Code Ann. § 20-59 (1901).

179 Pace v. Alabama, 106 U.S. 583, 588 (1883).

180 *Id.* at 591.

181 *Id.* at 593.

182 *Id.*

183 *Id.* at 599.

184 *Id.* at 601.

185 *In re Monks' Estate,* 120 P.2d 167, 172 (Cal. Dist. Ct. App. 1942).

186 *Id.*

187 Cal. Civ. Code § 60 (1944) which provided that "[a]ll marriages of white persons with Negroes, Mongolians, members of the Malay race, or mulattoes are illegal and void."; *See also* Cal. Civ. Code § 69 (1944) which stated that "... no license may be issued authorizing the marriage of a white person with a Negro, mulatto, Mongolian, or member of the Malay race." At the time of the Monk case, California's anti-miscegenation statute had banned interracial marriage since 1850, when it first enacted a statute prohibiting whites from marrying blacks or mulattoes.

188 Cal. Civ. Code § 60 (1944).

189 *In re Monks' Estate,* 120 P.2d 167, 172 (Cal. Dist. Ct. App. 1942).

190 Loving v. Virginia, 388, U.S. 1 (1967).

191 The Racial Integrity Act, codified as Va. Code Ann. § 20-59 (1901).

192 Loving v. Virginia, 388, U.S. 1 (1967).

193 *Id.* at 12.

[194] "Mildred Loving, Key Figure in Civil Rights Era, Dies," PBS ONLINE NEWS HOUR, May 6, 2008.

[195] Naim v. Naim, 87 S.E.2d 749 (Va. 1955).

[196] Lawrence v. Texas, 539 U.S. 558 (2003).

[197] Martin v. Ziherl, 607 S.E.2d at 369 (Va. 2005) (citing *Lawrence,* 539 U.S. at 567 (2003)).

[198] Every state in the United States fixes the age of consent in the form of statutory rape laws. Luisa A. Fuentes, *The 14th Amendment and Sexual Consent: Statutory Rape and Judiciary Progeny,* 16 WOMEN'S RTS. L. REP. 139 (1994).

[199] *Id.*

[200] DAVID GARLAND, THE CULTURE OF CONTROL: CRIME AND SOCIAL ORDER IN CONTEMPORARY SOCIETY (2001).

[201] Lawrence v. Texas, 539 U.S. 558 (2003).

[202] Bowers v. Hardwick, 478 U.S. 186 (1986).

[203] Loving v. Virginia, 388, U.S. 1 (1967).

Chapter Three

Illegal Nonconsensual Sex:

Sexual Assault, Rape,

Voyeurism, Frottage

"All forcible sex offenses are crimes of violence; it does not follow that no nonforcible ones are."

United States v. Shannon
United States Court of Appeals, Seventh Circuit
110 F.3d 382 (1997)[1]

Legal Background

N onconsensual sexual activity is always controversial and usually illegal, depending on the specific facts of the case. Where the first two chapters considered various activities that may be legal in other nations (polygamy), or that were once legal but are now illegal in the U.S. (marital rape), or offenses that have only recently become constitutionally protected (sodomy), this chapter examines criminal offenses that do not entertain notions of legitimacy in law or society under any circumstances (rape) and where one party is deceived or forced into sexual contact without consent (frottage).

Consent is what makes sexual expression safe for the parties involved. Safety provides the freedom for couples to go through the process of getting to know one another, develop continuity in their sexual sharing, and experience a unique form of human bonding and attachment. A lack of consent runs directly counter to the experience of human bonding in sexual expression. Lack of consent is disturbing and often terrorizing to the victim, placing the victim in an emotional and psychological condition of confusion and sometimes irreparable pain and suffering.[2] Many victims will never fully recover from a case of nonconsensual sex, hence, the legal regulation prohibiting all forms of nonconsensual sexual contact. In cases of nonconsent where force is used and intercourse ensues (rape), the case is a felony in the first degree and the convicted offender will be sentenced to prison.

Since cases where consent is lacking rise to the level of assault, the legal background of the cases is more straightforward relative to sex crimes that are more subjective in their morals such as prostitution or adultery. Someone who is punched in the face and harmed is similarly situated to someone who is grabbed sexually and harmed—both offend reasonable standards of social civility, are deterred by law, and have no type of legitimized support in law or society.

Historically, the manner in which rape cases were prosecuted was somewhat inexplicable and degrading to females. Early laws in Europe prohibiting rape were aimed at protecting the victim's father or brothers' family prestige rather than the woman herself.[3] In a rape case, a convicted rapist had to pay retribution to the father for damaging his goods, and pay nothing to the victim for brutalizing her. The same logic applied to a victim who lost her virginity in a rape. The victim was fined along with her perpetrator since the family had lost the value of the girl's chastity due to the female's involvement in the crime.[4] The rape of a prostitute was no crime at all since chastity was not lost and the family name was not blemished.

By 1776 and the founding of the United States, rape cases were felonious, but did not necessarily pay much respect to the victim. As stated in the first chapter, the rape of a spouse was formerly legal. In addition, the law in early America wanted to see "a continued state of physical resistance" by the victim for a conviction to hold. Courts in those days were influenced by the influential British judge Sir Matthew Hale who stated, "rape ... is an accusation easily to be made and hard to be proved, and harder to be defended by the party accused, tho never so innocent."[5] Lord Hale is also the origin of the remark, "In a rape case it is the victim, not the defendant, who is on trial."[6]

Interestingly, no laws existed in England or Colonial America that outlawed sexual assault. In fact, sexual assault was not a crime in the U.S. until the 1960s. This is because females did not receive much accord in the law and were considered property and second-class citizens. Where a woman may be touched or similarly offended against her will, at common law, the male offender tended to be viewed as actually deserving of such liberties.[7] For the first 175 years of the U.S., the law focused mostly on various forms of violent and/or immoral penetration such as rape and also various forms of sodomy, but not the sexual assault and unwanted touching of a woman.

The law of sexual assault, rape, and other nonconsensual offenses have evolved substantially in the U.S. and constitute good examples of sexual politics or the politics of sex cases, consensual or nonconsensual. The state will prosecute cases of nonconsent today that were legally permissible before 1970 because the law did not recognize the cases as socially harmful.

The 1960s era of free speech, anti-war movements, and equal rights provided the catalyst for a feminist political agenda that served to modernize sexual assault and rape laws. American society became more liberated and challenged the conventional wisdom surrounding the traditional roles of men and women that had dominated the social landscape throughout the history of the U.S.

While large populations of middle class Americans continued to prefer marriage, family, and suburban living, much greater numbers chose to remain single or engage in shifting, long-term monogamous relationships. The corporate model of work still dominated, but more numbers of people worked as sole proprietors, or worked from home telecommuting. Importantly, many more women chose to delay or forego childbearing and, instead, enjoy the lifestyle of employment and career success.

Parallel to familial and career autonomy was the concept and lifestyle of sexual autonomy. Since more people decided to remain single, the law could no longer confine itself to marital relations, sex out of wedlock, or suppressing the demand for effective birth control. Where social values supported individual autonomy, the law also came to support sexual autonomy.

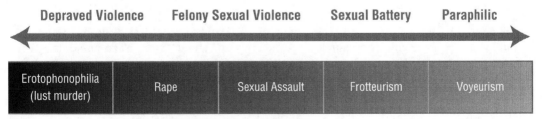

Figure 1 Continuum of Harm: Illegal Nonconsensual Acts.

Throughout the 1970s and 1980s, an extensive effort by legal scholars, judges, political organizations such as N.O.W. (National Organization of Women), and other entities strongly supported laws to create equality in marriage, the availability of birth control, and to prosecute and convict offenders of nonconsensual sex acts directed primarily toward women.

Rape law reform represents some of the most dynamic change in the area of sexual politics and law. Not only has the playing field been leveled by ending the second-class citizenship of females, but the orientation of rape cases was modified. Legal scholars such as Susan Estrich[8] and Katherine MacKinnon[9] demonstrated how rape is not only about a male who is desperate for sex. In addition, they argued more broadly that rape is about a sinister form of hegemony that males seek to preserve in relation to females. Rape was shown to be less a matter of sex and more a matter of violence. Rape cases are more accurately viewed as a form of kidnapping, coercion, and enslavement rather than merely fleeting, illegal sexual pleasure.[10]

Additional Legal Background: Child Sexual Abuse

The felonious nature of nonconsensual sex is unequivocal in cases of child sexual abuse. Child sex abusers are clinically known as pedophiles—someone with a sexual attraction to prepubescent children. Pedophilia, or child sexual abuse, by definition implicates a severe degree of mental imbalance or mental illness since under most any reasonable circumstance, an adult would not be compatible with a child sexually or in any other manner. The legalities of child sex abuse imply a "paraphilic" condition, discussed in chapter 6. However, since child sex abuse is a nonconsensual form of sexual assault, legal applications will be discussed in this chapter on nonconsensual crimes.

The umbrella of offenses that constitute child sexual abuse includes most fundamentally the legal dimensions of age, consent, and touching.[11] When it comes to a "child" the law typically refers to a prepubescent child (13 and under) and is distinguished from "youth," "minor," or "underage" person that most often refers to a teenager. The consent of a child is not an element in the law since a prepubescent child is legally and developmentally incapable of forming consent. Insofar as "touching" is concerned, the law will look at (1) touching of intimate body parts; and (2) for purposes of sexual stimulation, whether clothed or unclothed.

While the law applies to obvious cases of child sexual abuse, it is important to note the other forms of abuse that are inobvious, but seriously harmful to a child. Other forms of child sexual abuse include asking or pressuring a child to engage in sexual activities even if no such contact occurs. This aspect of abuse also includes carrying on a conversation about sex with a child as though the child were an adult. Conversations about sex between an adult (18 and over) and a child (13 and under) is abusive to the child and rarely are there any circumstances that would justify such a discussion. Viewing the child's genitalia without physical contact, or similarly viewing the child dressing for purposes of sexual arousal also constitute an inobvious form of child sexual abuse as the child can sense the violation and impropriety even if no words

Table 1 Various forms of child sexual abuse. Some are subtle and inobvious.

Moral Violation	Legal and Moral Violation
1. Leering or looking (fully clothed)	1. Showing pornographic images to a child
2. Viewing naked or while dressing	2. Using a child in pornographic pictures or videos
3. Sexual discussion and conversation, general	3. Sexual touching of nonintimate body parts
4. Undue focus and commentary on body parts (sexual objectification)	4. Touching or fondling of intimate body parts
5. Suggestive discussion (propositioning) without a result	5. Penetration (oral, anal, vaginal)
6. Sexualizing cartoons, or G-rated movies	

are spoken. Lastly, looking or leering at a child for purposes of sexual attraction is frightening and abusive to a child. These inobvious contexts are good examples of strategies deployed by offenders/paraphiliacs who are clever enough to refrain from actual touching.[12]

Legal definitions and labels will vary from state to state. Child rape is defined in most jurisdictions as any form of penetration of the child but may also include penetration upon the perpetrator. "Rape" of a child may also include any form of oral sex, use of objects for penetration, or any form of masturbation either upon the adult or by the adult upon the victim. Other jurisdictions may exclusively use the label "sexual assault" for all forms of abuse. "Sexual assault" of a child usually implies touching only (without any form of penetration), but in some jurisdictions all forms of sexual contact or penetration are referred to as sexual assault. Depending on the jurisdiction, other terms may also apply for child sexual abuse such as "criminal sexual conduct" (Michigan) any time any form of sex involves a prepubescent child.

Pedophile Priests. Some of the most notorious cases of child sexual abuse in the United States are those of "pedophile priests."[13] In the mid 1980s, information began to surface about child sex abuse worldwide in the Catholic Church, especially dioceses in Ireland and the United States. As part of its mission, the Catholic Church the world over established schools and boarding care facilities for youths. While confined to its care, large numbers of youths were sexually molested by priests and nuns in the Church; the priests and nuns held a sacred duty to provide for the safety and well-being of the youths in their care and abused that duty of care.[14]

As reports began to surface, all signs pointed toward a morbid and deranged criminogenic and sexualized atmosphere in various Catholic Church dioceses and parishes across the U.S. Court orders manifest and documents were subpoenaed that revealed some of the worse abusers were not turned over to the civil authorities and prosecuted, but rather, reassigned to another diocese where they began abusing children in their new location. Higher-ups in the Church did nothing to halt the abuse even though they had clear and convincing evidence of it.[15]

In the face of a global scandal, the Church finally took action and in June 2002, the United States Conference of Catholic Bishops met in Dallas and created a National Review Board that was assigned responsibility to study, with the full cooperation of the dioceses/eparchies, the nature and scope of the problem of sexual abuse of minors by clergy. The National Review Board engaged the John Jay College of Criminal Justice of the City University of New York to conduct the study. The time period covered by the John Jay study was to be 1950–2002. The study was eventually titled "The Nature and Scope of the Problem of Sexual Abuse of Minors by Catholic Priests and Deacons in the United States" and commonly referred to as the "John Jay Report.."[16]

The John Jay Report catalogued more than twenty types of sexual abuse of minors ranging from verbal harassment to penile penetration. It indicates that most of the abusers engaged in multiple types of abuses and that only 9 percent of the accused performed acts limited to improper touching over the victim's clothes. Slightly more than 27 percent of the allegations involved a cleric performing oral sex and 25 percent involved penile penetration or attempted penile penetration. Most of the allegations involved touching over or under clothing. Of the 4,392 priests who were accused, police were contacted regarding 1,021 individuals and of these, 384 were charged resulting in 252 convictions and 100 prison sentences; 3,300 were not investigated because the allegations were made after the accused priest had died. Civil liability lawsuits have also been filed against the dioceses and parishes for negligence and negligent care. As of this writing, the Church in the U.S. has paid out approximately $2 billion in damage awards to victims.[17]

Sexual Assault

Touching someone's body for purposes of sexual gratification is known as a sexual assault. If the two parties are a romantic couple and each consents to the touching, of course, this form of sexual touching is not a crime. However, if someone grabs a sexual body part without consent, it is a serious violation of the person and constitutes the offense of sexual assault. This crime does not involve intercourse or ejaculation and is not as serious as an incident of rape, but is frightening and alarming and more serious than a case of, for example, voyeurism or nonsexual assault.

As with many sex crimes, the details that surround an incident of sexual assault can be ambiguous. Types of sexual assault include grabbing of breasts, buttocks, or genitals for purposes of sexual arousal, but rarely are the cases clear-cut. Meaning, consent may be questionable, inobvious, or veiled. The two parties may experience a misunderstanding and have seriously conflicting intentions and values when it comes to the enjoyment of sex. A mutual understanding between the two people involved may imply consent, when actually the touching is completely unwanted. To compound the misperception and ambiguity, the police, prosecution, or judge involved may each have different beliefs, values, and experiences when it comes to sexual touching and petting and may add to the number of delicate considerations that surround a case of sexual touching.

Examples of types of cases abound. A flagrant example may be where two people are on a date, and while stopped in a vehicle waiting for the light to turn green, the man reaches over and grabs the woman's breast. Is this sexual assault? It is if the woman did not consent. As with all situations of sexual touching, both parties must be certain that the advances are welcome. Should there be the slightest question that the other party may not want to be touched, no touching should occur. Obviously, both parties must thoroughly communicate to each other their preferences when it comes to physical and sexual sharing.

Definition of the Offense

Sexual assault is typically defined as knowingly engaging in sexual conduct with another person without the other person's permission.[18] Sexual conduct is typically defined as any touching of the sexual or intimate parts of a person for the purpose of arousing or gratifying sexual desire.[19]

Elements of the Offense

The elements of the crime of sexual assault that must be proven beyond a reasonable doubt are:

1. the actor intended to arouse or satisfy his own sexual desires;
2. by touching the victim;
3. the victim was compelled to submit to touching by force or threat of force.[20]

Sample Statute

The State of Alaska sexual assault statute reads as follows:

Alaska Revised Statute, Sec. 11.41.420. Sexual Assault in the Second Degree.

    (a) An offender commits the crime of sexual assault in the second degree if

        (1) the offender engages in sexual contact with another person without consent of that person;

        (2) the offender engages in sexual contact with a person

            (A) who the offender knows is mentally incapable; and

            (B) who is entrusted to the offender's care

                (i) by authority of law; or

                (ii) in a facility or program that is required by law to be licensed by the Department of Health and Social Services;

    (3) the offender engages in sexual penetration with a person who the offender knows is

        (A) mentally incapable;

        (B) incapacitated; or

        (C) unaware that a sexual act is being committed; or

    (4) the offender engages in sexual contact with a person who the offender knows is unaware that a sexual act is being committed and

        (A) the offender is a health care worker; and

        (B) the offense takes place during the course of professional treatment of the victim.

  (b) Sexual assault in the second degree is a class B felony.[21]

Arguments Made By The Prosecution

The main aspect of a sexual assault case for the state is the element of consent. No matter what kind of touching occurs, the case cannot be prosecuted as an assault if both parties consent. Lack of consent, however, has to be beyond a reasonable doubt and can be difficult to prove. The prosecutor has to show, through a totality of the circumstances, that the accused had no permission, right, or implied understanding to put his/her hands on another person's body for purposes of sexual gratification.

Arguments Made By The Defense

Defending a case of sexual assault is easier than prosecuting one. The defense merely has to show that some degree of mutual affection was the intended context of the transaction. The defense will argue that the accused meant no harm, and had no reason to believe that the victim would be offended by the kissing or touching. In a case of relative aggressiveness, the defense can explain to the jury that the two were "just messing around" and that no harm was intended.

Variations of the Law of Sexual Assault

A. Unwanted Kissing

The act of kissing provides a good example of legal line-drawing, personal boundaries, and consent. Often, a kiss starts out consensual, but can get carried away and end up being an experience that was nonconsensual. At other times, someone may initiate a kiss that is so abrupt and unexpected, the surprised party may concede so as not to catalyze an even more unfortunate, unwanted scenario. At its most basic level, can an overly aggressive kiss constitute the crime of sexual assault?

In *People v. Rivera,* the defendant moved upon the victim, kissed her, and inserted his tongue into her mouth, all of which the victim said was against her will.[22] The victim stated that she felt defenseless to stop the aggressive action. The offender was charged and convicted of sexual assault and appealed his conviction.

The reviewing court examined the law in the State of New York on the subject of sexual abuse. The court noted that the unwanted sexual touching of another constitutes such abuse. The challenge was to determine if the mouth was a body part that was "intimate and personal" and hence could be involved in a case of sexual assault. Adding to the analysis, the court stated that intimacy could occur with a body part in one context, but the same body part could be used non-intimately in a different context. Kissing, a handshake, or similar touching may or may not be intimate and sexual, or it may be, depending on the intentions and actions of the parties involved.

To argue that kissing could not be a sexual assault, the defendant made prominent a precedent case that held that an overly-aggressive kiss cannot constitute the crime of sexual assault. In the case, *People v. Kittles,* the court dismissed the charges because it did not define sexual abuse in terms of kissing. The Kittles' court stated:

> Sexual abuse in the first degree (Penal Law, § 130.65, subd 1), is committed when a person subjects another person to sexual contact, which is any touching of the sexual or other intimate parts of a person for the purpose of gratifying the sexual desire of either party (Penal Law, § 130.00, subd 3), by forcible compulsion; the term "touching" applies only to those instances where there is digital manipulation or manual handling or fondling, and the term "intimate parts" does not include a person's mouth. Accordingly, where the only facts alleged to support two counts of sexual abuse in the first degree in an indictment are that defendant on two occasions kissed the victim against her will and inserted his tongue in her mouth, said counts were dismissed upon the ground that the acts alleged therein do not constitute a crime.[23]

In the instant case, however, the Rivera court disagreed with the Kittles' ruling and made an opposite ruling. The court here considered the mouth to indeed constitute a sexual part of the body and hence kissing could be sexual assault, depending on the type of kiss. The court stated:

An incident that begins with "apparent playfulness" can inadvertently become a case of sexual assault.[26]

> In the opinion of this court, very few things can be more personal or private than the
> mouth (cf., People v Kittles, supra; People v Belfrom, supra). The court takes note that
> the vast majority of people are very discriminating in who they allow to touch; and in
> what they permit to enter this bodily orifice.

The court discussed the distinction between sexual body parts, i.e., genitals, and "intimate body parts," i.e., leg, thigh, navel, hip, etc. The court held that the mouth was an intimate part of the body and that the kissing was sexual contact with an intimate body part and affirmed the conviction.[24] The court stated:

> To this court a fair import of the term "intimate part" must include, by any rational stan-
> dard, the interior of a person's mouth.[25]

B. Inobvious Touching

Doctors and other medical professionals by necessity have to touch the bodies of their patients. Other professional contexts such as dentistry, chiropractic services, and especially massage therapists by necessity touch the bodies of their clients and patients. Consent is implied in such cases and the law will use a degree of assumption of risk, assuming that the patient is aware they will be touched as a part of the service and procedure. If the patient or client does not wish to be touched by their doctor, they have the freedom to not visit the doctor. However, a gray area exists between the necessary touching of a patient and the subtle, inobvious sexual touching of a patient. The line between consent and a lack of consent is blurred in cases of inobvious sexual touching.

In *People v. Teicher*, a dentist engaged in a practice of sexual touching with his patients. The defendant, Mr. Teicher, would have some of his patients come in for a procedure that would require a dose of anesthesia. After sedating some of his patients, the offender would engage in illegal sexual touching. Once sedated (but still conscious), he would place their hand against his genital area. After one patient was alert enough to discover the crime and file a complaint, an investigation revealed a similar concern among other patients of the dentist. Teicher was charged and convicted of sexual abuse pursuant to the sex abuse statute in the State of New York. The statute read: § 130.65. Sexual abuse in the first degree. A person is guilty of sexual abuse in the first degree when he or she subjects another person to sexual contact:

1. By forcible compulsion; or
2. When the other person is incapable of consent by reason of being physically helpless.[27]

After his conviction, on appeal, Teicher argued that he did not do anything wrong—that he did not sexually touch anyone or anyone's intimate body parts, but rather, the victim placed her hand near his intimate body part. As a result, he cannot be charged because the law only sanctions those who touch others and that he did not touch anyone. The appellate court was not persuaded and stated:

> Defendant also argues that even if the element of sexual gratification and the victim's incapacity were established, his act of placing Carson's hand against his genital area could not possibly constitute the crime of sexual abuse, since the statute proscribes only the act of a defendant who touches the intimate parts of his victim and not the act of a person who places his victim's hand against his own intimate parts. As we have held, this argument must be rejected because it requires an overly restrictive and improper reading of the statutory language.

In affirming the conviction of the trial court, the appeals court judge stated,

> when the other person is incapable of consent by reason of being physically helpless, [the law] was made out where the defendant placed the victim's hand against his genital area, although this involves the victim touching the defendant rather than the reverse; further, such contact, while it was fleeting because the victim withdrew her hand, establishes the necessary element of sexual gratification as the purpose of the touching and, although the woman, who was heavily sedated when the original touching occurred, had enough control over her body to pull her hand away, the trier of fact was entitled to infer that she lacked capacity to consent to the touching because of her generally weakened condition.[28]

C. Intimate Body Part

The touching of another person's body is often a regular part of routine social interaction, albeit done with a degree of care and respect. The greeting with a handshake or a friendly hug are not inordinary social gestures and are often done with an instinct toward innocent affection and politeness. When the touching is not routine, questions may arise. What was the intent? Why did it happen? Was it a social gesture or was there a romantic or sexual overtone? The context and circumstances that surround the touching will determine the lawfulness of the act. In sexual assault cases, the law has to define what parts of the body are "intimate body parts" for purposes of a crime. Obviously, a handshake involving the hands cannot constitute assault, even if it were somehow shown to be without consent. A pat on the back is similarly not likely to rise to the level of sexual touching. At the other end of the spectrum, the unwanted touching of the reproductive organs is obviously criminal and a case of sexual assault.[29]

In the case of *In re Adams,* a male and female youth had secreted to a little-used area of a high school facility whereupon the parties tussled together and both unbuttoned the female's slacks and pulled them down to her mid-thigh.[30] The defendant then placed his hands around her waist apparently without her consent. While in the midst of their encounter, the two were discovered by a school counselor. On getting caught, both parties modified their stories, including the female who stated the incident was nonconsensual. To gain some clarification as to what actually happened, a more definitive description of the posture of the parties was given by the school counselor who happened upon the scene. He stated:

> I'm not sure where his hands were. He may have had one on the floor and the other to-wards her shoulder, but I'm frankly not sure. I know his body was prone, outstretched, and he was trying to rock and work his way into her, apparently to submit or something.

The male was charged and convicted of sexual assault, specifically, violating the state's indecent liberties statute.[31] The statute reads in part:

(1) A person is guilty of indecent liberties when he knowingly causes another person who is not his spouse to have sexual contact with him or another:

    (a) By forcible compulsion; or …

(2) For purposes of this section, "sexual contact" means any touching of the sexual or other intimate parts of a person done for the purpose of gratifying sexual desire of either party.

The defendant appealed, arguing that the two may have wrestled some, but nothing overtly sexual occurred between the two. He stated that he may have grabbed her around the waist and touched her hips, but the touching of the complainant's waist and hips were not "intimate body parts" for purposes of the indecent liberties law. The accused conceded that the genitals are, of course, intimate body parts, but not the hips and waist areas. The appellate court disagreed and cited previous court cases that addressed the exact same question. The court stated:

> the hips were a sufficiently intimate part of the anatomy that a person of common intel-ligence would have fair notice that the nonconsensual touching of them was prohibited, particularly if that touching was incidental to other activities which were intended to promote sexual gratification of the actor.[32]

Additional Court Cases: Sexual Assault

In re A.B. (a juvenile)

556 A.2d 645 (1989)

CASE SUMMARY

PROCEDURAL POSTURE: Appellant juvenile challenged an order of the Superior Court of the District of Columbia, which convicted him of simple assault for unlawfully assaulting and threatening in a menacing manner a 12-year-old girl in violation of D.C. Code Ann. §§ 16-2305, 22-504 (1981).

OVERVIEW: The juvenile, a 15-year-old male, was found guilty of nonviolent sexual touching for grabbing and squeezing the 12-year-old girl's buttocks on a public street. The court affirmed the conviction, holding that the definition of a nonviolent sexual touching was not limited to genital contact and that the crime did not require proof of the juvenile's specific intent to gain sexual gratification. The court refused to hold that the unconsented touching of the buttocks was not a sexual touching as a matter of law because the commonly accepted community sense of decency, propriety, and morality did not necessarily exclude the buttocks as an intimate part of the body deserving of protection from wandering hands. The court found that the evidence was sufficient to support the finding that the grabbing and squeezing of the girl's buttocks constituted a nonviolent sexual touching where the juvenile and the girl were not of the same peer group, the girl did not like the juvenile, and the playful beginnings of the incident did not render the subsequent touching playful.

OUTCOME: The court affirmed the juvenile's conviction for simple assault for unlawfully touching and threatening in a menacing manner a 12-year-old girl based on an unconsented, nonviolent sexual touching.[33]

Rape

One of the most underreported crimes, rape is also one of the most harmful of all criminal acts.[34] Similar to murder, rape finds no acceptance in any civilization in human history. The act of rape may be so damaging to the mental and emotional condition of the victim, even an attempted murder may be more desirable from the victim's point of view. A victim of an attempted murder may be able to understand the nature of the crime more easily than a rape victim can.

Acknowledging rape in certain contexts provides further recognition of the seriousness of the impact of rape. The savagery of international war has included raping the women of the enemy as part of the ultimate strike at the heart of the opposition. Prison rapes symbolize the brutality inside the walls and are used as a destructive weapon in the absence of knives and guns. Rape combines both violence against a person, and also, a tortured subjection and violation of the most sensitive part of the human make-up. Accordingly, the law has evolved and today distinguishes among different types of rape cases (acquaintance, date, spousal, etc.).

For a long time, rape was legally defined as unlawful intercourse with a female without her consent. The term "unlawful" was necessary because the rape of one's wife was lawful. Until the 1970s in the U.S., it was embarrassingly difficult to get a conviction for rape even for those who were flagrantly guilty.[35] The law in all fifty states required that the allegations be corroborated, even though witnesses are rarely present in these cases and its one person's word against the other's.[36] Jurors didn't believe acquaintance contexts could result in a rape, and the criminal justice system insisted on a clear showing of evidence of a struggle. Horrified victims took the witness stand, were forced to recount events, were blamed for their complicity, then walked away humiliated as the accused was acquitted. Jurors were invested with the idea that the female party who made the complaint was just being vindictive or was seeking an eventual civil suit for damages that could be supported with a conviction in criminal court.

Many necessary reforms have been made to the law of rape, especially the legal acknowledgment that physical force is not a requirement for a rape to occur. Today the victim does not have to say "no" for a rape to happen, and the offender can use threats or duress; actual force is not a required element for conviction.[37] All fifty states have removed their corroboration requirement and medical evidence such as scratches, bruises, or hospital personnel may legally provide testimony and evidence.[38] In most states, law reform accounts for "penetration" to mean oral or anal, and not only vaginal intercourse. The law also prevents consent from occurring in cases of alcohol intoxication or other impairment. Date rape acknowledges that a prior history is largely inapplicable to a charge of rape and, of course, it is no longer legal to rape one's spouse. Rape shield laws can prevent the introduction of prejudicial evidence and lurid tales of the prior sexual activities of the victim. Substantial improvements have been made to the law of rape.[39]

The federal criminal code has also been reformed when it comes to offenses related to sexual assault. As with many state codes, rape and sexual abuse laws in the federal system are gender neutral.[40] Immunity from prosecution for the rape of one's spouse was removed, and the federal code enacted degrees of sexual assault to account for aggravating factors such as the use of a weapon, the incidence of a kidnapping, or serious bodily injury that may have occurred during the sexual assault.[41]

Degrees of Rape. Like a lot of criminal offenses, most states break down rape into several degrees. For example, rape in the first degree is the most severe in terms of aggravating factors (see below). Rape in the second degree is arguably less severe, and rape in the third degree even less, or possibly referred to as simple rape. Some of the possible aggravating factors that turn a third degree rape into a first degree rape include: the victim is a child, the offender uses a weapon, or the offender is part of a group (gang) of accomplices during the commission of the offense.

Definition of the Offense

Rape, sometimes referred to as sexual assault, is an assault by a person involving sexual intercourse with or sexual penetration of another person without that person's consent.[42]

Additional Definitions: Consent

Consent means cooperation in act or attitude pursuant to an exercise of free will and with knowledge of the nature of the act.[43] A current or previous relationship is not by itself sufficient to constitute consent. Just because the parties know each other well does not mean consent is automatic.[44] Submission to advances under the influence of fear does not constitute consent, including nonverbal facial gestures that induce fear. Assent does not constitute consent if it is induced by force, duress, or deception.[45] Persons under the age of consent cannot consent and neither can someone under the influence of drugs or alcohol or otherwise mentally impaired. Specific relationship contexts are also considered for aspects of coercion such as teacher/student, employer/employee, prison guard/inmate, etc.

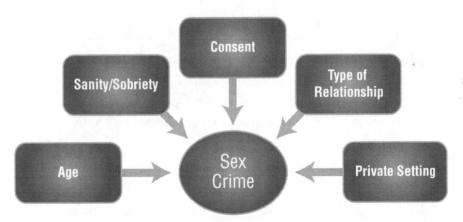

Figure 2 Primary considerations for a legal determination of consent.

Additional Definitions: Penetration and Intercourse

Penetration and intercourse are terms that may be used synonymously when it comes to the legalities of a sexual encounter. The terms refer to vaginal intercourse, anal intercourse, fellatio, or cunnilingus between persons regardless of gender. Their meaning is not limited to married persons. Penetration, however slight, is sufficient to complete vaginal intercourse, anal intercourse, or fellatio or cunnilingus and does not require emission of semen for penetration or intercourse to have occurred. Penetration may also occur with variations of vaginal intercourse, anal intercourse, fellatio, or cunnilingus. In *Chambers v. Lockhart*, the convicted offender made the victim lick the shaft of his penis.[46] The trial court interpreted this act as "penetration.." The offender appealed, arguing that penetration did not occur. The appellate court disagreed and affirmed the ruling of the trial court. Penetration may be committed by an object manipulated by the actor into the genital or anal opening of the victim's body, such as with a sex toy.[47]

Elements of the Offense

The elements of the crime of rape that must be proven beyond a reasonable doubt are:

1. unlawful
2. sexual intercourse (carnal knowledge)
3. by force or fear
4. without the consent or against the will of the victim.[48]

Sample Statute

The state of Iowa rape statute reads as follows:

Iowa Statute § 35-42-4-1 (1998). Sec. 1.

(a) Except as provided in subsection (b), a person who knowingly or intentionally has sexual intercourse with a member of the opposite sex when:

    (1) the other person is compelled by force or imminent threat of force;

    (2) the other person is unaware that the sexual intercourse is occurring; or

    (3) the other person is so mentally disabled or deficient that consent to sexual intercourse cannot be given; commits rape, a Class B felony.

(b) An offense described in subsection (a) is a Class A felony if:

    (1) it is committed by using or threatening the use of deadly force;

    (2) it is committed while armed with a deadly weapon;

    (3) it results in serious bodily injury to a person other than a defendant; or

    (4) the commission of the offense is facilitated by furnishing the victim, without the victim's knowledge, with a drug (as defined in IC 16-42-19-2(1)) or a controlled substance (as defined in IC 35-48-1-9) or knowing that the victim was furnished with the drug or controlled substance without the victim's knowledge.[49]

Arguments Made By The Prosecution

In a rape case, the victim will allege to have been forced, in some manner, to engage in sexual intercourse. Hence, the prosecutor will argue that the victim did not consent and that the perpetrator used some type of force. When it comes to the issue of consent, the evidence will be sparse and consist only of the victim's testimony "I did not consent.." A rape case is a "he said, she said" case. Assuming a male offender and female victim, the woman will say, "I did not consent," and the man will say, "She did consent," and the parties will argue back and forth with no real resolution. The prosecution often has more to work with when it comes to the issue of force or threat of force.

Actual physical force is more easily understood in these cases. A physically stronger male can subdue a physically smaller victim. However, force is a broad concept and the case can turn on a much more subtle variation of the term. For example, the prosecution will often argue that the perpetrator used "constructive" force, by using veiled threats such as "You don't want me to get upset, do you?" or "You don't want to become homeless, do you?" The offender may use latent threats and manipulations to an even greater degree if dependent children are involved, e.g., "You don't want you and your children to suffer harm, do you?" All of these statements can constitute force for purposes of a rape conviction.

Arguments Made By The Defense

Multiple strategies exist to defend a rape case, and these difficult-to-counter reasonings can fill a rape trial with unfortunate speculations. The most likely defense argument is that the victim initiated and/or cooperated in the act. The defense will argue consent and lack of force. When it comes to the issue of "constructive" force, the defense will argue that mere conversation does not constitute force, constructive or otherwise. The focus can be shifted to the victim's mental state and accusations of being "overly sensitive" or "overreacting" on the part of the victim are common.

The defense also has other avenues to pursue. Past relationship history is a prominent strategy because, with this line of reasoning, it becomes unmistakable that the victim voluntarily had sex with the offender, at least once in the past, and hence obviously was fond of the perpetrator at least at some time in the past. The defense will also seize on the debilitating effects of the act and suggest that the victim could have called the police, screamed, or run away and failing to do so implies a degree of consent. This argumentation, often persuasive, takes advantage of the immobility that occurs with severe fear and psychological traumatization; the victim may be paralyzed to do anything but submit.

Legal compliance dictates that the person who initiates the sexual contact take responsibility for obtaining the other participant's verbal consent as the level of intimacy increases.

Variations of the Law of Rape

A. Evidence of Prior Sexual Contact

A great majority of rape cases involve a "he said, she said" scenario where it's one person's word against the others. The victim may allege a forcible rape and the accused may allege that it was mutually consensual and that the parties have enjoyed sexual relations in the past. Typically, no witnesses are present to substantiate either of the claims made.[50]

Prior to 1970, it was legally permissible to introduce into evidence a history of the complainant's sexual lifestyle or preferences.[51] The introduction of this evidence was allowed because, at the time, it was thought to help clarify the matter of consent where ambiguity was present. The logic was that having sex with the accused in the past, or having a history of promiscuity, lent itself to consent in the present case. This logic, however, has only a limited application and tends to compound, rather than clear up, confusion about consent. The tendency of prior sexual history is to inflame speculation and incite moral disapprobation, both of which may be completely irrelevant to the case at hand. What happens is that the victim's history becomes subject to indictment rather than the accused's behavior. This is a serious error since past history can have no relevance to the guilt or innocence of the defendant in the present case. Opening the door to an examination of the complaining witness's prior sexual conduct shifts the balance of power to the accused who is now armed with a set of strategies with which to make the victim look bad. Allowing such evidence presents a strong disincentive to rape victims to come forward since they hardly want to be placed under a spotlight to explain the details of their sex life to a group of strangers in a courtroom. An evil man can be the victim of a hate crime just like a prostitute can be a rape victim.

Reflective of the increasing fairness of the law surrounding rape cases was the advent of rape shield laws in the United States throughout the 1970s. Rape shield laws prohibit some or all evidence relating to the past sexual behavior of the plaintiff/victim from being introduced into evidence. This encompasses evidence of specific instances of the victim's prior sexual conduct including opinion evidence or reputation evidence.

In the 2010 rape case of *Gagne v. Booker*, the defendant was convicted for participating in a gang rape of the victim.[52] The accused and alleged victim lived together for approximately six months unmarried, but were not cohabitating at the time of the incident. On the night in question, the defendant showed up at the victim's house, and later two other men (mutual acquaintances) also came by. Hence, at around 11:00 p.m., the four were drinking substantially and visiting together socially, under no duress, threat, or coercion. The complainant testified that she had drunk approximately ten beers that evening and a half-pint of vodka a little earlier in the day. Late in the evening and early the following morning, all four began engaging in various sexual activities together. According to the court record:

The defense's version of events differed primarily on the issue of consent. According to Gagne and Swathwood, the group purchased and smoked some crack cocaine at around midnight. Clark then began talking with the men about engaging in group sex, and in large part instigated the group sexual activity, first in the living room and then later in the bedroom. Their description of the sexual activities differed only in that Clark consented to them. They concede for instance, that they spanked Clark. At about five a.m. Gagne and Clark agreed that Gagne should leave and purchase more crack with money withdrawn using her ATM card. All three men left in Clark's car. Gagne dropped Stout off at home, withdrew $300 from an ATM using Clark's card, and then drove to a street corner and purchased crack. The defendants became nervous when they saw police cars in the area, so instead of returning home, they drove to a cemetery and smoked the crack. The defendants testified that they returned to Clark's house later that morning and Gagne returned her ATM card. Clark was angry and told Gagne to leave, so he did.[53]

Clark filed a police report the next day and Gagne was convicted at trial pursuant to the State of Michigan Sexual Assault Statute § 750.520b(1)(f):

Sec. 520b.

(1) A person is guilty of criminal sexual conduct in the first degree if he or she engages in sexual penetration with another person and ...

    (f) The actor causes personal injury to the victim and force or coercion is used to accomplish sexual penetration.[54]

The defendant appealed, claiming that the State of Michigan Rape Shield Law prevented the admissibility of evidence that the victim consented to a nearly identical episode of sex on two prior occasions and in fact, requested a type of multiple-person sexual interaction.[55] The defendant stated that he was unable to provide himself an adequate defense without the opportunity to present this evidence of the alleged victim's prior sexual activity.

The appeal was a request pursuant to a habeas plea to free the accused who was in prison due to the rape conviction. The appeals court judge agreed with the accused and granted the habeas request. The defendant was released from prison and ordered a new trial so that the accused could present a more complete defense.

First, the court referenced the state of Michigan's Rape Shield law:[56]

Evidence of specific instances of the victim's sexual conduct, opinion evidence of the victim's sexual conduct, and reputation evidence of the victim's sexual conduct shall not be admitted under sections 520b to 520g unless and only to the extent that the judge finds that the following proposed evidence is material to a fact at issue in the case and that its inflammatory or prejudicial nature does not outweigh its probative value.[57]

Second, the court held that the evidence of prior sexual activity was material and probative. The court stated:

> [The trial court must be] mindful of the significant legislative purposes underlying the rape-shield statute and should always favor exclusion of evidence of a complainant's sexual conduct where its exclusion would not unconstitutionally abridge the defendant's right to confrontation. [In this case, the exclusion did unconstitutionally abridge the defendant's right to confront his accuser].[58]

Third, the court used a constitutional justification to order a new trial, and stated,

> The Supreme Court has repeatedly recognized that the right to present a complete defense in a criminal proceeding is one of the foundational principles of our adversarial truth-finding process: 'Whether rooted directly in the Due Process Clause of the Fourteenth Amendment or in the Compulsory Process or Confrontation Clauses of the Sixth Amendment, the Constitution guarantees criminal defendants a meaningful opportunity to present a complete defense. *Holmes v. South Carolina,* 547 U.S. 319 (2006).

B. Resistance to the Utmost

The law of rape has been substantially modified since the time of the old "utmost resistance standard.."[59] With this legal provision, a rape conviction could not hold unless the victim resisted the attacker to the utmost. Up until the 1970s, a lack of consent could only be proven if the victim engaged in a struggle or fight to resist the attack. In the absence of such a struggle, the law assumed that the victim gave consent, otherwise she would have resisted.

The element of resistance proved to rest upon faulty assumptions. First, many victims were smaller and weaker than their attacker thus making any resistance an exercise in futility. Second, many victims—even if they could put up a fight—are unwilling to set off the anger of an attacker who has already proven to be lawless and violent. Resisting could easily invite death or serious bodily injury to the victim. Third and finally, the shock and trauma of such an attack can easily cause the victim to feign compliance and consent. The victim may even appear willing, all of which is part of a false affront to minimize a horrible ordeal. In sum, victims may fail to resist for many reasons and none of them may imply consent to sexual intercourse with the accused.[60]

In *Brown v. State,* a neighbor tripped a 16-year-old girl walking across a field and then raped her. She testified that she had tried as hard as she could to get away and had screamed as loudly as she could but that her attacker had put his hand over her mouth until he almost strangled her. She testified:

> I tried as hard as I could to get away. I was trying all the time to get away just as hard
> as I could, I was trying to get up; I pulled at the grass; I screamed as hard as I could,
> and he told me to shut up, and I didn't, and then he held his hand on my mouth until I
> was almost strangled.[61]

In the jurisdiction at the time, the rape law required that the victim resist, otherwise the case could not be a rape. The court transcript read:

> Not only must there be entire absence of mental consent or assent, but there must be
> the most vehement exercise of every physical means or faculty within the woman's
> power to resist the penetration of her person, and this must be shown to persist until
> the offense is consummated.[62]

The accused was convicted at trial. The judge and jury found that the victim resisted and that there was no consent. The defendant appealed, arguing that the victim did consent and that there was no actual resistance. The appeals court sided with the accused and ordered a new trial. The court believed that the girl had not resisted enough, citing medical authority for the proposition that a truly determined woman of normal size can nearly always fend off an attack by adroit use of her hands, limbs, and pelvic muscles.[63]

> Among the corroborating circumstances almost universally present in cases of actual
> rape are the signs and marks of the struggle upon the clothing and persons of the par-
> ticipants, and the complaint by the sufferer at the earliest opportunity. In the present
> case the former is absolutely wanting, for the one-inch rip in prosecutrix's underwear
> was not shown to be of a character or location significant of force or violence. Not a
> bruise or scratch on either was proved, and none existed on prosecutrix, for she was
> carefully examined by physicians. Her outer clothing not only presented no tearing, but
> no disarray, so far as the testimony goes. When one pauses to reflect upon the terrific

resistance which the determined woman should make, such a situation is well-nigh incredible. The significance of the other corroborative circumstance, that of immediate disclosure, is much weakened in this case by the fact that prosecutrix turned from her way to friends and succor to arrange her underclothing and there discovered a condition making silence impossible. Such facts cannot but suggest a doubt whether her encounter would ever have been disclosed had not the discovery of blood aroused her fear that she was injured and must seek medical aid, or at least that she could not conceal from her family what had taken place. Nor is this thoughtfulness of the disarrangement of her clothing consistent with the outraged woman's terror-stricken flight to friends to give the alarm and seek aid which is to be expected. We are convinced that there was no evidence of the resistance which is essential to the crime of rape, and that the motion for new trial should have been granted on that ground.[64]

This old, former standard had the effect of inducing the victim into a physical brawl with the assailant lest he be free of guilt.[65] Further, the culpability of the accused became contingent upon the ability of the victim to put up a fight, rendering obvious the culpability of the attacker. Today, none of the fifty states have the utmost resistance standard in their rape or sexual assault laws. Many states have gone to the other extreme, for example, in Michigan, the victim need not resist the attacker at all for a conviction to hold. The balance will be in between the two models. For example, the Delaware statute requires reasonable resistance under the circumstances to communicate nonconsent.[66] Logically, a rape conviction will be easier to obtain if there is at least some degree of communication concerning the nonconsent of the victim.

C. Intoxication and Consent

What if two college students have too much to drink and engage in sex? Is this a case of lawful, consensual sex? What if any two persons engage in sexual activity and one of them is legally drunk? Is it consensual? Cases where the parties are both intoxicated are especially difficult when it comes to the determination of consent and the legality of the episode. Historically, the data indicate that many men will try to get a woman drunk in an attempt to lower her inhibitions and scruples and have sex. "Date rape" drugs have been notoriously used in this manner. GHB (gamma-hydroxybutyric acid) and benzodiazepines (such as flunitrazepam, also known as *Rohypnol*, or "roofies") are two common date rape drugs. However, the research indicates that alcohol still remains the drug most frequently implicated in substance-assisted rape.[67]

In a context where the victim is under the influence, an overly aggressive male may even be told to stop or told "no" by the female, but he knows the cry of rape would never be taken seriously since they were both drunk. Many prosecutors won't take a rape case if the victim was drunk because it is so easy for the defense to create doubt over the issue of consent. In this context, the female bears the responsibility for staying sober. On the other hand, many commentators argue that intoxication automatically nullifies consent since a person must be of sound state of mind to legally consent. In this situation, any party can allege a lack of consent and be correct, so long as they can prove they were drunk. In sum, it is probably best to not have sex with someone who is drunk.[68]

In *People v. Giardino*, the male defendant engaged in sexual intercourse with an intoxicated woman and she alleged it was a rape.[69] These cases are controversial since there are no witnesses and it is one person's word against the other's. In the state of California at the time, the rape law specifically addresses contexts where one of the parties is intoxicated. The record noted the statute and annotated:

> Rape by Intoxication and Oral Copulation by Intoxication. In a prosecution for rape by intoxication (Pen. Code, § 261, subd. (a)(3)) and oral copulation by intoxication (Pen. Code, § 288a, subd. (i)), the trial court properly denied defendant's request for a consent instruction, since lack of actual consent is not an element of offenses proscribing sexual intercourse or oral copulation with persons who lack the capacity to give legal consent. In the context of rape and other sexual assaults, consent is the positive co-operation in act or attitude pursuant to an exercise of free will (Pen. Code, § 261.6).[70]

After a trial, the jury returned a verdict of guilty and the defendant was sentenced to prison. On appeal, the defendant argued that the woman consented and that the jury should have been instructed to understand exactly how the woman consented. The appellate court ruled that there can be no consent by a woman who is intoxicated.[71] The court stated:

> A. Lack of Actual Consent Is Not an Element of Offenses Proscribing Sexual Intercourse with Persons Who Lack the Capacity to Give Legal Consent. To give consent, a person must act freely and voluntarily and have knowledge of the nature of the act or transaction involved. The fact that the supposed victim actually consented to sexual intercourse disproves rape only if he or she had sufficient capacity to give that consent. If the charge is that the victim lacked the capacity to give legal consent, then actual consent is irrelevant.[72]

Additional Court Cases: Rape

Smith v. State

500 N.E.2d 190 (1986)

CASE SUMMARY

PROCEDURAL POSTURE: Defendant challenged a judgment of the Marion Superior Court, Criminal Division VI (Indiana), which entered a jury verdict convicting defendant of rape. Defendant argued that the evidence was insufficient to support the verdict because it did not identify him as the perpetrator who forcibly compelled the victim to have sexual intercourse.

OVERVIEW: Defendant also argued that his confession was induced by an officer's promise to obtain mental health assistance for him. On appeal, the court disagreed. As to defendant's first claim, the victim identified defendant as her attacker in court and testified that cataract surgery she had before the rape had not precluded her from clearly seeing defendant for identification purposes because it only affected her ability to see distant objects. That evidence was sufficient to support the finding that defendant was the perpetrator. Moreover, the fact that the victim did not resist defendant's attack did not preclude the State from establishing that the act of intercourse was compelled by force. Rather, the evidence that defendant pulled a knife and remained armed with it while engaging in intercourse justified the jury in inferring that the act was compelled by force. Finally, the officer's statement to defendant during interrogation that he would get mental health assistance for defendant did not constitute a promise of immunity or mitigation of punishment sufficient to support a finding that defendant's confession was induced by improper influences that overcame his free will.

OUTCOME: The court affirmed the judgment of the trial court.[73]

Voyeurism

On the street, a voyeur is often thought of as a "peeping tom.." Clinically, this sexualized practice is known as voyeurism.[74] Deriving sexual gratification from looking at someone without their permission is not the most serious of nonconsensual sex crimes, but it can become serious and criminal. More importantly, the physiology behind voyeurism provides evidence that a voyeur is also possibly a bigamist (chapter 1) or adulterer (chapter 2) or rapist (chapter 3). Meaning, the psychiatric qualities present in the voyeur combine to make plausible the possibility that the voyeur commits other breaches of traditional sexual propriety. It would be

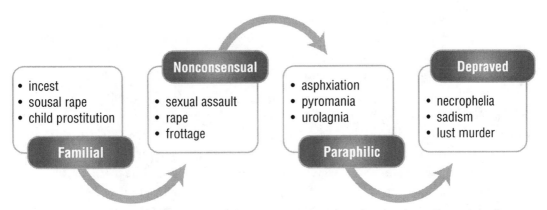

Figure 3 Continuum of deviancy; one act does not stop there but often involves other acts or the contemplation of other acts ("multiple-affected offender").

unusual for a bona fide voyeur to confine their sexual deviancy strictly to voyeurism, much like a person who is fond of scotch to not also be fond of other alcoholic beverages. Hence, voyeurism may be considered a more important offense for the law and the courts than first meets the eye.

The clandestine practice of voyeurism has a long history.[75] To one degree or another, everyone is a voyeur or pseudo-voyeur, or at least has resembled one at one time or another. It is unusual to find someone who does not enjoy "people watching" to observe another's hairstyle, jewelry, taste in clothes, body shape, etc. Notice how quickly fashion trends spread. This is strictly a result of the observations others make of the sex appeal—sexuality—of the fashions worn by others. The difference between the casual people-watcher and the voyeur is often a fine line, but is characterized by the voyeur's overly intense desire to obtain sexual stimulation from the observing, something often completely absent with the casual people-watcher.

Voyeurism may be thought of as a sexual disorder or a form of sexual deviance, one that varies greatly by degree. Sigmund Freud, in an essay on sexual aberrations, wrote that the "pleasure in looking [scopophilia] becomes a perversion if it is restricted exclusively to the genitals, or if it is connected with an overriding sense of disgust (as in the case of voyeurs who look at excretory functions), or if, instead of being preparatory to the normal sexual aim, it supplants it."[76]

Voyeurism and similarly deviant sexual practices are analyzed more appropriately in the medical field than the field of law and justice. The American Psychiatry Association defines voyeurism as a sexual disorder or paraphilia that

> involves the act of observing unsuspecting individuals, usually strangers, who are naked, in the process of disrobing, or engaging in sexual activity. The act of looking ('peeping') is for the purpose of achieving sexual excitement, and generally no sexual activity with the observed person is sought.[77]

Diagnostic criteria for this condition include recurrent behavior of the kind described above over a six-month period coupled with intense, sexually arousing fantasies or sexual urges, as well as significant distress or impairment in one's social, occupational, or other important areas of functioning caused by the fantasies, urges, or behavior.

In part, voyeurism brings us to the first "paraphilia" discussed in the book. **Paraphilias**, defined as aberrant sexuality—sexual deviance, often do not produce actual harm to anyone, as with voyeurism, but are deterred by law due to the underlying compulsion, intensity, and ritualism and, hence, threatening nature of the act.[78] It is threatening and disturbing to find, for example, someone peeping through a window in our home in the nighttime to watch us undress. In addition, the research tends to confirm that one paraphilia can lead to another and, hence, paraphilias have the ability to become dangerous, such as participating in pyromania or sadism.

Coverage of paraphilias here will be brief because chapter 6 is devoted entirely to the subject. Sex acts such as foot fetishism animate the field of psychiatry and, hence, paraphilia is a clinical term rather than a legal term. Sexual expression that strays from a moral standard of convention is often viewed with suspicion by medical authorities. Someone with a foot fetish, for example, is modestly considered to be sexually off balance and hence amenable to psychiatric review to a degree. All of these types of cases are assessed by degree. Sexuality labeled "paraphilic" should be viewed with a grain of salt. The medical field often attaches pejorative labels to activities that are merely sexual preferences. The tendency to view sex through a psychiatric lens is known as the "medicalization" of an otherwise personal preference. Said differently, maybe someone with a foot fetish is very much in touch with their sexuality and the medical authorities may be repressed sexually; the debate goes on.

Diagnostic and Statistical Manual of Mental Disorders. For the most part, the world of sexual paraphilias is governed by the medical authority of the *DSM-IV*. The *DSM (Diagnostic and Statistical Manual of Mental Disorders)* is published by the American Psychiatric Association and provides a common language and standard criteria for the classification of mental disorders such as sexual paraphilias.[79] It is used in the U.S. and in varying degrees around the world, by clinicians, researchers, psychiatric drug regulation agencies, health insurance companies, pharmaceutical companies, and legislative policy makers.

The *DSM* has attracted controversy and criticism as well as praise. There have been five revisions since it was first published in 1952, gradually including more mental disorders, although some have been removed and are no longer considered to be mental disorders, most notably homosexuality. In the 1980 revision of the *DSM*, the term "paraphilia" replaced the term "perversion" (which is where the term pervert was derived). The last major revision was the fourth edition *(DSM-IV)*, published in 1994, although a "text revision" was produced in 2000. The fifth edition *(DSM-5)* is currently in consultation, planning, and preparation, and is due for publication in 2013.

The *DSM* defines **paraphilia** as sexual arousal to objects, situations, or individuals that are not part of normative stimulation and that may cause distress or serious problems for the paraphiliac or persons associated with him or her. A paraphilia often involves sexual arousal and gratification toward sexual behavior that is atypical and possibly extreme. Some of the more common paraphilias include voyeurism, exhibitionism, fetishism and certain uses of pornographic material. According to the Glossary of Psychiatric Terminology, "voyeurism" is:

> Peeping; one of the paraphilias, characterized by marked distress over, or acting on, urges to observe unsuspecting people, usually strangers, who are naked or in the process of disrobing, or who are engaging in sexual activity.[80]

Definition of the Offense

Voyeurism is most often defined as the pleasurable, illicit observation of someone else's intimate acts, usually but not necessarily sexual. The unguardedness of the person(s) observed is key to the observer's thrill. When sexual, voyeurism is a deviant[81] manifestation of sexuality that involves looking without being seen in order to obtain sexual pleasure.[82]

Elements of the Offense

The elements of the crime of voyeurism that must be proven beyond a reasonable doubt are:

1. trespass or otherwise surreptitiously invade the privacy of another,
2. to spy or eavesdrop on another,
3. for purposes of sexually arousing or gratifying oneself.[83]

Sample Statute

The state of Indiana voyeurism statute reads as follows:

Indiana Statute § 35-45-4-5 (1998). Voyeurism.

Voyeurism is the peeping into an occupied dwelling of another person without the consent of the other person. "Peeping" is any looking of a clandestine, surreptitious, prying, or secretive nature.[84]

Arguments Made By The Prosecution

As with the other sex laws in this chapter, proving that someone was "peeping" when they may have been just "looking" is a difficult task in law and justice. Additional facts will be needed beyond mere "looking" and the state usually will not take the case if supporting and corroborative evidence is not available. The state will take the case if the accused was trespassing onto the property of another to look through a window. Also helpful to the state will be any type of video or digital images that clearly demonstrate that the watching was to view sexual body parts or sex acts.

Arguments Made By The Defense

Obviously, the defense will argue that the looking was not for purposes of sexual arousal and, therefore, no voyeuristic activities took place. Even if digital pictures or images can be admitted into evidence, unless they are flagrantly sexual, the defense can argue they may appear sexual but were nothing more than pictures that admired the scenery, generally, and were in no way personal. The defense will also have an advantage if the event was an allegedly one-time incident. If the arrest was part of a larger pattern, the defense will be at a relative disadvantage.

Variations of the Law of Voyeurism

A. Legal Inference from the Facts

In many cases of sexual deviancy, a suspect will claim that they did not know what they were doing was wrong. This may be true with possession of certain pornographic materials, or concern interactions with a prostitute, etc. In such cases, the criminal justice system, law, and the courts will make a legal inference of guilt from the attendant factual circumstances that surround the case. Said differently, the law will assume guilt in situations that are clearly outside the boundaries of routine behavior. Ignorance of the law is no excuse, in many cases.

In 2002, in *Saxton v. Indiana,* Scott Saxton was sentenced in 1993 to twenty years in prison for an aggravated battery conviction.[85] At a later sentencing hearing, he had his sentenced reduced to three years probation. While serving his term of probation, the accused went over to a neighbor's property at 5:00 a.m. and stood atop an outside air conditioning unit in order to voyeur into the bathroom of a woman who lived in the house with her husband. A neighbor happened to see the unusual circumstances, called the police, and ran outside to apprehend the trespasser. The offender was caught and charged with voyeurism pursuant to the State of Indiana Voyeurism statute:

35-45-4-5. Voyeurism.

(a) A person:

(1) who:

(A) peeps; or

(B) goes upon the land of another with the intent to peep;
into an occupied dwelling of another person; or

(2) who peeps into an area where an occupant of the area reasonably can be expected to disrobe, including:

(A) restrooms;

(B) baths;

(C) showers; and

(D) dressing rooms;

without the consent of the other person, commits voyeurism, a Class B misdemeanor.

A fine line can separate people watching from illegal voyeurism.

(b) However, the offense under subsection (a) is a Class D felony if:

(1) it is knowingly or intentionally committed by means of a camera, a video camera, or any other type of video recording device; or

(2) the person who commits the offense has a prior unrelated conviction:

(A) under this section; or

(B) in another jurisdiction, including a military court, for an offense that is substantially similar to an offense described in this section.

(c) "Peep" means any looking of a clandestine, surreptitious, prying, or secretive nature.[86]

Saxton appealed his conviction and probation revocation. His argument focused on the issue of consent and he stated that that there was no way to prove a lack of consent—that he had no notice to not look into the bathroom window, no one explicitly said for him not to do so, and the woman who used her bathroom did not explicitly communicate a lack of consent. While the argument was factually true—no one communicated a lack of consent to him—he should have known to obtain explicit consent beforehand and did not. He could not assume his actions of peering into the bathroom where residents typically disrobe was invited and approved of by the woman who uses her bathroom at 5:00 a.m. The court stated,

> Put in terms of sufficiency of the evidence, the question becomes: can a trial court infer that someone caught standing on an air conditioner staring into a woman's bathroom at 5 a.m. who runs off rather forcefully when challenged was a person peeping without the permission of the target? We say yes, and affirm the judgment of the trial court.[87]

B. Digital Voyeurism

Advanced technology has come to facilitate criminal voyeurism. High powered lenses and miniature, concealable video recording devices that are remotely timed and operated allow for the watching of others without their consent in more locations and more secretly than ever before. Offenders use these devices as a way to avoid detection and maintain a degree of anonymity while surreptitiously committing a sexual offense.[88]

In 2003, the elected sheriff of Madison County, Mississippi named Eddie Gilmer engaged in a nighttime pattern of driving over to a probationer's apartment complex purportedly to ensure that she was following the conditions of her probation. He drove an official police vehicle with his name prominently displayed on the side of the car. However, while legally monitoring the activity in the neighborhood of a probationer, the sheriff used a high-powered camera from relatively short range (87 feet) to record images of the probationer while she was out on the deck of her apartment. On examination of the digitized images, it was revealed that the pictures were specifically of her "chest and crotch area."[89] After this episode repeated itself more than once, the victim/probationer called the police. Local, municipal officers set up five separate undercover operations in the neighborhood and witnessed the sheriff engaging in video voyeurism. The undercover officers corroborated the victim's claims and accusations against the sheriff. The sheriff was charged and convicted under a new law in the state of Mississippi regarding video voyeurism. The law reads:

> Miss. Code Ann. § 97-29-63. Any person who with lewd, licentious or indecent intent secretly photographs, films, videotapes, records or otherwise reproduces the image of another person without the permission of such person when such a person is located in a place where a person would intend to be in a state of undress and have a reasonable expectation of privacy, including, but not limited to, private dwellings or any facility, public or private, used as a restroom, bathroom, shower room, tanning booth, locker room, fitting room, dressing room or bedroom shall be guilty of a felony and upon conviction shall be punished by a fine of Five Thousand Dollars ($ 5,000.00) or by imprisonment of not more than five (5) years in the custody of the Department of Corrections, or both.[90]

On appeal, the defendant/sheriff claimed that his actions were not done in secret. After all, he was in a police vehicle with his name on the side of the vehicle. He was required, as a law enforcement official, to make visits to the neighborhoods and residences of various probationers as part of their custody as probationers. In addition, the defendant argued that the victim was not "in a place where a person would intend to be in a state of undress and have a reasonable expectation of privacy"[91] since she was outside on the balcony of her apartment. The accused implicitly suggested he was not peeping through a bathroom window or doing something similarly odd and threatening, but rather, something that was his job to do as sheriff.

Despite the plausibility of the arguments, the Supreme Court of Mississippi did not accept them and affirmed the conviction of the sheriff for video voyeurism. Regarding his first claim that he was not engaged in anything "secret," the court stated:

> The undisputed facts are that [Sheriff] Gilmer recorded [the victim] Clayton starting around 9:00 at night, sitting inside his vehicle, the interior of which was dark, about 87 feet away from Clayton's apartment, using a camera and its zoom feature and carrying in his vehicle two sets of binoculars. The time of day, dark location, distance from Clayton's apartment and equipment for producing close-up recordings from such a distance clearly indicate an attempt by Gilmer to conceal his actions and elude observation or detection. Therefore, the facts were sufficient to support a jury finding beyond a reasonable doubt that Gilmer acted "secretly" in recording Clayton.[92]

As for the second claim, that the victim was not in a location where she had a reasonable expectation of privacy, the court stated that any private dwelling is a place of privacy.

> [T]he second category of places consists of public and private facilities, a number of which are named. Without question, proof that Gilmer recorded Clayton while she was in her apartment is equivalent to proving that she was recorded while in her private dwelling.[93]

C. Public Places Exception

When out in public such as in a shopping mall or at a sporting event, taking a quick picture of a famous athlete or movie star will usually not constitute criminal voyeurism. This is primarily due to the legality of taking pictures of people out in public. Famous athletes and movie stars, in particular, are aware that the public will pay attention to them out in public and therefore have a greatly reduced privacy expectation. The same is true for everyone else. Photos may be taken in public without explicit authorization, agreement, or consent. If a member of the public does not want to be looked at or photographed, according to the logic of the law, they should not go out in public.

"Upskirt voyeurism," however, is a different case and involves a different level of privacy expectation.[94] In *State v. Glas*, two defendants strategically used a shopping mall to take pictures up the skirts of unwitting female victims.[95] After walking around the mall, the offenders would locate inside a crowded store, sit on the ground nearby or behind the victim, and reach the camera forward, pointing it upward and take images of the women's legs and undergarments.

Due to the unusual and unconventional manner of using the premises of a clothing store, the offenders drew attention to themselves, were caught relatively easily, and convicted at trial of upskirt voyeurism.[96]

On appeal, the defendants used a familiar argument to exculpate themselves from guilt. They stated that the location was public and therefore, the victims had no reasonable expectation of privacy in such a location, despite having personal privacy wishes. Their argument was subject to critique. Meaning, unless a woman at the mall has taken some voluntary step that she knows will expose her underwear to public view, there should be an expectation of privacy, even while in a public place. Further, if a person's underwear can only be seen with the use of a visual enhancement device, such as a video camera, and awkwardly placed in a position where a person would not normally be sitting or standing—people do not normally lie down on shopping mall floors next to women to look up their skirts—then an expectation of privacy should be fairly obvious. It is logical to conclude that the typical victim of upskirt voyeurism in a public place does not expose her genitals or anus to anyone and instead covers them up with both underwear and a skirt.

Somewhat surprisingly, the appellate court agreed with the defendants and held that the victims had no such expectation of privacy while in a public mall. The court reversed their convictions and set them free. The court stated:

> Both [defendants] Glas and Sorrells contend that the voyeurism statute was misapplied in their respective cases because the victims were in public places and therefore did not possess a reasonable expectation of privacy. In Glas, both women were employees working in the public area of a shopping mall, while in Sorrells, the woman was standing in a concession line at the Bite of Seattle at the Seattle Center. Although Glas' and Sorrells' actions are reprehensible, we agree that the voyeurism statute, as written, does not prohibit upskirt photography in a public location.[97]

The court concluded the case by urging the State of Washington legislature to modify its voyeurism statute to include upskirt voyeurism in public places.[98]

> [A]lthough the legislature may have intended to cover intrusions of privacy in public places, the plain language of the statute does not accomplish this goal … Other state courts have faced similar frustration when confronted with acts of voyeurism, but with no statute clearly covering the challenged violations. See generally Lance E. Rothenberg, Re-Thinking Privacy: Peeping Toms, Video Voyeurs, and Failure of the Criminal Law to

Recognize a Reasonable Expectation of Privacy in the Public Space, 49 AM. U. L. REV. 1127 (2000).[99]

Additional Court Cases: Voyeurism
Bankhead v. State
626 So.2d 115 (1993)

CASE SUMMARY

PROCEDURAL POSTURE: Defendant sought review of a decision of the Lowndes County Circuit Court (Mississippi), which entered judgment on a jury verdict and convicted defendant of voyeurism.

OVERVIEW: Defendant was charged with voyeurism. At trial, a witness testified seeing a man peeping into an upstairs bathroom window in an apartment complex and called 911. The witness never saw the man's face, however, and lost sight of him for awhile. The officer that responded stated that he saw defendant walk behind the building and then go sit on a downstairs step. Defendant testified that he had car trouble. Seeing a man behind the apartment building, he went behind the building to ask for help. When the man refused to help, defendant testified that he sat on a step so that he could keep an eye on his car. The jury returned a verdict of guilty, and defendant sought review. The court disagreed with the jury verdict. The court held that because the State's case was based solely on circumstantial evidence, it had the burden of proving guilt beyond a reasonable doubt and to the exclusion of every reasonable hypothesis consistent with innocence. The court found that the State failed to meet its burden of proof considering the fact that there was a reasonable hypothesis, consistent with defendant's innocence, for his being in the area at the time a "Peeping Tom" was reported.

OUTCOME: The court reversed and remanded the judgment of the trial court.[100]

Frottage

Another form of deviant paraphilia is frotteurism.[101] Frotteurism is French for "to brush or rub."[102] In street jargon, the frotteur "cops a feel" or "gropes" another for purposes of sexual gratification in a compulsive and odd manner. This offender, to a degree, requires bizarre imagery or activities such as frottage as a necessary condition for sexual excitement. The medical reasoning suggests that the activities associated with frottage take the place of a loving, integrated, monogamous partnership.

A frotteur is easily camouflaged as an ordinary traveler and their actions easily defended as an accident.

© Konstantin Sutyagin, 2011. Used under license from Shutterstock, Inc.

The behavior of the frotteur tends to be involuntary and repetitive. A frotteur very often begins a career as a paraphiliac with fantasy and masturbatory activities and then progresses to sexual activity with or against strangers and unsuspecting victims. This nonconsensual activity can easily be done discreetly without being discovered, or in circumstances where the victim cannot respond quickly, typically in a public place such as a crowded train or at a rock concert where crowds of people are forced to bump against one another. Crowded trains or rock concerts are also perfect venues for the frotteur because the crime is easily defended as an accidental bumping into someone.

Frotteurism is so prevalent in the crowded Tokyo subway system in Japan that the subway authority had to establish female-only train cars to protect those who are frightened by the prospect of being victimized by a frotteur.[103]

As a medical matter, the *DSM-IV* looks upon frotteurism as a sexual paraphilia. The *DSM*, in part, observes the quick, reaching over and touching, patting, or rubbing as a failure to integrate one's sexuality and involves a case of someone who is in need of personal adjustment and counseling. Like other paraphiliacs, the frotteur has not used his or her sexuality in a personally fulfilling manner and instead attempts to experience the sexual self in a confused and offensive way, one that is not satisfying to the frotteur and terribly offensive to the victim.

Unwanted, nonconsensual touching in this manner is addressed in the criminal law with statutes pertaining to assault, sexual assault, sexual abuse, forcible sexual abuse, or assault and battery laws. The offender's behavior can be disturbing and repugnant to the victim and the activity can escalate into more threatening and harmful forms of physical contact such as a retaliatory blow with a fist. The offense is an obvious trespass upon a person.

Definition of the Offense

Frottage is defined as "The act of rubbing against the body of another person ... [to] attain sexual gratification."[104]

Elements of the Offense

The elements of the crime of frottage that must be proven beyond a reasonable doubt are:

1. the nonconsensual touching or rubbing up against the body of another person either naked or clothed,

2. for purposes of sexual gratification.

Sample Statute

The State of Kansas Sexual Battery statute for frotteurism reads as follows:

Section 21-3517. Sexual battery.

(a) Sexual battery is the intentional touching of the person of another who is 16 or more years of age, who is not the spouse of the offender and who does not consent thereto, with the intent to arouse or satisfy the sexual desires of the offender or another.

(b) Sexual battery is a class A person misdemeanor.

(c) This section shall be part of and supplemental to the Kansas criminal code.[105]

Arguments Made By The Prosecution

The state does not prosecute too many of these cases due to the ambiguity that surrounds them. If someone brushes up against us, it seems odd, but how can we prove it was a frotteuristic type of molestation? Witnesses will be helpful to the state. If a witness can testify that they saw someone grope the victim and run away, the testimony can corroborate the claim of frotteurism/sexual assault. Otherwise, the victim can only cry foul.

Arguments Made By The Defense

The defense can have a field day defending a case like this. The defense will begin with the argument that the touching that occurred was merely an accident, one that happens all of the time on a crowded subway or sold-out rock concert. The defense can also argue that the touching was not meant for a sexual body part, but rather, was meant to be like a pat on the back, but accidentally touched a sexual body part. Hence, the defense can get a lot of mileage out of legal intent, and the showing that there was no intent to obtain sexual gratification from the accidental collision with the victim.

Variations of the Law of Frottage

A. Intent to Obtain Sexual Gratification

In many cases, a gray area exists between a welcome gesture of affection and an inappropriate, unwanted touching. If such a case goes to court, the tribunal will examine the totality of the circumstances that surround the case for the purpose of clarifying the intentions of the parties involved. In many situations, the case turns on the intent to obtain sexual gratification.

In *Hamm v. State,* a 50-year-old church worker, Sunday school teacher, father, and husband befriended several prepubescent children at the church where he and the children participated in the church community.[106] "Lock-ins" and "sleepovers" were common in the church community and appeared safe to everyone involved, including the children's parents. On one occasion, the accused arranged for an all-children overnight stay at the church. During the event, at one point, the defendant had one of the 9-year-old girls he was "friends" with sit on his lap straddling and facing toward him where they remained in the position for a few moments. It is alleged that he was engaged in the act of frottage with the girl. Both were fully clothed. An adult witnessed the event and made a complaint.[107]

The offender was convicted of several crimes, one of them sexual assault for the paraphilic act of frottage. The frottage conviction was appealed on the grounds that the defendant had no intention to experience sexual feelings when the child sat on his lap. The case exemplified the difficulty of proving that the fully clothed interaction was sexual, especially when no part of the body was touched with the hands. The court had to rely on circumstantial evidence and explained that the details surrounding the incident were suggestive of sexual intent on the part of the accused. The court stated:

> The contact between the appellant and the little girl described by [the witness who made the complaint] involved a fifty-year-old man who was a Sunday school teacher and a church worker. It occurred at a lock-in, a church function where there were sure to be children, but at which no children of the appellant's were in attendance. There he held a little girl of unspecified age in an inappropriate manner, straddling his pelvic area.

> The appellant asserts that what occurred at the lock-in between the appellant and the little girl was non-sexual conduct. As the State points out, the conduct in question could constitute the sexual act of "frottage." Frottage is defined as: "The act of rubbing against the body of another person ... to attain sexual gratification." *The American Heritage Dictionary of the English Language* (4th ed. 2000).[108]

> We agree with the dissent to the denial of petition for rehearing in the Court of Appeals, 'There is nothing innocent about an adult male lying on his back and having a young girl straddle him, even when they are fully clothed, so that their pelvic regions are in contact.'[109]

B. Frottage as Sexual Harassment in the Workplace

When frottage is consensual, the act is no longer termed frottage, but rather "affection" and the line between the two can be thin. The frotteur is not always obviously psychologically imbalanced. In fact, some paraphiliacs are known for having above-average intelligence. Hence, they may be accomplished professionals who are lauded for their professional success, all the while engaging in deviant sex in secret, away from the workplace. Some frotteurs, however, will engage in a subtle form of frotteurism at work. Such practices can easily give rise to the claim of sexual harassment in the workplace, if not the bringing of criminal charges for sexual assault. The white collar workplace is a prime location for the participation in sexual fantasies as white collar professionals arrive at work well presented and attractively dressed, often wearing body fragrances, and interact in the work setting in proximity and relative intimacy to other workers.

In *Downes v. FAA*, a government agency (Federal Aviation Administration) supervisor who had worked in the same unit with the same personnel for a discernible period, among other things, touched the hair of a female subordinate on at least two occasions in the work-place setting.[110] Under most circumstances, there is never a reason for a male supervisor to touch the hair of a female subordinate in a bureaucratic and office setting. In response to the touching, the woman felt violated and filed a complaint, alleging a violation of federal regulations governing such workplace behavior between employees and also between supervisor and subordinate.[111] At issue were both the rules and regulations of the workplace, and also the traditional legal parameters of the intent of the supervisor (was it sexual?), and the consent of the subordinate (was the touching invited/accepted?). The regulations embodying these activities are found in 29 C.F.R. § 1604.11(a) and (b), which read as follows:

> (a) Harassment on the basis of sex is a violation of Sec. 703 of Title VII. Unwelcome sexual advances, requests for sexual favors, and other verbal or physical conduct of a sexual nature constitute sexual harassment when (1) submission to such conduct is made either explicitly or implicitly a term or condition of an individual's employment, (2) submission to or rejection of such conduct by an individual is used as the basis for employment decisions affecting such individual, or (3) such conduct has the purpose or effect of unreasonably interfering with an individual's work performance or creating an intimidating, hostile, or offensive working environment.[112]

The accused testified at trial to the following:

> I told them I recalled one time. This had to do with the time that we had discussed, or I discussed with [Ms. Jones], or she and I discussed her dress, where she had told me that her two previous chiefs had told her she had to dress like a man because she was doing a man's job, and it would be appropriate for the job she was doing. I told her that she was a lady, and as far as I was concerned she could dress like any other lady would, commensurate upon the job she had to do that particular time.

Up to that time, she had been wearing her hair more or less piled—whatever you call it. I don't understand women's hairdos, but piled up on top of her head, more or less. We also talked about that. I told her that she could wear her hair in any style that she felt was appropriate for a lady to wear her hair. The result of that was she did start wearing her hair down in whatever you call it, and the other type of clothing that she bought and started wearing.

Now, I remember one time going by her desk and taking these two fingers on a couple of strands of hair about the first time she did, and said, '[Ms. Jones], your hair looks great that way.' I told her that, and I kept on walking.

It was a gesture of friendliness or whatever you want to call it, or understanding or appreciation of her hair. I might tell a man he had a nice necktie on that day. That's all it amounted to, as far as I was concerned.

I never heard any repercussions from it at all, one way or the other, until this thing came up.

If Downes' testimony is true—and it was not found incredible—(indeed, the presiding official relied on it as an admission) it illustrates that touching a woman's hair may or may not be a sexual gesture.[113]

In making its determination, the appellate court relied heavily on evidence of phone conversations between the two parties when both were in their respective homes in the evening. These phone calls were initiated by the complainant, appeared to be amicable and at times friendly. The court ruled that the touching of the woman's hair was not obviously sexual, and that it was not obviously unwelcome/without consent, especially in view of the friendly phone conversations that took place between the parties. The decision to sanction the supervisor was reversed and the claim for sexual harassment dismissed.[114]

C. Civil Commitment

Persistent frottage (and persistent voyeurism) are more indicative of a mental abnormality than of simple affection, sexual experimentation, religious ritual, or flagrant criminality. If such behavior continues into adulthood from that of an adolescent passing phase, the individual is not likely to cease the behavior without a medical intervention. The paraphiliac is thus distinguished from the burglar or thief, who in many cases, once enough loot is stolen, can cease their criminal offending. The disturbed psychiatric condition of the paraphiliac, within degrees, can be helpless to stop the pattern of activity and hence may be subject to civil commitment proceedings where the state will incarcerate the person in a mental health hospital for an indefinite period.[115]

To commit a person, the State need only prove to the satisfaction of a jury or a judge that a sex offender has substantial volitional impairment. Certain psychiatric diagnoses, defined in the *DSM-IV*, are generally used to support a claim by the State that a sex offender suffers from a substantial volitional impairment, most commonly one of the paraphilias or personality disorders such as antisocial personality disorder. The American Psychiatric Association has disavowed the use of the *DSM-IV* to categorize persons as disordered for the purpose of predicting future behavior, or for any other forensic use, but these warnings have gone unheeded.[116] The *DSM-IV* is used by various parties in civil commitment proceedings.

In the case of *In re Hodges*, a frotteur was sexually molested as a child and this set of early childhood experiences may have contributed to his own involuntary, recurrent pattern of sexual offending.[117] With no other alternatives, the State of Iowa subjected Hodges to civil commitment hearings to determine if the State had the authority and the justification to incapacitate the accused in a state mental hospital so he could receive mental health treatment resources. At the civil commitment hearings, a panel of medical authorities deemed Hodges a sexually violent predator and he was civilly committed. The court found the following facts upon which to base the determination:

> After his father sexually molested him at age ten, Hodges began molesting his sister. Around the same time, he began peeping into the girls' locker room at school to watch girls undress and shower. He also peeped into the bathroom at home to 'watch women or other girls use the rest room.' He soon began peeping through windows in various houses in his community and even 'entered a few of the homes to rifle through the female occupant's underwear drawers.' On one occasion, after mowing a woman's lawn, he 'asked her if she could take her nightgown off for' him. Hodges was placed in the children's unit at Cherokee Mental Health Institute following the incident.
>
> Hodges remained at Cherokee for two years. While there, he continued peeping into the girls' locker rooms and bathrooms. After he was released, he continued his voyeuristic activities until he was placed in a children's home at age fifteen. While there, Hodges testified he would pull down girls' bed covers to look at their naked bodies as they slept. He was later returned to the Cherokee Institute after threatening to kill himself.

After his release from Cherokee, Hodges was placed in the Boys and Girls Home in Sioux City until he was seventeen. While on passes from the home, Hodges began to engage in frotteurism. He would randomly grab 'women inappropriately on the streets of downtown Sioux City.' He 'was arrested and charged with 26 different counts, roughly' over a 'two to three month period.' While at the Boys and Girls Home, he would clandestinely watch the house counselors take showers and would take their underwear. As a result of these activities, Hodges was placed in the State Boys Training School until he was eighteen.

Hodges described "frotteurism" as follows: 'I might notice their breasts or their butt and I might grab their breasts for sexual pleasure. Just to grab them. Not really to harm them. Just to grab them for my own gratification.'

When Hodges was twenty-one, he served thirty days in jail for fondling a woman without her consent. Between the ages of twenty-one and twenty-four, he frequently took women's underwear from clotheslines and laundromats. He also molested his twelve-year-old cousin for two to three months during this time.

The State filed a petition seeking to have Hodges deemed a sexually violent predator and civilly committed under Iowa Code chapter 229A. After a trial, the jury concluded Hodges was a sexually violent predator under Iowa Code section 229A.2(11), and the district court ordered him committed to the Civil Commitment Unit for Sexual Offenders at Oakdale in the State of Iowa.[118]

Additional Court Cases: Frottage

Commonwealth v. Berkowitz

609 A.2d 1338 (1990)

CASE SUMMARY

PROCEDURAL POSTURE: Defendant appealed from judgment of sentence imposed following convictions of rape and indecent assault in the Court of Common Pleas of Monroe County, Criminal (Pennsylvania).

OVERVIEW: Defendant was convicted of rape and indecent assault and sentenced to serve a term of imprisonment of one to four years on the rape and a concurrent term of six to twelve months for indecent assault. The court reversed defendant's conviction for rape because it found that the incident between defendant and victim did not meet the statutory definition of rape, 18 Pa. Cons. Stat. Ann. § 3121. Specifically, the court found that even in the light most favorable to the commonwealth, the victim's testimony as to the physical aspects of the encounter could not serve as a basis to prove "forcible compulsion." No evidence was adduced which established that mental coercion, or a threat, or force inherently inconsistent with consensual intercourse was used to complete the act of intercourse. The court further found that a new trial was warranted on the indecent assault charge because the trial court erroneously applied the Rape Shield Law to exclude evidence that tended to show the charges may have been fabricated, thus the evidence should have been deemed relevant.

OUTCOME: The court discharged defendant on the rape conviction because it found that the commonwealth did not establish that mental coercion, or a threat, or force inherently inconsistent with consensual intercourse was used to complete the act of intercourse. The court reversed and remanded for a new trial on the indecent assault conviction because it determined that the exclusion of evidence of victim's motive to fabricate the charge was improper.[119]

Chapter Three Summary

Many forms of human sexuality thus far covered in the book have, at one time or another, or in one country or another, been morally or socially accepted such as preserving family lines with incest or abiding by religious duty with polygamy. Oppositely, some forms of sexual expression were once verboten, but are now more accepted, such as domestic partnerships. In this chapter, however, the deviance behind nonconsensual sex has never found social, moral, or legal acceptance in conventional society.

To violate a person's sphere of personal privacy with a robbery, burglary, theft, or assault is trouble enough. To violate a person's sphere of personhood with unwanted sexual advances, touching, or rape is arguably a lot worse. The sexual dimension of a person's physiology involves neurological and psychological functions that, if abused, create a discord in the psyche that science and medicine to this day, are unable to fully address and remedy.

Not only are nonconsensual sex crimes particularly harmful to the victim, they can also be difficult to detect. A voyeur may peer clandestinely across the room and "take liberties" with someone sexually without their consent. The criminal law is helpless to address such instances of "abuse" since an offender cannot be prosecuted based on fantasies or glances alone. The principle of *actus reus* requires an offender to both intentionally motivate and also physically act before an arrest can be made. Nonconsensual sex crimes require the use, attempted use, or threatened use of force as a necessary element of the offense. Mere thoughts are not enough.

Where a physical act ensues, the law moves swiftly. Due to the actual or conceptual violence inherent in nonconsensual sex crimes, the justice system is relatively quick to examine cases where a victim reports the activity of unwanted, inexplicable sexual gestures or outright assault and violence. Due to patriarchal cultural values and the inferior status of women in an earlier era, statutes prohibiting sexual assault did not exist before 1970.[120] Change came slowly to the social roles for men and women in the workplace, family, and other areas. Led by reformers such as Maragret Sanger, Alfred Kinsey, Susan Estrich, and others, fundamental changes took place within the legal framework for sexual assault and especially rape cases. Today, nonconsensual sex crimes are taken more seriously than they were in the past.[121]

The contemporary modifications to the law of rape cases and rape statutes is one of the better examples of the legal changes made to respond to the injustices of nonconsensual sex crimes and achieve equitable and just results for victims. In rape cases, the spousal exemption for rape cases was abolished so that a rapist could be convicted regardless of their marital status. Most jurisdictions also removed the "utmost resistance standard" from the books. Today, a victim does not have to put up a fight with their attacker to demonstrate a lack of consent. Resisting the attack of a violent sexual predator stands a good chance of making matters worse for the victim, not to mention that the victim is not likely as strong as the attacker.[122]

Rape shield statutes have also been adopted to make the adjudication of rape cases fairer by eliminating prejudicial evidence that may be unrelated to the case at hand. While sometimes evidence of a couple's prior sexual exploits is probative and necessary to understand the pattern of sexual activity in a relationship, in earlier times, a female victim was easily portrayed as consenting when the defense highlighted her willingness to have sex with numerous partners in the past. One's history is often completely irrelevant as to whether a rape has occurred. Rape shield statutes even the playing field for rape trials where there are usually no witnesses and it's one person's word against the other's.[123] Lastly, the law of rape has also addressed the issue of consent and intoxication. Consent requires having a sound state of mind and the ability to make conscious decisions. Intoxication negates the possibility of consent in the same way as the status of minor, unconsciousness, drug-impaired, or insane persons. If two persons engage in sex and one of them is legally intoxicated, the state can pursue the case as a forcible rape even if the victim party would have consented while sober. The burden is on the sober party to walk away from an encounter with someone who is legally intoxicated.

The analysis of nonconsensual sex also includes paraphilia-related sexual activities. Highlighted by the medical community for their recurrent, involuntary, and hyper-intense qualities, paraphilias are thought to be relatively common, even though most paraphiliacs have enough cognitive control to avoid a violation of the criminal law. These individuals may, for example, involve themselves in fetishistic-related activities in the privacy of their own home and possibly alone, without another person present.

The paraphilias of voyeurism and frottage usually never hint at a relationship-based encounter, but rather suggest a sexual imbalance where the actor seeks to fuel a vivid fantasy life, ritualistically invading the sexual privacy of another, without consent, in a manner hoping to evade detection while still obtaining the objective of sexual leering or touching.

Paraphilias are complicated medical conditions to the extent many paraphiliacs hope to be seen during their escapade, but also hope to avoid apprehension, all of which is part of the obsessive game the actor desperately plays, each time seeking a new level of fear and excitement. In a small number of cases, paraphiliacs double as sociopaths and have no regard for laws, sexual customs, or respect for others and eventually commit heinous criminal acts such as lust murder.[124] Civil commitment laws are one legal possibility for addressing potentially dangerous sexual predators. Civil commitment proceeding will include a large quantity of medical evaluations where a determination can be made as to the dangerous nature of the offender to himself and the community. A positive determination from a civil commitment hearing will result in the offender being incapacitated in a state mental hospital for an indefinite period.

Key Terms

Sexual Assault 00

Rape 00

Force and Consent 00

Voyeurism 00

Paraphilia 00

Frottage 00

Civil Commitment 00

Privacy 00

Legal Inference 00

Sexual Harassment 00

Concepts & Principles

Purposes of Sexual Gratification 00

Consent 00

Intimate Body Parts 00

Penetration Requirement 00

Rape Shield Law 00

Utmost Resistance 00

Communication of Nonconsent 00

Date Rape and Intoxication

Public Places Exception 00

Circumstantial Evidence 00

Chapter One Select Court Cases	
Case	**Point of Law**
People v. Rivera 00	Kissing as an unwanted sexual touching
People v. Teicher 00	Doctor's touching of a patient and sexual assault
Gagne v. Booker	Applicability of Rape Shield Law
Brown v. State	"Resistance to the Utmost" standard in rape cases
People v. Giardino	Alcohol intoxication nullifies consent
Saxton v. Indiana	Guilt can be inferred from the facts
Gilmer v. State	Voyeurism and the use of high-powered cameras
State v. Glas	Voyeurism and a "public places" exception
Hamm v. Arkansas	Proof of intent to gain sexual gratification is required for a conviction for frottage
Downes v. FAA	Gestures of affection in the workplace and the crime of unwanted sexual touching
In Re Hodges	Uncontrollable acts of frottage may result in a court-ordered state civil commitment

Questions for Review

1. What is the legal definition of sexual assault?

2. Why was sexual assault not a crime at common law?

3. What factors contributed to the many changes in the law of rape?

4. What is the purpose of a rape shield statute?

5. How is the element of "resistance to the utmost" used in rape cases today?

6. How do the courts treat "consent" when a person is legally drunk?

7. What is the difference between people-watching and voyeurism?

8. Is voyeurism legal in a public place such as a shopping mall?

9. What is frotteurism?

10. What criminal law prohibits the practice of frotteurism?

1   United States v. Shannon, 110 F.3d 382, 388 (7th Cir. 1997).

2   A. Grubb & J. Harrower, *Understanding Attribution of Blame in Cases of Rape: An Analysis of Participant Gender, Type of Rape and Perceived Similarity to the Victim,* 15 J. Sexual Aggression, 63 (2009).

3   Anna Clark, Women's Silence Men's Violence: Sexual Assault in England 1770–1845 56 (1987).

4   In Rome at the time of Christ, a rape victim was expected to commit suicide since she had been so fouled and was no longer of value.

5   Sir Matthew Hale, The History of the Pleas of the Crown 635 (London Professional Books 1971) (1736). Hale was the Chief Justice of the Court of King's Bench in England. This treatise was first published in 1736 and has been significant in the development of American law.

6   *Id.*

7   John Henry Wigmore, A Treatise on the Anglo-American System of Evidence in Trial at Common Law (3d ed. 1940).

8   Susan Estrich, *Rape,* 95 Yale L.J. 1087 (1986).

9   Catharine A. MacKinnon, Feminism, Marxism, Method, and the State: Toward Feminist Jurisprudence 171–83 (1983).

10 Although sexual assault may seem "sexual" in nature, many sexual assaults have less to do with sexual desire inasmuch as they concern sexual humiliation. As one perpetrator stated, "I had the guy so frightened I could have made him do anything I wanted. I didn't have an erection. I wasn't really interested in sex. I felt powerful, and hurting him excited me. Making him suck me was more to degrade him than for my physical satisfaction." In another instance, a perpetrator raped his victim as a form of punishment for asking the assailant if he was "a homo." According to the perpetrator, "it wasn't for sex. I was mad and I wanted to prove who I was and what he was." In these instances, the perpetrators' "satisfaction" had less to do with erotic or sexual desire as much as it had to do with power and humiliation. S. F. Fuch, *Male Sexual Assault: Issues of Arousal and Consent,* 51 Cleve. St. L. Rev. 93, 107 (2004).

11 Scott D. Easton, Carol Coohey, Patrick O'leary, Ying Zhang & Lei Hua, *The Effect of Childhood Sexual Abuse on Psychosexual Functioning During Adulthood,* 26 J. Fam. Violence 41 (2011).

12 Julie M. Arnold, Note, *"Divine" Justice and the Lack of Secular Intervention: Abrogating the Clergy-Communicant Privilege in Mandatory Reporting Statutes to Combat Child Sexual Abuse,* 42 Val. U. L. Rev. 849 (2008).

13 Donileen R. Loseke, *We Hold These Truths to Be Self-Evident: Problems in Pondering the Pedophile Priest Problem,* 6 Sexualities 6 (2003).

14 Michael N. Kane, *Investigating Attitudes of Catholic Priests Toward the Media and the US Conference of Catholic Bishops' Response to the Sexual Abuse Scandals of 2002,* 11 Mental Health, Religion & Culture, 579 (2008).

15 *Id.*

16 John Jay College of Criminal Justice, The Nature and Scope of the Problem of Sexual Abuse of Minors by Catholic Priests and Deacons in the United States ix–x (2004), *available at* http://www.jjay.cuny.edu/churchstudy/main.asp.

17 *Id.*

18 18 U.S.C. § 2244 (1992).

19 N.Y. Penal Law § 130.55 (2002).

20 Bailey v. State, 764 N.E.2d 728 (Ind. Ct. App. 2002).

21 Alaska Stat. § 11.41.420 (1994).

22 People v. Rivera, 525 N.Y.S.2d 118 (N.Y. Sup. Ct. 1988).

23 People v. Kittles, 423 N.Y.S.2d 107 (N.Y. Co. Ct. 1979).

24 *Rivera,* 525 N.Y.S. 2d 118.

25 *Id.* at 123.

26 *In re* A.B., 556 A.2d 645 (D.C. 1989).

27 N.Y. Penal Law § 130.65 (2001).

28 People v. Teicher, 422 N.E.2d 506 (N.Y. 1981).

29 People v. Blodgett, 326 N.Y.S.2d 14 (N.Y. App. Div. 1971).

30 *In re* Adams, 601 P.2d 995, 999 (Wash. Ct. App. 1979).

31 Wash. Rev. Code § 9A.88.100 (1988).

32 *In re* Adams, 601 P.2d at 999.

33 *In re* A.B., 556 A.2d 645 (D.C. 1989).

34 Jody Clay-Warner & Callie Harbin Burt, *Rape Reporting After Reforms,* 11 Violence Against Women 150 (2005).

35 Meredith J. Duncan, *Sex Crimes and Sexual Miscues: The Need for a Clearer Line Between Forcible Rape and Non-Consensual Sex,* 42 Wake Forest L. Rev. 1087, 1095–1108 (2007).

36 *Id.*

37 Michelle J. Anderson, *All-American Rape,* 79 St. John's L. Rev. 625, 625–28 (2005).

38 *Id.*

39 Nicholas J. Little, Note, *From No Means No to Only Yes Means Yes: The Rational Results of an Affirmative Consent Standard in Rape Law,* 58 Vand. L. Rev. 1321, 1341–44 (2005).

40 18 U.S.C. § 109A (2006).

41 *Id.*

42 Conn. Gen. Stat. § 53a-65(2) (2000).

43 Donald Dripps, *After Rape Law: Will the Turn to Consent Normalize the Prosecution of Sexual Assault?,* 41 Akron L. Rev. 957 (2008).

44 Lise Gotell, *Rethinking Affirmative Consent in Canadian Sexual Assault Law: Neoliberal Sexual Subjects and Risky Women,* 41 Akron L. Rev. 865, 869 (2008).

45 Colo. Rev. Stat. § 18-3-401(1.5) (2005).

46 Chambers v. Lockhart, 872 F.2d 274 (8th Cir. 1989).

47 Conn. Gen. Stat. § 53a-65(2) (2000).

48 John Klotter, Criminal Law 130 (7th ed. 2004).

49 Ind. Code § 35-42-4-1 (1998).

50 Richard Klein, *An Analysis of Thirty-Five Years of Rape Reform: A Frustrating Search for Fundamental Fairness,* 41 Akron L. Rev. 981 (2008).

51 *Id.*

52 Gagne v. Booker, 596 F.3d 335, 339 (6th Cir. 2010).

53 *Id.*

54 Mich. Comp. Laws § 750.520b(1)(f) (2006).

55 *Gagne,* 596 F.3d 335.

56 Mich. Comp. Law §§ 750.520j(1)–(2) (1989).

57 *Gagne,* 596 F.3d at 339.

58 *Id.* at 346.

59 Michelle J. Anderson, *Reviving Resistance in Rape Law,* 1998 U. Ill. L. Rev. 953, 957 (1998).

60 *Id.*

[61] Brown v. State, 106 N.W. 536 (Wis. 1906).

[62] *Id.*

[63] *Id.*

[64] *Id.*

[65] *See* State v. Rusk, 424 A.2d 720, 728 (Md. 1981). "That a victim did not scream out for help or attempt to escape, while bearing on the question of consent, is unnecessary where she is restrained by fear of violence."

[66] Del. Code Ann. tit. 11, § 761(g)(1) (1987).

[67] Philip N. S. Rumney & Rachel Anne Fenton, *Intoxicated Consent in Rape: Bree and Juror Decision-Making,* 71 Mod. L. Rev. 279 (2008).

[68] Valerie M. Ryan, Comment, *Intoxicating Encounters: Allocating Responsibility in the Law of Rape,* 40 Cal. W. L. Rev. 407, 411–12 (2004).

[69] People v. Giardino, 98 Cal. Rptr. 2d 315, 326 (2000).

[70] *Id.*

[71] The appeals court reversed the conviction on a technical matter, but did not agree with the defendant and ruled in favor of the female/victim. *Giardino,* 98 Cal. Rptr. 2d 315.

[72] *Id.* at 326.

[73] Smith v. State, 500 N.E.2d 190 (Ind. 1986).

[74] Clay Calvert, Voyeur Nation: Media, Privacy and Peering in Modern Culture 202 (2000).

[75] Marjorie A. Caner, Annotation, *Validity, Construction, and Application of Stalking Statutes,* 29 A.L.R. 5TH 487 (1995).

[76] Sigmund Freud, The Interpretation of Dreams (Random House) (1950).

[77] 4 Am. Psychiatry Ass'n, Diagnostic and Statistical Manual of Mental Disorders (2000) [hereinafter DSM-IV].

[78] The most common authority on sexual paraphilias is the DSM-IV, written and organized by the American Psychiatry Association. The DSM defines paraphilia, in part, as a subtype of psychosexual disorder involving unusual or bizarre fantasies or acts that are necessary for full sexual excitement. 4 Am. Psychiatry Ass'n, Diagnostic and Statistical Manual of Mental Disorders 522–23 (4th ed. 1994).

[79] DSM-IV, supra note 77.

[80] John F. Abess, *Glossary: Terms in the Field of Psychiatry and Neurology,* Abess.com, http://www.abess.com/glossary.html#V (last visited May 9, 2010).

[81] "Deviant" is defined as departing from the normal: aberrant, abnormal, anomalistic, anomalous, atypic, atypical, divergent, irregular.

[82] Abess, *supra* note 80.

[83] Ohio Rev. Code Ann. § 2907.08 (West 2002).

[84] Ind. Code §§ 35-45-4-5(a)–(b) (1998).

[85] Saxton v. Indiana, 790 N.E.2d 98 (Ind. 2003).

[86] Ind. Code § 35-45-4-5 (2005).

[87] *Saxton,* 790 N.E.2d 98.

[88] Clay Calvert & Justin Brown, *Video Voyeurism, Privacy, and the Internet: Exposing Peeping Toms in Cyberspace,* 18 Cardozo Arts & Ent. L.J. 469 (2000).

[89] Gilmer v. State, 2004-KA-02236-SCT, 955 So. 2d 829 (Miss. 2007).

[90] Miss. Code Ann. § 97-29-63 (2006).

91   *Id.*

92   *Gilmer,* 955 So. 2d at 837.

93   *Id.* at 841.

94   Andrea Simakis, *Skirt-Peeping Video Suspect Blames Net,* PLAIN DEALER, Sept. 14, 1999, at 1B (quoting Andrew Drake, creator of a website called Upskirt.com that reportedly receives 1 million visitors each month).

95   State v. Glas, 54 P.3d 147 (Wash. 2002).

96   *Id.*

97   *Id.* at 157.

98   The court referenced as an example the State of California's modern voyeurism statute, which if in effect in this case, would have resulted in affirmed convictions for the defendants. The California statute reads: Any person who uses a concealed camcorder, motion picture camera, or photographic camera of any type, to secretly videotape, film, photograph, or record by electronic means, another, identifiable person under or through the clothing being worn by that other person, for the purpose of viewing the body of, or the undergarments worn by, that other person, without the consent or knowledge of that other person, with the intent to arouse, appeal to, or gratify the lust, passions, or sexual desires of that person and invade the privacy of that other person, under circumstances in which the other person has a reasonable expectation of privacy. CAL. PENAL CODE § 647(k)(2) (West 2007).

99   *Glas,* 54 P.3d at 162.

100 Bankhead v. State, 626 So. 2d 115 (Miss. 1993).

101 The DSM-IV defines frotteurism as: "Over a period of at least 6 months, recurrent, intense sexually arousing fantasies, sexual urges, or behaviors involving touching and rubbing against a non-consenting person." DSM-IV, *supra* note 77 at § 302.89.

102 Stephanie Neumann, Dawn Alley, Anne Marie Paclebar, Catherine Sanchez, & Brianna Satterhwaite, *Frotteurism, Piquerism, and Other Related Paraphilias,* in SEX CRIMES AND PARAPHILIA 237, 237 (Eric W. Hickey ed., 2006).

103 J. Mark Ramseyer & Eric B. Rasmusen, *"Why Is the Japanese Conviction Rate So High?",* 30 J. Legal Stud. 53 (2001).

104 Hamm v. State, 232 S.W.3d 463, 472 (Ark. 2006).

105 KAN. STAT. ANN. § 21-3517 (1993).

106 *Hamm,* 232 S.W.3d 463.

107 *Id.*

108 *Id.* at 478.

109 *Hamm,* 232 S.W.3d 463.

110 Downes v. FAA, 775 F.2d 288 (Fed. Cir. 1985).

111 29 C.F.R. § 1604.11(a)(3) (2010). This section discusses sexual harassment by engaging in a pattern of abusive and offensive sexual behavior directed to female employees.

112 29 C.F.R. §§ 1604.11(a)–(b) (2010).

113 *Downes,* 775 F.2d 288.

114 *Id.*

115 John Matthew Fabian, *Paraphilias and Predators: The Ethical Application of Psychiatric Diagnoses in Partisan Sexually Violent Predator Civil Commitment Proceedings,* 11 J. FORENSIC PSYCHOL. PRAC., 82 (2011).

116 Brief for Am. Psychiatric Ass'n as Amicus Curiae at 4, Barefoot v. Estelle, 463 U.S. 880 (1983) (No. 82-6080) ("The unreliability of psychiatric predictions of long-term future dangerousness is by now an established fact within the profession."). Despite the APA's position, the Court in *Barefoot* found that the DSM diagnostic categories could be used to make such predictions. Barefoot v. Estelle, 463 U.S. 880, 896–903 (1983) (affirming the district court's conclusion that the accuracy of psychiatric predictions is "within the province of the jury to resolve").

[117] *In re* Hodges, 689 N.W.2d 467, 481 (Iowa 2004).

[118] *Id.*

[119] Commonwealth v. Berkowitz, 609 A.2d 1338 (1990).

[120] Vivian Berger, *Man's Trial, Woman's Tribulation: Rape Cases in the Courtroom,* 77 Colum. L. Rev. 1, 58 (1977).

[121] Hendrick Hartog, Man and Wife in America 306–07 (2000).

[122] Wallace D. Loh, *The Impact of Common Law and Reform Rape Statutes on Prosecution: An Empirical Study,* 55 Wash. L. Rev. 543, 556–62 (1980).

[123] J. Alexander Tanford & Anthony J. Bocchino, *Rape Victim Shield Laws and the Sixth Amendment,* 128 U. Pa. L. Rev. 544, 579–81 (1980).

[124] Dinesh Bhugraa, Dmitri Popelyukb & Isabel McMullen, *Paraphilias Across Cultures: Contexts and Controversies,* 47 J. Sex Res., 242 (2010).

Chapter Four

Sex Workers: Prostitution, Pimping, Strippers/Nudity, Sex Tourism

---

"Nude dancing is expressive conduct within the outer perimeters of the
First Amendment, though we view it as only marginally so."

Barnes v. Glen Theatre, Inc.
United States Supreme Court
501 U.S. 560 (1991)[1]

Legal Background

S ex work and the legalities of the commercial sex industry have a long history. What makes this class of sex offenses distinct from more socially deviant cases of sex offending such as frottage or incest is the profit motive and economic benefits.[2] The business activities associated with sex work are far too lucrative for them to go away anytime soon and the profits help explain the long history behind sex work.[3] Hagner notes that the sex industry is a multi-billion-dollar operation per year.[4] As an example, systems operators who own sex-related digital chatrooms and charge a fee for user accounts net over $100,000 per month for merely running a set of servers. Farley indicates that the mere associated revenues such as cab rides, hotels, tips, and monies paid to bellmen, valets, or bartenders for information about where to find commercial sex generates over $1 billion a year in economic activity in the city of Las Vegas alone.[5] The Association of Club Executives estimates that annual revenues at adult clubs in the U.S. are approximately $14 billion.[6]

Under most circumstances, the activities related to sex work such as stripping or cybersex chat are not as harmful, for example, as sexual assault, nor as morally controversial, for example, as sodomy cases. Nor are sex-for-a-fee cases imbued with as much religious sentiment as with adultery or polygamy cases. To the contrary, sex work is legal in small parts of the U.S. and many people advocate making it legal, but regulated, nationwide. In her book, *Criminal Law*, Sue Reid notes:

> [I]n societies that permit premarital and postmarital sexual behavior by men with women who are not their marital partners, while insisting that women should not engage in sex outside of marriage, prostitution has been considered essential. Some people have even argued that prostitutes serve the role in society of preserving families and the chastity of women other than prostitutes.[7]

Hence, today, the moral approbation over sex work is less than many of the offenses we have covered so far or that come on to the radar of the criminal justice system.

When these particular cases come to the attention of the police, they tend to be treated as nuisance offenses, activities that local police hope to antagonize to the point where they will go away and relocate to a neighboring jurisdiction. The legal regulation of massage parlors, brothels, and escort services is largely a function of management and control rather than any hope of eradication. Undercover male officers will patronize a massage parlor and as soon as the masseuse suggests sex as part of the transaction, an arrest will be made. Undercover female officers will dress scantily and walk the streets. As soon as someone drives by and asks for sex for a fee, an arrest will be made there. The same police arrest procedure applies to Internet website dialogue, a subject covered in chapter 7. Political leaders and news reports will use the language of "ending" or "stopping" the sex trade, but veterans of the law enforcement community understand that the only hope is to govern a set of persistent offenses on behalf of public health and safety and that includes the protection of sex workers themselves from being ripped off or mugged.

Often, the enforcement of laws against sex workers such as prostitutes, escorts, or call girls is a low priority for the government. Sometimes the laws are not enforced at all, and in other contexts, the laws purposely do not apply. For example, U.S. military bases in places such as Thailand and the Philippines contract with the local police for American servicemen to patronize local prostitutes without fear of arrest. These arrangements, while admittedly controversial, condone the industry of sex work and fornication, and facilitate the unimpeded transaction between sex worker and client.[8]

With the digital age and advent of the Internet in the early 1990s, the market of customers has increased substantially due to the anonymity afforded. Formerly, many persons would not risk being seen in a brothel, strip club, massage parlor, or adult bookstore. Today, cell phones and the Internet allow for secretive and expansive arrangements that enable parties to meet for the exchange of sex for a fee or to engage in phone or cybersex in a digital medium. With much less risk of being seen or getting caught, certain formerly repressed sexual needs are less locked away and are being met, albeit in an office-like, business, and rational manner.

In the main, sex workers have responded to the expanded market for sexual outlets and have found the commerce and profits to be dependable and relatively satisfying. Although the example of a wealthy call girl leading a life of leisure is more myth than reality, sex work can constitute a reasonably decent living. Sex workers often set their own working hours, pick and choose their own customers, can relocate easily, shelter the profits, and come in and out of the business at will. Most sex workers are female and there is no doubt that the sex trade can be a superior alternative to many forms of work offered to females in the history of women and work.[9]

On the downside, around the world, a discernible number of sex workers are low-income females who come from violent homes and are drug-dependent. Like any worker without an adequate education or social skills, these women work in the lower echelons of the trade and in many cases have no alternative to sex work. They cannot afford the luxury of hotel rooms and security and have to walk the streets at their own peril. A substantial percentage of sex-related work is performed by women who are in a deep cycle of degradation and despair. This reality, one easily supported with statistical data,[10] has led to a successful Sex Workers Movement which attempts to provide support and protection to vulnerable females who choose sex work as employment because other avenues of making a living are not feasible or available.[11]

Whether or not a sex worker comes from a low-income setting, ample evidence exists that reflects the unfavorable conditions often faced by sex workers. In particular, violence visited upon a sex worker is treated differently from violence visited upon, for example, someone working in a white-collar business office. In most cases, a sex worker who is robbed or mugged cannot tell the police without revealing their own participation in criminal activity. Even in cases of nonpayment, no legal recourse is available to many sex workers. To the contrary, the criminal justice system is more of a foe than a friend to sex workers, unduly targeting them as a social ill when the only actual harm caused by a sex worker is consensual sex between adults in a private setting.

Cognizant of these injustices, the Sex Worker Movement has resulted in the formation of the English Collective of Prostitutes, the US PROStitutes Collective, and other organizations.[12] These organizations are part of the International Prostitutes Collective and constitute an international force for the advancement of legal protections of sex workers. The first European Conference on Sex Work, Human Rights, Labor and Migration was held in Belgium in 2005 where the Conference passed the Declaration of the Rights of Sex Workers and endorsed a "Sex Workers in Europe" manifesto.[13]

Asian nations have similar organizations. Following the closure of dance bars in the state of Maharashtra in India in 2005, Indian sex workers, led by the National Network of Sex Workers, pledged to intensify their campaign for the legalization of their profession. Contemporary Sex Worker organization is a combination of human rights such as the right to be free of scapegoating by the justice system, and of labor rights, such as the right to safe and healthy working conditions. Today, the Sex Worker Movement incorporates males, and transgender groups in the effort to recognize that in many ways sex work is work just like any other and should be treated as such.[14]

As for the historic legalities of sex work in the United States, it should be noted that the commerce of sex was not illegal at Common Law in England and neither was it when the United States was founded in 1776. A prostitute, for example, would be run off by local merchants if her presence detracted customers from patronizing the area. Men who solicited the services of a sex worker were mostly thought to have what they were entitled to as men and were not subject to arrest for facilitating a crime.

While discreet forms of sex work performed indoors were not a priority for the police, in a type of double standard, the advertisement of the sex trade was verboten. Early forms of strip clubs and similar adult entertainment were considered at the time to be flagrant advertising of sex (pornography) and came under the catch-all prohibition of obscenity.[15] Obscenity, covered more thoroughly in the next chapter on pornography, is a legal doctrine that has evolved substantially in the U.S.[16] Obscenity is a vague term and is highly similar to other vague legal terms such as "indecent," "amoral," "prurient," or "tends to the corruption of morals.."[17] Sex work such as table dancing, striptease, or cabaret fell under the legal umbrella of the obscenity doctrine and were all illegal by the middle of the 19th century in the U.S.[18] Today, adult entertainment (SOBs—Sexually Oriented Businesses) has gained a degree of legal ground with the First Amendment protection of speech and expression.[19]

The first notable shift in laws concerning sex workers was around 1900. Massive immigration and industrialization gave rise to concerns about new lifestyles in urban America, including wayward lifestyles. Numerous women found a living in prostitution and many foreigners came to the U.S. to work as prostitutes. Drunkenness and debauchery increased as single, hard-working, hard-drinking immigrants flooded American cities.[20] Without automobiles, airplanes, etc., they looked for entertainment right in the neighborhood where they lived and worked and much of it was sex related. These changes in urban life alarmed the proper-living bourgeoisie of New England at the time and they wanted to pass laws to deter untoward moral behavior and promote their version of healthy, decent, and proper living. They believed that the very fabric of society was threatened by "degenerate classes" in general, and prostitutes in particular.[21]

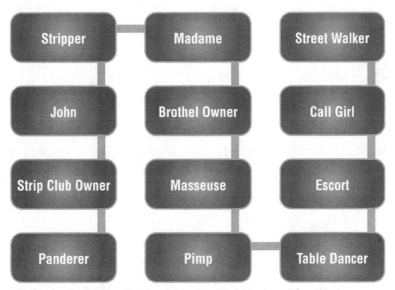

Figure 1 Numerous Entities Comprise the Industry of Sex Work.

Amid this environment of great change, the "Progressives" Jane Adams, Robert LaFollette, and others led the way in generating numerous, unprecedented social and political reforms.[22] Progressive reforms were beneficent and aimed at creating the greatest good for the greatest number. For example, the first income tax system was created in 1913 as the Sixteenth Amendment to the Constitution and Prohibition was passed in 1919 as the Eighteenth Amendment.[23] The first juvenile court was created in 1900. These and other reforms in the Progressive Era were aimed at social betterment and equality in addition to traditional notions of morality and the corresponding principles of decency.[24]

In response to prostitution-related activity around 1900 was the passage of the Mann Act of 1910.[25] This act, also known as the White Slave Traffic Act, is good law today and allowed the state to criminalize traveling with a prostitute. The law seeks to deter the evolving network of supply and demand when it comes to sex worker activities. Next, the Progressives targeted prostitutes themselves. Most American cities, including many small ones, had red-light districts and women who confined their activities to these areas could generally practice their trade free of police interference. For every famous red-light district such as San Francisco's Barbary Coast or New Orleans's 1986 Storyville, there were dozens of local red-light districts in places such as Sioux City, Iowa and Waco, Texas.[26] Although laws against prostitution, solicitation, and pandering existed, "segregated" red-light districts continued to function with the tacit consent of the police and public. With the Progressive Era, however, red-light districts were targeted as immoral and indecent with the passage of local Red Light Abatement Laws (similar to Liquor Abatement Laws). The tide of these laws was effective and few opposed them. By 1950, there were no more red-light districts in the U.S.[27]

The relationship between the military and sex workers traditionally occupies the time of policymakers. During World War I, Congress enacted several laws to regulate indecent sexual activity in military-training zones. The "Act of July 9, 1918" provided:

> During the present emergency, it shall be unlawful within such reasonable distance of any military camp, station, fort, post, canton, training or mobilization place which the Secretary of War … shall designate and publish in general orders or bulletins to engage in prostitution or to aid and abet prostitution, or to procure or solicit for the purposes of prostitution, or to keep or set up a house of ill fame, brothel, or boarding house, or to receive any person for the purpose of lewdness, assignation or prostitution into any vehicle, conveyance, place, structure, or building.[28]

Between World War I and World War II, arrests of women for prostitution fell off, and domestic and coercive sex crimes by men became more prominent in the statistics: Rape arrests doubled, sodomy arrests went up tenfold, and men started being arrested in significant numbers for offenses such as enticing girls into immoral activities. Prostitution arrests fluctuated wildly between 1921 and 1946, but arrests for rape and sodomy steadily increased. Historically, it's always a challenge for the law to figure out who is being more sexually deviant in any given period. Where prostitutes were the focus around 1900, in 1930 the buzzword was "sexual psychopath" a sensational term advanced by the psychoanalytic theories of Sigmund Freud. Freud attributed a great deal of human behavior to psychosexual development.[29]

With "perverts" taking center stage and attention to prostitutes waning, the first sexual psychopath laws were enacted in Michigan in 1935 and Illinois in 1938.[30] The Michigan law created special procedures for identifying people convicted of "disorderly conduct" and other sex offenses, who "appear to be psychopathic, or a sex degenerate" or a "sex pervert."[31] These laws chilled both sex workers and customers of the sex trade from engaging in their preferred activities for fear of a criminal prosecution.[32]

The groundbreaking work of Alfred Kinsey in 1950 tended to normalize Freud's alarming claims.[33] Nakedness and sexual desire gained greater legitimacy from Kinsey's credible academic research findings. The Free Speech era of the 1960s further legitimized nudity and sexuality and the Supreme Court opened up to defend expression in areas such as flag-burning, Vietnam War protest, and nudity. The 1960s was also an era of renaissance in artistic expression, such as nude painting and erotic pictures. This brought nudity into conflict with older legal standards and led to the important 1973 case of *Miller v. California,* a Supreme Court case that defines "obscenity" when it comes to, among other things, dancing and stripping.[34]

With a more modern society, but with not-so-modern perspectives, the Supreme Court has had difficulty with banning nudity, and instead, has tried to craft a "secondary effects" doctrine when it comes to local laws that prohibit nudity.[35] These local laws are grounded in the constitutional prerogative that the states can enact regulations that further a legitimate government interest. For example, in states that banned nude dancing, the Supreme Court upheld such restrictions as "an important or substantial governmental interest" of "protecting societal order and morality.[36] *Barnes v. Glen Theatre,* decided in 1991 after *Bowers v. Hardwick*[37] in 1986 (upholding bans of sodomy), reinforced current morals standards about what the American public considered decent, healthy, and proper.[38]

The 1991 Barnes decision, however, was not clear cut and was too conservative for many segments of society. Nine years later in 2000, the Pennsylvania Supreme Court ruled against Barnes and struck down an ordinance that banned nude dancing, stating, "we can find no point on which a majority of the Barnes Court agreed."[39] More applicable, however, is the current "secondary effects doctrine" crafted by the U.S. Supreme Court. In this doctrine, the legal focus applies less to morals and nudity and more to states' time, place, and manner restrictions when it comes to facilities of adult entertainment.[40] Some of the secondary effects recognized by the courts have included higher crime rates, a decline in real estate values, and overall neighborhood decline and the existence of these effects can justify government prohibition of an SOB.[41]

In the 21st century, prostitution, like stripping, has come to be viewed through a different lens, one more associated with public health and less laden with notions of morality. Decriminalization campaigns in the United States have grown from the sex workers' rights movement, which has advocated for decriminalization of sex work since the late 1970s.[42] The State of Nevada decriminalized prostitution in 1971, but kept it illegal in four counties in the state, including the two largest counties, Clark (Las Vegas) and Washoe (Reno).[43] Other sex worker campaigns have not been as successful. In 2004 the "Angel's Initiative" in Berkeley, California called on police to decrease the emphasis placed on the enforcement of prostitution laws, but was defeated soundly. In 2008, sex workers organized to place Proposition K on the ballot in San Francisco to eliminate the power of local police to enforce prostitution statutes against local sex workers. The proposition was defeated after securing 42 percent of the vote. Though there is considerable variation among state antiprostitution statutes, all state courts have held that laws criminalizing prostitution are constitutional. All states, at least to

Many varieties of sex work exist but so do various laws to regulate them.

some extent, also appear to view antiprostitution statutes as desirable.[44]

In response to deleterious levels of child prostitution in poverty-stricken, developing nations of the world, starting in 2003, federal sex law prohibits U.S. citizens or admitted aliens from engaging in illicit sexual conduct (such as certain sexual acts with persons under 18 years of age) in foreign nations.[45] Congress passed the prohibition on illicit sexual conduct with minors in foreign nations in 2003 as part of the Prosecutorial Remedies and Tools Against the Exploitation of Children Today Act of 2003 (PROTECT Act).[46] The PROTECT Act stiffened individual penalties for sex tourism activities by increasing the maximum imprisonment term from fifteen to thirty years.[47] The act also decreased the government's burden in prosecuting defendants accused of engaging in illicit sexual conduct in foreign states; the government is only required to show that the defendant engaged in illicit sexual conduct in a foreign place, and not that they were necessarily "traveling" to do so.[48] The Act also criminalized the activities of sex tourism operators, where such operators could act with impunity before the law was enacted.

Prostitution

When sexual contact or intercourse is performed between parties who are not friends, partners, or spouses and in exchange for an immediate fee or favor, it may be known as prostitution; illegal in all states except Nevada where it is regulated on a county-by-county basis and Rhode Island, where there is no prohibition.[49]

As with all forms of sexual expression, the contexts for prostitution-related activities abound, such as times, places, manners, and also parties such as male-to-male, or female patrons of male prostitutes.[50] There are also the more subtle contexts of escort services where nothing more happens besides an actual escort and call girls, a white-collar variation of prostitution. The overwhelming majority of cases involve female prostitutes with males as clients.

Persons who work in traditional occupations such as business or construction do not always understand why someone would sacrifice their bodily privacy and integrity for the sake of money. It should be noted that business workers and construction workers are thought to engage in their own form of sacrifice—the giving up of their time and talent for the same reason—for the sake of money. Sex workers, like other workers, are able to separate their heart from the transaction and merely do what is asked of them in order to make a living. In this sense, sex work is like any other work such as Wall Street banking, oil production, or suburban real estate development. The harms caused by the workers are overlooked for the sake of monetary gain. What makes prostitution different is an inability to legitimize the selling of one's soul for money.

In addition to traditional objections based on morality and decency, prostitutes are thought to present numerous practical nemeses to the locations where they work. Drugs and alcohol abuse can be a part of the lifestyle and further add to the objections of those with strict moral standards as well as local merchants and shopkeepers. Sexually transmitted disease and the spread of AIDS are notorious in the sex trade. The prospect of unwanted pregnancies are also an obvious potential problem inherent in the trade for sex. If the prostitute is young, pregnancy presents a question as to whether the young person can adequately care for the baby and provide financial support.

Mostly due to the nuisance-related "secondary effects" noted above, numerous forms of law exist to deter prostitution and prostitution-related activities. These statutes include:

1. **Patronizing a Prostitute** ("John"). Delaware Criminal Code: A person is guilty of patronizing a prostitute when: Pursuant to a prior agreement or understanding, the person pays a fee to another person as compensation for that person's having engaged in sexual conduct with the person.[51]

2. **Keeping a Place of Prostitution** ("Brothel" or Massage Parlor). Florida Criminal Code: It is unlawful to let or rent any place, structure, or part thereof, trailer or other conveyance, with the knowledge that it will be used for the purpose of lewdness, assignation, or prostitution.[52]

3. **Loitering for the Purpose of Engaging In or Advancing Prostitution** ("Walking the Streets"). Hawaii Criminal Code: Any person who remains or wanders about in a public place and repeatedly beckons to or repeatedly stops, or repeatedly attempts to stop, or repeatedly attempts to engage passers-by in conversation, or repeatedly stops or attempts to stop motor vehicles, or repeatedly interferes with the free passage of other persons for the purpose of committing the crime of prostitution as that term is defined in section 712-1200, shall be guilty of a violation.[53]

4. **Transportation for Purposes of Prostitution** ("Traveling with a Prostitute"). Michigan Criminal Code: Any person who shall knowingly transport or cause to be transported, or aid or assist in obtaining transportation for, by any means of conveyance, into, through or across this state, any female person for the purpose of prostitution or with the intent and purpose to induce, entice or compel such female person to become a prostitute shall be guilty of a felony, punishable by imprisonment in the state prison for not more than 20 years; any person who may commit the crime in this section mentioned may be

prosecuted, indicted, tried and convicted in any county or city in or through which he shall so transport or attempt to transport any female person as aforesaid.[54]

5. **Pimping** ("Pandering," Receive the Earnings of a Prostitute, Inducing Someone to Become a Prostitute and Remain One). Illinois Criminal Code: Any person who receives any money, property, token, object, or article or anything of value from a prostitute, not for a lawful consideration, knowing it was earned in whole or in part from the practice of prostitution, commits pimping.[55]

6. **Promoting Prostitution** ("I know where you can get a prostitute").
   Kansas Criminal Code:

   (a) Promoting prostitution is:

   (1) Establishing, owning, maintaining or managing a house of prostitution, or participating in the establishment, ownership, maintenance, or management thereof;

   (2) permitting any place partially or wholly owned or controlled by the defendant to be used as a house of prostitution;

   (3) procuring a prostitute for a house of prostitution;

   (4) inducing another to become a prostitute;

   (5) soliciting a patron for a prostitute or for a house of prostitution;

   (6) procuring a prostitute for a patron;

   (7) procuring transportation for, paying for the transportation of, or transporting a person within this state with the intention of assisting or promoting that person's engaging in prostitution; or

   (8) being employed to perform any act which is prohibited by this section.[56]

Definition of the Offense

The act or practice of engaging in sex acts for hire. The act or an instance of offering or devoting one's talent to an unworthy use or cause.[57]

Elements of the Offense

The elements of the crime of prostitution that must be proven beyond a reasonable doubt are:

1. Engaging in or offering to perform,

2. a sexual act,

3. for money.[58]

Multiple infractions may occur upon an interaction with a prostitute.

Sample Statute

The State of Nebraska prostitution statute reads as follows:

State of Nebraska Criminal Code Section 28-801: Prostitution.

(1) Any person who performs, offers, or agrees to perform any act of sexual penetration, as defined in subdivision (6) of section 28-318, with any person not his or her spouse in exchange for money or other thing of value commits prostitution.

(2) Prostitution is a Class I misdemeanor.[59]

Arguments Made By The Prosecution

Many prostitutes are street wise and familiar with how to ply their trade without breaking the law in an obvious manner. They can reconstruct a sex-for-a-fee episode into one that looks like a happy couple doing merely what many happy couples do; the exchange of money can be meant for groceries or the like. Hence, the prosecution often has actual cases of prostitution, but not that much evidence to work with. An undercover vice officer is often employed in these cases and he/she knows what to do/not do to capture the necessary evidence for a conviction. Any language that suggests sex for a fee is all it takes for the state to get a conviction.

Arguments Made By The Defense

The defense can use the letter of the law to defend these cases. Even the jury may sense guilt, but if the case does not fit the statute, the defendant can be acquitted. For example, the letter of the law states that the sex must be exchanged "for money or other thing of value." The defense can try to show that no money traded hands (the sex worker can try to collect the money at a later date), nor was any gift or favor exchanged for the sex. The defense also has a potentially strong strategy when it comes to the nature of the relationship between the two parties. The defense can argue that the two have been friends for a long time and were merely enjoying each other's company.

Variations of the Law of Prostitution

A. Walking Idly Down the Street

Municipal ordinances and state statutes govern and manage offenses related to prostitution for a variety of reasons, especially to prevent the spread of AIDS and STDs. Hence, prostitutes and their patrons, when caught in an activity prohibited by law, will be cited. What about the case of someone who looks like a prostitute, but might not be one, who is walking down the street from Point A to Point B? Can they be arrested for prostitution and related offenses? What if the police are wrong and the suspect is not a prostitute? Don't we all have the liberty right to move freely down the street without government interference? To deter activities related to prostitution, the long arm of the law reaches out relatively far.

In *People v. Smith*, a woman named Toni Smith was arrested when walking down the street, minding her own business. She was suspected by the police as being a prostitute and hence in violation of New York Penal Law 240.37, a law that prohibits loitering for purposes of prostitution.[60] The main provision of the law reads:

> 2. Any person who remains or wanders about in a public place and repeatedly beckons to, or repeatedly stops, or repeatedly attempts to stop, or repeatedly attempts to engage passers-by in conversation, or repeatedly stops or attempts to stop motor vehicles, or repeatedly interferes with the free passage of other persons, for the purpose of prostitution, or of patronizing a prostitute as those terms are defined in article two hundred thirty of the penal law, shall be guilty of a violation and is guilty of a class B misdemeanor if such person has previously been convicted of a violation of this section or of sections 230.00 or 230.05 of the penal law.

Smith had appeared to do no wrong except for walking down the street and also standing in front of an address at which there had been numerous arrests for prostitution in the past, and doing so at 2:00 a.m. She had also approached three men who walked past, touched each man's arm and said something, according to a police officer who was making observations undercover. Upon being arrested, Smith argued that the law was completely unfair and a violation of her civil liberties to walk around freely without being harassed by the police. She prepared a defense and asserted her rights during the trial. At trial, Smith prevailed and the trial court dismissed the case and found the law to be a violation of her civil liberties and of the U.S. Constitution. She argued in court:

> [The law] encourages police to use unfettered discretion in making arrests solely on circumstantial evidence, requiring them to infer criminality from wholly innocent or ambiguous activity in which free citizens must necessarily engage to lead normal lives.[61]

The state does not always appeal a case in which they lose because it becomes cost prohibitive. In this case, however, the state appealed and won; the appeals court held for the state. The case was reinstated, and 240.37 was once again ruled to be fair, valid, and constitutional. The judicial branch of government is often conservative and sides with law enforcement a lot of the time, knowing that the goal of the police is to serve and protect. The courts are also empathetic with the difficulties in trying to police activities related to prostitution and will often give the police a lot of latitude in regulating prostitution. In the Smith case, the court supported the discretionary action of the police and upheld the application of the law to Smith's walking down the street, stating:

> Hypotheticals notwithstanding, the actual observances of the police and their promulgated guidelines advising of the need for probable cause, as evidenced here, lend support to the view that officials in that calling do not regard the statute as granting them an impermissible measure of discretion. The loitering charges were reinstated and Smith must face the charges of loitering for purposes of prostitution.
>
> Section 240.37 of the Penal Law, which prohibits loitering for the purpose of engaging in a prostitution offense, does not violate the exercise of First Amendment freedoms for it is limited to behavior which has never been a form of constitutionally protected free speech.[62]

B. Gifts

Traditionally, one of the elements for a conviction for prostitution is the exchange of sex for money—a monetary transaction must occur for a conviction. Those who are experienced with the sex worker trade will never mention the words, such as "how much will the sex cost?" because that verbal statement is incontrovertible evidence of the crime of prostitution. Instead, the parties will use a type of secret language or code such as "how much money do you have?" or a similar euphemism. In addition, the money is handed from one person to another, but rather, it is placed on, for example, a table by one party, and picked up off the table by another. Both parties know how to get around the law. Each state, even in Nevada where prostitution is legal in some counties, has a slight variation on the types of activities that may or may not constitute criminality when it comes to being with, communicating with, traveling with, or having sex with a prostitute and those involved in the trade come to find out how to work with the law to avoid being arrested and convicted.

Gifts will also be used as part of a transaction in the sex worker industry. While it is common for couples to give each other gifts, and equally common for couples to engage in monogamous sex, if gifts and sex are not part of a loving relationship, and instead part of a commercial sex transaction, a criminal charge may follow. In *Muse v. U.S.* the defendant (male) and undercover police officer (female) engaged in a brief conversation while the defendant offered to give the officer a gift of a gold necklace.[63] According to the court transcript:

On Sunday June 30, 1985 ... the following conversation took place between the under-signed officer and the defendant [at the corner of 14th and Rhode Island Avenues, N.W.]:

DEF: Hi you want to buy some gold?

OFF: No.

DEF: Well do you think I can give you some gold for a date?

OFF: I don't know.

DEF: I need some loving and I think you will get a good deal and so will I.

OFF: Is that so. I don't think my man would like that.

DEF: Is that your man over there?

OFF: Yes, it is.

DEF: I'll go and ask him myself ... Defendant then engaged in a conversation with [the observer]. Defendant then responds back to the undersigned officer after the conversa-tion ends.

DEF: Your man says it's alright. He gives you the green light.

OFF: What exactly do you want?

DEF: I want to have sex. I want to make love to you.

OFF: Okay.

DEF: The defendant gives the undersigned officer the chain of yellow metal rope type and says let's go. While the undersigned officer and the defendant walk north on 14th St. N.W., [the two observers] approach him and he is placed under arrest.[64]

The accused was convicted at trial and appealed the conviction, stating that a conviction for soliciting a prostitute has to include the offer to exchange money and does not include gifts. The court record states:

While acknowledging that he gave the undercover police officer a gold necklace in ex-change for anticipated sexual intercourse, appellant argues that insufficient evidence supported his conviction because, he asserts, the term 'fee' in D.C. Code § 22-2701.1(1) refers only to money.[65]

The appeals court disagreed and made direct reference to the legal precedent and the prostitution laws of the District of Columbia and stated:

> Our cases have repeatedly recognized that solicitation for purposes of prostitution involves 'an invitation to commercial sexual intercourse' in the context of a purely commercial venture. Here, appellant offered to exchange his gold necklace for a 'date' with the undercover police officer. Appellant's statement, 'I need some loving and I think you will get a good deal and so will I,' clearly illustrates the commercial nature of the proposed exchange. Although no money was involved in appellant's suggested bargain, this transaction is precisely the type of purely commercial exchange of sexual acts for a 'fee that is encompassed by the definition of prostitution in D.C. Code § 22-2701.1(1). Conviction affirmed.[66]

C. Outrageous Government Conduct Defense

Only a few defenses are available to defendants charged with prostitution. Those defenses typically include that the parties are married to each other and are not strangers, police entrapment, and that the police coerced the transaction. In this case, the defendant raised the defense of "outrageous government conduct."[67]

The police need to have the flexibility to investigate cases, but when law enforcement exceeds its mandate and becomes reckless, the courts will dismiss the case, even if the defendant is otherwise culpable. In this manner, the courts are a check and balance on the power of the state. In *Commonwealth of Pennsylvania v. Sun Cha Chon*, a massage parlor and salon owner supervised several employees who provided massages to fee-paying clients of the salon. The owner of the salon arranged for his employees to offer clients sex after receiving a massage, an illegal practice in the massage industry that has a long history.[68] Some massage parlors are better known for their sex services than for their massages, while other massage parlors have nothing to do with sex-for-a-fee services. Anecdotal evidence indicates that massages and sex are referred to as a massage with a "happy ending." These episodes are illegal in most every state and constitute the crime of prostitution. Salon owners who permit such practices in their salon can be guilty of the promotion of prostitution. Many salon owners do it anyway and consider the price of the conviction merely another cost of doing business.

The relationship between the police, sex workers, and their customers is uneasy. The police are frustrated with the nuisance crimes of prostitutes and johns.

© Jack Dagley Photography, 2011. Used under license from Shutterstock, Inc.

The police who were involved in the Sun Cha Chon case merely had to use one undercover officer with a hidden microphone to obtain sufficient evidence for an arrest and conviction, but the police went way beyond this standard operating procedure. They contacted a local patron of the salon, someone who frequented the salon for a massage and sexual favors. The patron was provided with various sums of money by the police who then instructed the patron to enter the premises, receive a massage, and after the massage, engage in sexual intercourse with the masseuse. The police authorized this activity on four separate occasions when a single episode was hardly necessary. Authorizing and orchestrating this type of transaction is a distinct violation of professional policing ethics because it fosters criminal offending (rather than decreasing crime, it increases crime) and the police have numerous alternatives at their disposal. The police should never commit a crime to solve a crime. Doing so is reckless and abusive police work.

The police also paid their insurgent a fee of $180 for the man's trouble (in addition to paying for his massage and sex).[69] Apparently, the officers did this for a few laughs.[70] Many observers were incensed that the police would support an action where a low-income, young female would be subject to the abuse of sexual intercourse with a complete stranger for the purposes of fighting crime. The woman was not only used by the john, she was used by the police as well. During the trial, the trial court judge allowed a female expert witness to testify that "when police officers act as johns, and they traumatize an individual unnecessarily, it's outrageous."[71]

The salon owner was charged and wisely, his attorney insisted on a trial, where the details of the case were explained to the judge. The trial court judge dismissed the case based on "outrageous government conduct." The State appealed and the appellate court judge also dismissed the case (affirmed the trial court order) on the basis of outrageous government conduct/denial of due process for the accused. Knowing that the judicial branch of government is often partial to the State, the State appealed again, this time to the Pennsylvania Supreme Court (specifically referred to as the Pennsylvania Superior Court). Once again affirming the dismissal of an otherwise guilty defendant, the court stated:

> The [appeals] court upheld the trial judge's determination that the case required dismissal for a violation of defendant's due process rights predicated on outrageous government conduct in its investigation of the spa. The court agreed with the trial judge's

finding that the police used sex as a weapon in its investigatory arsenal, that they permitted the sex to continue even after having enough evidence for an arrest, and that the sexual conduct was entwined with the investigation. The court noted that the mere agreement to perform sexual acts for money would have satisfied the statute for which defendant was charged and would have permitted the police to secure a search warrant. The dismissal of the case is affirmed.[72]

Additional Court Cases: Prostitution
Harwell v. State
821 N.E.2d 381 (2004)

CASE SUMMARY

PROCEDURAL POSTURE: Defendant appealed her conviction by the Marion Superior Court (Indiana) for prostitution. Defendant argued that the State did not present sufficient evidence to sustain her conviction for prostitution.

OVERVIEW: A police officer stopped at the side of the road and inquired if defendant needed a ride. Without responding, defendant entered the car and asked the officer was a police officer. After denying he was a police officer, the officer specified he was looking for fellatio. Although defendant agreed to perform fellatio, she refused to discuss money. Instead, she directed the officer toward an alley. When they arrived in the alley, the officer asked defendant if the act would be more than $20. Defendant simply responded "no." The officer then arrested defendant. Defendant argued that she never agreed to accept money. The appellate court held that by indicating that the sexual service would not be more expensive than $20, defendant emitted an inference that there was a cost involved and that she would accept money. Thus, a meeting of the minds existed between the officer and defendant that she would perform fellatio for money, with a more specific price to be determined somewhere between one penny and $20, but definitely not more than $20. There was substantial evidence of probative value to support the judgment of the trial court.

OUTCOME: The judgment of the trial court was affirmed.[73]

Pimping

Somehow assisting a woman, or anyone, to get involved in a commercial transaction for sex can result in a charge of "pimping." Pimping is known legally as "pandering" and can include the related offenses of "human trafficking" and "solicitation" cases.[74] Typically, pimping is to encourage or induce someone to be a prostitute/sex worker.[75] Stereotypically, pimps are men who control female sex workers through intimidation and coercion. A pimp will inflict physical injury on a sex worker who fails to abide by his orders and the woman feels helpless to do anything about it. However, since a pimp need only encourage or assist in an act of prostitution performed by someone else, a brothel owner or manager is also a pimp and can be found guilty of pandering.

Pimps such as a brothel owner, manager of a massage parlor, or local drug lord expand the network of customers for sex workers. A lone sex worker may not be able to generate as much business on their own, but can increase the volume of sales with the help of others, such as a pimp. In some cases, the sex worker owes a debt of gratitude to the pimp for introducing the sex worker to wealthy clients that the sex worker would otherwise have never met. In other cases, the pimp stands in the way of the sex worker being able to earn more than they would without the pimp since the pimp will always take a cut of the profits and may not allow the sex worker to visit certain wealthy clients.[76]

Since prostitution is illegal in most parts of the U.S., a pimp has a great deal of latitude when it comes to orders and demands placed upon the sex worker. A prostitute cannot file a grievance with the local labor board or even go to the police, but rather is at the mercy of the pimp. This painful form of pseudo-servitude is why many people call for the decriminalization of sex work.[77] If a sex worker were employed in a licensed facility, the owner of the facility would be legally obligated to provide healthy and safe working conditions and a failure to do so would result in a fine or worse.

Pimping can mean profits and prestige for persons otherwise eclipsed from the legal job market.

© emin kuliyev, 2011. Used under license from Shutterstock, Inc.

Definition of the Offense

[An] Illinois statute describes two kinds of panderers, one being someone who merely "arranges" a situation in which a person may practice prostitution and the other being someone who "compels" a person to become a prostitute. Although both types of panderers must act "for money" and both are guilty of Class 4 felonies in Illinois if they do so, it is obvious that the "compeller" is a more serious violator of the law than a mere "arranger."[78]

Elements of the Offense

The elements of the crime of pimping that must be proven beyond a reasonable doubt are:

1. causes, induces, persuades, or encourages,
2. a female,
3. to engage in an act of prostitution.
4. The consent or willingness of the female is immaterial.[78]

Sample Statute

The state of Arizona pimping statute reads as follows:

> Arizona Revised Statutes, Title 13 Criminal Law. Chapter 32 Prostitution. § 13-3209. Pandering; definitions; methods; classification.
>
> A person is guilty of a class 5 felony who knowingly:
>
> (1) Places any person in the charge or custody of any other person for purposes of prostitution.
>
> (2) Places any person in a house of prostitution with the intent that such person lead a life of prostitution.
>
> (3) Compels, induces or encourages any person to reside with that person, or with any other person, for the purpose of prostitution.
>
> (4) Compels, induces or encourages any person to lead a life of prostitution.[79]

Arguments Made By The Prosecution

The language of pimping and pandering statutes favors the state. Any type of "encouragement" by one party toward someone inclined to prostitution is all it takes for a conviction. Of course, an undercover officer posing as a prostitute is a strong law enforcement strategy for the state. The state holds a few other cards as well. If a prostitute went through with an act of prostitution due to the encouragement from the pimp, the state can offer a reduced or dismissed charge to the prostitute in exchange for her testimony that the pimp encouraged her.

Arguments Made By The Defense

Pimps, like prostitutes, are not exactly sympathetic witnesses and the jury smells guilt right away. An accused pimp can always argue that it is not illegal to carry on a conversation with someone. But if that someone happens to be a prostitute, the circumstantial evidence is certainly incriminating. The pimp can also try to show he has a job or other forms of legal income, and therefore, would never be someone who needs to work in the world of prostitution.

Variations of the Law of Pimping

A. Human Trafficking

The seriousness of human trafficking spans a long time and is still a critical problem around the world.[81] Human trafficking can refer to forced labor or slavery, but for purposes of this chapter refers to the trafficking in persons for purposes of prostitution. Victims of human trafficking for sex are generally found in dire circumstances and become targeted by traffickers, known as pimps. Individuals, circumstances, and situations vulnerable to the exploitive practices of traffickers include homeless individuals, runaway teens, refugees, and drug addicts. While it may seem like trafficked people are the most vulnerable, victims are consistently exploited from any ethnic and social background.[82]

Traffickers, also known as pimps or madams, exploit the lack of opportunities of the victim, while offering promises of things such as marriage, employment, education, and/or an overall better life. However, in the end, traffickers usually force the victims to become prostitutes or work in the sex industry and provide nothing in return. Victims are hunted down and punished if they refuse to cooperate with the traffickers. Various work in the sex industry includes prostitution, dancing in strip clubs, performing in pornographic films and pornography, and other forms of demeaning and involuntary servitude.

"White Slave Traffic" is synonymous with human trafficking, but is an older and controversial term that refers to the alleged indiscretion of traveling with a woman who may be a prostitute, or a girlfriend, or just a friend who is unmarried. "White Slave Traffic" is a term created during the Purity Movement of the Progressive Era from 1900 to 1920, the White Slave Traffic Act (also known as the Mann Act)[83] was passed in response to social hysteria over an influx of immigration and unprecedented period of industrialization in the U.S. At the time, prostitution flourished in the chaos of teeming cities like Chicago and Boston where thousands of newly arrived immigrants looked for ways to spend their money after working all day in a factory.

The Mann Act is a federal statute making it a crime to transport a woman across state lines for "immoral" purposes.[84] At the time, self-seeking journalists and politicians claimed that girls and women were being forced into prostitution by unscrupulous pimps and procurers. The term "white slavery" became a sensational and popular term to describe the predicament these females faced. It was alleged that evil men were tricking, coercing, and drugging females to get them involved in prostitution and then forcing them to stay in brothels (what could be more dramatic for the public to contemplate?). Hence, the Mann Act targeted these alleged provocateurs, but also the females who worked as prostitutes. New immigrants also included single females who chose to live single, something that ran quite contrary to the moralism of the time. The Progressives equated a woman who enjoyed a sex life to be about the equivalent of a prostitute. In sum, the Mann Act was a tool to criminalize any consensual sex between unmarried persons as well as a tool for the government to harass people it did not approve of morally. Famous actor Charlie Chaplin traveled with his girlfriend and was arrested under the Mann Act, and singer Chuck Berry went on a weekend vacation with his long-term, committed partner and was arrested under the Mann Act.[85]

Because of its inherent biases mentioned above, the Mann Act was challenged all the way to the Supreme Court.[86] In *Caminetti v. United States*, Drew Caminetti, the son of a prominent California politician, and a friend, Maury Diggs, both married but having respective affairs with women, took their mistresses by train from Sacramento to Reno. Their betrayed wives found out about the caper and tipped off the police. Both men were arrested on their arrival in Reno. Caminetti and Diggs were tried and found guilty under the Mann Act for transporting unmarried women across state lines for

Neglected and abandoned teenage girls are prime targets for human traffickers.

"an immoral purpose." Caminetti and Diggs appealed their conviction, arguing that "an immoral purpose" lacks specific meaning, there was no type of commercialized sex, monetary payments, or any form of fee-for-service transaction taking place. The defendants were confused as to what they were guilty of since they were merely traveling with the women. The Supreme Court stated:

> The power of Congress under the commerce clause, including as it does authority to regulate the interstate transportation of passengers and to keep the channels of interstate commerce free from immoral and injurious uses, enables it to forbid the interstate transportation of women and girls for the immoral purposes of which the petitioners were convicted in these cases. Pecuniary gain, either as a motive for the transportation or as an attendant of its object, is not an element in the offenses defined. Convictions affirmed.[87]

B. Inchoate Crimes: Attempted Pandering

In the most basic case, it is not easy to know the role a panderer plays in a case of prostitution. Even in clear-cut cases of pandering, the evidence is relative easy to challenge and many panderers are able to get acquitted. Pandering raises many questions. When a pimp tries to get a woman to work as a prostitute, how can it be proven conclusively that it was the pimp that was the main influence? How do we know that the woman did not decide by herself, independent of external influences? To what degree do our friends and acquaintances determine our actions and behaviors? To ascribe a large role to the pimp is to say that the prostitute is incapable of deciding for herself.

If pandering cases can be legally tricky, attempted pandering cases can be even trickier. Attempt (or inchoate offense) cases require evidence that shows that some "overt act" was taken in furtherance of the commission of some criminal act. The "overt act" is a necessary element of any attempt offense. Even if a suspect never commits the act, they can be found guilty of attempting to commit the act, so long as an "overt act" was taken to perpetrate the offense. In a case involving attempted pandering, the evidence must show that some overt act was taken to influence a sex worker to take on clients as a prostitute. In such a case, not only can the alleged panderers deny any such attempt ever took place, but even if an overt act was committed, how can it be proved that such an act could ever be one in furtherance of prostitution if the prostitution never took place? Those were the lines of defense used to appeal the conviction in the following case.

In *People v. Charles,* a husband and wife team agreed with each other to try and induce and persuade two local cocktail waitresses to be "call girls" at their Los Angeles "call house" to "meet, entertain, and have intercourse with the call at the house."[88] The defendant husband and wife spoke to the two girls on five separate occasions about the plans, including a 60/40 split of the fees (60 percent to the house, 40 percent to the sex workers).

The two women never went to the house and never had sex with any of the Charles' house calls—were never prostitutes. Instead, the two women went to the police where a sting operation was arranged. At a predetermined location, all of the parties assembled to discuss the plans, at which time the police recorded the conversation and after, made the arrests. The Charles' were convicted at trial for attempted pandering. They appealed and argued that the evidence was not sufficient to prove an attempt to commit the offense of pandering. They stated that the evidence only shows intention and preparation but does not show the existence of a house of prostitution and the placement of the females therein, which, they claimed, are necessary factors in proof of the offense charged.[89] The appeals court did not buy their arguments and upheld and affirmed the convictions, stating:

> In the instant case the evidence shows that the defendants, by their promises to split the fees on a sixty-forty basis, of a $50 guarantee, and to furnish transportation, by their telephone calls, by their visits, and otherwise, attempted to persuade and encourage the two waitresses to become inmates of a house of prostitution and would have succeeded in doing so except for the latter's refusal to participate in the proposed plan; thus proves that the defendants had a specific intent to commit the offense of pandering

as described in clauses (a) and (b) of section 266i; establishes direct, unequivocal acts toward that end; and supports the verdict returned by the jury.[90]

C. "Johns"—Solicitation of a Prostitute

"John" is the euphemism applied to men who solicit prostitutes for sex for a fee. Johns are easy prey for the police and, similar to the new generation of men who solicit minors over the Internet for sex, johns always seem to forget they could be talking to a police officer when they ask a sex worker for sex for a fee. In most states, johns can be convicted of solicitation—the act of directing or asking someone to exchange money for sexual activity. Johns contribute to a crime problem by fostering prostitution and the associated risks of STDs, unwanted pregnancies, marital infidelity and female oppression.

Since Johns also compel, induce, or encourage prostitution, they can be charged as a panderer instead of a solicitor or possibly both. The exact charge will depend on the statutes of the state in which the episode occurred. In *Turner v. State,* the defendant propositioned an undercover police officer for sex in exchange for money.[91] He was arrested for the offense of pandering pursuant to the criminal laws of the state of Georgia.[92] Easily convicted at trial, the defendant appealed, stating that the pandering laws were a violation of his rights to due process and equal protection as guaranteed by the U.S. Constitution.

Specifically, Turner took aim at gender inequality. He argued that the pandering law only applies to males and does not apply to females and thus reinforces harmful stereotypes about men, women, and sex. He argued,

> the pandering statute is based upon the outmoded beliefs that males are more sexually aggressive and that females are more embarrassed by sexual advances. Hence, it is claimed, this gender classification rests only upon "old notions," "archaic and overbroad" generalizations, and "the baggage of sexual stereotypes," prohibited by rulings in other court cases.[93]

The appeals court judge took judicial notice of the argument but was not about to dismiss the case on the basis of gender-specifics since many laws apply to one gender and not the other or are disproportionate to one gender rather than the other. In addition, the appeals court cited precedent set by the U.S. Supreme Court while crafting the argument that females are already socially stigmatized and thus deterred from approaching male prostitutes and that is why the Georgia pandering law applies only to males—because the law does not need to be applied to females. The court upheld the conviction and stated:

Johns are illegal in 48 out of 50 states and highly regulated in the other two.

At stake is more than the 'embarrassment by sexual advances,' to which the appellants allude. As Justice Stewart's concurring opinion in *Michael M.*, 67 LE2d 437, supra, p. 449, points out, 'the pregnant unmarried female confronts problems more numerous and more severe than any faced by her male partner. She alone endures the medical risks of pregnancy or abortion. She suffers disproportionately the social, educational, and emotional consequences of pregnancy.' Justice Rehnquist observes in *Michael M.*, id., p. 445, that 'the risk of pregnancy itself constitutes a substantial deterrence to … females. No similar natural sanctions deter males. A criminal sanction imposed solely on males thus serves to roughly 'equalize' the deterrents on the sexes.' Moreover, besides the above risks, prostitution exposes the female to risks of physical harm and sexual violence (to which she is more susceptible than are males) and contracting (and consequent transmittal) of venereal disease.[94]

Additional Court Cases: Pimping

People v. Hashimoto

54 Cal. App. 3d 862 (1976)

CASE SUMMARY

PROCEDURAL POSTURE: Defendant appealed from the judgment of the Superior Court of Los Angeles County (California), which convicted him in a nonjury trial for pandering in violation of Cal. Penal Code § 266i, which statute condemned, among other things, the inducing, persuading or encouraging a female to become a prostitute.

OVERVIEW: Defendant was convicted of pandering in violation of Cal. Penal Code § 266i. The statute condemns, among other things, the inducement, persuasion, or encouragement of a female to become a prostitute. An officer represented herself to be a model. Defendant asked for a telephone number that he would provide to clients of the Japan Travel Bureau that desired to obtain her services as a prostitute. According to defendant's proposal, the officer would have sex with Japanese tourists. Defendant's interest in the plan was not the receipt of any remuneration but rather the satisfaction of the travel agency's clientele by augmenting the usual services that were offered. The court affirmed because the absence of financial gain was not fatal to the conviction because the statute covered all ramifications of the evil of the crime. The court found that the evidence supported the conviction and that the statute was not vague or overbroad because the statute was not susceptible to being interpreted to cover any activity beyond that of pandering and defendant's conduct met the commonly accepted definitions of the words of the statute.

OUTCOME: The court affirmed the judgment of the trial court, convicting defendant of pandering because it found that the evidence at trial was sufficient for the conviction even though defendant was not to receive any money from prostitution. The court also found that the statute was not unconstitutionally vague or over broad because it was not reasonably susceptible of being interpreted to cover any activity beyond that involved in the evil of pandering.[95]

Stripping/Nudity

Sex work in the adult entertainment industry often takes the form of partially nude or fully nude performances and the Supreme Court has consistently held that certain forms of **nude** dancing are expressive conduct protected by the First Amendment.[96] Facilitating the relative popularity of this form of sex work is that **stripping** and seminude dancing is legal, but regulated, throughout the United States, often with statutes pertaining to indecent exposure. Stripping has a long history, even gaining mention in Biblical accords, and is related to European and American burlesque, a form of dancing that is provocative and oriented to art and literary themes.[97] More closely related to sex work, stripping is also a part of striptease, an artistic performance by an "erotic dancer" who gradually undresses in a seductive and sexually explicit manner for the entertainment of the audience.[98]

Obviously, stripping and public nudity are more innocent than prostitution or pimping in that it is legal everywhere and does not involve any touching, nor any fondling or coercive sexual intercourse. Stripping and public displays of nudity are nevertheless meticulously regulated. For example, some cities have a "six foot rule" where it is illegal for a member of the audience to move closer than six feet to the dancer.[99] Other jurisdictions allow members of the audience to get close enough to the dancer solely for purposes of placing money in his/her belt/strap. If any form of sexual touching, caressing, or fondling were to occur, the episode would immediately rise to a case of prostitution. Hence, men's clubs, or male dancers for a bachelorette party are careful to keep the event one strictly for purposes of entertainment and not sexual contact.

Stripping, lapdances, or similar performances may be done at a gathering in the privacy of someone's home, at a private club, public club, or even large auditorium. Wherever stripping occurs, the event must obtain a form of licensure and approval from the local government or the dance can cross the line and be illegal and subject to criminal sanction.[100] As an example, it is illegal to undress (strip) on a public street (charged as lewdness or public indecency), but legal to do so in a legally authorized enclosed structure where minors are not present and the ages of the patrons are confirmed prior to admission to the event.

Other legal regulations across the U.S. include the requirement that females cover breast nipples with pasties, although males do not have to do the same.[101] Some cities and counties allow for fully nude dances where a license has been granted, while others require the dancer to wear a g-string to cover the penis or vaginal area. Lastly, some jurisdictions regulate poses. For example, the spreading of the dancer's legs can cross the line from performance art to indecent expression and is thusly regulated by law.[102] As the quote on the first page of the chapter refers to, nudity is a form of speech or expression protected by the First Amendment. However, state and federal courts permit all jurisdictions to highly regulate nudity.[103]

Aside from the work of strippers who perform for a fee, nudity in public by anyone is highly regulated by law as is any form of sex with oneself or a partner in public. As a historical matter of law and policy, nudity and sex in public are aggressively regulated by the state to protect minors who may see it and adults who don't want to see it. The display of nude body parts without a permit, or outside in public view may be criminalized in a variety of ways, such as with laws pertaining to "open lewdness" or "nuisance." Older statutes were titled "Lewd and Lascivious Behavior" or even "Appearing on the Highway in Bathing Garb."[104] Some jurisdictions can use a "lewdness" law to prohibit, for example, nude sun bathing on a public beach where such nudity is legally prohibited. Nude sunbathing in the privacy of one's backyard may be criminal if minors or adults could somehow see it. In cases of a "flasher" or "streaker" where an individual appears to derive satisfaction from an abrupt and unexpected display of nudity, the offender will have engaged in a more threatening and sexually aggressive act and therefore may be diagnosed as an exhibitionist (paraphiliac) and charged pursuant to a public lewdness or indecent exposure statute. Lewdness, indecency, vulgarity, lasciviousness, and obscenity take on similar meanings when it comes to sexual deviancy. The bottom line is that nudity and sex in public are highly regulated and always have been in the U.S.[105]

A conviction for indecent exposure or related activity relies primarily on three elements:[106]

1. **Intent.** The nudity must be deliberate, purposeful, and intentional. Accidents, wardrobe malfunctions, etc., are insufficient to establish intent. In general, the state can demonstrate willfulness and intent in one of two ways: (1) the exposure occurs in a place "so public that it must be presumed it was intended to be seen by others," or (2) the exposure is "accompanied by some action by which [the accused] draws attention to his exposed condition." Singer and actress Janet Jackson accidentally exposed one of her breasts during a 2009 performance at a Super Bowl football game watched by millions

of viewers. Her nudity was deemed an accident and, thus, she did not face charges for indecent exposure.

2. **Indecent.** The exposure must be grossly vulgar, obscene, and repugnant to common propriety, and one that tends to excite lust, and deprave the morals with respect to sexuality. Various gesticulations or the simulation of obvious sexual acts are good examples of "indecent." Jim Morrison, a famous and notorious rock star blatantly simulated acts of fellatio and masturbation, as well as exposing his penis during a musical performance by The Doors in 1969. Since the event was licensed solely for musical entertainment, he was charged with lewd and lascivious behavior and indecent exposure and convicted.

3. **Public View.** To make out the element of public view, first, the nudity must occur in a public place. This obviously includes public lands or public buildings, but also includes those "places so public and open … that they are certain to be observed by the general population." Courts also recognize that indecent exposure can occur in private locations, such as inside a privately owned home; however, the conduct must be "in the view of the public." The focus of the offense is on the victim, not the location of the crime.

Bearing in mind the three-part analysis above, is revealing female breasts in public against the law? What if it is done for sunbathing in one's backyard? In a strip club? How about a mother breastfeeding her newborn in a shopping mall? What if only part of the breast is visible, such as with a low-cut sweater? What if part of the areola is showing? These are always challenging questions for the law to address.

Legal regulation of nudity is conducted state-by-state and city-by-city. In a narrow majority of cities and states (approximately thirty states), the showing of a female breast in public is a violation of the law and charged as lewdness, indecency, or nuisance. Since breastfeeding mothers could be charged (but may not be convicted) under the thirty state laws, nearly every state legislature has affirmatively passed a law that specifically allows for breastfeeding in public.

Having Sex in Public? Nudity on a beach, in a cocktail bar, at a summer music festival, etc., is distinguished from sexual contact or sexual interactions with oneself or a partner in public. Sexual contact on a nude beach, for example, is an easier case to analyze because having sex in public is rarely, but sometimes, allowed depending on the jurisdiction, and therefore has some legitimacy in the Constitution.

Public sexual activity is risky legally and will fall within the classification of crimes known as "indecent exposure" or "public lewdness."[107] Having sex in locations such as a hotel elevator, empty subway car, back seat of a cab, restaurant

Sex in public, such as in an automobile parked on the street, is rarely permissible as a matter of law.

© YanLev, 2011. Used under license from Shutterstock, Inc.

bathroom, business office, or under a blanket in a park invite a different legal sanction from mere nudity.

Sexual contact in public nevertheless has defenders. Meaning, some argue that consensual sex between adults in public should have the backing of the Constitution under a right of privacy. The Supreme Court has yet to rule on the matter. While it is legal for two unrelated adults to verbally agree to have sex without a fee, a verbal agreement is different from actual touching. In 2007, a U.S. senator from Idaho, Larry Craig, was arrested for lewdness when he solicited a police officer to have sex in a stall in a public restroom in the Minneapolis–St. Paul Airport facility.[108] At the time, Craig was a husband and father of three children.[109] Craig entered a guilty plea to a lesser charge of disorderly conduct and announced his intention to resign from the Senate.[110] Since it is legal for two adults to discuss being together sexually, why wasn't Craig's gesture also protected speech?

In addition, in *State v. Bryant*, the Minnesota Supreme Court ruled that two men engaged in sexual activity in a department store restroom with the stall door closed had a reasonable expectation of privacy. The court held that the men were acting in a private, not public space.[111] In *State v. Limberhand*, the defendant was arrested for masturbating in a closed toilet stall. The court there found that the defendant had a legitimate expectation of privacy in a closed toilet stall and that a police officer's warrantless observation of him from an adjoining stall violated his privacy interests.[112] While some cases have found a legal right to public sex, the favorable court rulings arguably are inconsistent with the laws covering nudity in public.

Definition of the Offense

Except where licensed and legally authorized, variations on the form of nudity may be defined as:

I. Nudity

   (A) the appearance of a human bare buttock, anus, male genitals, female genitals, or female breast; or

   (B) a state of dress that fails to opaquely cover a human buttock, anus, male genitals, female genitals, or any part of the female breast below the top of the areola.

II. Seminudity a state of dress in which clothing covers no more than the genitals, pubic region, buttocks, and any part of the female breast below the top of the areolae.

III. Simulated Nudity a state of dress in which any device or covering, exposed to view, is worn that simulates any part of the genitals, buttocks, pubic region, or any part of the female breast below the top of the areolae.[113]

Elements of the Offense

The elements of the crime of public indecency that must be proven beyond a reasonable doubt are:

1. Exposes his person, or the private parts thereof;

2. in any public place, or in any place where there are present other persons to be offended or annoyed thereby;

3. procures, counsels, or assists any person so to expose himself or take part in any model artist exhibition, or to make any other exhibition of himself to public view, or the view of any number of persons, such as is offensive to decency, or is adapted to excite to or thoughts or acts, is guilty of a misdemeanor.[114]

Sample Statute

The State of Indiana Indecent Exposure statute reads as follows:

Public indecency; indecent exposure: Sec. 1.

(a) A person who knowingly or intentionally, in a public place:

    (1) engages in sexual intercourse;

    (2) engages in deviate sexual conduct;

    (3) appears in a state of nudity; or

    (4) fondles the genitals of himself or another person; commits public indecency, a Class A misdemeanor.

(b) Nudity' means the showing of the human male or female genitals, pubic area, or buttocks with less than a fully opaque covering, the showing of the female breast with less than a fully opaque covering of any part of the nipple, or the showing of the covered male genitals in a discernibly turgid state.[115]

Arguments Made By The Prosecution

In a sense, there is not much question about someone who is nude in public where such nudity is prohibited. Since the prosecution is not going to take a case of someone, for example, wearing a low cut blouse, the state will be working with a case of someone flagrantly nude and that is all that is necessary for a conviction. Examples of cases the state will take are streakers and exhibitionists. These types of cases are easy for the state to get a conviction, especially if an audience is present because the audience would all be eyewitnesses.

Arguments Made By The Defense

Outside of obvious cases of streakers and exhibitionists, the defense can always use the strategy of intent. Meaning, the defense can argue that the accused was nude, but did not enter a nude state knowingly or intentionally to be nude, but rather, was merely changing one's clothes at the time. The defense may also try the strategy of "ignorance of the law" and say that s/he didn't know nudity was illegal in the location of the episode. Lastly, the defense may try to argue that the pants were baggy and fell down by accident or that the blouse unbuttoned by accident, etc.

Variations of the Law of Stripping/Nudity

A. Indecent Exposure

Nudity in public where children and others are present is typically referred to as "indecent exposure" or "public indecency" and was a criminal offense at common law. Common law "prohibited the public exhibition of a person's private parts which instinctive modesty, human decency, or self-respect requires to be customarily kept covered in the presence of others."[116] Although such laws are more relaxed today, as a general matter, the law seeks to protect the public from shocking and embarrassing public displays of sexual body parts. Indecent exposure statutes reflect a general moral disapproval of people appearing in the nude among strangers in public places.[117]

The display of naked body parts may be done only where the law allows, such as at a specially designated beach. Signage is usually required and thus the public (and their children) has notice to avoid the area if they do not wish to view public nudity. It should be noted that the Constitution does not guarantee a right to nudity in public places and defers to local laws. Local cities and towns may allow for public nudity if the context is created in a reasonable manner. As discussed above, certain adult entertainment facilities or SOBs may obtain a legal permit to allow nude dancing, within certain legal limits and regulations. The same is true for nude beaches for swimming or sunbathing. Local laws apply and nudity or "clothing-optional" areas are only permitted in specially designated areas and are otherwise regulated by law. In addition, each jurisdiction will regulate specific forms of nudity (topless, partially topless, etc.).[118]

As a general matter, opinions vary, but many women find it odd that men can walk around in public barechested but women cannot. In *People v. Santorelli*, Romona Santorelli enjoyed a warm afternoon in Rochester Park in New York City barechested with four female friends who were also barechested.[119] All five individuals were sitting together minding their own business, not flaunting their nudity, when a passing police officer noticed the nudity and cited all five women. The women were arrested and convicted under N.Y. State Penal Law § 245.01 Exposure of a Person:

> A person is guilty of exposure if he [or she] appears in a public place in such a manner that the private or intimate parts of his body are unclothed or exposed. For purposes of this section, the private or intimate parts of a female person shall include that portion of the breast which is below the top of the areola. This section shall not apply to the breastfeeding of infants or to any person entertaining or performing in a play, exhibition, show or entertainment.[120]

Romona Santorelli was convicted in Rochester Municipal Court and ordered to pay a small fine. She appealed to the Monroe County Court and the county held for her and dismissed the charges. The People (in this case, the City of Rochester) appealed to the New York State version of their Supreme Court (the New York Appeals Court).

Santorelli argued that the law was a violation of her equal protection with men, and therefore violated her right to Equal Protection as guaranteed by the U.S. Constitution.[121] The New York Appeals Court held for Santorelli, dismissed her citation, and made female topless nudity legal throughout the state of New York. The court reasoned:

Where authorized, public nakedness is legal, but public sexual acts are almost always illegal.

> Appellants and the five other women who were ar-rested with them were prosecuted for doing some-thing that would have been permissible, or at least not punishable under the penal laws, if they had been men—they removed their tops in a public park, exposing their breasts in a manner that all agree was neither lewd nor intended to annoy or harass. ... Since the statute prohibits the public exposure of female—but not male—breasts, it betrays an underlying legislative assumption that the sight of a female's uncovered breast in a public place is offensive to the average person in a way that the sight of a male's uncovered breast is not. It is this assumption that lies at the root of the statute's constitutional problem. ... Defendants contend that apart from entrenched cultural expectations, there is really no objective reason why the exposure of female breasts should be considered any more offensive than the exposure of the male counterparts. They offered proof that, from an anatomical standpoint, the female breast is no more or less a sexual organ than is the male equivalent. ... Accordingly, the gender-based classification established by Penal Law § 245.01 violates appellants' equal protection rights and, for that reason, I concur in the majority's result and vote to reverse the order.[122]

B. Lewd Performance

The use of dance to express a sexual message has existed for quite some time. In Biblical times, Salome, daughter of Herodias, danced for King Herod in a provocative manner that persuaded Herod to offer her anything she desired, even half of his kingdom. In other ancient societies, dance was used as a way to encourage marriage and procreation. Nude dancing at strip clubs has also existed for a long time and has been recognized by the Supreme Court as a valid form of communication subject to First Amendment protection.[123]

Indoors or outside, for a few friends or for a large audience, any type of dance or performance that comes up to the line of being overly sexually suggestive can constitute a criminal offense, even when legally permissible at the start of the performance, but which later turns obscene. This includes pole dances, strip shows, table dancing, or a bachelor party in a private home. Under these circumstances, the activity/performance began as a legal interaction but became illegal over the course of the performance. About the only fool-proof legal way to perform an erotic dance with no suspicion of illegality is to do so for one's spouse in the privacy of their home with no other persons able to observe.[124] When a sex-related performance is conducted for an audience, the performance is legally bound to its artistic components and cannot cross the line to becoming obscene and, hence, illegal.

In *Morris v. U.S.,* a performer named "Carroll" was hired for a fee by the owner ("Morris") of the Gaiety Theatre in Washington, D.C. to provide a strip tease dance and performance for an audience interested in adult entertainment at an SOB.[125] Once underway, the event and performance proceeded as expected and during the performance, Carroll stripped naked and provided various forms of dance movements, gesticulations, and postures one would expect at a strip show. In the audience were two undercover police officers who observed the performance, found several legal objections to the stage act, and immediately arrested the actress Carroll for engaging in the presentation of an indecent performance, and also Morris, the theatre owner, for facilitating the performance.[126] Carroll and Morris were convicted at trial under a D.C. indecency statute that reads:

D.C. Code, § 22-2001

(1) It shall be unlawful in the District of Columbia for a person knowingly

(2) to present, direct, act in, or otherwise participate in the preparation or presentation of, any obscene, indecent, or filthy play, dance, motion picture, or other performance;

(3) For purposes of paragraph (1) of this subsection, the term "knowingly" means having general knowledge of, or reason to know, or a belief or ground for belief which warrants further inspection or inquiry of, the character and content of any ... performance ... which is reasonably susceptible of examination.[127]

The fact pattern occurred as follows: Carroll appeared on stage in a white gown that exposed her buttocks. Accompanied by music she rubbed her hand over a cape covering her breasts, turned around and then rubbed her buttocks. She then performed a "bump and grind type dance" and removed her gown, which left her wearing a white bra and panties and shoes. She moved to a small platform at center stage where she removed the rest of her clothes, retaining only a patch that covered her pubic area. She then lay down on her back on the platform moved her hips in an up and down motion and rubbed the end of a long feathery tail around her pubic area, between her breasts, and put it into her mouth. She then moved her legs toward the right side of the stage, held one up in the air, pulled the patch aside exposing her vaginal area and, at the same time, yelled, "Let's see it all." She then got on her hands and knees with her buttocks and vaginal area exposed to the audience and moved her hips in an up and down motion.[128]

Carroll and Morris argued that neither of them knew that the performance would be viewed as "indecent" or "offensive," and it was not their intention that the performance be viewed as such. From their perspective, it was just another adult performance and one that was oriented in an artistic manner. They also argued that not only did they lack intent to offend, the dance was presented in an artful and erotic manner and was not an illegal "filthy" dance as the undercover police officers might have suggested. They noted that the First Amendment protects freedom of expression, such as dance, and also protects artistic speech and expression.

The appeals court judge seemed bothered by the facts that were alleged and ruled for the state and against Carroll and Morris. Although the appellate court was an impartial arbiter, it may have felt disgusted by the description of the stage performance. The court concluded:

> In the case at bar, the performer, appellant Carroll, obviously had enough knowledge about the performance to properly hold her responsible for further inquiry or inspection into its character and content. She knew or should have known that the performance in question might violate the statute since she was the performer, and that is all that is needed to satisfy the requirement of scienter under the statute. After examining this record, we hold that reasonable men could conclude only that acts simulating fellatio and the intentional exposure of the vaginal area, in the manner and circumstances as in the case at bar, are obscene per se.[129]

C. Time, Place, and Manner Restrictions
The Secondary Effects Doctrine

The state police power reserves to the fifty states the right to regulate people and places for the health, safety, morals, and general welfare of the people. As early as 1926, the Supreme Court recognized zoning as a proper use of the state police power. The Supreme Court in *Euclid v. Ambler Realty Co.* recognized the power of local governments to enact zoning ordinances to preserve the quality of life of its citizens.[130] In general, the Court has interpreted the state zoning power broadly, giving the states a lot of latitude to regulate. States are permitted to zone for aesthetic reasons, to improve urban life, to reduce noise and traffic, to reduce crime, and to increase the quality of neighborhoods. States can also use their power of eminent domain to legally take property if doing so can benefit the state as a whole.

In addition, cities are permitted to zone to protect public morals as defined by the community. However, the Constitution places limits on city and state police power. For example, when zoning threatens freedom of speech and expression, the First Amendment is invoked and states do not receive the same deference as they do when regulating, for example, automobile traffic. The First Amendment protects a wide variety of "expressive conduct," including adult entertainment facilities.

Despite these constitutional protections, SOBs are often local lightning rods that reflect a moral backlash within the communities that house them. As a result, local governments have historically been aggressive in time, place, and manner restrictions when it comes to SOBs. Originally, the restrictions were simple and limited to bans on total nudity or a ban on the distribution of alcoholic beverages at establishments that exhibited totally nude dancers. Over time, however, these restrictions were expanded to include restricting the hours of operation, requiring a minimum distance between patrons and dancers, and eliminating all contact between dancers and patrons. The Supreme Court consistently upholds time, place, and manner restrictions that limit adult entertainment establishments to operate only at certain **times**, in certain **places**, and only in certain **manners**.[131]

Today, the *Barnes Theatre* case[132] (see below), and *Renton v. Playtime Theatres, Inc.* case[133](immediately following) are the leading cases that guide the lower courts as to the constitutionality of government time, place, and manner restrictions of SOBs.

Much controversy has befallen the Supreme Court's appeasement of local government restrictions on SOBs. In upholding the restrictions, essentially the government is infringing on the First Amendment. Yet, the Court does not seem to view this as harmful to democracy and free speech. Backpeddling from the criticisms, the Supreme Court no longer justifies the validation of time, place, and manner restrictions on morality alone, but more so, rests its decisions on the "secondary effects doctrine."[134]

The secondary effects doctrine suggests that cities are not suppressing speech, but rather, regulating secondary effects. Secondary effects refer to the potential for SOBs to attract pimps, prostitutes, drug dealers, or petty thieves who may increase crime in the areas where a SOB locates. With crime comes another secondary effect of lowered property values, or a flight of stable residents away to another city. Property values may decrease by demeaning the quality of a community in which an SOB is located. The secondary effects doctrine has proven to be fertile ground for abuse because it enables local government officials to conceal their thinly disguised dislike for SOBs behind claims of harmful secondary effects.[135]

In 1988 Justice William Brennan warned in his dissent in *Boos v. Berry* that the secondary effects doctrine "could set the court on a road that will lead to the evisceration of First Amendment freedoms."[136] As an example, in *Renton v. Playtime Theatres, Inc.*, two individuals purchased two theaters (SOBs) in Renton, Washington, a town of approximately 32,000 people near Seattle.[137] The two parties bought the theatres with the intention of exhibiting adult films at the locations. At the same time, they filed suit in Federal District Court, seeking injunctive relief and a declaratory judgment that the First and Fourteenth Amendments were violated by a City of Renton ordinance that prohibits adult motion picture theaters from locating within 1,000 feet of any residential zone, single- or multiple-family dwelling, church, park, or school.[137] The theatre owners argued that they couldn't find any other location that was in their price range or that was available at the time. The Supreme Court ruled in favor of the City of Renton and allowed the time,

The Internet is a unique public domain when it comes to stripping, nudity, and sexual gestures. See chapter 7: Digital Sex Crimes.

place, and manner restriction that the city had created and imposed. The court noted that a tight real estate market does not make the city ordinance a violation of the First Amendment. The court concluded:

> Since the ordinance does not ban adult theaters altogether, it is properly analyzed as a form of time, place, and manner regulation. 'Content-neutral' time, place, and manner regulations are acceptable so long as they are designed to serve a substantial governmental interest and do not unreasonably limit alternative avenues of communication.

> To be sure, the ordinance treats theaters that specialize in adult films differently from other kinds of theaters. Nevertheless, the District Court concluded, the Renton ordinance is aimed not at the content of the films shown at 'adult motion pictures theatres,' but rather at the secondary effects of such theaters in the surrounding community.[139]

Additional Court Cases: Stripping/Nudity

Barnes v. Glen Theatre, Inc.

501 U.S. 560 (1991)

CASE SUMMARY

PROCEDURAL POSTURE: The case was before the court on a writ of certiorari to United States Court of Appeals for the Seventh Circuit, which had concluded that nude dancing performed for entertainment was expression protected by U.S. Const. amend. I and that Indiana's public indecency statute, Ind. Code § 35-45-4-1, was an improper infringement of that expressive activity.

OVERVIEW: Respondents, establishments wishing to provide nude dancing as entertainment, and dancers employed at these establishments, claimed Indiana's public indecency statute violated First Amendment's guarantee of freedom of expression, and sued in district court to enjoin enforcement of the statute. The district court concluded that the type of dancing respondents wished to perform was not expressive activity protected by the constitution, and rendered judgment for petitioners. The court of appeals concluded that non-obscene nude dancing performed for entertainment was expression protected by the First Amendment, and that the public indecency statute was an improper infringement of that expressive activity because its purpose was to prevent the message of eroticism and sexuality conveyed by the dancers. The Supreme Court reversed, holding that the statute requiring dancers to wear pasties and g-strings did not violate First Amendment since there was a sufficiently important governmental interest in regulating non-speech element of the expressive conduct, i.e., prevention of public nudity.

OUTCOME: The Supreme Court reversed holding that the Indiana statutory requirement that nude dancers wear pasties and g-strings did not violate the First Amendment since prevention of public nudity was a sufficiently important government interest to justify regulating the nonspeech element of the expressive conduct.[140]

Sex Tourism

S ex tourism—vaguely defined as traveling to a foreign nation for purposes of purchasing commercial sex from a minor—has reached epidemic proportions around the world and has warranted the active role of the United Nations and other global justice organizations to curb the prevalence of this form of deviance. Sex tourism is a procedure for sexual deviants to obtain the object of their desire with relative anonymity, and with the tacit acquiescence of the host nation. While not all persons who travel abroad to visit tourist destinations and engage in sex for a fee are necessarily "deviant" or "perverted" individuals, as this section will highlight, tremendous controversy and illegality are present when it comes to the subject of sex tourism.

A Norwegian study of men's participation in buying sex found that 80 percent of those who bought sex or consumed sex acts did so abroad.[141] Certain poverty-stricken areas of the Philippines, Laos, and Thailand have become notorious for sex tourism. Western white males from Britain or the United States seeking sexual contact with minors have become the main purchasers and Asian citizens have become the providers.[142] The unprecedented growth in sex tourism has drawn more human traffickers into the realm of misconduct. Dealers and traffickers are undeterred by local, national, or international laws, especially when those who enforce the law, such as the police, can be bribed to look the other way. Among the hierarchy of global criminal black markets, only illegal drugs are more widely available or consumed. After the 2005 tsunami struck Indonesia, the Indonesian government immediately prohibited minors from leaving the country. This rule went into effect because human traffickers flocked to Indonesia to prey upon orphaned Indonesian minors as a supply to export back to their illegal sex markets. Today, certain airlines have in-flight commercials warning passengers of the legal consequences of traveling to purchase sex with minors. Tourist agency trainings worldwide alert staff to the potential for criminal liability when booking travel plans for wealthy clients who may be traveling for purposes of sex tourism.

Counteracting the trends in sex tourism has proved difficult. Sex tourism destinations such as Burma or Vietnam do not have a criminal justice system to adequately deter sex tourism rings. As a result, the criminal black market is synonymous with illegal drug markets: the police and courts are bribed and the lord of the ring operates with highly paid, loyal, and violent underlings who stop at nothing to kidnap and traffic minors back to the home country to expand the sex market and hence the profits. Life can be cheap in some Asian regions and some parents are content to offer a young daughter into the trade if it means a new television or computer, even if the family can already afford to purchase such consumer products. INTERPOL indicates that a young woman can bring in from $75,000 to $250,000 per year for her sexual exploitation.[143] As a general matter, low income, undereducated, and unskilled persons in certain Asian cities could never rake in the sums that they can selling minors to western tourists.[144] A tremendous number of interests seek to maintain the lucrative conditions of sex tourism.

The efforts to combat the conditions of sex tourism have been continuous. When the League of Nations was created in 1917, the supervision of agreements regarding trafficking in persons was included in its mandate. In execution of that responsibility, the League oversaw the conclusion of the Convention for the Suppression of Traffic in Women and Children in 1921 and the International Convention for the Suppression of the Traffic in Women of Full Age. The Universal Declaration of Human Rights of 1948 and the 1966 International Covenant on Civil and Political Rights also addressed issues pertaining to forced labor and exploitation of minors as did the 1984 Convention Against Torture and Other Cruel, Inhuman or Degrading Treatment or Punishment. Lastly, the Fourth World Conference on Women in Beijing in 1995 addressed the degradation of females caught in a web of human trafficking and prostitution activities.[145] While the United Nations has served a valuable role in sex tourism, it should be noted that the U.N. itself was drawn directly into anti-trafficking issues by the revelation that members of U.N. peacekeeping missions were engaging in human trafficking, directly or by creating demand for prostitutes, in West Africa.

Recently, numerous human rights groups have visited sex tourism areas, gathered data and issued reports, in particular ECPAT (End Child Prostitution, Child Pornography and Trafficking of Children for Sexual Purposes), and Human Rights Watch.[146] Since relatively wealthy Americans and other westerners are a large part of the demand side, subtle pressure has been placed on the American government to address the situation in some manner. The American government is also asked to respond due to the complicity of the U.S. in the historical development of sex tourism. During World War II and beyond, thousands of women were trafficked to U.S. military bases in the Philippines for forced prostitution. The women and children were lured from poor towns with the promise of a lucrative job and a better life. Trafficking was so widespread in the Philippines that certain U.S. military officers "owned" prostitutes.[147] In an inter-generational cycle, many of the approximately 50,000 Amer-Asian children who were mothered by women who were forced to prostitute themselves and fathered and abandoned by United States military personnel since World War II themselves became victims of trafficking.[148] In fact, many U.S. military personnel who engaged in sexual activity with girl children boasted about the youth of "their kid."[149]

The complicity of the American government is not relegated to an isolated historical era around World War II. In 1980 in Honduras, women and children were kidnapped, brought to the brothels near United States military bases, and forced to work as prostitutes to U.S. military personnel.[150] When the captive women would escape, Honduran policemen caught and returned them to the brothels.[151] In 2004 the U.S. Department of Defense proposed amending the UCMJ (Uniform Code of Military Justice) to include an offense under Article 134 for patronizing a prostitute. However, many military personnel argued in opposition to the proposed law and questioned the need for such a law and its impact on morale; others supported it as appropriate and long overdue. The rule was promulgated in 2005.[152]

The law covers the following elements: (1) that the accused had sexual intercourse with a person not the accused's spouse; (2) that the act was in exchange for money or other compensation; (3) that it was wrongful; and (4) that it was prejudicial to good order and discipline or service-discrediting under the circumstances. Prostitution patronage can thus be charged under either or both clauses of Article 134. The maximum authorized punishment is one year's confinement, forfeiture of all pay and allowances, and a dishonorable discharge.[153]

As a result of these practices knowingly engaged in by the U.S. military, the civilian American government has attempted to fashion various tools to help ameliorate the situation. The primary tool created by the government is the Prosecutorial Remedies and Tools Against the Exploitation of Children Today Act ("PROTECT") signed by President Bush in 2003.[154] The act creates harsher penalties and new rules that allow prosecutors to target American citizens who travel abroad either to have sex with children or to take pornographic pictures of children. The legislation is the first initiative to make it illegal for Americans to travel abroad with the intent of taking pornographic pictures of children. Prior to the act, no such prohibition existed and the activity was legal.

Additionally, the Military Extraterritorial Jurisdiction Act of 2000 allows for the civil prosecution and punishment of certain United States military personnel who engage in conduct outside the United States that would constitute an offense punishable by imprisonment for more than one year if the conduct had been engaged in the territorial jurisdiction of the United States.[155]

Lastly, in 2000, Congress passed the Trafficking Victims Protection Act (TVPA) to specifically address the problem of human trafficking.[156] TVPA's approach focuses on prevention, prosecution, and protection. The act constitutionally permits the government to impose sanctions and withhold non-essential foreign aid for those countries that fail to show "significant efforts" to eliminate human trafficking in their countries.

Definition of the Offense

Tourism with the intention of exploiting permissive or poorly enforced local laws concerning sex, especially sex with minors or children.[157]

Elements of the Offense

The elements of the crime of sex tourism that must be proven beyond a reasonable doubt are:

1. United States citizen,
2. travel in foreign nation,
3. engages in illicit sexual activity,
4. with another person.[158]

Sample Statute

The federal sex tourism statute reads as follows:

Title 18 of the United States Code (the Federal Code): Crimes and Criminal Procedure. Title I: Crimes. Sections 1-2725. 18 U.S.C. 2252 contains the PROTECT Act. The purpose of the law is to make it a crime for a U.S. citizen to travel to another country and engage in illicit sexual conduct with a minor. Section 2252(B)(b) reads as follows:

[The PROTECT Act] authorizes fines and/or imprisonment for up to 30 years for U.S. citizens or residents who engage in illicit sexual conduct abroad, with or without the intent of engaging in such sexual misconduct.[159] [Pursuant to the PROTECT Act, law enforcement can arrest and prosecute sex offenses committed by a U.S. citizen pursuant to U.S. laws but committed on foreign soil regardless of whether the act was a crime in that country].[160]

Sex Tourism is facilitated with cell phones and other advanced technologies.

© Darren Baker, 2011. Used under license from Shutterstock, Inc.

Arguments Made By The Prosecution

International cases present numerous practical difficulties for the prosecution, as well as typical legal challenges. The state has to rely on the cooperation of foreign law enforcement personnel and with cultural differences, those persons may not agree with what the American authorities are trying to do. Further, political differences or stalemates may also handcuff the case. The foreign nation may refuse to cooperate because, for example, the U.S. did not agree to some unrelated type of commercial trade agreement. Language barriers may combine with cultural and political differences to make the case exceptionally labor intensive for the state.

Arguments Made By The Defense

In a sex tourism case, penalties are severe for sex with a minor and since the accused is already used to foreign travel to developing nations, she or he can always abscond and become a fugitive. Similarly underhanded, the accused can bribe potential witnesses (doing so, however, can result in an additional charge of witness tampering or obstruction of justice). Since sex with a minor is a strict liability offense with no available defenses, and the PROTECT Act does not require that the American national be actually a traveling tourist, the only other possibility is for the accused to demonstrate that he was a citizen of the nation he was captured in, and therefore, American laws do not apply.

Variations of the Law of Sex Tourism

A. Extraterritorial Criminal Jurisdiction

The role of the government in international affairs calls into question issues pertaining to constitutional authority. Does the Constitution allow the U.S. government to arrest American citizens vacationing in a foreign country for an act that would not be a crime where the act took place? This legal question is a good example of "the long arm of the law" where, yes, under certain circumstances, U.S. laws, civil or criminal, can apply to American citizens in a foreign nation. In one example, a 48-year-old millionaire, Kent Frank, was charged under the PROTECT Act with traveling as a tourist abroad for purposes of sexual encounters with minor girls. In part, the PROTECT Act authorizes fines and/or imprisonment for up to 30 years for U.S. citizens or residents who engage in illicit sexual conduct abroad, with or without the intent of engaging in such sexual misconduct.[161]

As part of his sex tourism, Frank picked up local minor girls in Cambodia and paid them for sex in his hotel. His attorney, Jamie Benjamin, said, "[T]he case calls into question the government's authority to charge a U.S. citizen for his conduct in another country." Benjamin further stated:

> If anybody else from any other country in the world did what Kent is accused of, it wouldn't be a crime. The only thing that makes it a crime is that Kent is a U.S. citizen. I'm going to argue vehemently that they (the prosecution) don't have the power to charge him.[162]

The U.S. Supreme Court has settled the matter, at least for now. The most referenced legal authority is the 1949 case of *Foley Bros, Inc. v. Filardo*, a case regarding the application of U.S. employment laws to American workers who worked overseas, but with an American firm. The Supreme Court held: "Congress has the authority to enforce its laws beyond the territorial boundaries of the United States."[163] The one caveat concerns the language of the law. Meaning, Congress must explicitly describe the law in terms of its extraterritorial application. Not just any law may apply overseas, only those specifically intended to do so. Hence, the PROTECT Act, and similar laws, are constitutional as applied to American citizens abroad because that was the intent of Congress in writing the law. The PROTECT Act seeks to stem the tide of child sexual exploitation abroad.

B. Tourist or Permanent Resident?

To be convicted of a crime related to sex tourism, the accused needs to be a tourist in some way, shape, or form. If an individual is a permanent resident of the nation where the crime takes place, the allegations pertaining to sex tourism cannot apply. Many offenders who are engaged in misdeeds abroad will attempt to arrange for the appearances of a permanent residence in the nation they visit so as to deflect the application of a sex tourism law that prohibits engaging in illicit sex while traveling in a foreign nation.

In *U.S. v. Clark,* Michael Clark, a 71-year-old retired military veteran participated in a routinized pattern of visiting Cambodia for, among other things, sexual contact with minors, whom he paid for the transactions.[164] Clark attempted to establish various forms of residency in Cambodia even though he was not a citizen of that nation. Even though he was able to show certain types of permanent contact with Cambodia, he simultaneously maintained a U.S. passport, U.S. bank account, driver's license, and property ownership. These contacts with the U.S. were used as sufficient evidence to demonstrate that he was overseas for purposes of sex tourism rather than him being a resident of Cambodia.

As he continued his participation in illicit sexual contact, one of Clark's victims reported an incident to a local social worker who then reported the activity to the Cambodian police. Clark was arrested in Cambodia and the law enforcement officials in Cambodia contacted the U.S. Dept. of Justice. Cambodia agreed to turn over Clark to the U.S. and grant extradition. Clark was tried and convicted in U.S. courts and appealed his conviction.[165]

One of his arguments was that he was not a tourist, not traveling, and that he was living in Cambodia and therefore, the PROTECT Act, Section 2423 (c) and (e) cannot apply because it only applies to tourists. He argued that his conviction was a violation of his Fifth Amendment rights to due process because he was being arbitrarily and unfairly singled out as someone living in a foreign nation. Clark argued that there is an insufficient nexus between himself and the United States to make him a tourist for purposes of the sex tourism law. The appellate court judge did not agree and stated:

Although Clark's citizenship alone is sufficient to satisfy Due Process concerns, his U.S. investments, ongoing receipt of federal retirement benefits and use of U.S. military flights also underscore his multiple and continuing ties with this country.[166]

> In *Blackmer v. United States,* 284 U.S. 421, (1932), the Supreme Court explained that the extraterritorial application of U.S. law to its citizens abroad did not violate the Fifth Amendment. The Court declared that despite moving his residence to France, the U.S. citizen defendant continued to owe allegiance to the United States. By virtue of the obligations of citizenship, the United States retained its authority over him, and he was bound by its laws made applicable to him in a foreign country.[167]

C. Civil Remedy for Human Trafficking Victims

In many cases, after a criminal case has ended, the victim in the case can sue the offender for damages in civil court. For example, if someone's house is burglarized, the offender may be convicted for the crime of burglary in criminal court, and once the criminal case is over, the victim can sue the burglar in civil court to recover damages for items in the house that were stolen or destroyed as well as the possibility of collecting monetary damages for emotional pain and suffering as a result of the criminal victimization.

The Trafficking Victims Protection Reauthorization Act (TVPRA) of 2003, 18 U.S.C. 1581 et seq. acts as a deterrent to human trafficking and sex tourism and allows for victims to be compensated for the harm suffered at the hands of a sex tourist.[168] The main part of the law is Section 1595(a), which states:

> An individual who is a victim of a violation of section [this Act] may bring a civil action
>
> against the perpetrator in an appropriate district court of the United States and may
>
> recover damages and reasonable attorneys fees.[169]

With the passage of section 1595, trafficked victims can seek "a complete remedy," rather than the piecemeal approach required by common law torts [or federal employment and labor laws]. By targeting the actual harm suffered by trafficked persons, the TVPRA increases the potential for greater material recovery and makes possible the full expression of the trafficked person's painful experience.[170]

Section 1595 is aimed at trafficking victims and victims of slavery or forced labor. In *Roe v. Bridgestone Corp.*, two young children ages 9 and 11 were coerced and intimidated into forced labor in the nation of Liberia in between 1995 and 2000. The children were allegedly kidnapped from their homes and forced to work for a rubber plantation that was owned by Bridgestone Corporation of America. The children were forced to work full-time at heavy lifting and dangerous jobs on defendants' plantation tapping raw latex from rubber trees.[171] The children's parents were also workers at the plantation but did not suffer the flagrant harms that the children did, and sued on behalf of their children.

The defendant naturally argued that the labor of the children was voluntary and that no harm was intended and even that the locals were grateful to have the opportunity to earn the money that otherwise would be absent. Count Number 65 of the civil complaint states:

> 65. The Plantation Child Laborers are forced to work to avoid the starvation of their
>
> families. These young children have not reached the legal age of consent by any defi-
>
> nition, and therefore could not possibly agree to become laborers for the Firestone
>
> Plantation. They suffer daily the deprivations of living a slave-like existence, including
>
> malnutrition, disease, physical ailments from exposure to chemicals, and the lack of
>
> decent educational opportunities.[172]

The court ruled in favor of the children by allowing their claims and for the case to proceed to a trial. At the outset, the court first noted that Congress has the authority to apply its laws, including criminal statutes, beyond the territorial boundaries of the United States, to the extent that extraterritorial application is consistent with the principles of international law.[173] The court then referenced prior cases on the same legal point[174] and stated:

> [In prior cases] the court denied a motion to dismiss forced labor claims under the law. The plaintiffs were young women who alleged they were fraudulently induced to come to the United States with promises of education and employment, but were then forced to work long hours under arduous conditions at illegally low wages, and that they were sexually abused, physically beaten, and threatened. The court found that the allegations stated claims for forced labor, debt bondage, and trafficking actionable under the statute. In reaching that conclusion, the court relied on the Universal Declaration of Human Rights and the International Covenant on Civil and Political Rights.[175]

Additional Court Cases: Sex Tourism

United States v. Jackson

480 F.3d 1014 (2007)

CASE SUMMARY

PROCEDURAL POSTURE: The United States sought review of an order from the United States District Court for the Western District of Washington, which granted defendant's motion to dismiss an indictment that charged him with violating 18 U.S.C.S. § 2423(c).

OVERVIEW: Defendant left the United States in November 2001 to relocate permanently to Cambodia. Cambodian authorities arrested defendant on charges of debauchery after he engaged in sex with three Cambodian boys in June 2003. While the Cambodian charge was pending, the United States revoked defendant's passport and agreed to take jurisdiction over the crime. A grand jury indicted defendant on three counts of violating 18 U.S.C.S. § 2423(c), which was enacted on April 30, 2003. Although the district court suggested that applying the statute to defendant might violate the Ex Post Facto Clause, it interpreted the statute narrowly to avoid any constitutional infirmity. The court concentrated on the statutory interpretation question, determined that travel and illicit sex were distinct elements of the crime, and held that defendant's actions fell outside the conduct that Congress proscribed. Under the plain language of the statute, the court held that 18 U.S.C.S. § 2423(c) only proscribes the conduct of an individual who "travels" in foreign commerce after the enactment of the statute. Because defendant's travel had ended by April 30, 2003, § 2423(c) did not apply to him.

OUTCOME: The court affirmed the dismissal of the indictment. [176]

Chapter Four Summary

The regulation of sex work represents paradoxes in the law. Few areas of sexual deviance are so meticulously criminalized, yet the laws go unenforced much of the time. Sex workers have no worker benefits, no meaningful political voice, and are socially frowned on for having a poor set of moral values. Yet, they are patronized today more than ever before, to the tune of billions of dollars annually, even by famous athletes, politicians, and television personalities. The U.S. military, and even personnel of the United Nations are complicit in fueling the demand for prostitutes, including minors. Consumer demand has become so pronounced, at the federal level, in 2003 Congress passed the PROTECT Act to address the pattern of American tourists who travel abroad for the purpose of patronizing underage prostitutes. Congress has also addressed human trafficking and the worldwide situation of child exploitation in poverty stricken regions. The PROTECT Act has resulted in arrests and convictions of American johns who engaged in illicit sexual activity while on foreign soil. The convictions have been appealed, but the appellate courts have upheld the provisions of the PROTECT Act. Section 1234 of the Act authorizes imprisonment for up to thirty years for U.S. citizens who engage in illicit sexual conduct abroad. The courts have upheld the Act and also the exercise of extraterritorial jurisdiction. The demand for legal regulation will continue to equal the demand for licit and illicit sex. Farley notes that the economics of the sex worker industry have created an unusual interplay between the police, sex workers, and the legal enactments used to control sex workers. [177] The law seeks to make arrests while simultaneously protecting the cottage-type industries that sex work guarantees.

At the heart of the sex worker industry are prostitution and prostitution-related activities. In 1900 during the first significant era of American industrialization, unprecedented urban growth resulted in an unusual influx of foreign and American-born prostitutes to cities such as New York, Philadelphia, and Chicago. Community and political leaders responded with the White Slavery Act in 1910 (The Mann Act). This act began a trend to criminalize a multitude of activities as they relate to prostitution. Today, the pervasive framework for regulating prostitution means that a variety of associations with sex workers are criminalized. Loitering as a prostitute, traveling with a prostitute, encouraging prostitution, and making one's home available to a prostitute and other activities are all violations of the law in almost every state. Pimps, johns, and owners of a massage parlor or anyone else who facilitates the act of prostitution are drawn into the web of unlawful underworld crime.

With the number of laws and prosecutorial tools available to the state, typical police work with prostitutes, call girls, or escorts involves a basic strategy of undercover vice detail. Occasionally, police strategies are overly aggressive and defense work in prostitution cases often involves screening a case for entrapment activity or "outrageous government conduct" such as patronizing prostitutes as a means of making arrests. Police officers cannot commit crimes to solve crimes, lest they be subject to an arrest themselves.

Despite the overwhelming criminalization of prostitution in the United States, much debate still exists over the appropriate legal tools to use for prostitution. Three legal paradigms are considered: (1) **Criminalization** is the current legal framework whereby engaging in acts of prostitution is illegal and those convicted are subject to criminal penalties. (2) **Decriminalization** is an approach favored by many sex workers' advocates that would eliminate criminal penalties, but continue to leave prostitution regulated by the state. (3) **Legalization**—the legal paradigm that controls brothels in rural Nevada—would institutionalize sex work and require the state to regulate prostitution like other industries, such as providing licenses, requiring medical examinations, and collecting taxes.

Many legal scholars contemplate the future legalization of prostitution in the U.S. The 2003 *Lawrence v. Texas* Supreme Court decision may have implied a trend toward legalization. Lawrence ruled that states could not outlaw private, consensual sexual activities between adult members of the same sex because the Fourteenth Amendment protected private consensual sexual relations between adults.[178] Despite the Lawrence decision and greater acceptance of domestic partnerships, the trend toward legalization of prostitution does not seem to have much force. Legalization supporters in the U.S., such as the PROStitutes Collective, are part of the International Prostitutes Collective, a network of sex workers from around the world. This network lobbies for the legalization of prostitution within the realm of the sex trade to provide for a degree of protection to the mostly female work force. A large number of females are constructively forced into the world of prostitution and once there, are placed at risk of being trafficked or victimized in terms of rape, robbery, and eviction while having no protection unless prostitution is legalized and licensed as a business operation.

When sex work is performed legally in a commercial establishment it falls within the realm of an adult entertainment SOB. These facilities and establishments are legal and have First Amendment protection, but are heavily regulated. Originally conceived as rather innocuous such as burlesque shows or other fully clothed dance routines, SOBs can legally provide for fully nude dancing in half of the jurisdictions in the U.S. today. Where full nudity on stage is regulated, numerous aspects of the stage and theatrical performance are controlled, such as the distance that must come between the audience and the dancer, and the prohibition on anyone from touching the dancer. The dance routine itself is also regulated. A mildly erotic dance can start off as a legal activity, but if the dancer begins to engage in poses, gestures, and simulations that become overly erotic and hence obscene, the dancer can be arrested for giving an obscene performance and so can the proprietor of the facility for the promotion of lewd and lascivious behavior.

Many legal commentators express concern when an artistic dance routine is subject to state censorship and criminal control because these actions by the state represent state censorship of speech, a violation of the Constitution and the First Amendment. Legal scholars are not necessarily devotees of erotic dance, but rather, comprehend the slippery slope of the whittling away of protected speech and the corresponding degree of enhanced state control over speech and expression. This concern has been applied extensively to the manner in which local governments enact time, place, and manner restrictions on SOBs. Local government officials claim to push SOBs aside for fear of "secondary effects" of increased crime and decreased property values. However, the evidence suggests that local governments curtail the activities and speech of SOBs from a moralistic perspective rather than the purported problems of secondary effects. The Supreme Court has needed to address the balance between the First Amendment freedom of expression and the right of the states to regulate SOBs. The Supreme Court supports the "content-neutral" doctrine regarding "secondary effects." The cases of City of *Renton v. Playtime Theatres, Inc.*[179] and *Barnes v. Glen Theatres, Inc.*[180] constitute the current law on the secondary effects doctrine.

Away from an SOB, nudity in public, on the beach, in a park, etc., is legally regulated from city to city, and state to state so that children and innocent bystanders do not observe nudity if they are not comfortable doing so. Being nude in public is criminalized pursuant to a three-part analysis consisting of (1) the intent of the actor, (2) the form of the nudity, and (3) the extent of public exposure. An accidental exposure of oneself where no one is in the vicinity does not represent a serious violation. On the other end of the spectrum, a streaker who dashes naked onto the field at a crowded sporting event is an obvious case of indecent exposure. Depending on the surrounding facts of the case, some courts have held that bare-chested females are the legal equivalent to bare-chested males and are not offending the law. Public sexual acts by oneself or with another, however, draw greater legal scrutiny. Rarely is public sex legal. In 2007, Idaho Senator Larry Craig left the U.S. Senate due to a conviction for an attempt at public sex in a men's restroom at the Minneapolis–St. Paul airport. While two court cases were noted for allowing public sex accomplished in a discreet manner, the overwhelming majority of cases criminalize sex in public under a lewdness or public indecency statute.

Key Terms

Sex Worker 00

John 00

Pandering 00

Brothel 00

Loitering 00

Adult Entertainment 00

SOB 00

Sex Tourism 00

PROTECT Act 00

TVPRA Act 00

Extraterritorial Jurisdiction 00

Concepts & Principles

Public Health 00

Secondary Effects Doctrine 00

Commercial Transaction 00

Outrageous Government Conduct 00

Indecent Exposure 00

Lewd Performance 00

Public Sex 00

Human Trafficking 00

Human Rights Organization 00

Civil Remedy for Victims 00

Exploitation 00

Chapter Four Select Court Cases	
Case	**Point of Law**
People v. Smith 00	Prostitutes are legally prohibited from loitering
Muse v. U.S. 00	Gifts and money are synonymous for purposes of prostitution
Commonwealth v. Pennsylvania 00	Undercover police officers cannot further the practice of prostitution to catch a prostitute
Caminetti v. U.S. 00	Mere travel with a prostitute is illegal
People v. Charles 00	Inducing someone to work in prostitution is illegal
Turner v. State 00	Gender-specific prostitution laws are permissible
People v. Santorelli 00	Bare-chested females are no more illegal than bare-chested males
Morris v. U.S. 00	Stage performances must remain artistic and cannot cross the legal line to obscenity
Renton v. Playtime Theatres, Inc. 00	Adult theatres can be subject to content-neutral government regulation due to "secondary effects"
Barnes v. Glen Theatre, Inc. 00	Nude dancers can be required to wear pasties and g-strings during a performance
U.S. v. Clark 00	U.S. ties subject a U.S. citizen abroad to U.S. laws
Roe v. Bridgestone Corp. 00	Extraterritorial application of the law is constitutional

Questions for Review

1. What is the main reason sex workers have been around for so long?

2. Are sex workers as deviant as other sex offenders?

3. What are the public health and safety reasons to oppose prostitution?

4. How do the police usually investigate a "john," prostitute, or pimp?

5. What laws does a pimp violate?

6. How can a legal stripping performance suddenly become illegal?

7. Is it legal for men and women to be topless in public places?

8. What is the main objection to the practice of sex tourism?

9. What role has the United Nations played in sex tourism?

10. How has the U.S. military been involved in sex worker issues?

1   Barnes v. Glen Theatre, Inc., 501 U.S. 560, at 565-566 (1991).

2   Farley, Melissa, *Symposium: Sex for Sale: Prostitution, Trafficking, and Cultural Amnesia: What We Must Not Know in Order to Keep the Business of Sexual Exploitation Running Smoothly,* 18 Yale J.L. & Feminism 109 (2006).

3   Hagner, Drake, *Tenth Annual Review of Gender and Sexuality Law: Criminal Law Chapter: Prostitution and Sex Work,* 10 Geo J. Gender & L. 433 (2009).

4   *Id.* at 434.

5   Farley, Melissa, *Symposium: Sex for Sale: Prostitution, Trafficking, and Cultural Amnesia: What We Must Not Know in Order to Keep the Business of Sexual Exploitation Running Smoothly,* 18 Yale J.L. & Feminism 109 (2006), note 2.

6   The ACE is the trade association of America's adult nightclubs. Calvert, Clay and & Robert D. Richards, 7 N.Y.U. J. Legis. & Pub. Pol'y 287 (2003/2004), at 288.

7   Sue Reid, Criminal Law 323 (McGraw-Hill) (1998).

8   Let the Good Times Roll: Prostitution & the U.S. Military in Asia (Saundra Pollock Sturdevant & Brenda Stoltzfus eds.) (1992).

9   Scott Senjo, Book Review, Sex Roles : A Journal of Research, Vol. 60, No. 5, 435-438 (reviewing On the Game: Women and Sex Work, Sophie Day (Pluto Press 2007)) (2009).

10   Melissa Farley, Prostitution, Trafficking, and Traumatic Stress (Haworth Press) (2003).

11   Janice G. Raymond, Prostitution Is Rape That's Paid For, L.A. Times, Dec. 11, 1995, at B6. Adm. Macke was forced to resign after offering this opinion in a news interview.

12   COYOTE, an acronym for "Call Off Your Old Tired Ethics," began its movement 1973. It advocates the repeal of all laws prohibiting prostitution, pimping, pandering, and patronizing. COYOTE works in conjunction with a variety of national and international sex workers' rights organizations, such as Sex Workers' Action Coalition (SWAC), North American Task Force on Prostitution (NTFP), Hooking Is Real Employment (HIRE), and Prostitutes of New York (PONY). See Call Off Your Old Tired Ethics, available at http://www.walnet.org/csis/groups/coyote.html (last visited Dec. 2, 2003).

13   Int'l Comm. on the Rights of Sex Workers in Europe, Recommendations of the European Conference on Sex Work, Human Rights, Labour and Migration, Brussels, http://www.sexworkeurope.org/site/index. php?option=com_content&task=view& id=36&Itemid=200 (last visited Apr. 23, 2008) ("Sex work is work and a profession, sex workers are workers and must be recognized as such. We demand the protection of our labour, social and human rights on an equal footing with other workers, especially social rights such as access to social security, health care and minimum wages. ... Governments should ensure safe and healthy working conditions for sex workers, similar to other workers.").

14   Sarah Romans et. al., The Mental and Physical Health of Female Sex Workers: A Comparative Study, 35 AUSTRALIAN AND NEW ZEALAND J. OF PSYCHIATRY 75 (2001) (arguing that there is no difference in mental health or self-esteem of women who were sex workers and those who are not).

15   Lisa Malmer, *Nude Dancing and the First Amendment,* 59 U. Cin. L. Rev. 1275, 1276 (1991).

16   Free Expression in America: A Documentary History 150–208 (Sheila Suess Kennedy ed., 1999).

17   Commonwealth v. Sharpless, 1815 WL 1297 at 7 (Pa. Dec. 1815).

18   *Id.*

19   Barnes v. Glen Theatre, Inc., 501 U.S. 560 (1991).

20   John Pettegrew, Brutes in Suits: Male Sensibility in America, 1890–1920 (2007).

21   Lisa Lindquist Dorr, Gender, *Eugenics, and Virginia's Racial Integrity Acts of the 1920s,* 11 J. Women's Hist. 143, 144 (1999).

22   Barbara Leslie Epstein, The Politics of Domesticity: Women, Evangelism, and Temperance in Nineteenth-Century America 102 (1981).

23   Steven J. Diner, A Very Different Age: Americans of the Progressive Era (1998).

24   *Id.*

25   18 U.S.C.A. § 2421 et seq.

26 Hennigan, Peter C., Property War: Prostitution, Red-Light Districts, and the Transformation of Public Nuisance Law in the Progressive Era, 2004 Yale J.L. & Human. 123 (2004).

27 *Id.*

28 Act of July 9, 1918, 40 Stat. 886.

29 Freud, Sigmund, The Complete Introductory Lectures on Psychoanalysis (Norton Books) (1966).

30 Alan H. Swanson, *Sexual Psychopath Statutes: Summary and Analysis,* 51 J. Crim. L. Criminology & Police Sci. 215, 216 (1960).

31 Mich. Comp. Laws §§ 780.501-.509 (repealed 1968).

32 Edwin H. Sutherland, The Diffusion of Sexual Psychopath Laws, in Crime and the Legal Process 74 (William J. Chambliss ed.) (1969).

33 Alfred Kinsey, Sexual Behavior in the Human Male (Indiana University Press) (1998).

34 Miller v. California, 413 U.S. 15 (1973).

35 Barnes v. Glen Theatre, Inc., 501 U.S. 560, 585-586 (1991). (Souter, J. concurring) ("To say that pernicious secondary effects are associated with nude dancing establishments is not necessarily to say that such effects result from the persuasive effect of the expression inherent in nude dancing. It is to say, rather, only that the effects are correlated with the existence of establishments offering such dancing, without deciding what the precise causes of the correlation actually are.").

36 Barnes v. Glen Theatre, Inc., 501 U.S. 560 (1991).

37 Bowers v. Hardwick, 478 U.S. 186 (1986).

38 Barnes v. Glen Theatre, Inc., 501 U.S. 560 (1991).

39 Pap's A.M. v. City of Erie, 719 A.2d at 277-278 (2000).

40 City of Renton v. Playtime Theatres Inc., 475 U.S. 41 (1986).

41 Harman, Brigman, L., *Is a Strip Club More Harmful Than a Dirty Bookstore? Navigating a Circuit Split in Municipal Regulation of Sexually Oriented Businesses?,* 2008 B.Y.U.L. Rev. 1603 (2008).

42 Joyce Outshoorn, *The Political Debates on Prostitution and Trafficking of Women,* 12 Soc. Pol. 141, 145 (2005).

43 Alexa Albert, Brothel: Mustang Ranch and Its Women 174 (2001).

44 Belinda J. Carpenter, *Re-thinking Prostitution: Feminism, Sex, and the Self,* 53, 125–26 (2000).

45 Prosecutorial Remedies and Tools against the Exploitation of Children Today (PROTECT) Act of 2003, Pub. L. 108-21, 117 Stat. 650 (2003).

46 President George W. Bush, Remarks on Signing the PROTECT Act (April 30, 2003), in 39 Wkly. Comp. Pres. Doc. 502 (May 5, 2003), available at http://www.whitehouse.gov/ news/releases/2003/04/20030430-6.html. Prosecutorial Remedies and Tools against the Exploitation of Children Today (PROTECT) Act of 2003, Pub. L. 108-21, 117 Stat. 650 (2003). PROTECT Act at 106(e)(2) (referring to 18 U.S.C. 2242(1)-(2) (2000)).

47 *Id.*

48 *Id.*

49 Barbara Brents & Kathryn Hausbeck, *State-Sanctioned Sex: Negotiating Formal and Informal Regulatory Practices in Nevada Brothels,* 44 Soc. Persp. 307, 310 (2001).

50 It is estimated that 650,000 Western women have traveled to various foreign nations to engage in sex since 1980, many of them multiple times. By some estimates, 80,000 North American and European women visit Jamaica every year for sex. Retrieved from: http://www.canada.com/ottawacitizen/news/arts/story.html?id=6f1d0124-af59-431a-b9eb-f75a5aa47882, May 22, 2010. Sex Tourism: When Women Do It, It's Called "Romance Traveling." The Ottowa Citizen, January 27, 2007.

51 Del. Code Ann. § 1342-1352 (1997).

52 Fla. Stat. § 796.06 (1981).

53 Haw. Rev. Stat. § 712-1206(2) (1978).

54 Mich. Comp. Laws § 750.448-750.461 (1993).

55 Ill. Comp. Stat. Ann. § 11 19(a) (1986).

56 Kan. Stat. Ann. § 21-3513(a) parts 1-8 (1990).

57 http://www.answers.com/topic/prostitution. Retrieved May 19, 2010.

58 F. Schmalleger, Criminal Law Today 502 (3d ed. 2006).

59 Neb. Rev. Stat. Ann. § 28-801 (1996).

60 N.Y. Sess. Laws § 240.37 (1976). Loitering for the purpose of engaging in a prostitution offense.
1. For the purposes of this section, "public place" means any street, sidewalk, bridge, alley or alleyway, plaza, park, driveway, parking lot or transportation facility or the doorways and entrance ways to any building which fronts on any of the aforesaid places, or a motor vehicle in or on any such place.
2. Any person who remains or wanders about in a public place and repeatedly beckons to, or repeatedly stops, or repeatedly attempts to stop, or repeatedly attempts to engage passers-by in conversation, or repeatedly stops or attempts to stop motor vehicles, or repeatedly interferes with the free passage of other persons, for the purpose of prostitution, or of patronizing a prostitute as those terms are defined in article two hundred thirty of the penal law, shall be guilty of a violation and is guilty of a class B misdemeanor if such person has previously been convicted of a violation of this section or of sections 230.00 or 230.05 of the penal law.
3. Any person who remains or wanders about in a public place and repeatedly beckons to, or repeatedly stops, or repeatedly attempts to stop, or repeatedly attempts to engage passers-by in conversation, or repeatedly stops or attempts to stop motor vehicles, or repeatedly interferes with the free passage of other persons, for the purpose of promoting prostitution as defined in article two hundred thirty of the penal law is guilty of a class A misdemeanor.

61 People v. Smith, 378 N.E.2d 1032, 1049 (N.Y. 1978).

62 *Id.*

63 Muse v. U.S., 522 A.2d 888 (D.C. 1987).

64 *Id.*

65 *Id.* at 897.

66 *Id.* at 899.

67 Hagner, Drake, *Tenth Annual Review of Gender and Sexuality Law: Criminal Law Chapter: Prostitution and Sex Work,* 10 Geo J. Gender & L. 433, 451 (2009).

68 Commonwealth of Pennsylvania v. Sun Cha Chon, 983 A.2d 784 (2009).

69 *Id.*

70 The Superior Court opinion recounted how police and the informant were recorded laughing about the sexual encounter after one of the episodes. ABC News online. Retrieved from http://abcnews.go.com/US/wireStory?id=9017803, June 12, 2010.

71 Commonwealth of Pennsylvania v. Sun Cha Chon, 983 A.2d 784, 791 (2009).

72 *Id.*

73 Harwell v. State, 821 N.E.2d 381 (2004).

74 Karen E. Bravo, *Exploring the Analogy Between Modern Trafficking in Humans and the Trans- Atlantic Slave Trade,* 25 B.U. Int'l L.J. 207, 217 (2007).

75 David Vestal, *Pandering; Procuring; Pimping; Promoting Prostitution,* 63-C Am. Jur. 2d 17-23, 17-24 (1964).

76 *Id.*

77 Farley, Melissa, *Symposium: Sex for Sale: Prostitution, Trafficking, and Cultural Amnesia: What We Must Not Know in Order to Keep the Business of Sexual Exploitation Running Smoothly,* 18 Yale J.L. & Feminism 109 (2006).

78 U.S. v. Brown, 273 F.3d 747, 761 (2001).

[79] People v. Montgomery, 47 Cal. App.2d 1 (1941).

[80] Ariz. Rev. Stat. § 13-3209 (1978).

[81] Cynthia Shepard Perry, *The Menace of Human Trafficking in Africa and the U.S. Congressional Response Through the Office of the United States Executive Director of the African Development Bank*, 2 Loy. U. Chi. Int'l. L. Rev. 179 (2005).

[82] Karen E. Bravo, *Exploring the Analogy Between Modern Trafficking in Humans and the Trans- Atlantic Slave Trade*, 25 B.U. Int'l L.J. 207, 217 (2007).

[83] 18 U.S.C.A. § 2421 et seq.

[84] *Id.*

[85] Catharine A. MacKinnon, *Prostitution and Civil Rights*, 1 Mich. J. Gender & L. 13 (1993).

[86] Caminetti v. U.S., 242 U.S. 470 (1917). See also U.S. v. Bitty, 208 U.S. 393 (1908); Hoke v. U.S., 227 U.S. 308 (1913).

[87] Caminetti v. U.S., 242 U.S. 470, 482 (1917).

[88] People v. Charles, 218 Cal. App. 2d 812, at 820 (1963).

[89] *Id.*

[90] *Id.* at 827.

[91] Turner v. State, 282 S.E.2d 112 (1981).

[92] Ga. Code Ann. § 26-2016 (1968). A person commits pandering when he solicits a female to perform an act of prostitution, or when he knowingly assembles females at a fixed place for the purpose of being solicited by others to perform an act of prostitution.

[93] Turner v. State, 282 S.E.2d 112, at 119 (1981).

[94] *Id.* at 125.

[95] People v. Hashimoto, 54 Cal. App. 3d 862 (1976).

[96] Doran v. Salem Inn, Inc., 422 U.S. 922 (1975); Barnes v. Glen Theatre, Inc., 501 U.S. 560 (1991).

[97] Amy Adler, *Symptomatic Cases: Hysteria in the Supreme Court's Nude Dancing Decisions*, 64 Am. Imago 297 (2007).

[98] Amy Adler, *Girls! Girls! Girls!: The Supreme Court Confronts the G-String*, 80 N.Y.U. L. Rev. 1108 (2005).

[99] *Id.*

[100] *Id.*

[101] David Cole, *Playing by Pornography's Rules: The Regulation of Sexual Expression*, 143 U. Pa. L. Rev. 111, 124-31 (1994).

[102] *Id.*

[103] Barnes v. Glen Theatre, Inc., 501 U.S. 560 (1991).

[104] Katherine Liepe-Levinson, Strip Show: Performances of Gender and Desire (2002).

[105] David Cole, *Playing by Pornography's Rules: The Regulation of Sexual Expression*, 143 U. Pa. L. Rev. 111, 124-31 (1994).

[106] Duvallon v. State, 404 So.2d 196 (Fla. Dist. Ct. App. 1981) (explaining that even if the laws themselves do not change, interpretation is subject to continuous revision as a result of changes in public attitude). "An act which might have been considered by the general public a few years ago as an indecent exposure of the person and lewd and lascivious in its character might today not be frowned upon, nor condemned by upright, honorable and virtuous people." At common law, indecent exposure was a public nuisance and punishable as a misdemeanor. It was viewed as an offense against religion and morality, involving "open and grossly scandalous lewdness." Today, the common law crime has been supplanted by statutory offenses in almost every jurisdiction in this country. These statutes vary somewhat as to wording, but a survey of the case law indicates that many of the same elements of the common law crime have been retained. 276–277.

[107] *Id.*

108 Between May and August, 2007, 40 men were arrested at the Minneapolis–St. Paul International Airport bathroom for various forms of lewd and disorderly conduct, indecent exposure, or loitering.

109 Craig was arrested under MINN. STAT. ANN. § 609.72(1)(3) (2003) by an undercover officer for allegedly inviting the officer to have public sex. 609.72 DISORDERLY CONDUCT. Subdivision 1. Crime. Whoever does any of the following in a public or private place, including on a school bus, knowing, or having reasonable grounds to know that it will, or will tend to, alarm, anger or disturb others or provoke an assault or breach of the peace, is guilty of disorderly conduct, which is a misdemeanor: (1) engages in brawling or fighting; or (2) disturbs an assembly or meeting, not unlawful in its character; or (3) engages in offensive, obscene, abusive, boisterous, or noisy conduct or in offensive, obscene, or abusive language tending reasonably to arouse alarm, anger, or resentment in others.

110 See Brief of American Civil Liberties Union and American Civil Liberties Union of Minnesota as Amici Curiae supporting Appellant Larry Edwin Craig, State of Minnesota v. Larry Edwin Craig, No. A07-1949, (Minn. Ct. App. Jan. 15, 2008), 2008 WL 206295, at 6. The ACLU, who filed an amicus brief in support of Senator Craig, challenged the law as impermissibly overbroad and vague.

111 State v. Bryant, 177 N.W.2d 800 (Minn. 1970).

112 State v. Limberhand, 788 P.2d 857 (Idaho Ct. App. 1990).

113 City of Dallas, Texas, Municipal Code, Chapter 41(A), Ordinance 23137 (2002).

114 CAL. PENAL CODE §§ 314-318.6 (2000).

115 IND. CODE § 35-45-4-1 (1988).

116 Helen Pundurs, *Public Exposure of the Female Breast: Obscene and Immoral or Free and Equal?,* 14 IN PUB. INTEREST 1, 28 (1995).

117 Barnes v. Glen Theatre, Inc., 501 U.S. 560, 572 (1991).

118 Helen Pundurs, *Public Exposure of the Female Breast: Obscene and Immoral or Free and Equal?,* 14 IN PUB. INTEREST 1, 28 (1995).

119 People v. Santorelli, 600 N.E.2d 232 (1992).

120 N.Y. SESS. LAWS § 245.01 (1983).

121 People v. Santorelli, 600 N.E.2d 232 (1992).

122 *Id.*

123 David Cole, *Playing by Pornography's Rules: The Regulation of Sexual Expression,* 143 U. PA. L. REV. 111, 124–31 (1994).

124 These facts assume an episode of nonviolence where both parties are adults, mentally healthy, and not under the influence of drugs or alcohol.

125 Morris v. U.S., 259 A.2d 337 (1969).

126 *Id.*

127 D.C. CODE ANN. § 22–2001 (1958).

128 Morris v. U.S., 259 A.2d 337 (1969).

129 *Id.* at 348.

130 Vill. of Euclid v. Ambler Realty Co., 272 U.S. 365 (1926).

131 Joseph Gordon Hylton, *Prelude to Euclid: The United States Supreme Court and the Constitutionality of Land Use Regulation, 1900–1920,* 3 WASH. U. J.L. & POL'Y 1, 2 (2000).

132 Barnes v. Glen Theatre, Inc., 501 U.S. 560 (1991).

133 Renton v. Playtime Theatres, Inc., 475 U.S. 41 (1986).

134 Harman, Brigman, L., *Is a Strip Club More Harmful Than a Dirty Bookstore? Navigating a Circuit Split in Municipal Regulation of Sexually Oriented Businesses,* 2008 B.Y.U.L. Rev. 1603 (2008).

135 *Id.*

136 Boos v. Berry, 485 U.S. 312, 319 (1988).

137 Renton v. Playtime Theatres, Inc., 475 U.S. 41 (1986).

138 *Id.*

139 *Id.* at 51.

140 Barnes v. Glen Theatre, Inc., 501 U.S. 560 (1991).

141 Hughes, Donna (2004). Best Practices to Address the Demand Side of Sex Trafficking 30 (Aug. 2004), http://www.uri.edu/artsci/wms/hughes/demand sex trafficking.pdf.

142 Flowers, R. Barri, *The Sex Trade Industry's Worldwide Exploitation of Children,* 575 ANNALS AM. ACAD. POL. & SOC. SCI. 147, 148 (2001).

143 Cotter, Kelly M., *Combatting Child Sex Tourism in Southeast Asia,* DENV. J. INT'L & POL'Y 493 (2009).

144 *Id.* at 499.

145 Allison Marston Danner, *Bias Crimes and Crimes against Humanity: Culpability in Context,* 6 BUFF. CRIM. L. REV. 389, 450 (2002).

146 ECPAT International, Frequently Asked Questions About Child Sexual Exploitation: What makes children vulnerable?, at http://www.ecpat.net/eng/csec/faq/FAQ.pdf (last visited Mar. 10, 2005).

147 LET THE GOOD TIMES ROLL: PROSTITUTION & THE U.S. MILITARY IN ASIA (Saundra Pollock Sturdevant & Brenda Stoltzfus eds.) (1992).

148 SUSAN BROWNMILLER, AGAINST OUR WILL: MEN, WOMEN AND RAPE (Simon & Schuster) (1975).

149 Isabelle Talleyrand, *Military Prostitution: How the Authorities Worldwide Aid and Abet International Trafficking in Women,* 27 SYRACUSE J. INT'L. L. & COM. 151, 152 (2000).

150 *Id.*

151 Emily Nyen Chang, Comment, *Engagement Abroad: Enlisted Men, U.S. Military Policy and the Sex Industry* 15 NOTRE DAME J.L. ETHICS & PUB. POL'Y. 621 (2001).

152 The Uniform Code of Military Justice, 10 U.S.C. §§ 801-946 (West 1998 & Supp. 2004); The Military Justice System, http://sja.hqmc.usmc.mil/JAM/MJFACTSHTS.htm (last visited Jan. 19, 2006).

153 *Id.*

154 Prosecutorial Remedies and Tools Against the Exploitation of Children Today Act of 2003, Pub. L. No. 108–21, 117 Stat. 650 (2003) codified as 18 U.S.C. § 2423 (2003).

155 Military Extraterritorial Jurisdiction Act of 2000, 18 U.S.C. § 3261 (2000).

156 Trafficking Victims Protection Act, 22 U.S.C. §§ 7101-7110 (2000).

157 Sex Tourism. Collins English Dictionary—Complete and Unabridged. New York, NY: HarperCollins Publishers 2003.

158 18 U.S.C. § 2423(c) (2003).

159 Prosecutorial Remedies and Tools Against the Exploitation of Children Today Act of 2003, Pub. L. No. 108-21, 117 Stat. 650 (2003) codified as 18 U.S.C. § 2423 (2003).

160 *Id.*

161 *Id.*

162 Anthes, Jr., Meril E., Chester James Taylor 2005 Grand Prize Winner: *Regarding Women and Children: Using International Trade Relations to Stem the Tide of the Sexual Exploitation of Women and Children,* 14 CT. INT'L TRADE L. J. 69 (2005).

163 Foley Bros. Inc. v. Filardo, 336 U.S. 281 at 284-285 (1949).

164 U.S. v. Clark, 435 F3d 1100 (2006)

165 *Id.*

166 *Id.* at 1109.

167 Blackmer v. United States, 284 U.S. 421, (1932).

168 The Trafficking Victims Protection Reauthorization Act (TVPRA) of 2003, Pub.L. No. 108-93, 117 Stat. 2875 (2003). Codified at 18 U.S.C. 1581 et seq.

169 *Id.*

170 Nam, J.S., *The Case of the Missing Case: Examining the Civil Right of Action for Human Trafficking Victims,* 107 COLUM. L. REV. 1655 (2007).

171 Roe v. Bridgestone Corp., 492 F.Supp.2d 988 at 999 (S.D. Ind. 2007).

172 *Id.*

173 *Id.* at 1008.

174 Doe v. Reddy, 2003 U.S. Dist. Lexis 26120 (N.D. Cal. 2003).

175 Roe v. Bridgestone Corp., 492 F.Supp.2d 988 at 1018 (S.D. Ind. 2007).

176 United States v. Jackson, 480 F.3d 1014 (9th Cir. 2007).

177 Farley, Melissa, *Symposium: Sex for Sale: Prostitution, Trafficking, and Cultural Amnesia: What We Must Not Know in Order to Keep the Business of Sexual Exploitation Running Smoothly,* 18 YALE J.L. & FEMINISM 109 (2006).

178 Hagner, Drake, *Tenth Annual Review of Gender and Sexuality Law: Criminal Law Chapter: Prostitution and Sex Work,* 10 GEO J. GENDER & L. 433 (2009).

179 Renton v. Playtime Theatres, Inc., 475 U.S. 41 (1986).

180 Barnes v. Glen Theatre, Inc., 501 U.S. 560 (1991).

Chapter Five

The Law of Pornography:

Possession, Distribution, and Production

of Obscene and Child Porn

"This much has been categorically settled by the Court, that obscene material is unprotected by the First Amendment."

Miller v. California
United States Supreme Court
413 U.S. 15 (1973)[1]

Legal Background

*P*ornography Defined: The representation in books, magazines, photographs, films, and other media of scenes of sexual behavior that are erotic or lewd and are designed to arouse sexual interest.[2]

There is no doubt that large numbers of people enjoy reading pornographic material and looking at pornographic pictures, images, and videos. If revenues sustain the sex worker industry discussed in the previous chapter, revenues do much more than sustain the pornography industry. U.S. pornographers consider corporations such as Apple, Amazon, and Microsoft to be lesser competitors when it comes to profits. In 2006, the U.S. porn industry earned approximately $13 billion on video, website, and magazine revenues.[3] That total includes, according to Congressional testimony, "Internet distribution hitting $2.5 billion in 2005." That equates to over a $1 billion per month in porn sales.[4] The *Denver Post* observed in 2006:

> Pornography is a booming business. Online porn alone grew from $1 billion in 2002 to $2.5 billion by the end of 2005. Visits to adult websites have exploded in just a few years, rising to 34 million unique users in 2004, up from 23 million in 2001. Mobile pornography—porno for cell phones, PDAs and devices like video iPods—also is predicted to grow from $700 million last year to $2.1 billion by 2009.[5]

Since all pornography is legal (with the exception of "obscene" images that are illegal), the pornography industry will always remain a major player among the mightiest of U.S. industries.

Another thing that is certain about pornography, community standards vary when it comes to the subject of acceptability and that means a differential application of the law from case to case. Several cities in a single state can all have distinctly different levels of approval when it comes to the legitimization of pornography in their community. The First Amendment protects all legal porn, but a businessperson such as a grocery store owner can choose to ban products that appear pornographic from their business. In a town or city where large numbers of citizens adhere to a strict religious orientation, acceptance levels are lower.

Credible arguments exist that an overuse of porn, like an overindulgence in anything, is harmful. Logically, overuse of porn can foster a desensitization and objectification of bodies for sexual purposes and such a mindset is incongruent with the nurturing required for healthy sexual relationships. Important arguments also exist that porn contributes to the degradation of females and when children are involved, obvious harmful effects are present. Lastly, the research findings are still inconclusive, but many studies continue to explore the relationship between the consumption of pornography and the perpetration of sex crimes such as rape.[6]

Pornography, like the activities related to sex work, is consumed by large numbers. Yet, porn remains taboo, and this cultural phobia is a way to foster social solidarity among conventional, middle-class segments of society. Predictably, many religious, political, and business leaders decry the circulation of pornography while engaging in flagrant criminality themselves in some manner. One of the most famous cases is that of millionaire businessman Charles Keating. Keating crusaded vehemently against pornography in the 1980s. At around the same time, he was sentenced to prison for fraud, racketeering, and conspiracy convictions.[7]

Because it seems "decent" to oppose pornography, porn has a tradition as a political scapegoat. Meaning, local politicians will try to garner votes by declaring that pornography is "bad." It is nearly unheard of for a politician to openly declare his or her fondness for pornography. Many respectable people may favor porn in secret, but not very many do so in public since human sexual expression is typically a private matter. In both cases of religious leaders and political leaders, any campaign to stamp out pornography may be more of a strategy to garner public approval than a sincere dislike of pornography. Notorious cases of fallen leaders who secretly indulged in porn and adulterous affairs abound.[8]

If pornography consists predominantly of pictures of people that are meant to capture our attention through a youthful, athletic shape, seminude, or glamorously made up, it is easy to see that pornography is everywhere. As in the figure below, most obvious are pictures of young bodies used for the purpose of selling products such as cars, beer, exotic vacations, or life insurance. Internet sponsors, highway billboards, and local newspapers, without fail, all include pornographic images to sell their products. The models used for women's underwear ads in the local newspaper are often indistinguishable from models posing in a typical porn magazine. Business interests know that sex sells and if a consumer product is associated with a beautiful man or woman, that product takes on added luster and importance in the mind of the consumer.

In history, from a study of the preceding chapters, it is obvious that pornography runs counter to American ideals of family, chastity, and religious devotion. It also stands to reason that many groups throughout the history of the

The public is bombarded with subtle forms of pornography in advertisements for many consumer products such as automobiles, beer, and holiday vacations.

United States have sought to suppress expression related to erotic writings or nude pictures. Since looking at erotic photos takes on a realm of privacy and does not always involve harm as with a sexual assault, there are also many groups have supported the free expression of erotica.

When pornography is conceptualized as speech, it partners with principles of democracy and gains a tremendous foothold in the courts as subject matter deserving of legal protection. If the dissemination of ideas is an American ideal, so is the dissemination of other forms of expression such as film, books, and pictures, even if controversial or objectionable to the majority. To be sure, in history it is said that controversial speech (pictures or words) is the true test of the strength of the Constitution and the First Amendment.[9]

Regulating and criminalizing pornography falls under the legal umbrella of obscenity. Originally in the U.S., the Common Law of nuisance and obscene libel paved the way for censorship of speech and expressive pornographic art. Early American laws legitimizing the regulation of obscenity can be found in the laws of blasphemy, libel, slander, and the subsequent censorship of anti-slavery literature in the mid 1800s. Vermont adopted the first criminal statute banning obscenity in 1821.[10] Congress' first law to regulate obscenity was in 1842 when a provision was inserted into the Tariff Act banning the importation of "all indecent and obscene prints, paintings, lithographs, engravings, and transparencies."[11]

Congress and the courts were also influenced by the 1868 British court decision of *Hicklin v. Regina*.[12] This case defined obscenity as any material that tended to "deprave and corrupt those whose minds are open to such immoral influences."[13] Many books by poets and artists such as D. H. Lawrence were banned based on isolated passages in their works. One of the first distinct "anti-obscenity" crusades was led by Civil War veteran Anthony Comstock. Comstock established the New York Society for the Supression of Vice in 1873 because he experienced "deep-seated fears about the drift of urban life" among "transplanted provincials" in the U.S.[14] In this sense, Comstock was a precursor to the Progressive Era reforms of 1900 that were similar in orientation. Comstock and other wealthy male leaders of anti-vice societies were motivated by a nostalgic yearning for cohesiveness and order in a seemingly anarchic, increasingly dangerous and diverse world.[15]

Inspired by Comstock, Congress passed the Comstock Law in 1873 that was obscenity legislation making illegal the delivery or transportation of "obscene, lewd, or lascivious" material.[16] This law was used to investigate a play by playwright George Bernard Shaw titled *Mrs. Warren's Profession,* which first showed in 1893. Comstock was a postal inspector and used the law to prohibit anatomy books from being sent through the U.S. Mail to medical students around the country.[17] In 1874 the Woman's Christian Temperance Union, still active today, joined Comstock and became a part of Progressive Era reforms, including alcohol prohibition to address the "large number of seemingly rootless, unsupervised urban workingmen who thronged to the city." The Women's Christian Temperance Movement had within its organization a Department for the Suppression of Impure Literature.[18]

The eras of the two World Wars were not a time of expansive speech or artistic expression. The national consciousness was on the more serious matters of national security and the social conservatism inherent in time of war. But after the wars, social attitudes sought a small degree of freedom from the wartime conservatism.

After the wars, the prevailing legal status of obscenity was defined in *Roth v. U.S.* in 1957.[19] The Roth case began a historic evolution of the law of obscenity as we know it today. Samuel Roth owned a printing business in New York City and sent out a monthly newsletter with pictures of naked women inside. He was convicted for distribution of obscene material under a federal obscenity law and appealed his case to the Supreme Court. The U.S. Supreme Court was partly divided and held in a 6-3 decision for the state, defining obscenity even more strictly than the British court did in *Hicklin v. Regina*.[20]

The Roth majority stated that pictures, movies, books, etc., are obscene if: "The dominant theme taken as a whole appeals to the prurient interest of the average person, applying contemporary community standards."[21] The majority reaffirmed that obscene material is not protected by the First Amendment. But all was not settled. Justices Hugo Black and William O. Douglas dissented stating that all obscene material is protected by the First Amendment.[22] In fact, Justices Black and Douglas felt no need to view the porn videos that were subjects of future court cases on obscenity since they believed all porn was protected. The seven other justices, however, had to view the porn videos numerous times to determine if the content was obscene or not.

The next important test for the law of pornography continued to produce divided opinions. In *Jacobellis v. Ohio* in 1964, the Court was severely divided on what would and what would not be protected by the First Amendment. Jacobellis is a case containing a famous quote by Justice Potter Stewart, who stated:

> *Roth* protects all obscenity except "hard-core" pornography. I shall not today attempt further to define the kinds of material I understand to be embraced within that short-hand description; and perhaps I could never succeed in intelligibly doing so. But I know it when I see it, and the motion picture involved in this case is not that.[23]

As pornography law continued to evolve, in *Memoirs v. Massachusetts* in 1966, the court added the terms "patently offensive" and "utterly without redeeming social value" to determine what material would fall outside the protection of the First Amendment.[24] The Memoirs court fashioned a three-part test that would provide the foundation for the Miller decision to come in 1973. The three parts are: (1) the dominant theme of the material taken as a whole appeals to a prurient interest in sex; (2) the material is patently offensive because it affronts contemporary community standards relating to the description or representation of sexual matters; and (3) the material is utterly without redeeming social value.[25]

Despite the work done by the Supreme Court in settling the law of pornography, the police, courts, and pornographers were still confused. The most definitive ruling came in 1973 in the case of *Miller v. California*.[26] Marvin Miller operated a mail order business and distributed magazines containing serious adult content. He was convicted for the distribution of obscene material under a state obscenity law in the state of California. A California appeals court upheld Miller's conviction and he appealed to the U.S. Supreme Court.[27] The Supreme Court affirmed the conviction and used the case to shore up the law of obscenity. Even though Miller was guilty, the Court sent a clear message about the importance of freedom of speech and expression as protected by the First Amendment and explicitly acknowledged "the inherent dangers of undertaking to regulate any form of expression." The Court also noted that "state statutes designed to regulate obscene materials must be carefully limited."[28]

While paying due respect to the importance of free expression in a democratic society, the court repudiated part of the Memoirs ruling. The Miller decision vacated the standard that "all ideas having even the slightest redeeming social importance ... have the full protection of the guaranties [of the First Amendment]."[29] This part of the Memoirs decision was too great of a door for pornographers to walk through to freedom. In reframing obscenity standards, the decision seemed to provide greater clarity for the fifty state courts when it came to the regulation of the distribution or possession of pornographic materials. The Miller obscenity doctrine created in 1973 is good law today and consists of a three-prong test to determine if a material is obscene and hence illegal:

(1) whether the average person, applying contemporary community standards would find that the work, taken as a whole, appeals to the prurient interest;

(2) whether the work depicts or describes, in a patently offensive way, sexual conduct specifically defined by the applicable state law; and

(3) whether the work, taken as a whole, lacks serious literary, artistic, political, or scientific value.[30]

For adult movies, print magazines, books, and flyers, Miller has stood the test of time allowing each community to decide what is illegal porn by way of the "community standards" provision of the Miller ruling. Other contexts, however, are still open to legal debate. The law still has some ground to make up in the areas of virtual child porn on the Internet, and this and other contexts have been the subject of lengthy litigation.

The proliferation of child porn is problematic for society but not necessarily for the law. Any material suggesting a relationship between sex and prepubescent or minor children is obscene and an automatic violation of the Miller test. In 1982, the Supreme Court outlawed the distribution of child porn in the case of *New York v. Ferber*.[31] As an extension of Ferber, the Supreme Court held that mere possession of a single image of child porn was illegal in *Osborne v. Ohio* in 1990.[32] Despite these clear rulings, the problem of child porn has festered, due mostly to the advantages of the Internet and digital anonymity for peddlers of child porn.

The Internet is primarily unregulated due to its unique characteristics (regulating the Internet is also covered in chapter 7: Digital Sex Crimes). It is not controlled or administered by any one individual or organization, yet operates successfully only because those who send and receive electronic communications do so with compatible technologies. Because there is "no single point at which the Internet is administered," it is not technically feasible for any single entity to control the amount of pornography being transmitted.[33] Therefore, government regulation of Internet child porn is extremely difficult, if not impossible. First, regarding "community standards," what constitutes a "community" for the definition of pornography on the Internet? Secondly, software technology makes the creation of virtual porn easy. If no persons are pictured in porn images, can the picture ever violate laws that prohibit child porn?

Aware of these legal obstacles, Congress has made several attempts to address child porn and other obscene porn on the Internet. Despite these attempts, success has been elusive. Congress seeks to protect minors because minors flock to the Internet. However, despite the noble intentions of Congress, the symbolic gesture of protecting children comes with the not-symbolic reality of censoring valuable speech. As a result, the U.S. Supreme Court has had to rein in Congress from censoring speech in the name of protecting children.

In 1996, Congress passed the Child Pornography Prevention Act.[34] The act stated that "any visual depiction" including a virtual, computer-generated image that "appears to be ... or conveys the impression ... of a minor engaging in sexually explicit conduct" is illegal.[35] Because of the ambiguities of computer generated software visualizations, the CPPA was controversial and in 2002 was struck down by the U.S. Supreme Court as too broad and unenforceable, in the case of *Ashcroft v. Free Speech Coalition.*[36] The Court held that the CPPA "abridged the freedom to engage in a substantial amount of lawful speech."[37]

In a similar move to protect minors and stay abreast with advanced technology, Congress passed the Communications Decency Act in 1996 that outlawed the posting of indecent speech or images—such as swear words—on the Internet.[38] The FCC had already regulated television and radio when it came to obscene content, but cable TV and the Internet were as yet unregulated. With the CDA, Congress attempted to respond to this new digital medium that was obviously a magnet for porn distributors, as well as minors. Similar to the CPPA, the Supreme Court had to rule in favor of speech and the First Amendment. In the 1997 case of *Reno v. ACLU,* the Court struck the CDA as a form of Internet censorship.[39] A range of poetry, music, and medical information would all be illegal under the CDA if it were allowed to be enforced.

Continuing in its role to provide for the health, safety, and welfare of the American public, and still cognizant of the material circulating the Internet, Congress responded to the rescinding of the CDA with a new law in 1998 called the Child Online Protection Act (COPA).[40] COPA criminalized anyone who posted material to the Internet that was "harmful to minors." Once again too broad and an infringement on speech as protected by the First Amendment, COPA was stuck down in the 2002 case of *Ashcroft v. ACLU.*[41] Among other things, the Court noted the advances in pornography filtering software and suggested that these filtering techniques were a less restrictive alternative to the proposed law. COPA would prohibit and make illegal a wide range of innocuous material such as short stories, poetry, and musical lyrics.

In the exercise of its constitutional mandate, the Supreme Court has been a check and balance on Congress's zealousness when it comes to the media-driven hyperbole surrounding minors and pornography. Hence, responding to a learning curve, Congress's latest attempt has made it past the scrutiny of the Supreme Court. COPA requires all libraries that receive federal funding to have pornography filters installed on all library networks to block minors from viewing pornography in library facilities.[42] Passed in 2000, the act seeks to prevent young persons from seeing "visual depictions that are harmful to minors."[43] As with similar information-controlled enactments that came before it, the law was immediately subject to a legal challenge. The American Library Association sued in federal court to enjoin enforcement of the law because "no filtering software successfully differentiates constitutionally protected speech from illegal speech on the Internet."[44] The law was struck down at trial, but in an appeal to the Supreme Court in 2003, the Supreme Court upheld the law "only if, as the Government represents, a librarian will unblock filtered material or disable the Internet software filter without significant delay on an adult user's request" thus allowing for access to various legal material when requested.[45]

The most recent statutory activity by Congress to limit minors' access to pornography is the proposed Deleting Online Predators Act of 2007. Still working its way through Congress, this law would impose criminal penalties on any owner or operator of a social networking website, such as MySpace and Facebook, that permits a minor to create a profile or join the site without parental consent. In addition, the law would require public libraries to block access to minors to e-mail and social networking sites or deny minors access to the Internet in its entirety. It is not known if this proposed law will pass constitutional muster if it is enacted.

Reading or viewing pornography is enjoyed by millions of people in the United States. Unless ruled obscene under Miller, all adult pornography is legal and protected by the First Amendment.

The law of pornography and obscenity has been a dynamic field and continues to evolve. Today's litigation maintains the spirit of earlier decisions such as *Miller v. California* and the emphasis on protected speech. In 2009, a group of publishers, retailers, and website operators sued Ohio's Attorney General in

U.S. District Court.[46] The plaintiffs alleged that an Ohio law that prohibited the dissemination or display of "materials harmful to juveniles," was unconstitutional and violated both the First Amendment and the Commerce Clause of the Constitution.[47] Plaintiffs specifically challenged the statute's definition of "harmful to juveniles," as well as the provisions governing Internet dissemination of those materials. In the first wave of decisions starting in the Ohio courts, the decisions held the statute to be unconstitutional because the statute's definition of "material harmful to minors" did not comply with Miller. The State of Ohio has appealed to the U.S. Supreme Court and the case is pending as of this writing.[48]

Table 1 Chronology of the Obscenity Doctrine in the United States.

Year	Case or Statute	Cited As
Common Law	*Blasphemy and Nuisance*	Common Law
1868	*Hicklin v. Regina*	LR 3 QB 360 (1868)
1873	*Comstock Law*	17 Stat. 598 (1873)
1957	*Roth v. U.S.*	354 U.S. 476 (1957)
1966	*Memoirs v. Massachusetts*	383 U.S. 413 (1966)
1973	*Miller v. California*	413 U.S. 15 (1973)
1973	*Paris Adult Theatre I v. Slaton*	413 U.S. 49 (1973)
1978	*Protection of Children Against Sexual Exploitation Act*	18 U.S.C. § 2251 et seq. (1978)
1982	*New York v. Ferber*	458 U.S. 747 (1982)
1988	*Child Protection and Obscenity Enforcement Act*	18 U.S.C. § 2257 et seq. (2005)
1990	*Child Protection Restoration and Penalties Enhancement Act*	18 U.S.C. § 2257 et seq. (2005)
1996	*Child Pornography Prevention Act*	Overturned
1996	*Communication Decency Act*	Overturned
1998	*Child Online Protection Act*	Overturned
2000	*Children's Internet Protection Act*	20 U.S.C. § 9134 et seq. (2000)
2003	*PROTECT Act*	18 U.S.C. § 2252 et seq. (2003)
2007	*[proposed] Deleting Online Predators Act*	Pending

Table 2 First Amendment Challenges to Anti-Pornography Laws—Digital Era.

Challenged Statute	U.S. Supreme Court Case	Outcome
Child Pornography Prevention Act (1996)	*Ashcroft v. Free Speech Coalition (2002)*	Overturned the Law
Communication Decency Act (1996)	*Reno v. ACLU (1997)*	Overturned the Law
Child Online Protection Act (1998)	*Ashcroft v. ACLU (2002)*	Overturned the Law
Children's Internet Protection Act (2000)	*U.S. v. American Library Association (2003)*	Upheld the Law

Possession

The propriety of possessing obscene material (excluding child porn) by adults is a complicated legal question. First, in many cases there is no way of knowing if the material in question is obscene. Someone may write a book and never imagine that it would come up to, or cross the line as being without redeeming social value; what is obscene to one person is not to another. Who is to say that a picture, book, or website lacks artistic value? Helpful in addressing the ambiguity over the representations of the pornography is the knowledge requirement (intent). Meaning, in *Smith v. California,* the Supreme Court mandated a scienter (knowledge) requirement.[49] This means that accidentally coming into possession of illegal pornography cannot be a crime unless the possessor knew the material was obscene and hence illegal.

In Smith, the owner of a bookstore was convicted for violating a municipal ordinance that made it unlawful for any person to have in their possession any obscene or indecent writing, or book in any place of business where books are sold or kept for sale. This meant that a bookstore owner could be sentenced to jail for possessing a book he had no idea was obscene. The Supreme Court held that this form of strict liability in cases like this would seriously restrict the dissemination of books that are not obscene, by penalizing booksellers even though they had not the slightest notion of the contents of the books they sold. Every bookseller would be placed under an obligation to make themselves aware of the contents of every book in their shop—even every page in every book. It would be unreasonable to establish these requirements and would tend to limit the public's access to constitutionally protected material. Today, possession statutes must include a knowledge requirement pursuant to the Smith decision.

Second, community standards are amorphous and difficult to define. First decided in *Jacobellis v. Ohio,* the principle implies "a determination of the constitutional question of obscenity in each case by the standards of the particular local community from which the case arises."[50] Material that may be illegal in one town may be legal in the next town, even though both towns are in the same state and region. Third, legal rulings have decided that some forms of possession cannot be prohibited by law no matter how obscene (excluding child porn).[51] Hence, if uncertain, the owner of the questionable material is advised to maintain private personal ownership in one's own home and decline to lend it to a friend, sell it to a neighbor, show it to a passerby, or exhibit it on a wall in the living room.

Outside of possession, numerous other aspects of coming into contact with obscene material are legally regulated and present an easier legal question. For example, distribution and production with the intent to distribute are regulated, but not simple possession of obscene materials. An act that can be kept entirely private, then, and has no commercial gain involved, tends not to be a crime in most states. The sample statute below from the state of Oklahoma may not pass legal muster if the law was challenged before the U.S. Supreme Court.

Definition of the Offense

As a general rule, for a conviction for possession of obscene material, most states will conduct a threshold determination that a work or material is within the range of patently offensive "hardcore" sexual material defined in *Miller v. California*.[52] At that point, the three-prong Miller obscenity test must then be used to determine if the material is outside the ambit of U.S. Const. Amendment 1 protection.

A matter is not obscene unless, taken as a whole, an average person applying contemporary community standards would find that the work predominantly appeals to the prurient interest or a shameful or morbid interest in nudity, sex, or excretion. If the matter is obscene, a person knowingly in possession of the material can be subject to arrest for possession of obscene material.[53]

Elements of the Offense

The elements to the crime of possession of illegal pornography that must be proven beyond a reasonable doubt are:

1. Knowingly;
2. possessing obscene material.

Sample Statute

The state of Oklahoma possession of obscene pornography statute reads as follows:

Oklahoma Statute Title 21, Chapter 39, Section 1021, Part A, Subsection 3 and 4:A. Every person who willfully and knowingly either:

3. Writes, composes, stereotypes, prints, photographs, designs, copies, draws, engraves, paints, molds, cuts, or otherwise prepares, publishes, sells, distributes, keeps for sale, knowingly downloads on a computer, or exhibits any obscene material or

4. Makes, prepares, cuts, sells, gives, loans, distributes, keeps for sale, or exhibits any disc record, metal, plastic, or wax, wire or tape recording, or any type of obscene material … shall be guilty, upon conviction, of a felony and shall be punished by the imposition of a fine of not less than Five Hundred Dollars ($500.00) nor more than Twenty Thousand Dollars ($20,000.00) or by imprisonment for not less than thirty (30) days nor more than ten (10) years, or by both such fine and imprisonment.[54]

Arguments Made By The Prosecution

In those jurisdictions where possession of obscenity is illegal, most prosecutions will look for someone who is part of a larger network of circulation rather than someone with a single image, magazine, etc. Possession cases involve two steps. In the first, a grand jury or lone prosecutor will have to make the determination that the material in question is obscene—that is, violates community standards and has no redeeming social value. In the second step, the state will have to prove possession—that the accused knowingly came into possession of the material. The state will have to proffer evidence of a sales receipt, Internet download, etc.

Arguments Made By The Defense

One of the main lines of argument for the defense will be that the accused came into possession of the material solely for use in the home, thereby using the ruling in the Stanley case. If outside the home, the defense can argue that the accused did not "knowingly" come into possession, but rather, that the accused was somehow given, lent, or found the material and did not intentionally come into possession of obscene material. Occasionally Internet pop-ups automatically place pornographic material in files on the computers operating system. These scenarios are good examples where the accused did not knowingly acquire the images.

Variations of the Law of Possession of Illegal Pornography

A. Possession of Obscene Material in the Home

Pornography deemed obscene by community standards is illegal under the Miller Test. As noted in the Miller opinion, "This much has been categorically settled by the Court, that obscene material is unprotected by the First Amendment."[55] As a result of these legal regulations, obscene material cannot be made, sold, bought, circulated, or distributed in any manner. There is, however, one exception. The exception does not pertain to obscenity, but rather, to privacy.

In the case of *Stanley v. Georgia*, Robert Stanley was home alone one evening when the police came to his door with a search warrant, looking for illegal gambling supplies and paperwork.[56] None were found but, instead, the police found three reels of film from a desk drawer in an upstairs bedroom. The film was confiscated by the police, examined at headquarters, and later deemed to be obscene and, hence, illegal. Mr. Stanley was arrested and convicted for being in possession of obscene material, a violation of a Georgia obscenity statute.[57] He appealed his conviction, lost the appeal,[58] and took the case to the U.S. Supreme Court.

Before the Supreme Court, Stanley merely argued that his right to free speech meant he could have pornography in his home, but the case took on much broader implications. The Supreme Court supported the relationship between oneself and one's home/castle, but imported more from the arrest of Stanley. The case went in the direction of integrity of thought and sexual liberty.

The Supreme Court ruled that Stanley's right to receive information and ideas represents a broad, constitutionally protected right of privacy over one's thoughts—the lascivious as well as the pure, those formulated on the street as well as in one's bedroom. Obscenity laws such as the one used to convict Mr. Stanley should be carefully evaluated because they only serve to chill and reduce the amount of speech available in the marketplace of ideas. If drawn too broadly, an obscenity law will limit the ability of consenting adults to see, hear, and view other consenting adults engaging in sexually explicit acts or using sexually explicit language. Justice Thurgood Marshall wrote the opinion and stated, "[T]he right to receive information and ideas, regardless of their social worth, is fundamental to our free society."[59] If certain forms of sexually explicit content are not popular or profitable, then they will not be produced. Maybe it is better to leave such matters to marketplace economic forces than to leave them to taxpayer-funded government censorship and prosecutorial discretion.

Furthermore, when viewed as a sexual aid or stimulus, obscene material deserves additional consideration as part of an individual's interest in sexual autonomy and privacy. In reversing the decision of the lower courts and declaring part of Georgia's possession of obscenity law unconstitutional, the Court stated:

> These are the rights that appellant is asserting in the case before us. He is asserting the right to read or observe what he pleases—the right to satisfy his intellectual and emotional needs in the privacy of his own home. He is asserting the right to be free from state inquiry into the contents of his library. Georgia contends that appellant does not have these rights, that there are certain types of materials that the individual may not read or even possess. Georgia justifies this assertion by arguing that the films in the present case are obscene. But we think that mere categorization of these films as 'obscene' is insufficient justification for such a drastic invasion of personal liberties guaranteed by the First and Fourteenth Amendments. Whatever may be the justifications for other statutes regulating obscenity, we do not think they reach into the privacy of one's own home. If the First Amendment means anything, it means that a State has no business telling a man, sitting alone in his own house, what books he may read or

The First Amendment insists that citizens have the right to read or watch any material of their choosing, no matter how obscene, free from government interference, when in the privacy of their own home.

what films he may watch. Our whole constitutional heritage rebels at the thought of giving government the power to control men's minds.[60]

B. Possession of Obscenity Outside the Home, on the Street

The Stanley decision was narrow. It may be legal to have obscene pornography (excluding pornography involving minors) in the home, but it is nevertheless questionable as to whether someone can buy obscene pornography over-the-counter from an adult bookstore and walk outside to look at what was just purchased. Admittedly the law is inconsistent on the question of mere possession of obscenity outside of the home. States can outlaw obscenity, but exactly where the material is specifically prohibited is another question. Of course, the Stanley case above precludes making obscenity illegal in the home.

Additionally, legally, there is no question about selling, mailing, receiving through the mail, producing, importing from overseas, or carrying across state lines obscene material. All of these contexts are prohibited. But purchasing locally over-the-counter is not a settled matter. Local purchases for re-sale or further dissemination is illegal, but purchase for private consumption is another question.

Local purchase and possession of obscene material is traditionally a local matter that is a low priority for law enforcement. Only twelve states have laws that prohibit possession of obscenity, for example, while standing outside on the street.[61] It is a subtle, but important feature in a democratic society that the law and legislation not limit the amount of material they study and learn from because of a fear they may be arrested. One judge stated, "If a legislative prohibition of possession of books and papers is valid, it may discourage law abiding people from even looking at books and pictures and thus interfere with the freedom of speech and press guaranteed by the First Amendment."[62] The law tends to seek the interruption of channels of production and distribution rather than mere possession.[63] Possession of literature should be encouraged, not discouraged. In addition, a small number of states support the consumption of pornography, such as Oregon, which constitutionally supports mere possession of obscene material.[64]

Not only is mere possession less socially harmful in the eyes of the law, a purchaser can always make the argument they did not know the material they were purchasing was obscene. This is especially true since obscenity is based on a "community standard" and who knows what that is from one picture or cartoon to the next. Hence, since the law requires "knowingly receives" obscene material for a conviction, the case can easily be dismissed based on the fact the accused did not "know" the material had crossed the line to being obscene. If someone buys through the mail, the Internet, or downloads material he or she "should have known" was obscene, they could be found guilty of receiving obscene material—still not the same as purchasing locally at a legally operated adult bookstore.

In *Ohio v. Mapp,* a woman rented a room in her home to a man, but the man moved out suddenly and left most of his possessions behind.[65] The woman gathered up all of the man's possessions, including obscene magazines that she had discovered, and prepared the room for the next tenant. She stored the man's possessions in her basement hoping to return them to him at some future point in time.

Someone came across the obscene material and alerted the police who then came and made an arrest. The woman was convicted of possession of obscene material in a jury trial. She appealed to an Ohio Appeals court and lost the appeal, and hence appealed to the State of Ohio Supreme Court.[66] Her main argument concerned her use of the materials. She argued that she had no intention to ever use the obscene material (use, view, look at, distribute, etc.). The State Supreme Court had to use the state's obscenity statute and framed the legal question strictly in terms of "possession." The court stated:

> Defendant offered evidence to prove that these books and pictures belonged to a man who had rented from her and occupied a room in her home; that, when she learned he was not going to return or use the room for the balance of the last month for which he had rented it, she decided to use the room for herself and to pack up his belongings and store them until he came for them; that, in doing so, she found these lewd and lascivious books and pictures and packed them in a box and one of her suitcases with his other belongings with the purpose of storing them until he came for his belongings; and that she never looked at these books and pictures again before they were seized by the police.

> In our opinion, this evidence of defendant establishes that she had these books and pictures 'in [her] possession or under [her] control' within the meaning of those words as used in Section 2905.34, Revised Code [of Ohio]. Judgment affirmed.[67]

A dissenting judge stated:

> I cannot agree that mere private possession of … [obscene] literature by an adult should constitute a crime. The right of the individual to read, to believe or disbelieve, and to think without governmental supervision is one of our basic liberties, but to dictate to the

mature adult what books he may have in his own private library seems to the writer to be a clear infringement of his constitutional rights as an individual.[68]

C. Possession of Obscenity While Crossing State Lines

Possession of obscene material may be legal in the privacy of one's home, but the same sphere of privacy is not similarly applicable on leaving the home and crossing state lines. In *U.S. v. Orito*, George Orito, a known pornographer, took a flight from San Francisco to Milwaukee while in possession of numerous reels of obscene film purportedly for his own use. On landing at his destination, he was detained by security and had his bags searched again pursuant to law.[69] Presumably, airport security discovered the films, viewed them at some point, and arrested Orito for knowingly transporting obscene material by common carrier in interstate commerce, a violation of federal obscenity law.[70]

At trial, Orito argued that his personal travel with obscene material for private use should be protected under his right of privacy as guaranteed by the Constitution. After all, it was legal for him to look at the material in the privacy of his own home. To a degree, his argument was plausible since no one would see the material except Orito (minors would not see the material nor would unsuspecting adults). The trial court ruled for Orito and dismissed the case. The state appealed directly to the U.S. Supreme Court. The Supreme Court granted certiorari and took the case.[71] The Court reversed the decision of the trial court, holding against the accused. The Supreme Court noted two factors that weighed heavily against the accused. First, obscene material is illegal according to Miller.[72] Second, Congress has a long tradition of regulating highways, railways, maritime jurisdictions, airspace, etc., and controlling the various avenues of commerce in the country.[73] The Court stated:

> [W]e cannot say that the Constitution forbids comprehensive federal regulation of interstate transportation of obscene material merely because such transport may be by private carriage, or because the material is intended for the private use of the transporter. That the transporter has an abstract proprietary power to shield the obscene material from all others and to guard the material with the same privacy as in the home is not controlling. Congress may regulate on the basis of the natural tendency of material in the home being kept private and the contrary tendency once material leaves that area, regardless of a transporter's professed intent. Congress could reasonably determine such regulation to be necessary to effect permissible federal control of interstate commerce in obscene material, based as that regulation is on a legislatively

determined risk of ultimate exposure to juveniles or to the public and the harm that exposure could cause.[74]

Additional Court Cases: Possession of Illegal Pornography
Stanley v. Georgia
394 U.S. 557 (1969)

CASE SUMMARY

PROCEDURAL POSTURE: Appellant sought review of the judgment of the Supreme Court of Georgia, which affirmed his conviction for possession of obscene matter in violation of Ga. Code 1933, § 26-6301.

OVERVIEW: While searching appellant's home for evidence of bookmaking pursuant to a search warrant, federal and state agents discovered obscene films. Appellant was then convicted of knowingly having possession of obscene matter in violation of Ga. Code 1933, § 26-6301. The state supreme court affirmed the conviction. On appeal, the court held that while the State had an interest in the sale and distribution of obscene matter, it did not have any interest in appellant's mere possession of obscenity in his own home. The court found that Ga. Code 1933, § 26-6301 violated U.S. Const. amend. I and U.S. Const. amend. XIV in that it was an attempt to control a person's private thoughts. The court held that mere possession of obscene materials could not be a crime and, therefore, reversed the judgment and remanded the case.

OUTCOME: The court reversed the judgment and remanded the case.[75]

Distribution of Illegal Pornography

The front-end distribution of obscene material takes on some of the legal dimensions of those who traffick in controlled substances. Dealers and various sellers of pornography are looked down on socially as peddlers of smut and have been targets of moral panics, lawsuits, and even assassination attempts. In 1978 famous pornographer Larry Flynt was paralyzed from the waist down in an assassination attempt in Georgia. He was shot by a sniper while leaving a courthouse where he was fighting an obscenity charge. Distributors can be isolated as the cause of various social ills whether they've contributed to those ills or not. Lastly, distributors have a vested financial interest in the distribution function, and therefore, are not going away anytime soon. The state can only hope to manage and govern the problem rather than try to eradicate it altogether.[76]

A brick-and-mortar store selling obscenity or child pornography can be raided and the contraband removed. This tactic can cut off access to porn by consumers and slow the distribution. In such a case, little disruption occurs to innocent businesses. On the other hand, operators of illegal porn websites elude detection easily and will forever remain anonymous or outside of competent jurisdiction. In addition, in the digital realm illegal porn cannot be completely physically seized since other copies are almost assuredly floating around in cyberspace somewhere. Therefore, all law enforcement can realistically do, with the resources they have available, is minimize the number of locations where illegal pornography is available.

Because of the relatively easy sums of money to be made, pornography distributors use every channel possible to serve the demand. Traditionally this includes the postal service, and also over-the-counter bookstore sales. Movie houses, and cable television are also channels but are more easily regulated by the state. Where these historic avenues of commerce have become targets of law enforcement investigation, porn distributors have expanded to setting up shop in foreign nations where the laws are more relaxed. Lastly, Internet websites have emerged as the newer, preferred distribution channel.

The Internet affords numerous advantages to the distribution of pornography, obscenity, and child pornography. Secret domain names, impersonal coordination with fellow distributors, and the use of various bots and Trojan programs can close down the digital shop instantly and erase traces of evidence, making it cumbersome for investigators and the police to locate and prosecute distributors.

Distributors also have more legal room to maneuver on the Internet. Legislative attempts to regulate the Internet have been fraught with cumbersome failures, and distributors are aware of this. The rapid expansion of technology in the past few years has left states and the federal government struggling to keep up with the pornography industry in order to regulate obscenity. State governments have not been able to devise a plan capable of limiting the spread of contraband material online. State and federal laws have a number of inherent Constitutional problems and have been shown to simply not work. Monitoring devices are quickly detected, and forcing ISPs to become police agents has also not worked.

Blocking websites, a topic discussed more fully in chapter 7, is an option, but has been shown to run into unique difficulties. When laws have been passed, such as the CDA to block illegal porn websites, those targeted sites were successfully blocked.[77] However, if the only websites that were blocked were those that contained illegal porn there would be no problem. Complications arise however when websites that contain protected speech also get blocked by accident. Some blocked sites may have had erotic, but constitutionally protected, content while other sites that get blocked can be completely unrelated to adult material.

Definition of the Offense

Georgia Code Ann. § 26-2101 reads in relevant part: Distributing obscene materials.

(a) A person commits the offense of distributing obscene materials when he sells, lends, rents, leases, gives, advertises, publishes, exhibits or otherwise disseminates to any person any obscene material of any description, knowing the obscene nature thereof, or who offers to do so, or who possesses such material with the intent so to do. ...

(b) Material is obscene if considered as a whole, applying community standards, its predominant appeal is to prurient interest, that is, a shameful or morbid interest in nudity, sex or excretion, and utterly without redeeming social value and if, in addition, it goes substantially beyond customary limits of candor in describing or representing such matters. ...

(d) A person convicted of distributing obscene material shall for the first offense be punished as for a misdemeanor, and for any subsequent offense shall be punished by imprisonment for not less than one nor more than five years, or by a fine not to exceed $ 5,000, or both.[78]

Elements of the Offense

The elements to the crime of the distribution of illegal pornography that must be proven beyond a reasonable doubt are:

(1) sells, delivers, or provides or offers or agrees to sell, deliver, or provide any obscene writing, picture, record, digital electronic file, or other representation or description of the obscene;

(2) presents or directs an obscene play, dance, or other performance, or participates directly in that portion thereof which makes it obscene;

(3) publishes, exhibits, or otherwise makes available anything obscene to any group or individual; or

(4) exhibits, presents, rents, sells, delivers, or provides; or offers or agrees to exhibit, present, rent, or to provide: any motion picture, film, filmstrip, or projection slide, or sound recording, sound tape, or sound track, video tapes and recordings, or any matter or material of whatever form which is a representation, description, performance, or publication of the obscene.

Sample Statute

The federal distribution of obscenity statute reads as follows:

Title 18, United States Code, Chapter 71. Obscenity, § 1461. § 1461. Mailing obscene or crime-inciting matter. Every obscene, lewd, lascivious, indecent, filthy or vile article, matter, thing, device, or substance; and, Every article or thing designed, adapted, or intended for producing abortion, or for any indecent or immoral use; and, Every article, instrument, substance, drug, medicine, or thing which is advertised or described in a manner calculated to lead another to use or apply it for producing abortion, or for any indecent or immoral purpose; and, Every written or printed card, letter, circular, book, pamphlet, advertisement, or notice of any kind giving information, directly or indirectly, where, or how, or from whom, or by what means any of such mentioned matters, articles, or things may be obtained or made, or where or by whom any act or operation of any kind for the procuring or producing of abortion will be done or performed, or how or by what means abortion may be produced, whether sealed or unsealed; and, Every paper, writing, advertisement, or representation that any article, instrument, substance, drug, medicine, or thing may, or can, be used or applied for producing abortion, or for any indecent or immoral purpose; and, Every description calculated to induce or incite a person to so use or apply any such article, instrument, substance, drug, medicine, or thing: Is declared to be nonmailable matter and shall not be conveyed in the mails or delivered from any post office or by any letter carrier.

Whoever knowingly uses the mails for the mailing, carriage in the mails, or delivery of anything declared by this section or section 3001(e) of title 39 to be nonmailable, or knowingly causes to be delivered by mail according to the direction thereon, or at the place at which it is directed to be delivered by the person to whom it is addressed, or knowingly takes any such thing from the mails for the purpose of circulating or disposing thereof, or of aiding in the circulation or disposition thereof, shall be fined under this title or imprisoned not more than five years, or both, for the first such offense, and shall be fined under this title or imprisoned not more than ten years, or both, for each such offense thereafter.[79]

Arguments Made By The Prosecution

Possession cases may be controversial (there may not even be a statute, depending on the state), but all fifty states outlaw distribution. Prosecutors look for any variation on the theme of give, sell, rent, lease, loan, convey, publish, exhibit, transmit, send, etc. Easy cases for the state are grossly obscene movies, magazines, or pictures displayed or exhibited or sold in any public manner whatsoever. Solid evidence can include books, pictures on the wall of a saloon, movies shown in a theatre, etc. In any of these contexts, if the state can prove the product is legally obscene under the Miller test, the state can get a conviction for the distribution of obscene material.

Arguments Made By The Defense

"Knowingly" is an element to the offense of distribution. Hence, the defense can argue that, for example, a bookstore owner did not "know" anything in his or her book inventory was obscene.

The accused will argue that if they knew any material actually crossed the line from pornography to illegal obscenity, they would have immediately removed the material from their shelves. The same defense will be used for website systems administrators, owners of video stores, etc. They can argue the "knowingly" element. Distributors can always argue the Miller test as well and allege that the material in question has artistic value and hence is legal and protected by the First Amendment.

Variations of the Law of Distribution of Illegal Pornography

A. Adult Bookstore Sales of Obscene Material

Anytime a substance or material is illegal to possess, such as illegal drugs, anyone who sells such illegal material is subject to criminal prosecution in the same manner as one who is in possession of the matter. What about the sales of obscene pornography in an adult bookstore? The law regulates various features of an adult bookstore such as the location of the store (away from schools or where minors might congregate), size of the facility, and hours of operation. If the material is not obscene, the sales are legal and permissible. But if the material is legally obscene, the law is not clear when it comes to adult bookstores.

If illegal, obscene pornography may not be produced, presented, circulated, distributed, delivered, exhibited, etc. If that is the case, then of course, over-the-counter sales in an adult bookstore are illegal. However, the *Stanley v. Georgia* case declared that obscene material is legal in the privacy of the home.[80] Therefore, shouldn't sales be legal? In *Hawaii v. Kam,* a clerk in an adult bookstore named Brian Kam sold obscene material to an undercover police officer and was arrested and convicted. Kam appealed to the Hawaii Supreme Court.[81]

Kam's main argument centered on the Stanley case. He argued that he had a privacy right to sell obscene material just as someone has a privacy right to view obscenity in the home. The Supreme Court of Hawaii agreed with Kam and reversed his criminal conviction. The Court declared a broad right of privacy for Kam under the Hawaii State Constitution Article I, Section 6 that cannot be abridged without the state showing a compelling state interest for doing so.[82] This holding only applies to the State of Hawaii. So far, no other jusrisdiction has crafted a privacy right for sales of adult obscene material to other adults. The Court stated:

> It is obvious that an adult person cannot read or view pornographic material in the privacy of his or her own home if the government prosecutes the sellers of pornography pursuant to HRS 712-1214(1)(a) and consequently bans any commercial distribution.
>
> Since a person has the right to view pornographic items at home, there necessarily follows a correlative right to purchase such materials for this personal use, or the underlying right of possession in the home becomes meaningless.

Because the enforcement of HRS 712-1214(1)(a) has a similar detrimental impact on privacy rights, the State must demonstrate a compelling governmental interest exists to prohibit the sale of pornographic material. The State, however, has not met its burden.[83]

B. Dissemination of Obscene Materials Through the Mail

The mail cannot be used as a vehicle to conduct an illegal business. The statute noted above, U.S.C. Section 1461, prohibits the use of the mails for the distribution of obscene materials. In the case of *U.S. v. Reidel,* defendant Norman Reidel advertised in the newspaper the sale to persons over 21 years of age of booklet titled "The True Facts About Imported Pornography."[84] He believed he was in compliance with the law, even though he admitted the materials were obscene. He thought that since he was transacting with adults only, and in a private transaction, the materials were protected by the First Amendment just as obscene materials were protected by the First Amendment in the Stanley case.[85] At trial in federal district court, the district court agreed with Reidel and dismissed the case. The state appealed to the Supreme Court and the Supreme Court issued certiorari and agreed to hear the case.[86] The Court upheld the law as stated in Section 1461 and ordered the case back to a new trial where a conviction was imminent. The Court stated:

> The District Court gave Stanley too wide a sweep. To extrapolate from Stanley's right to have and peruse obscene material in the privacy of his own home a First Amendment right in Reidel to sell it to him would effectively scuttle Roth, the precise result that the Stanley opinion abjured. Whatever the scope of the 'right to receive' referred to in Stanley, it is not so broad as to immunize the dealings in obscenity in which Reidel engaged here—dealings that Roth held unprotected by the First Amendment.
>
> The right Stanley asserted was 'the right to read or observe what he pleases—the right to satisfy his intellectual and emotional needs in the privacy of his own home.' 394 U.S. at 565. The Court's response was that 'a State has no business telling a man, sitting alone in his own house, what books he may read or what films he may watch. Our whole constitutional heritage rebels at the thought of giving government the power to control men's minds.' Ibid. The focus of this language was on freedom of mind and thought and on the privacy of one's home. It does not require that we fashion or recognize a constitutional right in people like Reidel to distribute or sell obscene materials. The personal constitutional rights of those like Stanley to possess and read obscenity in their homes

and their freedom of mind and thought do not depend on whether the materials are obscene or whether obscenity is constitutionally protected. Their rights to have and view that material in private are independently saved by the Constitution.

Reidel is in a wholly different position. He has no complaints about governmental violations of his private thoughts or fantasies, but stands squarely on a claimed First Amendment right to do business in obscenity and use the mails in the process. But Roth has squarely placed obscenity and its distribution outside the reach of the First Amendment and they remain there today. Stanley did not overrule Roth and we decline to do so now.[87]

Most states legally prohibit the distribution of obscene material over-the-counter in adult bookstores.

C. International Importation of Obscene Materials

Although the Internet has become the primary realm for the distribution of pornography, the government will always seek to guard the nation's borders from the importation of illegal materials. In *U.S. v. Thirty-Seven Photographs,* Milton Luros flew from Europe into the United States with thirty-seven erotic photographs that he needed to prepare for a book on the subject of human sexuality.[88] In a random border search of Luros' luggage, U.S. Customs officials discovered the pictures, suspected they may be legally obscene and seized them pursuant to federal law.[89]

Luros felt his First Amendment rights protected his bringing the pictures across the border. He also relied on the law as formulated in the *Stanley v. Georgia* decision, which stated the possession of illegal obscenity in the home is protected. At a trial in federal district court, Luros won and his case was dismissed. However, the state appealed and the case went before the U.S. Supreme Court.[90]

The Supreme Court overturned the decision of the trial court and ruled in favor of the state. Although the Court had ruled two years earlier in Stanley that obscenity was legal to have in the privacy of one's home, the importation of illegal obscene materials was an entirely different context. In an attempt to secure the borders from such activity, the case was remanded for a re-trial in light of the Supreme Court's ruling. The Court stated, obscene materials may be removed from the channels of commerce when discovered in the luggage of a returning foreign traveler even though intended solely for his private use. That the private user under [our decision in] Stanley may not be prosecuted for possession of obscenity in his home does not mean that he is entitled to import it from abroad free from the power of Congress to exclude noxious articles from commerce. Stanley's emphasis was on the freedom of thought and mind in the privacy of the home.[91]

Additional Court Cases: Distribution of Illegal Pornography

United States v. Extreme Associates

431 F.3d 150 (3d Cir. 2005)

CASE SUMMARY

PROCEDURAL POSTURE: Appellant, the government, sought review of a decision from the United States District Court for the Western District of Pennsylvania, which dismissed an indictment brought against appellees, distributors of obscene materials over the Internet. The district court struck down the statutes in the indictment, 18 U.S.C.S. §§ 1461, 1462, and 1465, as unconstitutional restrictions on substantive due process privacy rights.

OVERVIEW: This appeal required the court to decide whether the district court erred by dismissing an indictment brought against a distributor of obscene materials under 18 U.S.C.S. §§ 1461 and 1465, on the ground that those statutes violated the privacy rights of the distributor's customers under the Fifth Amendment doctrine of substantive due process. At issue was whether the district court correctly analyzed Supreme Court precedent with respect to both obscenity laws and privacy rights. The district court concluded that the Supreme Court's decision in Lawrence v. Texas invalidated the primary rationale for the statutes regulating the distribution of obscenity because the Government's asserted interests, even if compelling, were not narrowly advanced by those statutes. On review, the court found that the district court erred because the Supreme Court's decisions in Reidel and its progeny, which repeatedly upheld the federal obscenity statutes, were directly applicable to the instant case. This case was not distinguishable simply because the distribution occurred over the Internet. Thus, the Supreme Court's decisions upholding the same federal statutes dictated the result in this case.

OUTCOME: The court reversed the order of the district court and remanded the case for further proceedings consistent with this opinion.[92]

Production of Illegal Pornography

Knowingly producing obscene material is a heightened focus for law enforcement because the production process lends itself to the overall consumption by society and that is something the law seeks to deter. If producers can become less active, the logic goes, the availability and consumption will be less. Hence, producers and manufacturers of obscene film, art, poetry, or magazines are sanctioned by the criminal law in an effort to reduce the overall supply of illegal porn that circulates in commerce.

Producers can include heavily financed Hollywood movie studios, but the label also attaches to a teenager who takes a picture of oneself nude with their telephone. The law is mainly concerned with the hard core XXX-rated video producer who seeks to employ young models for the purpose of making sex-related films that can be sold.

Reality porn producers have found a niche market.[93] Reality pornography is pornography as if made by small independent film-makers: The subjects are found on location, the camera is often handheld, and there is little embellishment. Like other reality shows, the overhead is low and often the images and plot are enjoyed by the audience. Reality porn producers, however, have not been meticulous in their ethics. In 2001, 22-year-old Brian Buck was approached by a group of pornographers known as Shane's World at his fraternity house at Arizona State University. They offered him the opportunity to participate in their porn videos.[94] Mr. Buck agreed and took part. When the pornographers published his videotaped exploits, he was forced to resign from student government, expelled from his fraternity, barred from university housing and employment, and disowned by his parents. When Mr. Buck asked for compensation from Shane's World, he received an offer of $500. Buck seemed to have paid a high price for his acting role in the pornographic film.[95]

For a deterrent effect to have a meaningful impact, the law implicates all parties associated with production, including producers, directors, and actors. Anyone who is tangentially related to the production process of an illegal film, such as camera personnel or make-up artists, can be held liable for aiding and abetting in the production process.

Despite the ever-present threat of having a product labeled obscene, manufacturers have moved quickly to take advantage of emerging technologies to make porn. The Internet explosion of the mid 1990s took law enforcement by surprise and it seems as though the police have yet to catch up. The number of host computers on the Internet exploded from 300 in 1981 to 9.4 million in 1996.[96] In a ten-year period, the number of host computers increased by a factor of 150.[97] Additionally, new technologies emerged that made it possible for pornographers to produce images that appeared to be actors and actresses and children engaging in sexual acts, but were created entirely by computer and did not involve actual persons, thereby evading many legal provisions. Pornography manufacturers could mount an affirmative defense to a charge under 18 U.S.C. § 2252A(a)(5)(b) by proving that the images used in the making of their pornographic material were not real. This tactic presented a substantial challenge to law enforcement, as even skilled online agents could not distinguish between a virtual "model" and a real model victim of sexual exploitation.

In 1988, Congress passed the Child Protection and Obscenity Enforcement Act that made it unlawful to use a computer to manufacture illegal pornography.[98] The act imposed record keeping and disclosure requirements on the producers of certain sexually explicit materials, even if the material is not obscene and hence legal. In 1994, federal pornography law was amended again to punish the production of sexually explicit depictions of a minor and to provide for mandatory restitution for the victims of child pornography.[99]

Producers are regulated in detail and not only by the Miller test. For example, having a minor female pull up her shirt for the pornographer is legal, unless the episode is part of a "sexual performance" in which case the act would be illegal under both state and federal law.[100] Much hinges on the definition of "sexual performance," or its primary component, "sexual conduct." As in obscenity law, an image produced of the adult female breast alone is not illegal. Under federal law, an exposed breast is only criminal if bared as part of simulated sexual intercourse, and it is described in gender-neutral terms.[101] In Florida, "sexual conduct" only occurs if a woman's breast is touched "with the intent to arouse or gratify the sexual desire of either party."[102] "Sexual conduct" is often limited to penetrative intercourse or sodomy, with a separate category of "exploitive exhibition" that makes criminal the exposure of the lower half of one's body with the purpose of sexually stimulating a viewer. Even if one exposed one's genitals to the camera, there is no guarantee that filming that act would be illegal. Producers are advised to stay abreast of the exact provisions of the law in the state where they are producing.

Definition of the Offense

Participation or engagement in, or management, operation, production, presentation, promotion, advertisement, sponsorship, electronic communication, or display of hard core sexual conduct.[103]

Elements of the Offense

The elements of the crime of the production of illegal pornography that must be proven beyond a reasonable doubt are:

1. to employ, use, persuade, induce, entice, or coerce;
2. any other;
3. to engage in, or assist any other person to engage in;
4. any sexually obscene conduct;
5. for the purpose of producing any visual depiction of such conduct is guilty of the preparation of obscene material.[104]

Sample Statute

The South Carolina production of illegal pornography reads as follows:

> South Carolina Obscenity Statute. Section 16-15-325. Participation in preparation of obscene material prohibited; penalties. Any individual who knowingly:
>
> (a) photographs himself or any other individual or animal for purposes of preparing an obscene film, photograph, negative, slide, videotapes, motion picture, or digital electronic files for the purpose of dissemination; or
>
> (b) models, poses, acts, or otherwise assists in the preparation of any obscene film, photograph, negative, slide, videotapes, motion picture, or digital electronic files for the purpose of dissemination is guilty of a misdemeanor and, upon conviction, must be imprisoned for not more than one year and fined not more than one thousand dollars.[105]

Arguments Made By The Prosecution

Producers are at the top of the food chain and logically targeted by the state. In the mind of the prosecution, if it were not for producers, there would be no distributors or consumers and all would be well. Hence, anyone who makes obscene porn will catch the eye of the state. Producers, however, are less visible than distributors or consumers and the state will have to go looking for them. On obtaining obscene material, the state has to find the parties responsible for the putting together of the film, book, cartoons, etc. Assuming the material fails the Miller test, once found, the accused will face charges as the party culpable for the creation and production of the obscenity.

Arguments Made By The Defense

"I didn't know it was 'obscene'" is a favorite line of illegal pornography producers. The defense can argue they were merely crafting artistic expression as they always have and that they meant no harm. The defense will argue the First Amendment aggressively and attempt to enlist the support of gigantic media conglomerates such as Times-Warner publications or Fox Entertainment who all want the First Amendment to protect all of their performance arts.

Variations of the Law of Producing Illegal Pornography

A. Production of Soft Porn Motion Pictures

All of us have gone to the movies and watched a film. Under most circumstances, the makers of the film are not criminals. The same holds true for adult, soft-porn films. Anyone is legally free to make, produce, and market such a film and famous movie producers have done so for a long time. But what if the actors and actresses agree to engage in activities for the film that would be illegal if the acts were not part of a movie?

In *New Hampshire v. Theriault,* Robert Theriault, a security officer for a local district court-house in New Hampshire approached a young couple whom he had seen in the courthouse before, and who were occasionally there to pay a fine.[106] Theriault asked them if they "needed employment" and could make a movie with them as the lead actor and actress. He stated that he would pay them just as any movie star is paid for their role in a film. The movie would be sex-related and the couple would be filmed having sexual intercourse with the defendant acting as movie director.

The couple declined the offer and, instead, called the police. Theriault was visited by the local police where he was arrested and convicted of a state prostitution statute, RSA 645:2 which states in part: A person is guilty of a misdemeanor if the person … pays, agrees to pay, or offers to pay another person to engage in sexual contact … with the payor or with another person.[107] The trial court judge determined that Theriault wanted to pay the victims so the victims could engage in sex and so that Theriault could experience sexual arousal and gratification from watching. He was found guilty.[108]

The accused appealed, however, since his goal was merely to make a movie and not to experience sexual arousal or gratification. He alleges that the prostitution statute does not apply to him, and additionally, that his right to make a movie is protected by the free speech provisions of both the state and federal constitutions.[109]

Since it was not possible to prove that the defendant was trying to do anything except make a movie, the appeals court held for the defendant and reversed his conviction. The court stated:

> The facts boil down to the defendant offering to remunerate the couple to have sexual intercourse while being videotaped. There was no evidence or allegation that the defendant solicited this activity for the purpose of sexual arousal or gratification as opposed to making a video. Thus, if the statute constitutionally prohibits the defendant's conduct, a request to pay two individuals to make a sexually explicit video would be unprotected under the free speech guarantees of the State Constitution.[110]
>
> To uphold the conviction in the instant case, where the only facts adduced at trial were that the defendant offered to pay two people to have sexual intercourse while being videotaped, would infringe upon an area of speech protected by the State Constitution.[111]

© artcalin, 2011. Used under license from Shutterstock, Inc.

The artistic expression factor in the Miller test shelters movie productions from allegations of producing obscene material.

B. Duty to Confirm Age of Models

The 1969 President's Commission on Obscenity and Pornography found that pornography producers, catering to the lucrative child pornography market, often use "very young-looking" performers to give the viewer the impression they are minors.[112] Except in the most obvious instances, no one can be certain whether the performers are really under the age of 18 or if they just look under age 18. That not only hindered prosecution of child pornography offenses but also provided an excuse to those in the distribution chain, who could profess ignorance that they were actually dealing in sexual materials involving children. Producers, too, could escape the laws' sanction by claiming they were misled about the performer's age or did not know the performer's true identity. Producers can always argue that it is difficult to determine when a person is under 18. Difficult or not, production personnel have a legal duty to be cognizant of the ages of actors and actresses.[113]

Even if it presents a burden to check ages, pornography producers are prohibited from using minors for models in their shows, websites, magazines, peep shows, etc., and it is the duty of the producer to confirm the ages of all models and participants. "I didn't know she was a minor" or "she said she was 18" are not valid defenses to the charge of exploitation of a minor for the purpose of producing pornography.

In *U.S. v. Thomas*, pornographer Charles Thomas used a minor in some of his pornographic magazines and mailed the magazines to customers who had contracted to receive them.[114] The magazines were actually ordered by the police and on receiving them, Thomas was arrested pursuant to a federal child pornography statute.[115] Convicted in federal court, Thomas appealed his case to federal circuit court and lost again. He appealed to the U.S. Supreme Court, but certiorari was denied and the U.S. Supreme Court felt no need to review the case.[116] Thomas was sentenced to prison.

While his case was not unique, the legal ruling was important concerning the duty to confirm ages. Thomas tried to argue that the law required him to have **knowledge** that the model he used in his magazines was underage, and, that he simply did not know and should not be punished for making a simple mistake.[117] Since a lot of criminals use the excuse "I didn't know" the appeals court was prepared to deal with Thomas's defense.

The court read the plain language of the federal pornography statute. In one section of the statute, the accused has to **knowingly** transport the illegal pornography to be convicted. In another section, the accused has to **knowingly** receive illegal pornography to be convicted. These two sections of the federal pornography law, 18 U.S.C. § 2252 are below:

(1) knowingly transports or ships in interstate or foreign commerce or mails, any visual depiction ... knowingly receives, or distributes any visual depiction that has been transported or shipped in interstate or foreign commerce or mailed or knowingly reproduces any visual depiction for distribution in interstate or foreign commerce or through the mails ...

Nowhere, however, does the law state that a producer or maker of porn has to know the age of his or her models. Meaning, mistake of age is not a defense because the law does not require knowledge of age for a conviction. When it comes to age, the law takes on strict liability—if a model is under 18, the accused is guilty and there are no defenses available.[118]

A final point on the duty to confirm ages is worth noting. The law needs to be flexible where possible and other courts have entertained mistake of age defenses, but only after it was proven that the accused was seriously misled. For example, in *U.S. v. U.S. District Court for the Central District of California*,[119] under the statute being used, an accused's awareness of a minor's age was not an element of the offense, just like in *U.S. v. Thomas* above. Thus, knowledge of a minor's age was not necessary for conviction. However, although Congress could punish those who knowingly, recklessly, or negligently subjected minors to sexual exploitation, it could not impose serious criminal sanctions on persons who formed a reasonable good-faith belief on the basis of a diligent investigation that their acts were protected by the First Amendment. Imposing severe sanctions on defendants without allowing them to present a reasonable mistake of age defense would chill protected speech. The mistake of age defense may only be used by those who have "diligently investigated" the performers' age, and that such an investigation requires the viewing of identification documents.[120]

C. The Proposed Pornography Victims Compensation Act

Not yet law, a proposition to compel producers of hard-core pornography to pay more attention to the effects of their trade is the proposed Pornography Victims Compensation Act.[121] This draft legislation would allow an aggrieved party to sue a pornographer in civil court if the party was somehow harmed by someone who came under the influence of pornography. An example would be for a wife to sue a pornographer because her husband assaulted her after consuming porn. The proposal was originally called the Bundy Bill because convicted killer Ted Bundy admitted that part of his motivation for killing women was his viewing of pornographic videos.

Vicarious, third-party liability like this is firmly established in the doctrine of legal culpability. Parents can be held liable for the actions of their children, whiskey bars can be liable for the overindulgence and accidents of their patrons, employers for the actions of their employees, and so forth. The law of product liability also contributes a model by holding producers liable for the effect of their product on the consumer. Other examples also exist.

The reason the proposal is not yet law is because some strong objections exist to oppose the legislation. First, science has not yet established a valid and reliable correlation between viewing pornography and subsequent criminal behavior.[122] Further, as with other First Amendment arguments concerning censorship, legal action taken as a result of someone looking at porn would cause many book writers and booksellers to take their material off the shelves for fear of being sued by someone who looks at their material, then commits a crime. Lastly, in a trial where evidence is presented to a jury, the assault on a vulnerable female may causally drive the jury to find the material in question "obscene" when it may not be, or may not have had anything to do with the motive behind the assault.

Aside from this proposal, victims of a sex offense can similarly bring suit against a pornographer in different ways, but the likelihood of success is lower. Another legal recourse would be the common law of torts. Under this course of action, the plaintiff must show that pornography was a substantial factor in the commission of the sex crime and that it was reasonably foreseeable that the pornography would lead to such an offense. In addition, the plaintiff must demonstrate that pornography was an invitation to commit the offense rather than "mere 'facilitation' of an unintended adverse result. Under these legal criteria, the defense can easily demonstrate the existence of dozens of intervening variables that explain why a sex offense occurred, and none of them may be related to viewing pornography.

In *Rice v. Paladin Enterprises,* Paladin Enterprises published a how-to manual titled *Hit Man.*[123] The publication was a detailed murder manual that encouraged people to be killers and showed them how to commit murder for hire. The manual had an effect on the behavior of a hit man hired by an estranged husband to murder his wife and handicapped son. At the trial, the trial court granted a motion for summary judgment and dismissed the case because of the tenuous link between the publication and the crime. On appeal, the appellate court reinstated the case and allowed it to go to a full trial before a jury. The murderer followed the content of *Hit Man* so closely that the appeals court held that the First Amendment did not preclude a cause of action against the manual's publisher. The Rice case suggests that if pornography instructs a sex offender how to carry out violent sexual fantasies, and shows how to act out fantasies and desires, a court may allow a cause of action against the producer of the material, irrespective of First Amendment protections.[124]

The same legal theory applies to sex offenses. In *Herceg v. Hustler Magazine,* a mother, Mrs. Herceg, brought a negligence and products liability action against Larry Flynt's *Hustler Magazine* for its publication of an article entitled "Orgasm of Death."[125] The magazine article described the paraphilia-related practice of autoerotic asphyxiation. In this practice, the participant arranges for a noose-like stranglehold to be placed on him- or herself and when the choking becomes intense, the person engages in sexual self-stimulation. The plaintiff's child accidentally killed himself while following the article's instructions on how to do erotic asphyxiation.[126] In a trial court victory, the jury awarded damages to the plaintiff.[127] On appeal, however, the appellate court reversed, and held that the publication was protected against a lawsuit by the First Amendment. In addition, the appellate court found that the article, among other things, advised against performing the dangerous act, thus the deceased incurred a degree of an assumption of risk.[128] The court stated:

> The constitutional protection accorded to the freedom of speech and of the press is
>
> not based on the naive belief that speech can do no harm but on the confidence that

the benefits society reaps from the free flow and exchange of ideas outweigh the costs society endures by receiving reprehensible or dangerous ideas. Under our Constitution, as the Supreme Court has reminded us, 'there is no such thing as a false idea. However pernicious an opinion may seem we depend for its correction not on the conscience of judges and juries but on the competition of other ideas.'[129] We rely on a reverse Gresham's law, trusting to good ideas to drive out bad ones and forbidding governmental intervention into the free market of ideas. One of our basic constitutional tenets, therefore, forbids the state to punish protected speech, directly or indirectly, whether by criminal penalty or civil liability.[130]

Additional Court Cases: Production of Illegal Pornography

People v. Freeman

758 P.2d 1128 (1988)

CASE SUMMARY

PROCEDURAL POSTURE: Defendant adult video producer appealed a judgment from the Superior Court of Los Angeles County (California) that convicted him of five counts of pandering pursuant to Cal. Penal Code §266I, based on the hiring of five actresses who performed sex acts in a film. Defendant was not charged with any violation of the obscenity laws, Cal. Penal Code §311 et seq., in connection with production or distribution of the film.

OVERVIEW: Defendant adult video producer was convicted of five counts of pandering under Cal. Penal Code §266i, after he hired and paid actors to perform in an adult film, which portrayed sexually explicit acts. The court of appeal affirmed his conviction and defendant sought review. The court held that there was no evidence that defendant paid the acting fees for the purpose of sexual arousal or gratification, his own or the actors, and that the payment of acting fees in a non-obscene film was the only payment involved. The court held that defendant did not participate in any of the sexual conduct, thus did not engage in either the requisite conduct nor did he have the requisite mens rea or purpose to establish procurement for purposes of prostitution. The court held that even if defendant's conduct was somehow found to come within the definition of "prostitution" literally, the application of § 266i to the hiring of actors to perform in the production of a non-obscene motion picture would impinge unconstitutionally on First Amendment values, that the governmental interest be unrelated to the suppression of free expression. The court reversed the court of appeal judgment.

> **OUTCOME:** The court reversed the court of appeal judgment convicting appellant of pandering because it was based solely on the payment of wages to the actresses in his film, which was not determined to be obscene. The court found that defendant did not engage in the requisite conduct to be found guilty of pandering and that he did not possess the mens rea for the crime.[131]

Child Pornography

Few crimes of late have raised the ire of American society as have the crimes associated with child pornography. Hence, the law is clear: Any party in possession of, or who in any way promotes, distributes, or produces this form of pornography is subject to an arrest and conviction.[132] Sentences are comparatively long and the convicted offender is placed on the Registry for all to see.[133]

Since most images of child pornography (including cartoons or stories) are located in cyberspace, accurate statistics are difficult to determine. According to one source, images of child porn circulated worldwide have increase by well over 1,000 percent in the last twenty years.[134] Approximately 20 percent of all Internet porn consists of child porn and approximately 20,000 new images are posted to the Internet weekly (these data do not indicate the number of images that come down from the Internet on a weekly basis).[135] A tremendous amount of money is made with this form of pornography and underworld child porn groups such as the Howard Nichols Society, Rene Guyon Society, Pedophile Information Exchange (PIE), and the NAMBLA (North American Man/Boy Love Association) coordinate with each other to increase the level of sophistication to their operations and production of child pornography.[136]

The laws banning child porn are ideological, but also rational. Meaning, research has touched on a causal link between the viewing of child pornography and child molestation. Though viewing child pornography does not, of course, inexorably lead to sex crimes against children, statistics suggest that the connection between viewing child pornography and committing subsequent sexual abuse against children is significant.[137] One study cited in congressional testimony found that at least 80 percent of purchasers of child pornography actively abuse children, and "a 1984 study by the Chicago Police Department confirmed that in almost 100% of their annual child pornography arrests, detectives found photos, films, and videos of the arrested individual engaging in sex with other children."[138] A 2000 study by the Bureau of Prisons revealed that, of sixty-two offenders convicted of either child pornography or traveling to engage in sex with a minor, 76 percent admitted to prior unprosecuted sex crimes against children.[139] A chief from the FBI's Crimes Against Children Unit testified that "there is a clear correlation between sexual abuse of children and the collection of child pornography," and cited an FBI sting operation that netted ninety-two collectors of child pornography, thirteen of whom admitted having sexually molested forty-eight children total.[140] He testified that images of child pornography "whet [child predators'] appetites for real world sexual encounters with children." Thus, child pornography is causally linked to actual child molestation: "[Researchers] believe that child pornography is central to pedophiliac psychology, social orientation, and behavior. … The trading of pornography with other pedophiles may lead to exchanging victims for their sexual services."[141]

The first comprehensive federal statute to address child porn was the Protection of Children Against Sexual Exploitation Act of 1977.[142] This law prohibited the use of a minor in the production of obscene materials. In addition, it prohibited the transportation, importation, shipment, and receipt of child pornography for the purpose of sale or distribution by any interstate means. The law also provided for enhanced penalties of up to ten years in prison and a $10,000 fine for a first offense and up to fifteen years and $15,000 fine for subsequent offenses.[143]

The main Supreme Court case to address child porn is *N.Y. v. Ferber*.[144] In this case, the Supreme Court removed the Miller test from the equation and held that child pornography is a strict liability crime not protected by the First Amendment. For someone to be convicted of the possession of child porn, a court does not need not find that the material appeals to the prurient interest of the average person, nor is it required that sexual conduct portrayed be done so in a patently offensive manner. Lastly, the material at issue need not be considered as a whole. Differing from adult porn laws, child porn laws may impose criminal responsibility without some element of knowledge on the part of the defendant. In upholding the anti-child porn statute at issue in the Ferber case, the Court reiterated a state's compelling interest in "safeguarding the physical and psychological well-being of a minor." A democratic society rests, for its continuance, upon the healthy, well-rounded growth of young people into full maturity as citizens.

The Child Protection Act of 1984 increased the age of minors for purposes of the law from a person under age 16 to one under age 18.[145] Also, fines increased ten-fold for a first-time offense to $100,000 and almost seventeen times for subsequent offenses to $200,000. Fines for organizations such as website affiliates that violate the law increased to $250,000 for a first-time offense. The Child Sexual Abuse and Pornography Act of 1986 banned the production and use of advertisements for child pornography and included a provision for civil remedies for personal injuries suffered by a minor who is a victim of pornographers.[146] It also raised the minimum sentences for repeat offenders from not less than two years to imprisonment to not less than five. The Child Protection and Obscenity Enforcement Act of 1988 made it unlawful to use a computer to transmit advertisements for or visual depictions of child pornography.[147] In 1990, Congress amended this law with the Child Protection Restoration and Penalties

Enhancement Act making it a federal crime to sell any visual depiction of child pornography by computer.[148] Congress amended the statute again with the Protection of Children from Sexual Predators Act of 1998 to expand the definition of child pornography by providing for the prosecution of persons for the production of child pornography if the image was produced with materials that have been mailed, shipped, or transported in interstate or foreign commerce, including by computer.[149]

Armed with sufficient statutory enactments, law enforcement has shown no reluctance in pursuing these cases. Not only do they receive accolades from the greater public, but the offenders are a classic example of the fish jumping into the boat; mentally disturbed men visit child porn websites and fail to comprehend the illegality of their actions. Another key reason for the law enforcement success with these cases is that the evidence is easy to obtain and none of the evidence is subject to an obscenity test. Child porn is strict liability, although in a small number of cases there is a question if the picture is related to pornography or not. A court has to determine, for example, if the image is an innocent family photo, or if the image is pornographic but portrayed as a family photo. The Supreme Court has indicated that a depiction of a nude minor, without more, does not automatically constitute child pornography. However, even nonnude visual depictions can qualify as child pornography because the federal child pornography statute contains no nudity or discernibility requirement. The definition of child porn can still be unclear and depend on subjective viewpoints.[150]

For the reasons above, the government has outposts in all possible locations for the monitoring of suspects who may show an interest in viewing, buying, possessing, and/or circulating child porn. The U.S. Postal Service watches the mail, including mail from abroad, the FCC (Federal Communications Commission) watches television programming, the FBI lurks around the Internet, and the local police act undercover as buyers of products in adult bookstores.[151]

Definition of the Offense

An individual commits the offense of sexual exploitation of a minor if, knowing the character or content of the material, he possesses material that contains a visual representation of a minor engaging in sexual activity.[152]

Elements of the Offense

The elements of the crime of child pornography that must be proven beyond a reasonable doubt are:

1. Any visual depiction,

2. of anyone under 18 years of age,

3. engaging in sexually explicit conduct.[153]

Sample Statute

The state of New Mexico child pornography statute reads as follows:

New Mexico 30-6A-3. Sexual exploitation of children.

A. It is unlawful for a person to intentionally possess any obscene visual or print medium depicting any prohibited sexual act or simulation of such an act if that person knows or has reason to know that the obscene medium depicts any prohibited sexual act or simulation of such act and if that person knows or has reason to know that one or more of the participants in that act is a child under eighteen years of age. A person who violates the provisions of this subsection is guilty of a fourth degree felony.[154]

Arguments Made By The Prosecution

One reason prosecutors love these cases is because they are relatively easy. If the accused is in possession of any media that depicts a minor and sex, it is illegal. No cumbersome Miller test is applicable. The laws do not allow for a mistake-of-age defense. There is no wrangling over whether the accused "knew" the material was illegal, and there is no possibility for arguing the First Amendment exists with cases of child porn. In addition, the laws are comprehensive and do not provide for loopholes and the voting public praises the state when they get an easy conviction for anyone in possession of, or working with, child porn.

Arguments Made By The Defense

The number of convictions for consumers of child porn would have you think they would stop, but the consumption continues. Consumers, distributors, etc., have few defenses and face stiff sentences. The only possibility for a defense is to argue that the media in question is not pornographic—not intended to arouse sexual interest. These defenses have been used for relatives who possess computer files of grandchildren swimming naked in the family backyard pool. For all other contexts, the presumption of innocence becomes tenuous and the public is warned when it comes to possessing pictures of minors not fully clothed.

Variations of the Law of Child Pornography

A. Child Porn and Strict Liability

Strict liability is a legal doctrine that imposes liability on the accused without the availability of any defense. For example, today anyone caught in possession of child pornography is guilty of a crime and the culpable party cannot raise any defenses. The only questions that may arise are: (1) is it a child, and (2) is it pornography? If theses two questions are answered in the affirmative, the accused is guilty. Questions about "obscenity" and "community standards" are inapplicable.[155]

The states and federal government experimented with various lewdness laws and obscenity statutes to prohibit the production, distribution, and possession of child porn up to and including the *Miller v. California* case in 1973, but questions still remained concerning classic art, literature, and poetry, medical texts, and other material that may reveal a minor naked in some manner. The U.S. Supreme Court cleared up much of the confusion surrounding the law of child porn in the 1982 in the case of *New York v. Ferber.*[156]

Paul Ferber owned an adult bookstore in Manhattan in New York and sold two videos to an undercover police officer that depicted minors engaged in sex. He was arrested and convicted under state law and the appeals court upheld his conviction.[157] The state supreme court, however, reversed his conviction and gave his sale of the material First Amendment protection. The state supreme court stated that the statute Ferber was convicted under did not meet the Miller test for obscenity and thus would "prohibit the promotion of materials which are traditionally entitled to constitutional protection from government interference under the First Amendment."[158] The State of New York appealed to the U.S. Supreme Court.

The U.S. Supreme Court held against Ferber and for the State of New York and decided that child pornography may be banned without first being deemed obscene under the Miller Test. The Court determined that statutes regulating child pornography are not unconstitutional under the First Amendment. Although it conceded that the Court of Appeals' decision "was not unreasonable in light of [previous Supreme Court] decisions," the Court found that this case constituted the "first examination of a statute directed at and limited to depictions of sexual activity involving children. As such, the Court established clear-cut reasons for the fifty states to pass laws prohibiting minors to be included in pornography. The five reasons are:

1. The government has a compelling interest in preventing the sexual exploitation of children.

2. Distribution of visual depictions of children engaged in sexual activity is intrinsically related to the sexual abuse of children. The images serve as a permanent reminder of the abuse, and it is necessary for government to regulate the channels of distributing such images if it is to be able to eliminate the production of child pornography.

3. Advertising and selling child pornography provides an economic motive for producing child pornography.

4. Visual depictions of children engaged in sexual activity have negligible artistic value.

Using children as beauty models is legally inadvisable in a legal environment suspicious of children and glamour photography.

© Oleg Kozlov, 2011. Used under license from Shutterstock, Inc.

5. Thus, holding that child pornography is outside the protection of the First Amendment is consistent with the Court's prior decisions limiting the banning of materials deemed "obscene" as the Court had previously defined it. For this reason, child pornography need not be legally obscene before being outlawed.[159]

B. Virtual Child Pornography

Bearing in mind the fundamental role of free speech in democracy, laws that restrict speech must have a compelling justification. In 1996 Congress passed the Child Pornography Prevention Act to outlaw the possession of child porn.[160] However, the Ferber (1982) and Osborne (1990) cases had already accomplished that objective. In the CPPA, Congress expanded the definition of child porn to include "any visual depiction" of a minor "that appears to be" involved in sexual activity.[161] The reason Congress felt the need to expand the definition of child porn was because technological advances had made it possible to create visual depictions that appear to be minors engaged in sexually explicit conduct that are virtually the same as actual photographs of real children engaged in identical conduct. Real pictures obviously would be a violation of the federal child pornography laws. However, computer-generated photographs that are make-believe or an alteration of a photograph in which real children were used or a photograph in which no real children were used at all pose a problem because under the existing laws, prosecutors must prove that a real child was used in the creation of the photograph.

While the goal of the law was the continued protection of children, the extent of the law was too broad. Any video or film, such as *Romeo and Juliet,* would be illegal. Some of the Disney Channel productions would run afoul of the law. A book publisher, several artists and virtual pornographers, and the adult entertainment trade association called The Free Speech Coalition sued in federal court to enjoin enforcement of the law before it was ever used.

In the case of *Ashcroft v. Free Speech Coalition,*[162] the trial court ruled against the plaintiffs and for the state, indicating that it was "highly unlikely" that a film such as *Romeo and Juliet* would be treated as criminal contraband under the statute. In addition, the trial court found that the government had a compelling interest in preventing harm to actual children and that the statute was sufficiently narrowly tailored to promote this interest. The trial court concluded that the government's interest was no less compelling where the images are virtually indistinguishable from those in which an actual child is used.

The decision of the trial court was appealed to the Ninth Circuit Court of Appeals and the decision was reversed. The Ninth Circuit ruled that the CPPA was overbroad because it would outlaw paintings, pictures, or virtual images that were neither obscene nor produced by exploiting real minors.[163] The Ninth Circuit found the CPPA to be a content-based restriction on protected speech that does not further any compelling governmental interest because the prohibited images do not include real children. The case was appealed to the U.S. Supreme Court for a final determination and the Supreme Court struck down the law as being overbroad, agreeing with the Ninth Circuit.[164] The Supreme Court recognized Congress' compelling interest in protecting children from abuse. However, in responding to the government's argument that the CPPA only prohibits images that are virtually indistinguishable from child pornography using real children, the Supreme Court reiterated its position in *N.Y. v. Ferber* where it upheld a prohibition on the distribution and sale of child pornography, as well as its production. The Court stated that it upheld the laws at issue in Ferber because "these acts were intrinsically related to the sexual abuse of children" by "creating a permanent record of the abuse" and supporting "an economic motive for its production." Further court decisions that reinforced this prohibition focus on the victim of the crime, not the actions themselves. The CPPA, however, prohibits speech that records no crime and creates no victims. The court stated:

> CPPA prohibits speech despite its serious literary, artistic, political, or scientific value. If these films [such as Rome and Juliet or American Beauty], or hundreds of others of lesser note that explore those subjects, contain a single graphic depiction of sexual activity within the statutory definition, the possessor of the film would be subject to severe punishment without inquiry into the work's redeeming value. This is inconsistent with an essential First Amendment rule: The artistic merit of a work does not depend on the presence of a single explicit scene.[165]

C. Cartoons, Written Words, and Minors

When it comes to minors and sexually explicit material, the law raises numerous red flags. When only adults are involved, a degree of leeway is provided because many classic works of art depict or suggest adults engaged in romance or sexual expression. Much less leeway, and often none at all, pertains to romance, sexual expression and children. The law seeks to protect minors until the age of majority and a developmentally suitable time for a young person to consider sexual expression.

In *U.S. v. Whorley*, Dwight Whorley was using computing resources at a Virginia job resource center called the Virginia Employment Commission.[166] Persons seeking work there were allowed to use the computers to scan help wanted ads. Whorley did not use the computers for employment, but rather, used them to download and print various Internet materials, including cartoons and written stories about minors and sexual expression, specifically twenty Japanese anime-style pornographic cartoons involving children. A supervisor at the site caught him at the computer and in possession of material he had just printed and he was escorted off the premises. The supervisor called the police and the police searched Whorley's login and gathered evidence of his browsing, downloading, and printing activities. His case was handed over to the FBI and he was arrested and convicted in federal district court pursuant to a federal statute.[167]

On appeal, Whorley used two arguments to defend himself. First, he stated that the material he downloaded and printed did not involve any pictures or images and only involved cartoons and short stories. He argued that to be convicted, he had to have material that used pictures or images that unmistakably showed minors in sexual activity. His second argument was that the material he viewed, downloaded, and printed may involve innocent cartoons or poetic short stories of minors, but nonetheless did not involve real human beings—real children—and, therefore, he committed no crime.[168]

The appeals court easily upheld Whorley's conviction and dismissed his two arguments. As for the first argument, the Court referred to the leading case on obscenity, *Miller v. California*, which defined obscenity in the context of "works," "taken as a whole"[169] and made clear that "works" include both pictorial representations and words such as the kind Whorley downloaded and printed such as cartoons and short stories.[170] The Court stated, "[O]bscenity can, of course, manifest itself in conduct, in the pictorial representation of conduct, or in the written and oral description of conduct."[171]

As for his second argument, that no real children were involved, the Court similarly dismissed. The Court stated:

> [The law] criminalizes receipt of 'a visual depiction of any kind, including a drawing, cartoon, sculpture, or painting,' that 'depicts a minor engaging in sexually explicit conduct.' In addition, the law unambiguously states that it is not a required element of any offense under this statute that the minor depicted actually exist.[172]

Additional Court Cases: Child Pornography
New Mexico v. Myers
207 P.3d 1105 (2009)

CASE SUMMARY

PROCEDURAL POSTURE: The State challenged a judgment of the New Mexico Court of Appeals that reversed defendant's convictions of seven counts of sexual exploitation of children under N.M. Stat. Ann. § 30-6A-3(D) (2001) for videotaping girls using the bathroom, arguing that the appellate court erred in concluding that the images were not lewd, sexually explicit, or manufactured for the purpose of sexual stimulation.

OVERVIEW: On appeal, the State argued that the appellate court erred in concluding that the images were not lewd or sexually explicit because they did not depict a child engaged in sexually provocative conduct and erred in concluding that N.M. Stat. Ann. § 30-6A-3 only prohibited hard-core child pornography. The court held that all child pornography was prohibited under the statute and that the photographs were lewd, explicit, or manufactured for the purpose of sexual stimulation as those terms were defined in N.M. Stat. Ann. § 30-6A-2 (2001). The photographs depicted female victims unclothed from the waist down, either before or after they used the toilet, and the perspective from which the images were shot gave a sense that the viewer was peering through a peephole. Because the images had a voyeuristic and deviant quality that rendered them sexual in nature, the images were lewd. Further, although the site of the photographs--a workplace bathroom--was not inherently sexual, the private nature of the setting, the intimate bodily function in which the victims were engaged, and the voyeuristic quality of the images combined to transform the setting into a fetishistic and sexualized one.

OUTCOME: The judgment of the appellate court was reversed, and the case was remanded to that court with instructions to consider the parties' remaining claims that the statute was avoid for vagueness as applied to defendant's conduct and that the trial court erred in staying defendant's obligation to register as a sex offender during the pendency of the appeal.[173]

Chapter Five Summary

© Yuri Arcurs, 2011. Used under license from Shutterstock, Inc.

The viewing of a single image of child pornography is a felony offense.

In many cases, pornography-related crimes are like other nuisance sex offenses: they have occurred for a very long time and are not apt to go away anytime soon. The criminal justice system can only hope to manage and govern this set of offenses and does not rationally hope to end illegal activity associated with pornographic material.

In earlier times, the concerns over porn revolved around the immorality of promiscuity, loveless sex, and a lifestyle where marriage, children, and fidelity were not prominent concerns. Today, in addition to those traditional concerns, pornography is thought to foster divisions within monogamous partnerships, promote the sexualized objectification of people, especially young adults, and contribute to lowered sexual hygiene and mental well-being. Another contemporary concern over pornography and its illegal variation, obscenity, is the statistical link between pornography and criminal behavior—does porn lead to crimes such as rape or sexual assault? Most of the research to date does not support this correlation.[174]

The primary reason for the ceaseless circulation of porn in society is not exactly the demand, but in addition, is the stunning financial incentives for those who produce and distribute pornography. The money that stands to be made from peddling erotic material is difficult to comprehend and the porn industry rivals any "pillar of industry" in the U.S. or around the world.

The advent of computing technology in the mid 20th century and computer networking technology in the 1960s paved the way for an unforeseen explosion in the porn trade. By the time the Internet became public in the 1990s, a home PC was commonplace and created the conditions for massive growth in the demand for erotic material that, heretofore, many consumers were disinclined to access by walking into an adult bookstore. Since the advent of the Internet, the trend has continued with consumers using handheld and other mobile computing devices to access pornography anonymously wherever they may be.

Many segments of society disapprove of porn materials, even though more subtle variations are found in mainstream society in nearly every direction. Corporate advertising, in particular, uses sex to sell products by having an attractive young model associated with a consumer product such as a car or clothing. Despite widespread skepticism over objectionable content, most pornography is legal. Pornographic books, magazines, and websites are forms of artistic expression and are considered speech. As such, most porn material is protected by the First Amendment and any law, rule, or regulation banning such "speech" is immediately scrutinized as an unconstitutional prohibition on the freedom of speech.[175] Those who defend pornography from government censorship are not necessarily advocates of porn, but rather, defenders of the Constitution and mindful of what can happen if speech is curtailed in a democratic society. What is important concerning the First Amendment and pornography regards the creation of ideas and information and the uninhibited circulation of those ideas and information. Anti-pornography proposals "chill" the freedom to speak. An educated civilization and a democratic society, without question, need a free flow of ideas and information. This unlimited material is used for growth, progress, intellectual and scientific achievement, and most of all, for the ability of citizens to evaluate government and make educated decisions about public policy in order to govern themselves and hold their elected leaders accountable. As one judge stated, "[T]he right of the individual to read, to believe or disbelieve, and to think without governmental supervision is one of our basic liberties."[176] To the extent that anti-pornography efforts decrease First Amendment protections, everyone in a democracy loses. Arguably, it is fortunate that the U.S. Supreme Court recognizes the importance of First Amendment protections in its statutory regulation of pornography and obscenity.[177]

Thus, pornography is protected speech and legal unless it is judged as "obscene." Obscenity is a vague term, but applies to pornography if the porn is determined by community standards as having no social value and seeks to appeal to prurient interests. How do we know if porn is obscene? The U.S. Supreme Court provides three criteria:

1. whether the average person, applying contemporary community standards would find that the work, taken as a whole, appeals to the prurient interest;

2. whether the work depicts or describes, in a patently offensive way, sexual conduct specifically defined by the applicable state law; and

3. whether the work, taken as a whole, lacks serious literary, artistic, political, or scientific value.[178]

A tremendous amount of time and effort has gone into the "obscenity doctrine" in the United States, but we cannot say that the law has necessarily evolved that much. For example, the three criteria enumerated above were established in 1973 in the Supreme Court decision of *Miller v. California* and created well before then. That 1973 case remains the law of obscenity today. Porn is illegal if it meets all of the three Miller test criteria. The Miller decision was a more refined formulation of the law of obscenity as first proposed in the *U.S. v. Roth* case from 1957.

Since Roth, then Miller, it has been quite a legal battle, one most intensely fought where porn meets the digital world. The Supreme Court decision in *Stanley v. Georgia* remains a pinnacle case because Stanley crystallizes the role of the First Amendment in the possession of illegal pornography. In a unique irony, illegal obscene pornography (which does not include child pornography) is legal when possessed in the privacy of one's home. Stanley was a constitutional declaration, not so much to let adults view porn, but more so to keep the door open on citizens' capacity to read what they want, write what they are inspired to write, and think broadly without government interference. While supporting cherished freedoms, Stanley simultaneously is a decision that made things difficult in other contexts. For example, if obscenity is legal in the home, it must also be legal to purchase, otherwise, what good is the right to keep it in the home? Despite the inherent conflict, most states prohibit the selling of obscenity at adult bookstores or over the Internet, thus making the Stanley decision somewhat empty.

Pornography has flooded the Internet and created a cause for alarm because minors and children can easily stumble on Internet porn sites. Nonlegal responses to this modern dilemma have been relatively effective. The use of Internet filters, encryption, password protection, and even cyber nanny's have all assisted in separating youths from the viewing of Internet porn. Congress has also been aggressive in the attempt to protect minors from accessing digital porn, but many laws passed by Congress have run up against the First Amendment. For example, the Supreme Court immediately ruled the CDA (Communications Decency Act) of 1997 unconstitutional in 1997.[179] It was a law that restricted the production and distribution of Internet porn, but also worked to limit the dissemination of thoughts, ideas, and speech. Similarly, COPA (the Child Online Protection Act of 1998) was ruled unconstitutional in 2002.[180] That act would have successfully deterred online pornography distribution, but would have also made a large volume of nonpornographic material illegal and subject to serious felony charges.

Child pornography, something oddly epidemic in proportion, is illegal as a matter of strict liability. Meaning, child porn is not subject to a Miller determination as to its relative obscenity. Child porn is not judged, but rather, is always illegal and knows no First Amendment protection. Any time a minor is depicted sexually, the material is illegal. With the advent of the Internet, this material has become a social and legal hot button. The odd proliferation and interest in child pornography makes one wonder if the legal and social attention to the cases is not itself spurring a morbid curiosity and subsequent interest in this form of illegal material.[181] As recently as 1970, the law seemed disinterested in child pornography cases.[182] Today, however, a type of moral panic has emerged and the effect has been laws, such as the CPPA (Child Pornography Prevention Act), COPA (Child Online Protection Act), CIPA (Children's Internet Protection Act), and the 2005 FBI Anti-Porn Squad, created to apprehend and convict those associated with child pornography.

Key Terms

Pornographic 00

Obscene 00

Possession 00

Distribution 00

Production 00

Child Porn 00

Anti-Pornography Activism 00

Porn Victims Compensation Act 00

Miller Test

Strict Liability

Concepts & Principles

Prurient Interest 00

Redeeming Social Value 00

First Amendment 00

Community Standards 00

Chilling Effect 00

Knowingly Distribute 00

Mistake of Age 00

Virtual Pornography 00

Written Words 00

Artistic Expression

Chapter Four Select Court Cases	
Case	**Point of Law**
Stanley v. Georgia 00	Obscene porn is legal in the privacy of one's home
Ohio v. Mapp 00	"Possession" is subject to a detailed legal analysis
U.S. v. Orito 00	Traveling with illegal pornography is unlawful
Hawaii v. Kam 00	Adult bookstore sales of illegal porn may be permissible
U.S. v. Reidel 00	The U.S. Mail cannot be used to distribute illegal porn
U.S. v. Thirty-Seven Photographs 00	Border crossings cannot be used to import illegal porn
New Hampshire v. Theriault 00	The law of free speech allows filmmakers to solicit parties to engage in sexual acts for purposes of a film
U.S. v. Thomas 00	"Mistake-of-age" is no defense when using minors for the manufacturing of pornography
N.Y. v. Ferber 00	The law does not permit possession of child porn
Ashcroft v. Free Speech Coalition 00	The Child Pornography Prevention Act was ruled overbroad and a violation of the First Amendment
U.S. v. Whorley 00	Obscenity law applies to cartoons and short stories

Questions for Review

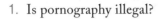

1. Is pornography illegal?

2. Which court case governs the law of obscenity?

3. Why is Stanley v. Georgia unique when it comes to the law of pornography?

4. Can an adult bookstore sell obscene material?

5. What type of porn is sold in an adult bookstore?

6. Can a citizen in the U.S. receive obscene material through the mail and read it in the privacy of their own home?

7. Can a foreign citizen come into the U.S. with obscene material made in their home country?

8. Why does the First Amendment protect people who make pornography?

9. How do TV show producers legally show scenes of romance between minors?

10. Can a pornographer claim "mistake of age" if s/he uses a model who said she was 18, but was younger than 18?

11. What defenses are available to somone who is arrested for downloading child pornography?

1   Miller v. California, 413 U.S. 15, 28 (1973).

2   MERRIAM-WEBSTER, MERRIAM-WEBSTER'S ONLINE DICTIONARY, http://www.merriam-webster.com/dictionary/marriage (last visited Mar. 19, 2010).

3   Gorman, S., Monk-Turner, E., & Fish, J. N., *Free Adult Internet Web Sites: How Prevalent Are Degrading Acts?*. 27 GENDER ISSUES 3/4, 131-145 (2010).

4   Jerry Ropelato, INTERNET PORNOGRAPHY STATISTICS. http://internet-filter-review.toptenreviews.com/internet-pornography-statistics. html. Retrieved on June 15, 2010.

5   Douglas Brown, PORNOPOLIS, Denver Post, July 9, 2006, at L-01.

6   Kingston, D. A., Fedoroff, P., Firestone, P., Curry, S., & Bradford, J. M., *Pornography Use and Sexual Aggression: The Impact of Frequency and Type of Pornography Use on Recidivism Among Sexual Offenders*. 34 AGG. BEH. 4, 341-351 (2008).

7   Plotke, A., *Trust Me: Charles Keating and The Missing Billions*. MAGILL BOOK REVIEWS (1994). Retrieved from EBSCO*host* on April 11, 2010.

8   Campbell, K., & Wright, D. W., *Marriage Today: Exploring the Incongruence Between Americans' Beliefs and Practices*. 41 J. COMP. FAM. STUD. 3, 329-345 (2010).

9   Clay Calvert & Robert D. Richards, *The Free Speech Coalition & Adult Entertainment: An Inside View of the Adult Entertainment Industry, Its Leading Advocate & the First Amendment*, 22 CARDOZO ARTS & ENT. L.J. 247, 257–302 (2004).

10 Dennis, D. I., & Erlanger, H. S., *Obscenity Law and the Conditions of Freedom in the Nineteenth-Century United States*. 27 L. & SOC. INQ. 2, 369 (2002).

11 5 Stat. 548, 566 (1842).

12 Hicklin v. Regina, LR 3 QB 360 (1868).

13 *Id.*

14 Dennis, Donna I., *Obscenity Law and the Conditions of Freedom in the Nineteenth-Century United States*. 27 L. & SOC. INQ. 369 (2002).

15 *Id.* at 381.

16 Comstock Act, 17 Stat. 598, enacted March 3, 1873. This Act was officially officially titled "An Act for the Suppression of Trade in and Circulation of Obscene Literature and Articles of Immoral Use."

17 Dennis, Donna I., *Obscenity Law and the Conditions of Freedom in the Nineteenth-Century United States*. 27 L. & SOC. INQ. 369 (2002).

18 McCarthy, T. M., *"The Humaner Instinct of Women": Hannah Bailey and the Woman's Christian Temperance Union's Critique of Militarism and Manliness in the Late Nineteenth Century*, 33 PEACE & CHANGE 2, 191-216 (2008).

19 Roth v. U.S., 354 U.S. 476 (1957).

20 *Id.*

21 Roth v. U.S., 354 U.S. 476, 489 (1957).

22 *Id.* at 496.

23 Jacobellis v. Ohio, 378 U.S. 184 (1964).

24 Memoirs v. Massachusetts, 383 U.S. 413 (1966).

25 *Id.* at 429.

26 Miller v. California, 413 U.S. 15 (1973).

27 *Id.*

28 *Id.* at 28.

29 *Id.* at 33.

30 *Id.*

31 New York v. Ferber, 458 U.S. 747 (1982).

32 Osborne v. Ohio, 495 U.S. 103 (1990).

33 Jasmin J. Farhangian, *A Problem of "Virtual" Proportions: The Difficulties Inherent in Tailoring Virtual Child Pornography Laws to Meet Constitutional Standards,* 12 J.L. & Pol'y 241, 280 (2003).

34 The Child Pornography Prevention Act of 1996. Public Law 104-208, 1996.

35 *Id.*

36 Ashcroft v. Free Speech Coalition, 535 U.S. 234 (2002).

37 *Id.* at 244.

38 Communications Decency Act, 47 U.S.C. § 230 (1996).

39 Reno v. ACLU, 521 U.S. 844 (1997).

40 Child Online Protection Act, 47 U.S.C. 231 (1998).

41 Ashcroft v. ACLU, 535 U.S. 564 (2002).

42 Children's Internet Protection Act, 20 U.S.C. § 9134 *et seq.* (2001).

43 U.S. v. American Libraries Association, 539 U.S. 194, 200 (2003).

44 *Id.* at 199.

45 *Id.* at 208.

46 American Booksellers Association for Free Expression v. Strickland, 560 F.3d 443 (6th Cir. 2009).

47 Ohio Rev. Code §§ 2907.01(E) and (J) (1999).

48 American Booksellers Association for Free Expression v. Strickland, 560 F.3d 443 (6th Cir. 2009).

49 Smith v. California, 361 U.S. 147, 172 (1959).

50 Jacobellis v. Ohio, 378 U.S. 184, 197 (1964).

51 Stanley v. Georgia, 394 U.S. 557 (1969).

52 Miller v. California, 413 U.S. 15 (1973).

53 *Id.*

54 Okla. Stat. § 1021 (2008).

55 Miller v. California, 413 U.S. 15, 28 (1973).

56 Stanley v. Georgia, 394 U.S. 557 (1969).

57 From the appellate court opinion that upheld Stanley's conviction at trial: Ga. Code Ann. § 23-6301 (1963). The indictment in this case that charged that the defendant on a specified date "did knowingly have possession of obscene matter," thereafter describing three rolls of motion picture film in detail and concluding with the allegation: "said accused having knowledge of the obscene nature of such motion picture film and matter; said motion picture films when considered as a whole and applying contemporary community standards that exist in this county, being obscene matter whose predominant appeal is to a shameful and morbid interest in nudity and sex; and accused should reasonably have known of the obscene nature of said matter, said act of accused being contrary to the laws of said state, the good order, peace and dignity thereof," sufficiently charged the defendant with an offense under the provisions of Code § 26-6301, as amended by the Act approved March 13, 1963 (Ga. L. 1963, p. 78 et seq.). It is not essential to an indictment charging one with possession of obscene matter that it be alleged that such possession was "with intent to sell, expose or circulate the same." Stanley v. State, 161 S.E.2d 309, 313 (1968).

58 Stanley v. State, 161 S.E.2d 309 (1968).

59 Stanley v. Georgia, 394 U.S. 557, 566 (1969).

60   *Id.* at 564–565.

61   Marcum, C. D., Higgins, G. E., Freiburger, T. L., & Ricketts, M. L., *Policing Possession of Child Pornography Online: Investigating the Training and Resources Dedicated to the Investigation of Cyber Crime.* 12 Intnt'l. J. Pol. Sci. & Man. 4, 516–525 (2010).

62   Ohio v. Mapp, 166 N.E.2d 387, 391 (1960).

63   Desai, Anuj C., *Filters and Federalism: Public Library Internet Access, Local Control, and the Federal Spending Power.* 7 U. Penn. J. Con. L. 3 (2004).

64   Or. Const. art. I, § 8 (2009). No law shall be passed restraining the free expression of opinion, or restricting the right to speak, write, or print freely on any subject whatever; but every person shall be responsible for the abuse of this right.

65   Ohio v. Mapp, 166 N.E.2d 387 (1960).

66   *Id.*

67   *Id.*

68   *Id.* at 393.

69   U.S. v. Orito, 413 U.S. 139 (1973).

70   18 U.S.C. § 1462 (1994).

71   U.S. v. Orito, 413 U.S. 139 (1973).

72   Miller v. California, 413 U.S. 15 (1973).

73   Citing to the precedent of North American Co. v. SEC, the Court stated, "It is sufficient to reiterate the well-settled principle that Congress may impose relevant conditions and requirements on those who use the channels of interstate commerce in order that those channels will not become the means of promoting or spreading evil, whether of a physical, moral or economic nature." North American Co. v. SEC, 327 U.S. 686, 705 (1946).

74   U.S. v. Orito, 413 U.S. 139, 151 (1973).

75   Stanley v. Georgia, 394 U.S. 557 (1969).

76   Baskin, Sienna, *Deviant Dreams: Extreme Associates and the Case for Porn.* 10 N.Y. City L. Rev. 155 (2006).

77   Communications Decency Act, 47 U.S.C. § 230 (1996).

78   Ga. Code Ann. § 26-2101 (1987).

79   18 U.S.C. § 1461 (1994).

80   Stanley v. Georgia, 394 U.S. 557 (1969).

81   Hawaii v. Kam, 748 P.2d 372 (1988).

82   *Id.*

83   *Id.* at 379.

84   U.S. v. Reidel, 402 U.S. 351 (1971).

85   *Id.*

86   *Id.* at 355.

87   *Id.* at 356.

88   Luros stated that the 37 photographs were intended to be incorporated in a hard-cover edition of *The Kama Sutra of Vatsyayana,* a widely distributed book candidly describing a large number of sexual positions. U.S. v. Thirty-Seven Photographs, 402 U.S. 363 (1971).

89   19 U.S.C. § 1305(a) (1988). The statute reads, in part, "All persons are prohibited from importing into the United States from any foreign country ... any obscene book, pamphlet, paper, writing, advertisement, circular, print, picture, drawing, or other representation, figure, or image on or of paper or other material, or any cast, instrument, or other article which is obscene or

immoral. ... No such articles whether imported separately or contained in packages with other goods entitled to entry, shall be admitted to entry; and all such articles and, unless it appears to the satisfaction of the collector that the obscene or other prohibited articles contained in the package were inclosed [sic] therein without the knowledge or consent of the importer, owner, agent, or consignee, the entire contents of the package in which such articles are contained, shall be subject to seizure and forfeiture as hereinafter provided. ... Provided, further, That the Secretary of the Treasury may, in his discretion, admit the so-called classics or books of recognized and established literary or scientific merit, but may, in his discretion, admit such classics or books only when imported for noncommercial purposes.

[90] U.S. v. Thirty-Seven Photographs, 402 U.S. 363 (1971).

[91] *Id.* at 380.

[92] U.S. v. Extreme Associates, 431 F.3d 150 (3d Cir. 2005).

[93] Tonya R. Noldon, *Challenging First Amendment Protection of Adult Films with the Use of Prostitution Statutes,* 3 Va. Sports and Ent. L.J. 310 (2004).

[94] Ken Hegan, *The New Sex Ed,* Rolling Stone, Sept. 18, 2003, at 66–67.

[95] Dateline NBC (NBC television broadcast, Nov. 2, 2003) ("Shane's World insists it does not buy alcohol, nor officially sponsor parties, though that is common practice for other web porn companies.").

[96] Tun, P. A., & Lachman, M. E., *The Association Between Computer Use and Cognition Across Adulthood: Use It So You Won't Lose It?* 25 Psychology & Aging 3, 560–568 (2010).

[97] *Id.* at 565.

[98] The Child Protection and Obscenity Enforcement Act of 1988, Pub. L. 100–690, title VII, subtitle N (§7501 *et seq.*), 18 U.S.C. § 2251 *et seq.* The Act places stringent record keeping requirements on the producers of actual, sexually explicit materials. The guidelines for enforcing these laws are in 28 C.F.R. Part 75. 28 C.F.R. Part 75 requires producers of sexually explicit material to obtain proof of age for every model they shoot, and retain those records. Federal inspectors may at any time launch inspections of these records and prosecute any infraction.

[99] 18 U.S.C. § 2251 (1994).

[100] 18 U.S.C. § 2257A (2009).

[101] *Id.*

[102] Fla. Stat. Ann. § 847.001 (2002).

[103] La. Rev. Stat. Ann. 14: § 106(2)(a) (2003).

[104] 18 U.S.C. § 2251(a) (1996).

[105] S.C. Code Ann. § 16-15-325 (1998).

[106] New Hampshire v. Theriault, 960 A.2d 687 (2008).

[107] N.H. Rev. Stat. Ann. § 645:2 (2010).

[108] New Hampshire v. Theriault, 960 A.2d 687 (2008).

[109] *Id.*

[110] *Id.* at 690.

[111] *Id.* at 692.

[112] Report of the Commission on Obscenity and Pornography, October 24, 1970. U.S. Dept. of Justice.

[113] U.S. v. X-Citement Video, 982 F.2d 1285 (1992).

[114] U.S. v. Thomas, 74 F.3d 701 (6th Cir. 1996).

[115] 18 U.S.C. §§ 2251-2252 (1989).

[116] U.S. v. Thomas, 74 F.3d 701 (6th Cir. 1996).

117 The defendant's awareness of the subject's minority is not an element of the offense. This omission was deliberate. Both Houses of Congress originally considered bills making it unlawful for any person "knowingly" to employ, entice, or coerce a minor to engage in sexually explicit conduct for the purpose of producing or promoting a film or other print or visual medium. Department of Justice representatives urged deletion of "knowingly" so as to avoid the inference that producers could be prosecuted only if they knew the minor's age.

118 U.S. v. Thomas, 74 F.3d 701 (6th Cir. 1996).

119 U.S. v. U.S. District Court for the Central District of California, 858 F.2d 534 (1988).

120 U.S. v. U.S. District Court for the Central District of California, 858 F.2d 534, 546 (1988).

121 Pornography Victim's Compensation Act, S. 983, 102d Cong., 1st Sess. 3(a) (1991); Stephanie B. Goldberg, 1st Amendment Wrongs: A New Approach to Fighting Pornography Says Free Speech Has Nothing to Do With It, Chicago Tribune, Mar. 17, 1993 (Tempo), at 1 (discussing federal anti-pornography legislation).

122 R. Karl Hanson & Monique T. Bussiere, *Predicting Relapse: A Meta-Analysis of Sexual Offender Recidivism Studies,* 66 J. CONSULTING & CLINICAL PSYCHOL. 348, 357 (1998). A later meta-analysis breaks down the studies according to these different recidivism criteria: "The recidivism criterion was arrest in 25 studies, reconviction in 24 studies, and reincarceration in 3 studies." R. Karl Hanson & Kelly E. Morton-Bourgon, *The Characteristics of Persistent Sexual Offenders: A Meta-Analysis of Recidivism Studies,* 73 J. CONSULTING & CLINICAL PSYCHOL. 1154, 1155 (2005).

123 Rice v. Paladin Enterprises, 128 F.3d 233 (1997).

124 *Id.*

125 Herceg v. Hustler Magazine, Inc., 814 F.2d 1017 (1987).

126 *Id.*

127 The jury awarded Diane Herceg $69,000 in actual damages and $100,000 exemplary damages. It also awarded Andy V. $3,000 for the pain and mental suffering he endured as the bystander who discovered the deceased's body and $10,000 exemplary damages to Andy V. Herceg v. Hustler Magazine, Inc., 814 F.2d 1017 (1987).

128 Herceg v. Hustler Magazine, Inc., 814 F.2d 1017, 1022 (1987).

129 Gertz v. Robert Welch, 418 U.S. 323, 339–340 (1974).

130 Herceg v. Hustler Magazine, Inc., 814 F.2d 1017, 1029 (1987).

131 People v. Freeman, 758 P.2d 1128 (1988).

132 Carlson, K., *Strong Medicine: Toward Effective Sentencing of Child Pornography Offenders,* 109 Mich. L. Rev. 1, 27-33 (2010).

133 *Id.*

134 Lam, A., Mitchell, J., & Seto, M. C., *Lay Perceptions of Child Pornography Offenders.* 52 CANAD. J. CRIM. & CRIM. JUST. 2, 173–201 (2010).

135 *Id.*

136 HOLMES, STEPHEN T. AND RONALD M. HOLMES, SEX CRIMES: PATTERNS AND BEHAVIORS 123–128 (3rd ed., Sage) (2009).

137 See, e.g., STOPPING CHILD PORNOGRAPHY: PROTECTING OUR CHILDREN AND THE CONSTITUTION: Hearing Before the S. Comm. on the Judiciary, 107th Cong. 60-61 (2002). (prepared statement of Ernest E. Allen, president and chief executive officer of the National Center for Missing & Exploited Children, and Daniel S. Armagh, director of the Legal Resource Division, National Center for Missing & Exploited Children) (testifying to 60,000 reports of child pornography in over four years since the establishment of an Internet "CyberTipline" site).

[138] Diane Schetky & Arthur Green, Child Sexual Abuse: A Handbook for Health Care and Legal Professionals 154 (1988); see also Kenneth V. Lanning, Child Molesters: A Behavioral Analysis for Law-Enforcement Officers Investigating Cases of Child Sexual Exploitation 31 (3rd ed. 1992), available at http://www.skeptictank.org/nc70.pdf ("The pedophile can also use the computer to troll for and communicate with potential victims with minimal risk of being identified... . The child can be indirectly "victimized' through the transfer of sexually explicit information and material or the child can be evaluated for future face-to-face contact and direct victimization."); ("In most cases the arousal and fantasy fueled by [child] pornography is only a prelude to actual sexual activity with children.").

[139] Stephen Fairchild, *Protecting the Least of These: A New Approach to Child Pornography Pandering Provisions,* 57 Duke L. J. 163 (2007).

[140] Enhancing Child Protection Laws after the April 16, 2002 Supreme Court Decision, Ashcroft v. Free Speech Coalition: Hearing Before the Subcomm. on Crime, Terrorism, and Homeland Security of the H. Comm. on the Judiciary, 107th Cong. 6 (2002) (statement of Michael J. Heimbach, unit chief, Crimes Against Children Unit, Federal Bureau of Investigation).

[141] *Id.*

[142] Pub. L. No. 95-225, 92 Stat. 7 (1977) (codified as 18 U.S.C. §§ 2251-2253 (2000)).

[143] *Id.*

[144] New York v. Ferber, 458 U.S. 747 (1982).

[145] Pub. L. No. 98-292, 98 Stat. 204 (1984) (codified as 18 U.S.C. §§ 2251-2254, 2256, 2516 (2000)).

[146] *Id.*

[147] Pub. L. No. 100-690 at tit. VII, Subtitle N, Ch. 1, 102 Stat. 4181 (1988) (codified as 18 U.S.C. §§ 2251-2256).

[148] 18 U.S.C. § 2252 (1990).

[149] Pub. L. No. 105-314, tit. II, 112 Stat. 2978 (1998) (codified as 18 U.S.C. § 2252(A)).

[150] M. Megan McCune, Comment, *Virtual Lollipops and Lost Puppies: How Far Can States Go to Protect Minors Through the Use of Internet Luring Laws,* 14 Commlaw conspectus 503, 512-13 (2006).

[151] *Id.*

[152] N.M. Stat. Ann. § 30-6A-3 (2002).

[153] U.S.C. § 2256 (1991).

[154] N.M. Stat. Ann. § 30-6A-3 (2002).

[155] New York v. Ferber, 458 U.S. 747 (1982).

[156] *Id.*

[157] N.Y. Law § 263.15. Promoting a sexual performance by a child. (1977).

[158] New York v. Ferber, 422 N.E.2d 523 (1981).

[159] New York v. Ferber, 458 U.S. 747, 758 (1982).

[160] The Child Pornography Prevention Act of 1996. Public Law 104-208, 1996.

[161] *Id.*

[162] Ashcroft v. Free Speech Coalition, 535 U.S. 234 (2002).

[163] Reno v. Free Speech Coalition, 198 F.3d 1083 (9th Cir. Cal. 1999).

[164] Ashcroft v. Free Speech Coalition, 535 U.S. 234 (2002).

[165] *Id.* at 252.

[166] U.S. v. Whorley, 550 F.3d 326, 341 (2008).

167 18 U.S.C. § 1462 (1983). Importation or transportation of obscene matters. Whoever brings into the United States, or any place subject to the jurisdiction thereof, or knowingly uses any express company or other common carrier or interactive computer service (as defined in section 230(e)(2) of the Communications Act of 1934 (47 USCS § 230(e)(2)), for carriage in interstate or foreign commerce— (a) any obscene, lewd, lascivious, or filthy book, pamphlet, picture, motion-picture film, paper, letter, writing, print, or other matter of indecent character; or (b) any obscene, lewd, lascivious, or filthy phonograph recording, electrical transcription, or other article or thing capable of producing sound; or (c) any drug, medicine, article, or thing designed, adapted, or intended for producing abortion, or for any indecent or immoral use; or any written or printed card, letter, circular, book, pamphlet, advertisement, or notice of any kind giving information, directly or indirectly, where, how, or of whom, or by what means any of such mentioned articles, matters, or things may be obtained or made.

168 U.S. v. Whorley, 550 F.3d 326, 341 (2008).

169 Miller v. California, 413 U.S. 15 (1973).

170 U.S. v. Whorley, 550 F.3d 326 (2008).

171 *Id.* at 341.

172 *Id.*

173 New Mexico v. Meyers, 207 P.3d 1105 (2009).

174 R. Karl Hanson & Monique T. Bussiere, *Predicting Relapse: A Meta-Analysis of Sexual Offender Recidivism Studies,* 66 J. Consulting & Clinical Psychol. 348, 357 (1998).

175 Clay Calvert & Robert D. Richards, *The Free Speech Coalition & Adult Entertainment: An Inside View of the Adult Entertainment Industry, Its Leading Advocate & the First Amendment,* 22 Cardozo Arts & Ent. L.J. 247, 257-302 (2004).

176 Ohio v. Mapp, 166 N.E.2d 387 (1960).

177 Ashcroft v. Free Speech Coalition, 535 U.S. 234 (2002).

178 *Id.*

179 Reno v. ACLU, 521 U.S. 844 (1997).

180 Ashcroft v. Free Speech Coalition, 535 U.S. 234 (2002).

181 Senjo, Scott, Child Pornography: Crime, Computers, and Society by Ian O'Donnell and Claire Milner. Portland, Oregon: Willan Publishing, 2007. 259 pp. 22 Criminal Justice Studies: A Critical Journal of Crime, Law and Society 1, 103–106 (2009).

182 In a 1970 issue of *Playboy* Magazine, actress Brooke Shields posed nude at the age of 10. The issue sold a regular number of magazines and the Department of Justice showed no interest in a prosecution of the magazine.

Chapter Six

Paraphilia and Legal Prohibitions:

Necrophilia, Erotic Asphyxiation,

Zoophilia, Sadomasochism

"This type of behavior is disturbing. It's disturbing to the public.
It's disturbing to the court."

People v. Hathaway
Superior Court of the State of Wisconsin, Douglas County
Case ID: 9881 (2006)[1]

Legal Background

This chapter discusses a more peculiar, and sometimes more threatening, world of sexual deviancy, that of sexual paraphilias. There are many types of paraphilias, some are innocuous, harmless, and legal while others are harmful, violent and, hence, banned in all fifty states. Paraphilia is a medical (not legal) condition and a medically ascertained paraphilia is often more serious than offenses discussed in previous chapters such as prostitution, adultery, or stripping because of the cognitive involuntariness that underlies the sexual act. Paraphilia is a complicated medical condition that continues to baffle medical science. This chapter focuses on only a select few paraphilias, such as zoophilia and erotophonophilia and examines their treatment in the law and courts.

Defined, a **paraphilia** is a form of aberrant sexual behavior that involves unusual fantasies or acts necessary for full sexual excitement such as exhibitionism or frotteurism, discussed in chapter 3.[2] A true paraphiliac in an advanced stage finds no satisfaction in a loving and supportive partnership with a monogamous spouse. For paraphilia, it is advised to obtain some kind of medical attention so that the condition does not lead to a crime such as frotteurism or worse.

Para denotes deviation and *philia* refers to attraction. The definitive source for this and other psychiatric aberrations is the American Psychiatric Association's *Diagnostic and Statistical Manual of Mental Disorders*, Volume 4 (*DSM-IV*, 1994). The *DSM-IV* provides that the essential features of a paraphilia are "recurrent, intense sexually arousing fantasies, sexual urges, or behaviors generally involving 1) nonhuman objects, 2) the suffering or humiliation of oneself or one's partner, or 3) children or other nonconsenting persons, that occur over a period of at least 6 months."[3] Tender sharing with one's husband or wife would not be considered paraphilic while sex with an animal would be.[4] Paraphilia is often associated with impulse control disorder and personality disorders.[5] It would be rare to find someone who engages in serial bestiality who does not also have a type of impulse control or personality disorder.

As suggested above, some paraphilias are dangerous, such as when choking, biting, whipping, or other abuse is part of the episode. Many other paraphilias, however, simply involve a predilection not understood and a tendency exists to label as "bad" that which is not understood or engaged in by the average person.[6] Paraphilias involving a third person, cross-dressing, or legal pornography are not harmful or necessarily illegal in themselves, but raise a suspicion as to other, more dangerous experimentation that may follow.[7] 1n its extreme form, some paraphilias are horrifying, such as killing someone for sexual arousal, or pyromania—setting a building on fire solely for purposes of sexual excitation. These paraphilias, of course, face the full brunt of the criminal justice system.

Table 1 Possible Charged Offense for Select Paraphilia

Paraphilia		Criminal Offense
Pyromania	charged as	Arson
Sadism	charged as	Aggravated Battery
Necrophilia	charged as	Defiling a Corpse
Frotteurism	charged as	Sexual Assault
Exhibitionism	charged as	Public Indecency
Zoophilia	charged as	Animal Cruelty
Erotic Asphyxiation	charged as	Attempted Suicide
Erotophonophilia	charged as	Murder

When correlating a medical condition with a legal prohibition, it is important to take any "psychosexual" disorder with a grain of salt. Historically, what is "sick and perverted" is a highly subjective determination. A psychiatric evaluation is merely one opinion. In the *DSM-IV*, the number of diagnosable mental disorders, sex-related and nonsex-related, has ballooned from about one hundred disorders in 1952 to almost three hundred today. From "caffeine intoxication" to numerous sexual behaviors, professional mental health treads on thin ice when it claims its science is free from political or other motives. It should be noted that some members of the APA board of directors have direct ties to the pharmaceutical industry and personally benefit if someone has a mental disorder and needs to purchase medication from one of the pharmaceuticals.

For this reason, it is important to note the bifurcated relationship between the *DSM* (as a medical reference), and various state criminal codes (as a legal reference). A *DSM* diagnosis does not meet the legal standards necessary for a criminal conviction nor for a legal civil commitment. To this end, the *DSM* contains in its literature a caveat to distinguish between medical diagnoses and legal definitions.[8] In all, there are eight named paraphilias listed in the *DSM*. These eight are merely a sample of the complete spectrum of all documented paraphilias. This chapter covers only a few paraphilias so as to provide a general understanding for the relationship between the criminal law and sexual paraphilias.

Historical Develoment of the Medicalization of Sexual Deviancy. The medical insight into sexual behavior did not start with the *DSM-IV*. As a frontrunner in modern western science is Richard Krafft-Ebing and his 1886 extensive anthology on sexuality titled, *Psychopathia Sexualis*.[9] Krafft-Ebing was a German psychiatrist who worked for a time in insane asylums where he interviewed and observed a large sample of asylum patients. This pioneering reference was found credible worldwide as it contained a tone of medical science and was free of moral judgment. It was the first of its kind in the U.S. that included well-developed medical explanations for sexual behaviors such as sadism and masochism. In 1886, topics like sadism or masochism were not understood or discussed in the U.S. Like any book that speaks openly about sexual experimentation, his book came under fire for many reasons, including his associating the desire for spirituality and martyrdom with hysteria and masochism, and for denying that homosexuality was a perversion. The book also introduced the western world to the terms heterosexual and homosexual and created the categories for what is referred to as paraphilia today. No other source had organized the material cogently, nor explained sex, and sexual deviations so thoroughly. Krafft-Ebing paved the way for future research on human sexuality such as that done by Sigmund Freud, Alfred Kinsey, Masters and Johnson, and Michael Foucault.

Freud, discussed in chapter 2, influenced law and policy on sexual deviancy with his *Three Essays on the Theory of Sexuality* in 1905.[10] Where Krafft-Ebing used the lens of biology, Freud used the lens of psychology. He persuasively argued that sexual "perversion" was present even among healthy (nonpathological) adults. He developed the Oedipus Complex where he asserted a young boy would go through a phase of being jealous of his father and sexually possessive of his mother.

With greater contemplation of human sexuality fostered by Krafft-Ebing and Freud, as the Progressive Era (1900–1920) developed, so did a new era in the confidence of medical science to fix or cure those who could not participate in mainstream American society, sexually or otherwise. The intersection of Freud, financial resources, and the Progressives led to the first sexual psychopath statutes in the U.S., a series of laws that were enacted in about half the states during the late 1930s to the 1960s to address what we now call paraphilias. These laws were influenced by Krafft-Ebing and Freud and were based on the assumption that criminal sexual conduct, or at least some forms of it, were the product of mental disorder, and that afflicted individuals were in need of medical help. Those initial sexual psychopath laws looked to the states to incapacitate sexual deviants by using civil commitment laws to place them in a locked down state mental hospital.

In the 1940s and 1950s, Alfred Kinsey undertook a path-breaking study of human sexuality in the spirit of Krafft-Ebing and Freud. However, one impetus for Kinsey's research on human sexuality was to demonstrate that "sexual pathology" was more common than was originally believed, and hence, maybe not so pathological after all.[11] Kinsey's research achieved a degree of normalization when it came to sexual behavior such as premarital sex, masturbation, and marital affairs. Just after Kinsey, in the 1960s, Masters and Johnson were a team of researchers and counselors who tended to celebrate human sexuality.[12] They came to assist clinic patients with developing an emotional comfort level with sexual expression and removing the shame and "baggage" around sex. In the 1970s Michael Foucault opened-up the discussion of sex behavior using the paradigm of social learning and social constraints.[13]

With the influence of Kinsey, Foucault, and Masters and Johnson as well as a generation of other credible researchers who studied sex and sexual deviancy, in 1977 the Group for the Advancement of Psychiatry (GAP) issued an influential report entitled *Psychiatry and Sex Psychopath Legislation: The 30s to the 80s.*[14] This report, along with other research, recommended the repeal of the sexual psychopath laws from the 1930s and 1940s. The GAP Report characterized sex offender commitment statutes as an "experiment [that] has failed."[15] The report alleged that professionals lacked adequate clinical skills to predict future behavior and to treat sexual violence effectively.[16] By the 1980s, most of the states with sexual psychopath laws had either repealed them, or had ceased actively using them.

The rescinding of the sexual psychopath laws created a public policy vacuum and impetus for a new series of approaches to governing and managing sexual deviants and paraphiliacs. In the late 1980s and early 1990s, the criminal justice systems in the states and at the federal level lessened reliance on the medical model and began leaning toward a sanction-based crime control model. It was as if the states took a break from trying to understand sexual deviancy and instead began to merely punish those acts that violated the law. As a result, the rate of incarceration for convicted sex offenders increased substantially and the states and federal government began using new tools for sex offenders such as registration, notification, and civil commitment. These new approaches are part of a management orientation to cases of criminal sexual deviance and represent a departure from the medicalization approach that began in the 1930s.

Table 2 Pioneers in the Study of Sexual Deviance.

Year	Researcher	Field of Study	Publication
1886	Krafft-Ebing	Psychiatry	*Psychopathia Sexualis*
1905	Sigmund Freud	Psychology	*Three Essays on the Theory of Sexuality*
1948	Alfred Kinsey	Biology	*Sexual Behavior in the Human Male*
1966	Masters and Johnson	Biology	*Human Sexual Response*
1978	Michel Foucault	Sociology	*The History of Sexuality*

Civil Commitment. Civil commitment today, briefly discussed in chapter 2, is based on legislation targeting sexually violent predators (SVPs). While the end result of SVP legislation is the same as the old sexual psychopath laws, namely incapacitation, today's civil commitment brings a great deal more science, as well as due process protections, to the process.[17] In 2010, twenty states had SVP laws, providing for the indefinite detention of about 2,700 offenders.[18]

Civil commitment, whether in 1930 or 2000, is a controversial approach to sexual paraphiliacs because it represents a substantial deprivation of liberty at the hands of a speculative arrangement. A paraphiliac is placed in a state mental facility because the state predicts the offender could harm him- or herself or another person at some time in the future. Civil custodial arrangements are additionally controversial because the state predicts that the mental health care will have a positive effect on the person subject to the commitment. It should be noted that a civil commitment by the state is indeterminate—the subject of the commitment may or may not ever be released.[19]

As a result of the controversy, the laws surrounding a civil commitment hearing are heavily litigated. Many legal challenges focus on the steps the state takes to commit someone, also known as due process. The law of due process imposes limits on state power to restrict the liberty of individuals without an adequate allowance for rights, rebuttals, and counterarguments. In a series of cases, the U.S. Supreme Court has defined some of the constitutional limits on civil commitment. In *O'Connor v. Donaldson,* 422 U.S. 563 (1975), the Court suggested that it would be unconstitutional for a state to confine a harmless though mentally ill person. In *Addington v. Texas,* 441 U.S. 418 (1979), the Court said that commitment can rest on both parens patriae and police power, but the Court did not clarify whether both powers are necessary, or either is sufficient, to support civil commitment. Some commentators read *United States v. Salerno,* 481 U.S. 739, 748 (1987), a case upholding a system of limited preventive detention of persons charged with criminal offenses, as approving preventive (noncriminal) detention based on dangerousness alone. This theory was rejected, however, in *Foucha v. Louisiana,* 504 U.S. 71 (1992), where the Court struck down dangerousness-based civil commitment in the absence of mental illness.

The most recent and pronounced case is *Kansas v. Hendricks.*[20] A paraphiliac named Leroy Hendricks was serving time in a Kansas State Prison and when his sentence expired, the state moved to have him civilly committed pursuant to the state's civil commitment statute. Hendrick's admitted he had an uncontrollable urge to molest children. In any event, Hendricks appealed the decision, arguing several issues, including the statute's definition of "mental abnormality." The Kansas Supreme Court held for him, but when the U.S. Supreme Court granted certiorari and heard the case, the high court ruled for the state and deemed the Kansas civil commitment law to be valid and constitutional. In the case, the U.S. Supreme Court set forth procedures for the indefinite civil commitment of prisoners convicted of an unlawful paraphilia whom the state deems dangerous due to a mental abnormality.[21]

Registration and Notification. In addition to arrest and incarceration, civil commitment, and other strategies of the civil and criminal justice system, all fifty states and the federal government began using a SORN to alert neighbors to the possible presence of a sex offender living in their neighborhood.[22] A SORN (Sex Offender Registration and Notification) website is legally required by the states for all convicted sex offenders.[23] States that fail to comply with the federal mandate risk losing substantial sums of federal criminal justice block grant funds. A failure for a convicted sex offender to register with a local SORN can result in an additional criminal charge similar to an obstruction of justice charge. In most states, failure to register or update information is a felony offense.

Congress promulgated the first SORN statute in 1994 after the abduction of a young boy named Jacob Wetterling. Wetterling has yet to be found. Named the Jacob Wetterling Crimes Against Children and Sexually Violent Offender Registration Act, this law[24] required all fifty states to implement a sex offender and crimes against children registry to be used solely by law enforcement agencies, excluding the public. The Act was amended two years later by Megan's Law in 1996, which mandated that the registry be made public and that sex offenders remain on the community registry for at least ten years. Under the Act, states may include any sex crime, e.g., sexting, prostitution, possession of child porn, as a predicate offense to being placed on the registry. The SORN as it is known today is most synonymous with Megan's Law since the SORN became public at this time.[25]

The Wetterling Act was amended once again in 1997. The Pam Lychner Sexual Offender Tracking and Identification Act of 1996 (the Lychner Act),[26] requires lifetime registration for recidivists and offenders who commit certain aggravated offenses. The Wetterling Act was amended one more time in 1998[27] to include registration of military offenders and nonresident workers and students. The Act was yet again amended in 2000 so that convicted sex offenders would have to report to the nearest law enforcement agency any enrollment or employment at an institution of higher education. In sum, what began as a private notification system in 1994 with the abduction of Jacob Wetterling has become a prominent public system, one likely to see other amendments and modifications in the future.

Despite quite a bit of legislative and media attention, the consensus does not bode well for the SORN. A SORN is neither effective as a legal tool nor a medical tool, and hence completely fails to address the root causes of paraphilia. SORNs have been operating for approximately ten years, allowing for formal research to have been completed during that time. The findings from formal studies indicate that SORNs are ineffective at best.[28] In many ways, SORNs do more harm than good. For example, many sex offenders who sought to integrate themselves back into mainstream society instead went underground to avoid vigilantes who found the SORN an expedient way to locate sex offenders and exact reprisals on them.

To this day, controversy continues to exist when it comes to how the state manages paraphiliacs, including civil confinement and post-conviction public displays, digital or otherwise. In some ways, sexual deviancy continues to vex the criminal justice system. There are not enough scientific studies to indicate that sexual paraphiliacs suffer from a specific psychological problem or that their choice of sexual behaviors interferes with their day-to-day functioning. Modern psychology has been unable to arrive at a clear diagnosis of most paraphiliacs because the behaviors are a "poorly understood phenomenon" in both its behavioral and biochemical aspects. Because there is such a wide range of activities falling within the rubric of "paraphilia,"[29] there is little consensus in psychological and psychiatric literature on the etiology of these acts. Absent a more definitive understanding, a valuable reference point for the criminal justice system is recidivism data.

Recidivism. The mystery and misunderstanding behind paraphilias contributes to the sterotype that sex offenders are habitual and repeat offenders. If there were ever a test case for the recidivism of sex offenders, the paraphiliac is the best possible test case because of the involuntary, impulsive return to the "act of choice" for full excitation.

The discussion surrounding sex offenders and recidivism goes back and forth, and the matter will likely never be fully settled. The discussion involves competing sets of data and the proponents of the data often use the data to advance a morals-based personal agenda. Since the data on recidivism are scattered, it is not possible to come to a definitive conclusion. One thing, however, is certain. Many controlled studies do not support the media-sensationalized stereotype that sex offenders are repeat offenders. The U.S. Department of Justice conducted a major study on the recidivism of sex offenders released from prison in 1994. According to the study:

> Compared to non-sex offenders released from state prison, sex offenders had a lower overall rearrest rate. When rearrests for any type of crime (not just sex crimes) were counted, the study found that 43 percent (4,163 of 9,691) of the 9,691 released offenders were rearrested. The overall rearrest rate for the 262,420 released non-sex offenders was higher, 68 percent (179,391 of 262,420).[30]

A study in Massachusetts conducted by the Urban Institute Justice Policy Center supports these national statistics. From a sample of inmates who served criminal sentences and were released in 2002, sex offenders had the lowest recidivism rates for any new crime: 22 percent. In contrast, the average recidivism rate for any released inmate was 39 percent. Thus, Massachusetts is in line with the national data: sex offenders, as a group, with the exception of murderers, have the lowest overall recidivism rates.[31]

Of course, in a sexually dangerous person's trial, the issue is not whether the individual will commit another offense, but rather, whether the individual will commit a new sexual offense. Here the recidivism statistics for sex offenders are even more different than the public perceptions. Over the period studied by the Department of Justice in regard to the recidivism of sex offenders released from prison in 1994, the re-arrest rate of former sex offenders released from prison for committing a new sex crime was 5.3 percent. In contrast, the re-arrest rate for robbers was 70.2 percent for any new offense, and 13.4 percent for a new robbery.[32]

Other researchers have combined individual studies into meta-analyses of sex offender recidivism. One author notes that the findings contradict the popular view that sexual offenders inevitably re-offend. Only a minority of the total sample (13.4 percent of 23,393) were known to have committed a new sexual offense within the average four- to five-year follow-up period examined in this study.[33]

This hard data have lent themselves to medical, legal, and social changes when it comes to many of the less serious paraphilic behaviors. The term paraphilia replaced the term perversion in 1980 in the *DSM-IV.* The reformed terminology represented a move away from the perjorative, value-laden term pervert and toward a more objective description of the reality of variegated sexual behavior in modern society. Homosexuality is no longer considered a mental illness in the *DSM.*

The Criminal Law and Sexual Paraphilias. The relationship between paraphilias and the law is a little tricky. For example, in the fifty states, there are typically no specific laws for sex acts that involve the use of insects, drinking blood, or wearing unusual costumes. While some laws exist that address the particulars when it comes to sex with animals, corpses, or familial relatives, the majority of paraphilias present a slight challenge to prosecutorial activity since there may be no specific laws regulating such activity. In such cases, the defense may make the argument that no such law existed proscribing the behavior the defendant is charged with. In this case, the defendant may go

Some paraphilic acts are legal; others are illegal. While common in society, the law, social constraints, and individual choice often conceal the existence of a paraphiliac.

free since there has been no law violated. On the other hand, if a threatening sexual act has been committed, but there is no specific statute, the prosecution may simply be able to use a different, nonsex-related statute, such as one related to public nuisance or lewdness.

When a paraphilia is specifically outlawed, such as with a serial rapist, it is relatively easy to examine the alleged illegality of the act. If force is involved along with a lack of consent, it is typically a rape case. However, when no law exists, it is not known if a different type of sex law can apply or if nonsex-related statute, such as kidnapping or assault, can be used to sanction and deter the accused. To further complicate the role of the law with paraphilias, many paraphilic acts do not come to the attention of the law because they can be done in relative or complete secrecy. These paraphilias may eventually be disclosed to the medical community and mental health treatment providers through participation in a mental health treatment program. The frequency of legal enforcement will depend on the existence of a specific law, potential for harm or injury, frequency of occurrence, and the social stigma involved. In many cases, such as a foot fetish, a paraphilia is legal or presents little harm to anyone and will not involve the criminal justice system.

It is useful to mention other parpahilias and how the law may typically apply, if at all. Hebephilia (attraction to teenagers) and pedophilia (attraction to prepubescent children) are punished severely in the United States in all jurisdictions and at both the state and federal level. Sexual contact with an unmarried person below the age of consent is a felony offense in all fifty states. Odaxelagnia (arousal from biting someone) and anophelorastia (arousal from defiling someone) may be injurious to another and, hence, may be prosecuted pursuant to a battery, attempted battery, or aggravated battery statute. Coprophilia (sexual attraction to human feces) and urolagnia (arousal due to urinating) can be accomplished alone and in private—not necessarily involving another person and are therefore relatively harmless and undetected and hence not prosecuted. Ochlophilia (arousal to crowds of people or being in a crowd of people) and actirasty (sexual arousal from exposure to the sun's rays) may involve a threat to innocent bystanders or minors if known to them, but are silent and expressionless and can easily avoid coming on to the radar of the police and the courts. Prosecutorial activity will vary depending on the type of act, the harm done, and the social approbation in any given period of time.

Most statutes that address paraphilic activity are written with broad terminology and use the language "abusive'" "indecent," or "dangerous" to address the deviance that comes under the purview of the police. These statutes are prepared to address illegal paraphilic behavior, but without more specific application, can become subject to appellate review. Anytime a law is overbroad and lacks specificity, an appeals court may invalidate the law based on the doctrine of "void for vagueness" or a similar constitutional protection of due process.

Necrophilia

Necrophilia is defined as an erotic attraction to a human corpse and constitutes one of the psychosexual disorders categorized as a paraphilia by the American Psychiatry Association's *DSM-IV*.[34] Necrophilic behaviors can include touching or stroking a corpse, rubbing dead body parts, including genitalia, masturbating on or near a corpse, or having sexual intercourse with a corpse.[35] All of these acts could be prosecuted per se, or, possibly under different but related statutes.

Other medical terms that refer to necrophilia include necrofetishism, Sleeping Beauty complex, and pseudonecrophilia (where a partner pretends to be a corpse during episodes of sexual contact). In addition to laws that prohibit necrophilia, law enforcement also sanctions any prostitute who, for a fee, will "ice themselves down, dust on white powder, and lay motionless with eyes closed in a casket," thus role-playing a necrophilia scenario.[36]

Like with many sex offenses, degrees of variation exist within the act of necrophilia. Some participants prefer only to fantasize about having sex with a corpse. Others wait for their husband or wife to fall asleep, then begin fantasizing while watching them sleep, or initiate sexual contact once their partner is asleep. Others use a prostitute to act out necrophilia while some others will exhume a corpse from a graveyard. In a study of 122 necrophiliacs, 57.1 percent admitted to taking a position of employment that allowed them access to corpses, such as a hospital or funeral home.[37] Rosman and Resnick reviewed information from thirty-four cases of necrophilia and described the individuals' motivations for their behaviors. The sample reported

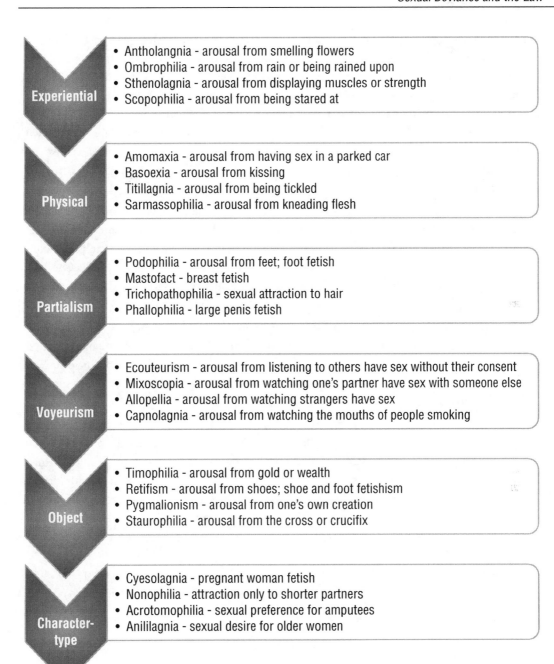

Experiential
- Antholangnia - arousal from smelling flowers
- Ombrophilia - arousal from rain or being rained upon
- Sthenolagnia - arousal from displaying muscles or strength
- Scopophilia - arousal from being stared at

Physical
- Amomaxia - arousal from having sex in a parked car
- Basoexia - arousal from kissing
- Titillagnia - arousal from being tickled
- Sarmassophilia - arousal from kneading flesh

Partialism
- Podophilia - arousal from feet; foot fetish
- Mastofact - breast fetish
- Trichopathophilia - sexual attraction to hair
- Phallophilia - large penis fetish

Voyeurism
- Ecouteurism - arousal from listening to others have sex without their consent
- Mixoscopia - arousal from watching one's partner have sex with someone else
- Allopellia - arousal from watching strangers have sex
- Capnolagnia - arousal from watching the mouths of people smoking

Object
- Timophilia - arousal from gold or wealth
- Retifism - arousal from shoes; shoe and foot fetishism
- Pygmalionism - arousal from one's own creation
- Staurophilia - arousal from the cross or crucifix

Character-type
- Cyesolagnia - pregnant woman fetish
- Nonophilia - attraction only to shorter partners
- Acrotomophilia - sexual preference for amputees
- Anililagnia - sexual desire for older women

Figure 1 Unusual Paraphilias. Most of these paraphilias are legal.

the following motives: desire to possess an unresisting and unrejecting partner (68 percent), reunions with a romantic partner (21 percent), sexual attraction to corpses (15 percent), comfort or overcoming feelings of isolation (15 percent), and seeking self-esteem by expressing power over a homicide victim (12 percent).[38] As a legal matter, the most dangerous necrophiliac will murder someone to have a deceased body available for sexual contact. Notorious serial killers are suspected of having tendencies for necrophilia when they participate sexually with their victims.

Necrophilia has a long history despite being an obscure form of sexual deviancy. In tribal areas of Indonesia, superstition and culture require that a man have sex with the corpse of a woman who died while still a virgin, otherwise she will be unable to transition to the heavenly bodies. The ancient Egyptians knew of necrophiliac tendencies and took precautions. They prohibited the corpse of a wife of a man of rank from being delivered immediately to the embalmers, for fear that the embalmers would violate them. Like with many paraphilias, however, much of mainstream American society considers necrophilia to be seriously deviant.[39]

Where a dead body is tampered with, including in a sexual manner, a variety of criminal charges may be filed against the perpetrator. For example, abuse of a corpse,[40] disorderly conduct, or vandalism. In 2006 in Grant County, Wisconsin, three 20-year-old men were caught trying to exhume the body of a 20-year-old female from a cemetery grave to have sex with it.[41] In absence of a necrophilia law, the men were charged with damaging cemetery property, attempted criminal damage to private property, and attempted third-degree sexual assault.[42]

Nine states have no law prohibiting necrophilia. In the forty-one states that address necrophilia, the statutes tend to be vague and lack specific meaning. For example, only four states (Arizona, Georgia, Hawaii, and Rhode Island) have the word "necrophilia" in the state criminal code. The laws in the forty-one states vary widely as to how sexual acts with dead bodies are defined and what kind of penalty should be administered for committing necrophilic acts. In Massachusetts the statute used for necrophilia is Crimes Against Chastity, Morality, Decency and Good Order.[43] Section 35 of the statute reads:

> Whoever commits any unnatural and lascivious act with another person shall be punished by a fine of not less than one hundred nor more than one thousand dollars or by imprisonment in the state prison for not more than five years or in jail or the house of correction for not more than two and one half years.[44]

In Mississippi, Unnatural Intercourse is the law used for necrophilia.[45] The vagueness of the laws makes the enforceability of the law difficult since the provisions can be easily circumvented by legal counsel during a trial.

Definition of the Offense

Sexual penetration of a dead human body, regardless of motive.[46]

Elements of the Offense

The elements to the crime of necrophilia that must be proven beyond a reasonable doubt are:

1. Intentionally, knowingly, or deliberately
2. engaging in sexual contact,
3. with a dead human body.[47]

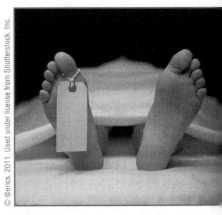

A distinct sexual attraction to a dead body is uncommon, but nevertheless has been present throughout history.

Sample Statute

The state of Nevada necrophilia statute reads as follows:

Nevada Revised Statute § 201.450. Necrophilia.

1. A person who commits a sexual penetration on the dead body of a human being shall be punished by imprisonment in the state prison for life, with possibility of parole, beginning when a minimum of 5 years has been served, or by a fine of not more than $ 20,000, or by both fine and imprisonment.

2. A person convicted of a violation of subsection 1 shall not be granted probation or parole unless a psychologist licensed to practice in Nevada or a psychiatrist licensed to practice medicine in Nevada certifies that the person is not a menace to the health, safety or morals of others.

3. For the purposes of this section, "sexual penetration" means cunnilingus, fellatio or any intrusion, however slight, of any part of a person's body or any object manipulated or inserted by a person into the genital or anal openings of the body of another, including sexual intercourse in what would be its ordinary meaning if practiced upon the living.[48]

Arguments Made By The Prosecution

Except in more flagrant situations, in many cases, the state will be challenged to gather enough evidence for a conviction for necrophilia. Many offenders are insiders such as employees of a hospital and can achieve their fantasy-oriented goal without detection. Many can achieve their goal simply from being in the presence of a corpse, even without touching it. Not only does the state have to discover the touching, there must be evidence that the touching was sexual or somehow related to the purpose of sexual gratification. The state must further demonstrate that the touching was without authorization, which may be difficult if the suspect is an employee who is authorized to manage the body.

Arguments Made By The Defense

In obvious cases, the defense can try to work with a desecration statute rather than a law on necrophilia specifically. A jury will be less appalled and the sentence may be lighter. Other than that, the defense may not have much to work with. The accused can assert that the touching was not sexual, but usually no witnesses will be present to corroborate such claims. Lastly, since there are often no witnesses, the defense can try to assert that there was no type of touching at all, but rather, simply an unusual curiosity to observe the dead body.

Variations of the Law of Necrophilia

A. Res gestae/Continuous Transaction

As a matter of strict definition, necrophilia is a nonviolent, nondestructive act that manifests more out of a secretive, deviant contemplation rather than an impulse control disorder. Arguably, acts of necrophilia or fantasies based on an episode of necrophilia will occur in a cemetery, morgue, mortuary, or hospital. The perpetrator is not necessarily interested in a power-driven sexual conquest, but rather, a silent, lurking interest in a highly specified type of sexual experience.

Necrophiliacs are usually distinguished from murderers, although both are interested in the death of another person. On the more violent side of crime, murderous offenders may indeed engage in other inhumane and felonious acts with those they kill, such as dismemberment or cannibalism. In cases where a murderer has sex with the victim of the murder, the law suspects a necrophilia act in addition to the murder and has a legal analysis in place for such cases. To separate necrophilia from a case of a murder and subsequent sexual contact with the dead body, the courts will examine the facts to determine whether the sexual contact with the dead body was a continuous aspect of the criminal episode—the res gestae of the act. If the sexual contact with the corpse was connected to the act of the killing, the case will be treated apart from a case of necrophilia.

In *Lipham v. State,* a violent offender broke into the home of a 79-year-old woman and went on a bizarre crime rampage, primarily looking for something to steal, such as jewelry.[49] After the break-in, he shot the woman in the head and eventually stole several pieces of jewelry. After the killing, in an apparent burst of haste, the killer engaged in sexual intercourse with the dead victim. The intercourse did not appear to be a contemplated act of necrophilia or a sexually ritualized part of the crime scene, but rather a demented aspect of an already dangerous and volatile criminal episode.[50]

The total charges of murder and rape brought by the prosecution were substantial and, as a result, the sentence of death was a distinct possibility. To avoid an execution, it was necessary for the defendant to get out of the rape charge. This legal scenario was similar to other previous cases where a killer appeals the case solely to avoid the sentence of death. There is nothing to lose by filing an appeal, and a lot to salvage. In such cases, the offender tries to argue that he could not be charged with rape because the rape and the murder convictions together can justify the sentence of death.

To get out of the rape charge, the defendant cited legal precedent that indicated rape can only occur if the victim is alive, and in the case at hand, he had killed the victim and had sex with her after he had killed her. She was not alive when the rape occurred, hence it was no rape, according to the defendant. The defense cited *Gibson v. Jackson* which states: "For the petitioner to be guilty of rape, the victim must have been a person, a living human being; if dead before the act—as terrible and disgusting as it may be—the act is not rape.[51]

Usually, a judge will follow legal precedent of prior cases. In this case, however, the judge may have been so disturbed by the facts involved that the judge basically ignored the legal precedent of Gibson and provided an interpretation of the law that would work against the defendant, rather than in his favor. The court stated:

> The offense of rape is defined in our Code as follows: A person commits the offense of rape when he has carnal knowledge of a female forcibly and against her will. Carnal knowledge in rape occurs when there is any penetration of the female sex organ by the male sex organ.[52]

> There is nothing in this code section which precludes a finding of rape if the victim is not alive at the moment of penetration. What the jury must find is that the defendant had carnal knowledge of the victim 'forcibly and against her will.'[53]

> If the element of force is satisfied where the defendant has used less than deadly force to overcome the victim's resistance so as to allow him to have carnal knowledge of the victim, the element of force is surely no less satisfied when the defendant has used deadly force to accomplish his aim.

> As for the remaining element, 'against her will', this has been interpreted to mean 'without her consent,' and has been satisfied in cases in which the victim was drugged, asleep, unconscious, or in a coma. See, e.g., *Brown v. State*, 174 Ga. App. 913 (331 S.E.2d 891) (1985). We see no reason why it should be any less applicable in a case in which the defendant has rendered the victim permanently unconscious by killing her.

> The facts here differ fundamentally from a case in which one happens upon the corpse of a female and engages in sexual intercourse with it. The use of force in the former and

the absence of force in the latter is the difference. One is rape and the other necrophilia. The evidence in this case supports the jury's finding that the defendant had carnal knowledge of Kate Furlow forcibly and against her will notwithstanding that it is unclear whether the defendant first raped the victim and then killed her, or first killed the victim and then raped her.[54]

B. Mortician Duty of Care

The domain of the necrophiliac is generally limited to obvious locations where a corpse may be present. Graveyards and mortuaries are likely locations. It is not uncommon for someone with necrophilia or necrophilia-related tendencies to seek some type of employment or association in a mortuary or funeral home to gather the sensation produced from being in the proximity of a corpse or in a position where the possibility of touching a corpse may exist.[55] The same logic is true for a patron of a strip club, or possibly a fitness center who seeks to be in the presence of certain bodies and experience various sensations from observing the bodies in the physical environment.

Business establishments, including mortuaries, have a legal duty to keep their premises safe and secure from unwanted intrusions or any type of harmful disturbance to visitors, guests, patrons, or customers. If someone is harmed as a result of the mismanagement of the business, the injured party may address the injury in civil court and sue for damages.[56] It is unlikely that mortuaries are vigilant about the potential for harm caused by necrophiliacs, however, mortuaries, like all businesses, may be sanctioned for a failure to exercise a duty to keep the business safe.

In the case of *Draper Mortuary v. Thomas*, defendant Draper Mortuary was formally and intentionally organized for the preparation, transportation, disposition of, and care of dead human bodies.[57] In so doing, the mortuary incurred a legal duty and obligation to "customers" and bereaved families to exercise reasonable care in the protection of corpses in its custody. The plaintiff in the case, Mr. Thomas, made an agreement with the mortuary to have the mortuary exercise temporary care of his deceased wife.

Most mortuaries have a chapel within the physical premises of the facility that is used for several purposes related to the death and passing of the body that has been brought to the mortuary. One evening, mortuary personnel failed to lock the chapel door and the unlocked chapel allowed for an intruder to enter the premises at night without authorization. On gaining access to the chapel and mortuary, the intruder located the corpse of Mrs. Thomas and engaged in sexual contact with the corpse. No property was taken nor was the building altered in any way. After sexualizing the corpse, the intruder left the building without detection.

On gathering evidence and discovering the sexual assault on the corpse and the unlawful entry of the intruder, the husband and family of the deceased filed a civil lawsuit against the

mortuary alleging a breach in the duty to care for the remains of their loved one and for negligence in the safekeeping of the body. Once in court, the mortuary tried to defend itself and
attempted to have the case dismissed, arguing that the failure to lock the chapel door was an
accident. The court rejected the defense and remanded the case to the jury. The court stated:

> Where a mortuary undertook to accept the care, custody, and control of a decedent's
> remains, the mortuary had a duty of care to the members of the decedent's bereaved
> family, and the question whether the duty was breached by the omission of the mortuary
> in failing to lock the door of the chapel in which the decedent's remains lay, resulting
> in a third party's unauthorized entrance therein and desecration of the remains, was a
> question of fact for the jury precluding summary judgment on the issue of the mortu-
> ary's negligence; though the existence of the mortuary's duty was a question of law, the
> foreseeability of the third party's act was a question of fact [for the jury].[58]

C. Insanity Implied by Necrophilia

Necrophilia raises concerns for the law and the criminal justice system, and also for medical
professionals. In the Western world, it is curious why anyone would consider an act of necrophilia. That said, necrophilia is not strongly opposed in other nations and is actually accepted if
not desired as important in other cultures throughout history. In addition, necrophilia is legal
in many states in the U.S., but this is more likely a matter of a lack of incidence than a matter
of decreased concern for the public health and safety.

Whatever the perceptions in other countries, or at other times in history, today in the
U.S. necrophilia is still largely viewed as deviant and suggests a mental abnormality since it is
such an extreme departure from what is viewed as "normal" sexual behavior.[59] In criminal cases
where a necrophiliac is involved, the insanity defense is called into question. For example, in
the case of *Robinson v. Maryland*, William Robinson, 26, entered the home of two relatives,
Florence and Eddie who were married, murdering them both. It appears that his goal was to
have sexual contact with Florence.[60]

Related to them both by marriage, Robinson was familiar with the two victims, as they
were with him. Even though they were related, not much background existed prior to the
murders. One day Robinson knocked on their door, entered the home when Florence answered
and after ascertaining that her husband was not home, asked to have sex with Florence. She
refused his advances. When she refused he assaulted her. Contrary to his understanding, the
husband was actually home, and when he intervened, he, too, was attacked by Robinson. One
of Robinson's confessions reads as follows:

> I turned around and came back down on Grafton Shop Road and knocked on Florence Bond's door. I asked if Eddie was home and she said no and I asked her for some and she said 'no'. Then we started wrasseling and she said she was going to give me some. And that's when I cut her and she was laying in the floor and Eddie came in and Eddie asked me what I was doing there. Then him and I got to wrasseling. Then I cut him. Then both was dead I went upstairs and got three dollars. Then I come back down the steps then I shut the light out and went out the kitchen door.[61]

The evidence indicated that Robinson stabbed both victims numerous times and that most of the stabbings occurred after the victims were dead. In addition, both victims had their jugular vein sliced open. Finally, Robinson had anal and vaginal sex with the female victim after she was dead. Robinson was charged with premeditated murder and faced the death penalty. On appeal, he tried to argue that his acts of having sex with the dead female was a necrophilia act, and therefore, he was insane and should not be subject to the death penalty.

As a result of his insanity plea, during the trial numerous medical and psychiatric experts took the witness stand to testify regarding the mental state of the defendant. The appellate court judge considered the testimony of one of the medical examiners

> The evidence relied upon by appellant, if it exists at all, must be found in the testimony of Dr. Rudiger Breitnecker, the medical examiner. Appellant [Robinson] tried very hard to get Dr. Breitnecker to say that the evidence compelled a diagnosis of necrophilia, which he defined as 'an abnormal desire to cohabit with a dead body.' He said he was not a psychiatrist and that he was 'not qualified [or] willing to discuss what [he thought] about it because [he didn't] know enough about it,' adding that he didn't 'know anybody who is a necrophiliac.' In any event appellant's sanity had to be measured by the McNaghten rule and evidence of some mental disorder or instability, *per se,* is insufficient proof to overcome the presumption of sanity. Jenkins v. State, supra. Necrophilia, as we understand the word, is a sexual deviation or aberration analogous to homosexuality, bestiality, sadism, masochism and the like. McNaghten sanity and necrophilia are not necessarily incompatible.

The opinion of the medical examiner weighed in favor of ruling the defendant insane and hence not legally capable of receiving the death penalty. However, many other experts took the witness stand and their evaluations seemed to carry more weight. In the end, the court found that necrophilia was more of a deliberate and willful act, one done with aforethought. The court did not find that necrophilia was related to insanity. The court stated:

> Appellant's present contention is aimed both at that statement and her statement in respect of his prior sexual activity. The thrust of his argument, of course, is that Dr. Simmons' testimony attenuates his claim that he is a necrophiliac and, therefore, insane. In our judgment, the record not only does not support a finding of necrophilia, it does not support a finding of any kind of sexual deviation. As Dr. Simmons observed, necrophilia (an erotic attraction to corpses) is a neurotic rather than a psychotic illness and a necrophiliac can be and usually is a responsible agent, aware of what he is doing.[62]

Additional Court Cases: Necrophilia
State v. Ryan
899 P.2d 825 (1995)

CASE SUMMARY

PROCEDURAL POSTURE: Defendants in consolidated appeals from the Superior Court of Snohomish County and the Superior Court of Superior County (both in Washington) challenged restitution orders imposed on their guilty plea or conviction, claiming that the restitution orders were not determined within the mandatory time limits of Wash. Rev. Code § 9.94A.142(1).

OVERVIEW: In the consolidated appeals, defendant sought a determination whether constitutional and statutory requirements were met when the trial court as part of a criminal sentence entered an ex parte order of restitution with the proviso that each defendant could have a restitution hearing if he or she objected to the amount that was set. One defendant, who broke into a funeral home and made sexual contact with several corpses, had his restitution hearing four months after the restitution order. He objected to about half the amount he was ordered to pay. The other defendant, who pleaded guilty to charges arising from a vehicular homicide, and the statutory time frame for a restitution order was also not followed in his case. The court vacated the restitution order with respect to the defendant charged with vehicular homicide, and vacated the portion of the restitution order to which the other defendant had objected. The court held that the statutory requirement of Wash. Rev. Code § 9.94A.142(1) that a trial court determine restitution within 60 days of sentencing was mandatory, not directory.

OUTCOME: One restitution order was vacated in part, and the other order was vacated entirely.[63]

Erotic Asphyxiation

At first glance, choking is not immediately associated with a warm sexual encounter with a loved one. Some would say choking could not possibly be a part of a loving encounter. A study of paraphilia, however, provides unequivocal evidence that aggression and violence are, in fact, very much associated with the sexuality of some people.[64] Of course, the law seeks to deter this type of activity for the health and safety of the parties involved. Even though the acts may be done in private by mature, consenting adults, the law will still seek to decrease the chance for anyone to get hurt.[65]

Erotic asphyxiation is sexualized choking. Other labels used for this practice include "scarfing," asphyxiophilia, and hypoxyphilia.[66] The *DSM* definition is "sexual arousal by oxygen deprivation obtained by means of chest compression, noose, ligature, plastic bag, mask, or chemical."[67] The primary reason that participants engage in this sex act is due to the heightened stimulation. On being choked or strangled, the asphyxiation and rapidly decreased oxygen level in the brain and body produce an intensified sense of arousal that can be sexualized. Specifically, the activity of strangulation decreases dopamine and increases endorphin in the brain, thereby enhancing sexual arousal.[68] Like the effects from certain controlled substances, participants can develop a tolerance level that leads to increased participation, increased risk taking, and hence, increased risk of death or accident.[69]

In the early 1800s in the Antebellum South, it was discovered unscientifically that men who were hanged to death for the commission of a felony offense developed a sexual response and erection on being strangled to death. These incidences led to further medical investigation for the relationship between choking and sexual response. Even earlier in time (the 1600s), choking was experimented with as a treatment modality for erectile dysfunction.[70]

Autoeroticism is any sex act practiced on a solo basis. In many cases of autoerotic choking, the participant slings a type of noose over a door, places the noose around their neck and tugs aggressively on the end of the rope with one hand while engaging in sexual self-stimulation with the other. Many deaths have resulted from this potentially lethal practice.

With a partner, like with other forms of sexual contact, the participants can zero in with great sensitivity the exact manner of the act for the purpose of optimal satisfaction. Each becomes intimately familiar with the subtle preferences of the other and caters to them for a heightened experience. Various cues are used to signal the partner to make certain adjustments in the midst of the encounter. Arguably, in the best of all circumstances, neither person is bashful about telling the other exactly what they want. The overall result is to make the encounter magnetizing in its effect and power. The intensity can both frighten the participants from ever doing it again or draw them back into the scenario for another, even better experience.

The criminal justice system cannot much grasp this offense when it results in harm. Hickey (2006) indicates that hundreds of deaths may occur each year from this dangerous practice.[71] However, many of the deaths are misclassified as suicide or accidental deaths and sometimes the deceased's family covers up the act because they are embarrassed about the sex involved or cannot comprehend it.[72] Family members may remove ropes and plastic bags from the scene or even write a fraudulent suicide note, thus confusing the scene for investigators and the police. Depending on the facts of the case, in the event of a prosecution, a battery statute may be used or a statute pertaining to assault. It is entirely possible that an assisted suicide law may be invoked if the prosecution has reason to believe that a partner assisted, encouraged, or otherwise aided and abetted the death by strangulation. Lastly, at the extreme end of the spectrum, rapists and sadists presumably would not hesitate to use smothering or strangulation as part of their heinousness and in such cases, a murder or attempted murder charge may apply.

Definition of the Offense

The intentional restriction of oxygen to the brain by choking, suffocation, or strangulation of oneself, or someone else for purposes of achieving sexual excitation.[73]

Elements of the Offense

Erotic asphyxiation is not criminalized per se. Where the act involves oneself, the law allows for the act of sexual self-stimulation, even in cases of injury or death. Solicitation or inducement, however, can result in criminal liability.[74] Assisted auto-asphyxiation therefore may be criminalized pursuant to statutes that prohibit the aiding or encouraging of lethal self-destructive acts. The elements that must be proven beyond a reasonable doubt are:

1. causes, induces, persuades or encourages,
2. lethal self strangulation or self asphyxiation.[75]

Sample Statute

The Model Penal Code provisions related to erotic asphyxiation reads as follows:

Model Penal Code § 210.5 Causing or Aiding Lethal Self Destruction.

(1) Causing Self-destruction as Criminal Homicide. A person may be convicted of criminal homicide for causing another to commit a self destructive act resulting in death only if he purposely causes such self destruction by force, duress, or coercion.

(2) Aiding or Soliciting Self-destruction as an Independent Offense. A person who purposely aids or solicits another to commit a lethal act of self-destruction is guilty of a felony of the second degree if his conduct causes such self-destruction or an attempted act of self-destruction.[76]

Arguments Made By The Prosecution

For many of these cases, the state only gets involved after someone has been injured or killed. If the state can intervene before death or serious bodily injury, a confession would certainly be helpful. A witness or partner may also be involved and they may provide a statement under oath and on the record and explain what actually happened. Various paraphernalia may be used in these cases and certain items used to cut off oxygen supply, such as a rope or strap of some kind, may be used as physical evidence. The state would also benefit if it can show a pattern of paraphilic behavior on the part of the accused. Such evidence would support a present claim of similar deviance.

Arguments Made By The Defense

The accused has a few avenues to work with if facing a type of assault charge. Mainly, the accused can argue consent and that the activities were desired rather than unwanted. The accused can also argue that no one was hurt, even if it seems like strangulation would be injurious. Lastly, the defense can claim that any injuries or alleged harm were all a part of consensual experimentation and that any injuries were expected and no cause for alarm.

Variations of the Law of Erotic Asphyxiation

A. Paraphilia or Reckless Disregard for Life?

Accidental deaths always raise the specter that the death may not be accidental after all. This historic clarification is especially pronounced in cases of rough play where it is thought that the parties should have known better—that someone could get hurt.[77] Rituals, ceremonies, sport, or unusual sexual acts that result in death by necessity will need to be examined for criminal intent.[78] If the facts of the case somehow don't add up, even a case of a truly accidental death cannot withstand the scrutiny of the criminal justice system and a prison sentence.

In the case of *Braswell v. State*, a couple who were married for seven years (and had two young sons) occasionally engaged in the practice of erotic asphyxiation in the privacy of their home and out of view and earshot of their children. On one occasion, the wife asphyxed beyond the point of return and died and her husband became the lead suspect.

On the night in question, after arriving home, Braswell and his wife took a bath together that eventually led to sexual activities. Afterward, she took a bath alone and then woke Braswell up at approximately 2:45 a.m. She wanted to have sex again and asked for a "fixie," her term for erotic asphyxiation and he complied with her request.[79] The couple got into the bathtub, turned on the air jets, and Braswell proceeded to choke his wife as she had requested. When her fingers grew limp (a sign for him to release his strangle-hold), he released his hold and laid her back in the water with an inflatable pillow beneath her head. Braswell said that he went back to bed and dozed off. He re-awoke between 3:45 and 3:50 a.m. and noticed that his wife had not come to bed. He went into the bathroom and found her submerged in the bath water, dead.

Mr. Braswell had a difficult time explaining to the police that his wife died in the course of a sexual experience that was engaged in willfully and knowingly, and even enthusiastically. He explained to the police that he and his wife had learned about various sexual practices from pornography and felt their experiments were "adventuresome." He stated that he and his wife frequented a "swingers club" in Shelby County and that his wife was the one who first suggested that they engage in erotic asphyxiation.[80]

In this practice, he stated, he would get behind his wife and place his arm around her neck, sometimes with his hands against the side of her neck. He stated that his wife would signal him with her fingers. If his hold was too tight, she would tap her fingers; if his hold was too loose, she would pinch him. When her fingers grew limp, he would release his hold. He stated that the choking sensation heightened sexual pleasure. Braswell added that after he released his chokehold, he would lay his wife down until she "came around." He said that they had engaged in the practice for approximately two years on a weekly basis.

An expert in sexual psychiatry testified during the case that Braswell's explanation of the use of hand signals to control the application and release of pressure around the neck supported his credibility because someone who had not engaged in erotic asphyxiation would not grasp the significance of anticipating a signal for release. The expert explained that the problem with the system described by Braswell was that, eventually, the partner waits longer and longer before signaling release, and it was a "lethal kind of system that they used."[81]

On the night in question, after they engaged in erotic asphyxiation, Braswell stated that he went to bed and his wife went to take a bath. But three hours later, when the police arrived, the bathwater was still warm, if as though Mrs. Braswell had taken a bath more recently than the defendant stated. When discovered, the police noted that the victim's arms and legs were stiff, and that she had bloodshot eyes consistent with strangulation. There appeared to be no signs of a struggle or fight in the home. At the crime scene, the defendant repeatedly told the first responders how horribly upset he was and that he should have never let his wife take a bath. However, for some reason, he made several phone calls during the initial investigation even though it was very early in the morning. In addition, at the investigation, the police found the couple's divorce papers and other evidence related to the couple's marital discord and imminent divorce. The original responder for the police, Baba Tanzy, gathered evidence and the court record included the following notation:

> Tanzy said that the water in the bathtub was warm when he arrived. Mr. Tanzy noticed small red marks on each side of the victim's neck and broken blood vessels in her eyes, which indicated to Mr. Tanzy that the victim had died by suffocation or asphyxiation. Mr. Tanzy said that the victim's arms were stiff.[82]

An autopsy was performed by a medical professional, Dr. Carter, which provided more evidence of what might have actually happened. According to the autopsy report:

> Dr. Carter said that she had performed autopsies on people who had died from erotic asphyxiation. Dr. Carter said that a crime scene investigation was very important to determine if the death resulted from such activity. Dr. Carter said that she usually looked for ligatures, pornography, or signs of a safe escape such as something that needs to be pulled to release the choking. Dr. Carter said that generally the victim is found in the position where they accidentally asphyxiated. Dr. Carter stated that the victim's injuries were not consistent with a death from erotic asphyxiation because there were multiple injuries to the victim's neck muscles as opposed to a pattern made by some type of ligature.[83]

Braswell denied that he intentionally killed his wife, or that he choked her to death in anger. When asked if the victim's death was an accident, he responded, "yes." Dr. Schwartz, the sexual psychiatry expert that testified during the case stated that as a result of his interview with the defendant and review of the material that had been introduced into evidence, it was his opinion that the victim's death was an accident due to erotic asphyxiation.

Nevertheless, the state charged Braswell with murder in the second degree. The offense of second-degree murder is defined as the knowing killing of another.[84] A person acts "knowingly" with respect to the result of the person's conduct when the person is aware that the conduct is reasonably certain to cause the result.[85] Braswell was convicted of murder at trial. On appeal, he argued that the evidence wrongfully portrayed the act of erotic asphyxiation as something meant to kill rather than an alternative form of sexual relations. However, the appellate court did not agree and affirmed his conviction for the murder of his wife. The court stated:

> [W]e conclude that the evidence was probative of both Defendant's intent and to rebut his theory of an accidental killing. Although the evidence was prejudicial, based on our review of the facts presented in this case, we do not find that the prejudice was unfair. Moreover, the trial court gave the jury a limiting instruction as to how to consider this evidence. See *State v. Jordan,* 116 S.W.3d 8, 18 (Tenn. Crim. App. 2003) (observing that jurors are presumed to follow the instructions given them absent evidence to the contrary). Thus, we conclude that the probative value of the evidence was not outweighed by the danger of unfair prejudice. Accordingly, this evidence was properly admitted.[86]

The jury heard Defendant's theory of defense that the victim accidently drowned in the bathtub following her engagement in the practice of erotic asphyxiation and, by its verdict, obviously found this explanation not credible as was their prerogative. Viewing the evidence in a light most favorable to the State, we conclude that a rational trier of fact could find beyond a reasonable doubt that Defendant was guilty of the offense of second degree murder. Defendant is not entitled to relief on this issue.[87]

B. Accidental Death of Exculpatory Witness

When two parties engage in activities such as wrestling, playful fighting, contact sports, or actual violent exchanges and someone dies, even if it appears to be an accident, the law has to respond. The friends and family of the victim will likely be upset and usually hope for a retributive justice response by the criminal justice system, and it is the role of the state to redress these grievances.

With this legal procedure in mind, when two people are not trying to hurt one another, but someone accidentally gets hit, for example, in the head and dies, the person who dies is often the most valuable witness. The deceased party is usually the one and only person with the intimate knowledge of the case and can be helpful in determining whether the situation was one of an unintentional accident or a case of reckless disregard for life.

In the case of *Washington v. Metcalf,* James Metcalf and his girlfriend were out on a type of "double-date" with another couple. The four of them went bar hopping one evening and had consumed a large volume of alcohol between them. In particular, Metcalf's girlfriend was legally intoxicated with a BAC of .24 (high).[88] Toward the end of the evening, Metcalf and his girlfriend went back to Metcalf's apartment. Once there, they apparently watched pornography on a television and engaged in sexual contact. Metcalf testified that during sex, his [intoxicated] girlfriend brought his hands to her neck and squeezed his hands around her neck. While doing this, she asphyxiated and died. Coroners examined her body and determined that she died as a result of asphyxia due to strangulation.[89]

The death alerted the authorities and the state charged Metcalf with the murder of his girlfriend.[90] Metcalf was convicted of murder with an aggravating sexual component. Specifically, the aggravating factors of sexual motivation and victim vulnerability due to intoxication. The aggravating sexual component created a sentence enhancement. Metcalf's standard range sentence was 123–220 months in prison, but the court enhanced his sentence to a minimum of 360 months and a maximum of life due to the aggravating factors.[91]

On appeal, Metcalf raised various standard defenses. For example, he alleged that the police did not adequately read him his rights and that some of the statements he made to the police should not be allowed as a part of the record. The issue was whether the trial court erred in denying Metcalf's motion to suppress his statements made to detectives at the time of his arrest. Metcalf contends the statements were made during a custodial interrogation, thus requiring Miranda warnings.

The entire time, Metcalf claimed the death was an accident and explained the activities that led to the strangulation, namely, erotic asphyxiation, were not a part of a malicious killing in the least. However, the state did not agree with Metcalf and the jury did not believe him, either. He had little or no exculpatory evidence. There is only one person who could testify that Metcalf was telling the truth and that person was dead: the victim in the case. The court ruled against Metcalf during the trial and again during his appeal. The appellate court stated:

> Evidence is sufficient to support a conviction if, after viewing the evidence in the light most favorable to the State, any rational trier of fact could have found guilt beyond a reasonable doubt; *State v. Green,* 616 P.2d 628 (1980). A claim of insufficiency admits the truth of the State's evidence and all inferences that reasonably can be drawn therefrom. Circumstantial and direct evidence are considered equally reliable. We defer to the trier of fact on issues of conflicting testimony, credibility of witnesses, and persuasiveness of the evidence.[92]

C. Ligature, Sadism, and Homicide

No matter what the context, choking someone is a violent act and only a few contexts, mainly sporting events such as octagon fighting, make such violence legal. In nearly all other contexts, the law will examine choking under traditional assault or aggravated assault statutes. In case of death, the episode will come under the purview of a homicide statute.

In the realm of sexual deviancy, choking may be done for a variety of reasons, not only for the practice of eroticized asphyxiation. For example, couples may touch one another in the neck or clavicle area as a form of affection or foreplay. Couples may engage in playfulness by softly biting one another on the neck. Hence, the realm of touching, choking, or biting the neck may be done for a variety of purposes when it comes to the physical sharing between partners. One other context—in the criminal realm—further exists when it comes to the neck and sexualized touching. Choking and asphyxiation may also be a part of the intentional infliction of pain and suffering for purposes of sexual satisfaction, also known as sadistic choking.[93]

In the case of *People v. Russo,* Patrick Russo was convicted by a Texas jury of capital murder for killing someone in the course of an alleged robbery. He was sentenced to life in prison. With nothing to lose, Russo raised several points of law on appeal and all of them were rejected by the appellate court.

The facts of the case are as follows: the murder victim, Diane Holik, worked out of her home in a relatively expensive suburb of Austin, Texas. She was engaged to be married and was selling her home to go live with her husband-to-be in the Houston area. She had a For Sale sign in front of her house and frequently let prospective buyers come in and look around so that she could sell the house as soon as possible.[94]

Russo contrived to pose as a buyer of Holik's house and he had been lurking around other homes for sale in the area posing as a buyer and did so for the purpose of targeting potential victims. In a depraved manner, he would ritualistically wander through the home while making observations of female targets and plans for what he would do to his victims. One such seller of a home testified that when Russo showed up to "preview" her home for purchase, he was noticeably nervous, trembling, and that when she shook hands with him, his hands were sweaty.[95] His criminality was thus ritualized, premeditated, sexualized, and dangerous.

Holik was found dead in an upstairs guest bedroom in her home. The cause of death was strangulation. Her hands had been bound behind her back and she was choked to death. She was fully clothed and had not been sexually assaulted. Her expensive engagement ring was missing as well as her jewelry box, which contained a few pieces of expensive jewelry. When the police queried the neighbors, a couple of neighbors reported seeing Russo enter Holik's house and one neighbor reported that Russo had been in her home posing as a buyer of her house. At trial, thirteen people who had their respective homes for sale testified that Russo came inside their home asking questions about the floor plan, looking around, and expressing an interest in buying the house.[96] The police located Russo at a nearby church where he was employed as a pastor's assistant and music director. He was placed under arrest, charged with Holik's murder, and as stated above, convicted and sentenced to life in prison.

In the course of the investigation, the police obtained a search warrant to search Russo's computer. The search produced evidence that Russo had studied various strangulation techniques and that he had purchased a six-month account for a pornography site related to the subject of sexualized strangulation, erotic asphyxiation, and sadistic choking. Approximately one thousand images of eroticized strangulation were retrieved from Russo's computer. At trial, an expert witness named Dr. Coons testified as to the relevance of the strangulation images pulled from Russo's computer. The record states:

> Dr. Coons explained that a sexual sadist is sexually stimulated with a fantasy life and becomes obsessive. The person will "play out" the fantasies, searching out potential victims. The person is aroused by watching and controlling another with knives or guns or injuring them by other methods, including ligature strangulation. In many such encounters, Dr. Coons explained, there is no completed sexual act. The underlying purpose

Sexual asphyxiation may be criminalized pursuant to laws relating to assisted self-destruction, assault, or in the case of death, murder.

can be killing, dominating, or humiliating another. The doctor testified that in his opinion, the hypothetical scenario strongly suggests that the defendant [Russo] in the scenario sought sexual gratification through ligature strangulation.[97]

On appeal, Russo argued that the information about strangulation taken from his computer and used against him in court was inadmissible. He argued that the case is about an alleged killing and stolen jewelry and that any information about sex and choking is irrelevant. The appellate court judge did not sympathize with Russo or his arguments. The judge ruled that the discovery of the files on his computer were part of a search incident to a lawful arrest and that the files were necessary to tie Russo to the killing of Holik. The judge reminded Russo that the images pulled from his computer pertained to strangulation and that the cause of death of Holik was strangulation. The judge stated:

The resulting [computer images] exhibits were obtained from an independent source without any tinge of illegality and were admissible into evidence. See *Murray v. United States,* 487 U.S. 533, 541-44 (1988). Moreover, there is no Fourth Amendment protection against the disclosure of subscriber information by Internet service providers. The touchstone of the Fourth Amendment is reasonableness. *Florida v. Jimeno,* 500 U.S. 248 (1991). Computer searches are no less constitutional than searches of physical records where innocuous documents may be scanned to ascertain their relevancy. *United States v. Hunter,* 13 F. Supp. 2d 574, 584 (D. Vt. 1998). Keeping in mind the particular facts of the instant case, we find no violation of the Fourth Amendment. The trial court did not abuse its discretion in admitting evidence of the contents of appellant's computer as contended. The sixth ground of error is overruled.[98]

Additional Court Cases: Erotic Asphyxiation

People v. Hashimoto

54 Cal. App.3d 862 (1976)

CASE SUMMARY

PROCEDURAL POSTURE: Defendant appealed a judgment of the Criminal Court for Shelby County (Tennessee) convicting him of second-degree murder in violation of T.C.A. § 39-13-210 and sentencing him to twenty-four years in prison.

OVERVIEW: Defendant was convicted for strangling the victim to death. On appeal, the court held that the evidence was sufficient to support defendant's conviction because: (1) the coroner testified that the victim's cause of death was manual strangulation; (2) he also testified that the victim's injuries were not consistent with strangulation by choke hold; (3) defendant did not contend that he was not present in the house when the victim died, or that anyone else, other than his two sons, was present; and (4) the jury heard defendant's theory that the victim accidentally drowned in the bathtub following her engagement in the practice of erotic asphyxiation and, by its verdict, obviously found that the explanation was not credible. The trial court did not err by admitting into evidence under Tenn. R. Evid. 404(b) defendant's girlfriend's testimony that defendant had assaulted her on two prior occasions because he sought to demonstrate to the jury his skill at successfully engaging in erotic asphyxiation and placed his relationship with his girlfriend at issue by submitting that they had engaged in erotic asphyxiation in the same manner as he and the victim, without adverse consequences.

OUTCOME: Defendant's conviction and sentence were affirmed.[99]

Zoophilia

The emotional and sexual attraction of humans to animals has a long history. Until 2005, a farm existed near Enumclaw, Washington that was an "animal brothel," where people paid to have sex with animals. After an incident on July 2, 2005, when a man died in Enumclaw community hospital after having been sodomized by a horse, the state legislature of the State of Washington, which had been one of the few states in the United States without a law against bestiality, within six months passed a bill making bestiality illegal.

Zoophilia may be defined as the affinity or sexual attraction by a human to a nonhuman animal.[100] A **zoophile** is a "person who has a profound emotional and/or physical attraction to animals."[101] It is worth speculating that persons who have sex with animals are prone to personality disorders and may have a tendency to commit other sex crimes or nonsex-related offenses against persons.

More recently, the term "zoosexuality" has been used to more accurately reflect the full spectrum of a "human/animal interactions."[102] The term "bestiality" is often used interchangeably with "zoophilia," though some suggest that this is inaccurate since the term bestiality does not encompass the entire set of dynamics that may occur between human and animal. The term bestiality is most often used too broadly to describe human–animal sexual activity, failing to specify the requisite sexual act. The term sodomy has also been used somewhat too broadly to cover sexual acts with animals but also covers certain human sexual acts.

Sexual acts with animals have occurred since prehistoric times as evidenced by cave drawings, ancient Egyptian artifacts, and Greek and Roman mythology, human perceptions of these behaviors have varied substantially over time and across cultures. By the time of the Common Law in England, British authorities had a law, drafted around 1290 that required anyone convicted of engaging in bestiality be burned. Between 1400 and 1800, it was commonplace in England to even charge the animal in cases of bestiality. The human abuser and animal were often sentenced to torturous deaths followed by the two being buried together in the same grave.[103] In early America, zoophilia was referred to as a "sin against God, Nature and the Law" and considered so detestable that Christians in Colonial America would not name the act.[104]

The legality of zoophilia is similar to the laws of necrophilia and is not controlled from the federal level. The only relevant federal law is the sodomy law under the military code. This law provides that "[a]ny person subject to this chapter who engages in unnatural carnal copulation with ... an animal is guilty of sodomy."[105]

As with most of the crimes covered in this book, the primary legal jurisdiction is at the state level. Kentucky, New Mexico, and West Virginia are the only three states lacking zoophilia-related statutes. Even today, the states differ widely in their terminology and use terms such as bestiality, cruelty to animals, interspecies sexual assault, crime against nature, or unnatural intercourse; buggery, sodomy, or sexual assault may also be laws used to prosecute human sexual contact with an animal. Arkansas, Connecticut, Iowa, Oregon, and Utah all consider the act to be a misdemeanor, while Nevada and South Carolina consider it a felony. Oklahoma and Mississippi both punish the act with up to ten years in prison, with the penalty in Louisiana ranging from $2,000 to $10,000 in fines and six months to five years in prison, depending on whether it is the offender's first, second, or subsequent offense. Colorado, Kansas, and Minnesota all consider the act a misdemeanor or a felony, depending on the specific offense.[106]

Consent, animal cruelty, and also the law of marriage represent three obscure legal issues when it comes to zoophilia. It is argued that zoophilia must be illegal since the animal cannot give consent and this argument parallels sex with minors. Others claim consent can be assumed due to the love the owner has for the animal (same logic used by pedophiles and children).[107]

Aside from consent, many persons construe zoophilia as the crime of animal abuse or cruelty to animals and earlier in history some feared that a pollution of the species (human and animal) would occur from zoophilia acts. Lastly, at least one church has formally organized to perform weddings between human and animal.[108] This form of marriage, however, also implicates the legal issue of consent, as well as not being a form of marriage constitutionally recognized by government.

Definition of the Offense

Sexual contact or penetration by a human with an animal.[109]

Elements of the Offense

The elements of the crime of sexual assault on an animal that must be proved beyond a reasonable doubt are:

Sexual Assault of an Animal (proposed).

1. A person commits the crime of Sexual Assault of an Animal if the person:

    (a) Touches or contacts, or causes an object or another person to touch or contact, the mouth, anus or sex organs of an animal for the purpose of arousing or gratifying the sexual desire of a person; or

    (b) Causes an animal to touch or contact, the mouth, anus or sex organs of an animal for the purpose of arousing or gratifying the sexual desire of a person.

2. Sexual assault of an animal is a class B felony.

3. Sexual assault of an animal is a sex crime.[110]

Sample Statute

The state of Louisiana zoophilia/sexual assault on an animal statute reads as follows:

Louisiana's Revised Statute, § 14:89(A)(1). Crimes Against Nature. The law of crimes against nature prohibits "unnatural carnal copulation," i.e., oral or anal sex between humans, or sex with animals.[111]

Arguments Made By The Prosecution

A medical veterinary examination would be very helpful to the state. Such evidence can show with little error that a sexual activity or stimulus was visited upon the animal in question. The state also benefits from the nature of the law when it comes to the sexual touching of animals. Specifically, consent, agreement, or experimentation is not an available defense and the state need only show that touching occurred.

Arguments Made By The Defense

Since a lot of people touch pets, such as petting a dog or cat, the defense can make the argument that the touching was not sexual and draw an analogy to all pet owners who are affectionate toward their pets. A lack of witnesses in these cases will also be a benefit to the defense. Hopefully for the defense, the accused can avoid a character examination that might show a history of animal cruelty or pattern of childhood developmental problems.

Variations of the Law of Zoophilia

A. Animal Cruelty

The act of zoophilia may be prosecuted in a number of ways. The most certain manner is with a bestiality statute that is right on point. Absent a bestiality law, the state can use an animal cruelty statute. Animal rights activists are relatively successful actors in the political process and have been aggressive in lobbying state and federal government for comprehensive laws to deter various forms of abuse targeted to animals. Sexual abuse is one of the forms of abuse considered by animal rights activists.

As a result of their lobbying efforts, at the federal level, Congress passed the Animal Welfare Act (AWA) in 1966 and has strengthened the law through amendments in 1970, 1976, 1985, and 1990.[112] The U.S. Dept. of Agriculture is charged with the administration of the act and has enforced the AWA to protect certain animals from inhumane treatment and neglect.[113] The AWA did not have zoophiliacs primarily in mind on the passing this piece of legislation, but neither is the legislation oblivious to the potential for harm to an animal by someone inclined to sexual abuse.

The AWA prohibits staged dogfights, bear or raccoon baiting, and similar animal-fighting ventures.[114] The act also requires that minimum standards of care and treatment be provided for certain animals bred for commercial sale, used in research, transported commercially, or exhibited to the public. This provision of the act requires the safe keeping of animals from human predators such as sexually motivated predators since zoophiliacs will most likely target a caged, rather than feral animal due to accessibility.

At the state level, approximately thirty-six states have bestiality laws. On conviction, some make sex with an animal a misdemeanor offense while others administer the crime as a felony. Some states require a psychological evaluation of the convicted offender as a part of sentencing and others require court-ordered psychological counseling, in particular if the convicted zoophile is a minor.[115]

In 2004 in Ocala, Florida, Randol Mitchell, 27, was caught by his then-fiancée having sex with her rottweiler dog.[116] On being caught, Mitchell admitted to having a life-long problem with his sexual attraction to animals.

The state of Florida, however, did not have a bestiality law to use against Mitchell. The legislature has attempted to pass a bestiality bill, but has failed thus far. Lawmakers said they didn't want to be accused of wasting time addressing a rare crime when Floridians needed them to help create jobs. Further, the legislature apparently "didn't want to debate the icky subject in public meetings occasionally frequented by children."[117]

Without a bestiality law, Mitchell was charged under the state Cruelty to Animals statute, which makes sexual contact with an animal a misdemeanor offense. Florida statute section 828.12 Cruelty to Animals reads:

(1) A person who unnecessarily overloads, overdrives, torments, deprives of necessary sustenance or shelter, or unnecessarily mutilates, or kills any animal, or causes the same to be done, or carries in or upon any vehicle, or otherwise, any animal in a cruel or inhumane manner, is guilty of a misdemeanor of the first degree, punishable as provided in s. 775.082 or by a fine of not more than $5,000, or both.[118]

Mitchell was convicted under the statute.[119] In addition to five years of probation, as part of his sentencing, Mitchell was ordered to undergo a mandatory psychological evaluation and was prohibited from owning pets of any kind while on probation and from having unsupervised contact with other people's pets. In addition to the probation and psychological evaluation, the judge ordered Mitchell to pay restitution to the dog's owner for any necessary veterinary treatment and furthermore prohibited Mitchell from possessing pornography of any kind. The judge commented:

> This is very disgusting, to tell you the truth, but I'm going to leave out my personal opinions and withhold adjudication unless you mess up. To a third party, the judge stated, 'He certainly needs some psychological help. For somebody to do something like this, they gotta have something wrong with them.'[120]

There was no evidence Mitchell had ever committed any sexual offense against a person.

B. Void for Vagueness (specificity requirement)

Courts have used a variety of terms to refer to zoophilia acts. For example, case law includes the terms bestiality, buggery, and sodomy to express a jurisprudential disgust for sex acts with animals. Legislatures have used the terms "unnatural intercourse"[121] or "aggravated criminal sodomy"[122] in reference to zoophilia. The medical community has used "zoorasty" and "zoosexuality" as applicable terminology. In earlier times, the law held tightly to odd euphemisms and would also refer to zoophilia as "the abominable and detestable crime against nature." This language was vague, not providing enough advance notice as to exactly what acts were against the law. At it's most illogical, the courts would refer to zoophilia as "unspeakable" and convict offenders without referring to what offense the conviction was for (since it was unspeakable).

Today, such reasoning would certainly be subject to a constitutional challenge based on the legal principle of vagueness. All laws must have a degree of clarity as to what acts are prohibited.

In the case of *State of Minnesota v. Bonynge*,[123] Robert Bonynge was found guilty under the law in Minnesota of one count of bestiality for masturbating a Rottweiller dog and four counts of aiding and abetting bestiality.[124] Under the Minnesota statute, an individual who "carnally knows" an animal is guilty of bestiality. However, the statute does not define the term "carnally know" and Bonynge claims that the law was vague and that his activities did not involve carnally knowing the dog, and therefore, he is not guilty of any crime.

There is no question that Bonynge's activities with the animal need to be deterred by law. However, the question remains: If Bonynge knew that he would receive a criminal sanction, would he have done the same thing? Since many paraphiliacs can satisfy their urges and curiosities in a manner that would not result in criminal liability, we may speculate that if he had greater notice in the law, he may have been deterred from committing his crime.

It is the role of the courts to interpret the law and make or advise corrections for shortcomings or vagueness in legislative statutes. This is particularly true in cases of sexual deviancy where the law takes a moral stand against deviant acts without explaining in specifics what acts are to be avoided. As a result of this historic role, many courts have had to strike down laws that are void for vagueness. A good example of one such court ruling is the following:

> It is authoritatively recognized that this statute provides a penalty for a crime, but fails to delineate what conduct will violate its terms.
>
> The blindfold upon our Lady of Justice is symbolic of impartiality, as being blind to all outside influences which would divert from the material facts and law applicable to the case in which justice is being sought upon its merits. Her blindfold in no way suggests that justice should be blind to the facts of life and of the times in which it functions; for the law, to be vibrant, must be a living thing, responsive to the society which it serves, and to which that society looks as the last true depository of truth and justice.
>
> A further reason dictating our reexamination here is the expansion of constitutional rulings on the invasion of private rights by state intrusion which must be taken into account in the consideration of this statute's continuing validity. The language in this statute could entrap unsuspecting citizens and subject them to 20-year sentences for which the statute provides. Such a sentence is equal to that for manslaughter and would no doubt be a shocking revelation to persons who do not have an understanding of the meaning of the statute.

Those who are versed in the law may understand the statute's meaning because of their knowledge of legal interpretations in court opinions, but it seems to us that if today's world is to have brought home to it what it is that the statute prohibits, it must be set forth in language which is relevant to today's society and is understandable to the average citizen of common intelligence which is the constitutional test of such language.

We are thoroughly in accord with upholding proper statutes, but a court must guard equally against those which offend constitutional standards and which constitute an infringement by the state upon the private rights of citizens. The statute, § 800.01, is void on its face as unconstitutional for vagueness and uncertainty in its language, violating constitutional due process to the defendants.[125]

C. Nonliving Animals

When the facts and circumstances of a case vary, so can the applicable law. Laws that prohibit sexual contact with an animal clearly apply if the animal is alive, but what about if the animal is dead? If the animal is dead, it may no longer be an animal, but rather, technically a carcass. What a corpse is to the human form, a carcass is to an animal. If the law only addresses sex with an animal, and not a carcass, no law may apply in a case of sex with a dead animal.

In 2009, a 20-year-old offender named James Hathaway was, at the time, a parolee from state prison. He had served an 18-month sentence for killing a horse. He pleaded no contest to one felony charge of mistreatment of an animal when he shot and killed a 26-year-old horse in order to have sex with it.[126]

In the present case, Hathaway was riding his bicycle along a country road when he spotted a dead deer in a ditch along the road. On seeing the deer, he approached it and engaged in a molestation of the carcass. He later admitted to becoming sexually aroused on seeing the deer in the ditch. He was seen by a passerby and subsequently reported to the police. The police located him at the halfway house where he was staying and questioned him about the incident. He had blood and deer hair on his clothes when confronted by the police. He originally stated that he had been helping his father clean a deer, but later admitted to the crime he was charged with.[127]

Hathaway was charged with sexual gratification with an animal, a misdemeanor crime in the state of Wisconsin pursuant to the state's Sexual Gratification statute.[128] The provision of the statute that applied to Hathaway is section 944.17(2), Whoever does any of the following is guilty of a Class A misdemeanor: 944.17(2)(c) Commits an act of sexual gratification involving his or her sex organ and the sex organ, mouth or anus of an animal.[129]

In the case, Hathaway originally entered a plea of not guilty.[130] It was not so much that Hathaway denied he engaged with the carcass, but rather, he focused on a legal technicality. His defense attorney aptly noted that the Wisconsin law did not refer to sex with a carcass. The defense made two arguments. Having sex with an animal is illegal in the state of Wisconsin, but the law does not say that having sex with a dead animal is against the law. Secondly, the defense argued that on death, the animal no longer is legally an animal and therefore, there was no sex with an "animal" since the deer was dead.[131]

Courts have a lot of discretion to make legal rulings and the case presumably could have gone either way. The judge rejected Hathaway's argument that the charge should be dismissed because the law against committing an act of sexual gratification with animals does not apply if they are dead. The court did not rule on the defense raised. Possibly upset by the whole ordeal, the defendant gave up the fight and entered a plea. The court stated:

> He rather convincingly contends that 'animal' means a living creature. However, Hathaway pled no contest to the charge. A plea of guilty or no contest waives all non-jurisdictional defects and defenses.[132]

Legally, we still do not know if sex with a carcass is permissible in the state of Wisconsin. We know the state can bring charges, but we are left wondering if those charges are permissible as a matter of substantive due process. Hathaway was sentenced to six months' probation and ordered to be evaluated as a sex offender and treated at the Institute for Psychological and Sexual Health in Duluth, Minnesota. Judge Michael Lucci stated: "This type of behavior is disturbing. It's disturbing to the public. It's disturbing to the court."[133]

Additional Court Cases: Zoophilia

People v. Haynes

760 N.W.2d 283 (2008)

CASE SUMMARY

PROCEDURAL POSTURE: The Calhoun County Circuit Court, Michigan, convicted defendant, pursuant to a no contest plea, of committing an abominable and detestable crime against nature with a sheep, MCL 750.158. The trial court sentenced defendant as a fourth habitual offender, MCL 769.12, to 30–240 months' imprisonment. Defendant was ordered to register under the Sex Offenders Registration Act (SORA), MCL 28.721 et seq. Defendant appealed.

OVERVIEW: Defendant argued that the trial court erred in requiring him to register as a sex offender. The appellate court found that when it applied the plain, ordinary, and generally accepted meanings of the words "if" and "individual" to MCL 28.722(e)(ii), a violation of MCL 750.158 required registration under the SORA for a listed offense only if the victim of the offense was a human being less than 18 years old. It was patent that the sheep that was the object of defendant's abominable and detestable crime against nature" was not a victim under MCL 28.722(e)(ii). Thus, the instant offense was not a listed offense pursuant to MCL 28.722(e)(ii). The appellate court rejected the prosecutor's argument that the age provision was not to exclude the bestiality component of the sodomy statute itself because such an interpretation would read language into the statute that it did not contain and thus not within the manifest intent of the Legislature as derived from the words of the statute itself. MCL 28.722(e)(xiv) did not apply to offense proscribed by the State of Michigan.

OUTCOME: The order requiring defendant to register under the SORA was reversed and vacated.[134]

Sadomasochism

Sadomasochism is defined as a web of control-oriented, sex-related activities, including sadism (arousal through inflicting pain or humiliation on others) and masochism (arousal by being controlled through bondage, regulations, commands, having pain inflicted upon oneself, or experiencing embarrassment or humiliation).[135] Also known as "S/M" these unusual practices were first formally described and categorized by Krafft-Ebing in the late 1800s. In his 1886 *Psychopathia Sexualis*, he defined sadism as

> [t]he experience of sexual, pleasurable sensations (including orgasm) produced by acts of cruelty, bodily punishment afflicted on one's person or when witnessed in others, be they animals or human beings. It may also consist of an innate desire to humiliate, hurt, wound or even destroy others in order, thereby, to create sexual pleasure in ones self.[136]

Freud and other sexologists have been drawn to analyze these practices because of the manner in which sex and violence can constitute sexual satisfaction. More recently, Fromm suggested that the "core of sadism ... is the passion to have absolute and unrestricted control over living beings. ..."[137]

The activities associated with S/M have received a slight degree of social acceptance through their popularization by television, movies, and art forms.[137] Today, arguably S/M is no longer universally considered to be a fantasy or fetish confined to the "sexually deviant." The Institute for Advanced Study of Human Sexuality estimates that at least one in ten adults has experimented with some form of S/M and that it is most popular among educated, middle- and upper-class men and women.

During the day, these men and women are businesspersons and blue-collar workers seen everywhere. At night, so the argument goes, they are master and slave in a carefully orchestrated erotic experience. Often, participants report a type of emotional breakthrough and integrative healing that they allege is attributed solely to violent sexual release, a type of satisfaction purportedly unattainable through any other means, including conventional sexual relations. In sum, an understanding has come to exist that S/M is not just an unusual form of sexual recreation, but rather, contains a unique logic. While consent is a primary issue of criminality for S/M, voluntariness is considered the "first law" of this practice and the formal engagements come with a full understanding that the parameters of sexual violence have been voluntarily agreed to.[138] In order for S/M to remain legal, and safe, during an S/M encounter, ongoing consent is periodically verified, and constructive consent is insufficient.[139] Consent must always be explicit in the S/M arena.

Despite a degree of social acceptance and a recent legacy of formal "rules and regulations" adopted by participants, S/M practices are forms of violence against a person just as is a case of assault and battery. Hence, the parameters of these activities are still highly questionable as a legal matter. The realm of sadism (pleasure from harming others) and masochism (pleasure from being dominated or harmed oneself) raises a red flag for the police, law, and courts. Aside from moral concerns about the propriety of violent sexual encounters, the aggressiveness inherent in sadomasochistic acts immediately invokes statutes pertaining to assault as well as the legal principles of intent, consent, and causation. Simply stated, persons who get involved with acts associated with dominating others, or being dominated, are taking a legal risk.

The central legal issue, among others, in these cases is the issue of consent. The aspect of consent is not whether consent occurred, such as in a rape case. In these cases, the aspect of consent concerns the ability for anyone to consent to an aggravated assault. In these cases, that is exactly what the parties do. However, if the law permits someone to consent to a battery or aggravated assault, the floodgates may be opened too wide. Meaning, every barroom brawl can be described as "just playing around" and that "consent was implied" in the give and take of the environment.

If the case gets to court, it is unreasonable to expect a judge to contemplate the subculture of S/M and hence entertain consent as a defense to violently whipping and beating someone. Cases solely concerning the art form of S/M have come before the courts and the accused had little to stand on, despite the testimony from psychiatrists who describe the legitimate aspects of S/M. One court sentenced the accused in an S/M case to ten years in prison for assault for a fully consensual act and stated, "[B]ecause assault is a general intent crime, the only intent required is an intent to do the act causing the injury; a showing of hostile purpose or motive is not required."[141]

Definition of the Offense

Sadomasochism may refer to flagellation or torture by or upon a person clad in undergarments, a mask or bizarre costume, or the condition of being fettered, bound, or otherwise physically restrained on the part of one so clothed.[142]

Elements of the Offense

The elements of the crime of sadomasochism that must be proven beyond a reasonable doubt are:

1. Exposes his person, or the private parts thereof; or thoughts or acts, is guilty of a misdemeanor.[143]

Sample Statute

Bondage and S/M have a long history within the parameters of sexual expression and suggest an underlying paraphilic condition. Numerous laws can apply to overt sadomasochistic acts such as assault, rape, and/or kidnapping.

The State of Ohio sadomasochism law reads as follows:

"Sado-masochistic abuse" means flagellation or torture by or upon a person or the condition of being fettered, bound, or otherwise physically restrained.[144]

Arguments Made By The Prosecution

Since sadomasochistic practices are inherently violent, these cases can provide the prosecution with a few things to work with. The mere admission of having engaged in sadomasochism implicates a participating party to the act of assault. In addition, two (or more) participants are usually involved and that means the presence of at least one eyewitness. Physical evidence such as whips and chains, etc., can further bolster the prosecution's case.

Arguments Made By The Defense

In light of recent court rulings (e.g., *Lawrence v. Texas*, and the Jovanovic case below), the defense in a case of sadomasochism can argue consent and the principle of liberty, privacy, and autonomy when it comes to agreed-on sexual exchanges. If possible, the defense will be assisted if the parties can demonstrate they have a familiarity with one another and that they have developed an understanding as to the nature of their physical sharing, even though it was violent. If they can make this argument, they can be no more guilty of assault than two people play-fighting or play-wrestling.

Variations of the Law of Sadomasochism

A. Use of a Prostitute for Sadomasochistic Acts

Paraphilias can place a paraphiliac in a double-bind. The person is not only possessed by an urge not likely shared by very many friends or family members, thus making them feel a degree of shame and rejection for being different, but also, the prospective romantic partners which emerge may be unwilling to allow the person to engage in their paraphilic behavior during physical sharing. For example, emetophilia is the paraphilia of sexual attraction to vomiting. We might assume that few spouses would be willing to use vomit as a form of sexual stimulation. Hence, the paraphiliac is left with no outlet and may experience frustration. The same may be said for coprophilia (use of feces for sexual arousal) and odaxelagnia (biting someone for purposes of sexual arousal). Not all lovers are going to be willing to engage in these acts. Then again, sexual frustration may be experienced between any couple, even the most conventional and mainstream. With a paraphiliac, however, the danger lies where frustration compels the offender to insist on finding a partner, including one who is nonconsenting. Sexual contact without consent is a serious felony offense.

With traditional avenues for sexual expression somewhat limited, it makes sense that a paraphiliac would pay a prostitute for the opportunity to give expression to their particular brand of paraphilia, their "drug of choice." In the case of *New Hampshire v. Higgins,* the defendant Jack Higgins hired the services of a prostitute for the purposes of engaging in his brand of paraphilia, which was a form of sadomasochism.[145]

In 1998 Higgins was a truck driver and picked up a prostitute in the region of Manchester, New Hampshire. The two of them proceeded to Higgins' apartment in Manchester and discussed two types of traditional sexual contact: oral sex and intercourse. In the middle of intercourse where Higgins was positioned behind his temporary partner, the woman looked back and saw that Higgins had come into possession of a gun from somewhere and had it pointed at her head from behind her. This began a two-hour episode of nearly unbelievable acts on the part of the defendant that reflected his desire to engage in sadomasochism. Higgins handcuffed her hands behind her back and also shackled her ankles, both of which turned the victim into a hostage and instantly invoked a kidnapping statute.

Even though she was now wearing handcuffs and shackles, Higgins also tied her wrists and ankles together with rope. None of these acts of bondage were remotely necessary since the woman was working as a prostitute and had fully consented to provide sex to the defendant. This was not a situation where tying up the victim was necessary to force her to have sex with him. When he had completely bound the victim, he then used a riding crop to beat her, and sodomized her while yelling profanities and saying, "I hate women." When the violence had ceased, he removed the restraints and asked the victim "What have I done to you?" as though what he had done was somehow unobjectionable.[146] They both dressed and went out to his truck. They drove a few miles and she got out at the earliest opportunity. The next morning, she filed a report with the police and a few days later, Higgins was arrested.

The trial court convicted Higgins of aggravated felonious sexual assault,[147] criminal restraint,[148] and criminal threatening[149] pursuant to the criminal code in the state of New Hampshire. The criminal threatening convictions came with a sentence enhancement,[150] and the judge, possibly quite upset by the case, imposed consecutive sentences rather than concurrent sentences. Higgins was ordered to serve 33½–67 years in state prison for his visit with the prostitute.

With nothing to lose, Higgins appealed his conviction and made two arguments. First he argued that the police did not read him his rights prior to questioning him. Therefore, his incriminating statements and confessions should not have been admitted into court. His second argument was that the trial court should have allowed evidence of the victim's prior sexual activity and that he was prejudiced by the use of the rape shield law during the trial.

The appeals court did not find for Higgins and argued away both of his points of law. As for his first argument, the court stated that his statements before his rights were read were just as incriminating as those he made after his rights were read, hence it made little difference that the statements he made before the Miranda warnings were admitted into court. The court stated:

> We conclude that the evidence before the trial court was sufficient to support its factual finding that the defendant was given his Miranda warnings before substantive interrogation began.[151]

As for his second argument, the judges sided with the prostitute and defended her victimization. They argued that just because a prostitute consents to intercourse, does not automatically translate to a consent to be tied up and sodomized. They deepened the argument by stating that even if the prostitute had consented to engage in sadomasochistic acts in the past, it does not automatically mean that she consented to sadomasochistic acts in this case. The court stated:

> Consent to sexual conduct with one person in no way implies consent to such activity with another. *Commonwealth v. Joyce*, 415 N.E.2d 181 (Mass. 1981); *State v. Patnaude*, 438 A.2d 402 (Vt. 1981). Each decision to consent is a new act, a choice made on the circumstances prevailing in the present, not governed by the past. Patnaude, 438 A.2d at 410. Whether a woman previously engaged in a particular type of sexual activity, such as anal intercourse or sadomasochistic role-play, with another person has no bearing, in and of itself, on whether she agreed to do so with the defendant.

Further, the victim's status as a prostitute does not necessarily mean that she will accept every opportunity that comes along to engage in sexual relations or relent to the desires of any paying customer, regardless of her motivation for engaging in prostitution in the first instance. See Harris, 362 S.E.2d at 213; Patnaude, 438 A.2d at 407. A prostitute does not lose the right of choice, and may consent or not consent according to her own will. Brewer,559 A.2d at 321.[152]

B. Sexual Violence as Legal Sexual Autonomy

Much is written about the intertwined relationship between pain, pleasure, and human sexuality. Older societies such as those in India and Japan are more familiar with the role of pain with sexual expression and some would go so far as to recommend the use of bondage in sex as a way to reach within oneself for healing or transcendence of some kind, as odd as that may seem.[153] As we have seen throughout this book, however, American courts are typically disinclined to excuse assaultive behavior justified on the grounds of attempting to have a personally transcendent sexual experience.

In the case of *People v. Jovanovic,* two upper-middle-class university students met online and shared with each other their thoughts and fantasies when it comes to being tied up, held hostage, bitten, choked, whipped, and so forth during sex.[154] Their fantasies basically pertained to sadomasochism. It was not the first time that either had met someone online to discuss these things and both had a degree of experience with the practice. After some familiarization with each other through e-mails and the communication of further specifics about what each would like done to oneself and the other, the two arranged for a face-to-face meeting. On meeting face-to-face, they began their experiment with the relationship between pain and sex and engaged in a multitude of acts in furtherance of this sexual ideal. He poured candle wax on her, bit her, inserted an object into her rectum, and did to her what she asked. However, on one occasion while tied up and placed in bondage, she felt threatened and asked to be untied. He thought she was joking and faithfully fulfilling her role as a helpless, desperately suffering victim and did not untie her even though she asked to be untied.[155]

On this occasion, since the victim felt that she was seriously violated and that Jovanovic exceeded the agreed-on terms of the exchange, she informed the police. When the police heard the story, they did not sympathize that this was a mutually agreed-on practice of S/M and Jovanovic was arrested.

The case turned on the issue of consensual sexual violence as a means for sexual autonomy. Jovanovic defended himself by saying that any violence was all part of the agreed-on deal—if there was no violence, neither would have gotten together. The purpose of having the violence was in having the sex, and conversely, the reason for the sex was to engage in violence. If it were not for the implicit agreements contained in the emailing weeks before, he never would have done what he did. Due to the e-mailing, he would more likely expect her to express satisfaction rather than try to have him prosecuted. To convict him would be to criminalize all bedroom behavior that involves tightly holding one's partner, pressing oneself upon another, or otherwise pinning down a partner as part of the exchange. The defense was trying to forge legitimacy in the practice of rough play when it comes to sexual contact.[156]

Jovanovic was charged with first degree felony kidnapping, first degree felony sexual abuse, and first degree assault—the prosecutor never imagining the two would consent to such activity. The jury was similarly unprepared to hear what had happened and convicted the accused on all counts after a jury trial. Perceiving a serious injustice, Jovanovic appealed the jury verdict.

The defense attorney in the case was the attorney who successfully defended the preppie murder case and he had success in this case as well. The appeals court was persuaded that the exchange was about sex and violence, and allowing for a conviction would be to indict human sexuality. "Rough play" was held to have some legitimacy and that if both parties were ready, willing, and able to engage in this kind of sport, the doctrine of assumption of risk would apply. Subtly, the case separated pain from violence and acquiesced that pain is part of sex and that to convict would say more about the court's misunderstanding of sex than it would about criminal liability.

As a legal matter, the appeals court pinpointed the use of the rape shield law during the trial and how it was used to convict the defendant. While a rape shield statute is useful to prohibit information about a woman's prior sexual activity that could unduly prejudice her in the eyes of a jury, in this case, the use of the eape shield law obfuscated the fact that the complainant agreed to engage in sadomasochistic acts with the accused. The appeals court stated:

> Defendant's conviction of kidnapping in the first degree, sexual abuse in the first degree and other related charges arising from a date between defendant and the complainant which took place after weeks of on-line conversations and e-mail correspondence must be reversed and the matter remanded for a new trial. The trial court's evidentiary rulings that statements made by complainant in e-mails sent to defendant indicating an interest in participating in sadomasochism were inadmissible under the Rape Shield Law (CPL 60.42) because they constituted evidence of complainant's prior sexual conduct, incorrectly applied that statute, and, as a result, improperly hampered defendant's ability to present a defense. The redacted e-mail messages were not subject to the Rape Shield Law, since they were merely evidence of statements made by complainant about herself to defendant, and did not constitute evidence of complainant's sexual conduct. Defendant's purpose in seeking to offer these statements in evidence was not

to undermine complainant's character or her honesty by demonstrating that she was unchaste. Rather, it was to highlight both the complainant's state of mind on the issue of consent, and defendant's own state of mind regarding his own reasonable beliefs as to complainant's intentions. The court's rulings precluded defendant from effectively challenging certain aspects of complainant's presentation, thereby improperly interfering with defendant's Sixth Amendment right to confront his accuser. Furthermore, in the absence of proof that defendant had reason to believe, prior to their meeting, that they both had intended to participate in consensual sadomasochism on the night of their date, his ability to testify in a credible manner as to his defense was irreparably harmed.[157]

The case was remanded for a new trial.

C. Erotophonophilia

Erotophonophilia technically is the paraphilia of lust murder. The offender derives sexual pleasure from killing someone, almost always a person the offender has an arousal toward. The act of killing, in and of itself, may be all that is required for the offender to derive pleasure, but in many cases of lust murder, the depraved offender engages in some form of sex with the person just killed. Lust murders also take on the characteristics of serial killing because the offender does not have the cognitive capacity to cease and is compulsively drawn to repeat the act.[158] This heinous crime, like most paraphilias, is heavily ritualized. Erotophonophilia is one step further down the road from sadomasochism in that a sadomasochistic act may never involve a killing. In addition, erotophonophilia is distinct from necrophilia in that an act of necrophilia often does not involve any violence, pain, or killing. Hence, erotophonophilia is in a relatively distinct class of its own, but is included in the section of sadomasochism due to the sadistic nature of the offense.[159] Jeff Dahmer is perhaps the most famous erotophonophiliac on record.[160]

In a different case, the case of *People v. Rundle,* David Rundle met two young women ages 18 and 15 at the time of their deaths. Each was met at a different point in time and each had a slightly different relationship with the defendant. After a couple of brief meetings, the defendant engaged in the acts of erotophonophilia with the respective victims.[161]

Rundle was, as a young child, sexually abused by his mother over a prolonged time. He was also mistreated, scorned, and treated like an animal by both his parents for the span of his childhood. As a result, Rundle had an intense dislike for authority and mainstream society and, in particular, a venomous hatred for women. In a way, he was domesticated to be a violent criminal offender and that is exactly what he became.

Both of Rundle's victims were nonthreatening persons who had kept company with Rundle for no special reason except to "hang-out," possibly smoke pot, and make-out romantically in a parked car. These modest encounters with the victims were enough to create a morbid arousal in Rundle and trigger the subsequent bizarre acting out of mentally deranged homicidal acts.

In each case, Rundle's victims were dragged into the woods, bound and tied up, choked and strangled to death, and subject to sexual relations after being killed. Thereafter Rundle returned to daily life as though nothing had happened and systematically lied to the authorities about the killings. Once the evidence was sufficient in quantity and quality, and the police made it clear to Rundle that he had been caught, Rundle confessed. Rundle was convicted of aggravated murder and sentenced to death.[162]

According to the court transcript, a person named Heather visited Rundle while he was in jail. The transcript reads:

> Heather Smith visited defendant on several occasions in the Placer County Jail after his
> arrest. During her last visit, Smith asked defendant why he killed Garcia and Sorensen.
> He said it was partly because he did not like 'sleazy women.' He then said, 'I had a good
> thing going while it lasted. Too bad I got caught.' Smith asked defendant why he had not
> killed her, and defendant replied he had no reason to kill her.[163]

Additional Court Cases: Sadomasochism

People v. Gacy
468 N.E.2d 1171 (1984)

CASE SUMMARY

PROCEDURAL POSTURE: Defendant brought numerous challenges to the judgment of the Circuit Court of Cook County (Illinois), which upheld his conviction on thirty-three counts of murder, as well as sexual assault, and indecent liberties with a child.

OVERVIEW: A boy's mother reported her son missing to the police. About the time the boy was missing defendant's truck was seen near the last-known location of the boy. The police found out the defendant had a history of sexually assaulting young men. They sought several search warrants for defendant's home. During the course of the investigation defendant confessed to having killed thirty people. He was tried and convicted of thirty-three counts of murder, among others charges. Defendant challenged his conviction on several grounds. The court affirmed and found that the search warrants sufficiently set out the items sought at the location and, therefore, defendant's motion to suppress the resulting evidence was properly denied. The confession was shown to be the product of free rational mind. The attorney's advice to confess given the fact that the police were on the verge of locating twenty-seven bodies in the crawl space of defendant's home was not ineffective assistance of counsel. The court's questioning of the jury was sufficient and in most instances the defense counsel had declined the opportunity to ask further questions of the jury and when they did request further questions, the court complied with the request.

OUTCOME: Judgment was affirmed because none of the errors defendant pointed to rose to the level of reversible error.[164]

Chapter Six Summary

Sexual paraphilias arguably are an oddity across the spectrum of sexual activity. A paraphiliac is often, but not necessarily, a loner who is unmarried and spends a relatively large amount of time contemplating sexual acts with others, the sexuality of others, and his or her lack of satisfying sexual outlets. Continuing with this overgeneralization, he or she is socially clumsy, a factor that drives the person toward aloneness and loneliness where more sexual fantasizing takes place. A medically "true" paraphiliac will have a preferred "drug of choice," a sex act that has been determined by the actor through repeated experimentation to involve the greatest possible stimulation.[165] However, by definition, this condition means the actor will entertain or involve him- or herself in multiple paraphilias and will stick with the one the offers the greatest payoff. Paraphilias are harmful to self and potentially to others, including children. Animals are also at risk. Hence, jokes pertaining to paraphilic cross-dressers and so forth are not funny for a true paraphiliac. It would be like cracking jokes about a violent rape case.

Thus, paraphilias can represent a relatively serious medical and psychiatric condition in which conventional sexuality as we know it today is placed secondary to more intense, ritualized, recurrent, and possibly life-threatening acts. Dozens of paraphilias exist, such as a foot fetish, and can be innocuous and present no cause for alarm in the law. However, as seen in this chapter, the potential for a paraphilic-related act to harm or injure someone obviously exists. The harm may involve breaking into a mortuary for a necrophiliac, choking someone to death as with a case of erotic asphyxiation, or killing someone sexually in cases of erotophonophilia.

The medicalization and formal study of sexual deviance can be traced back a thousand years in Chinese or Eskimo culture. When it comes to contemporary western culture, Richard von Krafft-Ebing receives credit for being among the first to treat sexual aberration. Sigmund Freud and Alfred Kinsey also made highly notable contributions to the research and understanding of this highly complicated medical condition.

While still somewhat obscure, paraphilias have been studied more in-depth and by the 21st century have been treated more as a medical problem rather than a problem of morality. In 1980, the term paraphilia replaced the term perversion/pervert in the leading authority on mental illness, the *DSM-IV.*

The *DSM* provides that the essential features of a paraphilia are

1. Recurrent, intense sexually arousing fantasies, sexual urges, or behaviors generally involving 1) nonhuman objects, 2) the suffering or humiliation of oneself or one's partner, or 3) children or other nonconsenting persons for a period of at least 6 months.

2. The fantasies, sexual urges, or behaviors cause clinically significant stress or impairment in social, occupational or other important areas of function.[166]

Although the *DSM* only mentions a handful of paraphilias, many others exist and were mentioned throughout this chapter. While greater objective science has been brought to bear on the subject of paraphilia, the underlying etiology is still mysterious. Law and medicine are still not sure what causes someone to be, for example, an ephebephiliac.[165] In addition, society is unwilling to entertain notions of legitimacy when it comes to paraphilias, even those that involve legal consent. Social mores and the law are threatened easily when it comes to sexual deviancy.

Paraphiliacs tempt the law quite often and this may be part of their overall thrill seeking. The legal system does not address a parpahilic condition directly, but rather, controls any byproduct of paraphilia where it presents a social harm. Ochlophilia, which is a sexual arousal from being in a large crowd, for example, is a paraphilia that does not have a socially harmful byproduct. In fact, it would be impossible to detect in many cases. Only when the paraphilia involves threatening or harmful behavior does the law intervene.

For those acts that are offensive, the law plays approximately three roles with paraphilias. First, the law may target a paraphilia specifically, such as with necrophilia. The states may outlaw such acts outright and use exact wording such as a prohibition on necrophilia in their state codes. In this chapter, the state of Nevada statute (NRS 201.450) on necrophilia was used. Secondly, the law may target the paraphilia indirectly, such as outlawing erotophonophilia with a murder statute instead of a statute related specifically to that particular paraphilia. As another example, pyromania is not legally prohibited as eroticized fire setting, but rather is made illegal with a felony arson statute in most states. Third, the law may not address a paraphilia at all, either because the act is considered harmless such as a sexual arousal to insects, or because the act is so infrequent, such as vampirism and drinking blood for sexual arousal, that the legislatures or Congress does not feel a need to address such a statute. In this chapter, it is noted that the State of Florida legislature has not banned bestiality, despite numerous legislative proposals to do so. One legislator noted that he didn't want to discuss an "icky" subject like bestiality.[168]

Most paraphilia-related criminal cases are handled at the state level. Each state has the prerogative to proscribe and regulate the sexual behavior of the citizens of the respective state. Obscure paraphilias are not regulated at all while extreme examples will be addressed by laws in all fifty states. Where laws are overly general and too vague to provide adequate notice as to what constitutes illegal behavior, an appeals court, even the U.S. Supreme Court can rule the law void for vagueness and unenforceability. In addition, laws that restrict mainstream conventional sex between consenting adults are also circumspect and may be subject to appellate review for a violation of due process.

Amid the roles and techniques the states may use in the decision to address paraphilias, two other tools used in the post conviction stage are civil commitment and registration and notification. Civil commitment began in the 1930s with the legal backing of sexual psychopath laws. These initial forms of civil commitment for sexual deviants tended to be crude forms of legislation directed more toward the clamor of moral entrepreneurs than the medical needs of the offending population. Formal empirical research debunked the foundation and purpose of these early laws and most were rescinded by the 1970s. In the 1980s, the U.S. criminal justice system adopted a "get tough" approach to crime, using laws such as "Three Strikes" as well as new minimum mandatory sentencing schemes, which came down the hardest on nonviolent drug offenders. At this time civil commitment laws were reintroduced in various states, this time with more direction provided to the mental illness of the offender. Today's civil commitment laws target the SVP (sexually violent predator). The focus today is tighter than in the 1930s, and also, the U.S. Supreme Court has ruled on the process used by the state civil commitment proceedings so that injustices do not occur. The leading case on civil commitment of SVPs is the 1997 case of *Kansas v. Hendricks*.[169] In the case, the U.S. Supreme Court upheld the constitutionality of Kansas's Sexually Violent Predator Act that states any person who, due to "mental abnormality" or "personality disorder," is likely to engage in "predatory acts of sexual violence" can be indefinitely confined in a state mental hospital.[170]

Starting in 1994, the states began using another post-conviction tool for sex offenders, a SORN (Sex Offender Registration and Notification) website. Passed after the abduction of Jacob Wetterling, the Jacob Wetterling Crimes Against Children and Sexually Violent Offender Registration Act[171] required all fifty states to implement a sex offender and crimes against children registry. While the fifty state and one federal SORN have been conclusively shown in the research to be ineffective, they tend to assuage the fears of the public when it comes to convicted sex offenders living in their neighborhood. Many members of the general public are convinced as to the habitual patterns of offending for sex offenders. However, the crimes associated with offenders involved in a sex-related case are so varied, recidivism data is nearly impossible to use to make safe conclusions. If recidivism studies are employed, many suggest that sex offenders are not habitual repeat offenders as many would like to believe.

In the future, the justice system will likely remain objective about the condition of paraphilia, sanctioning only those cases where offenders threaten the health, safety, and welfare of themselves or others. However, the medical community will likely continue to play a greater role in addressing treatment issues for those who seek treatment for the complex condition of paraphilia. Trying to logically decipher why someone would want to touch a corpse so badly that they unlawfully break in to a mortuary indeed presents a formidable task for a treatment provider. But then again, so do many criminal acts. The bridge between the law and the treatment community may be formed as the trend toward specialized courts and the drug court model come to include sex offender treatment as part of its overall caseload.

Key Terms

Paraphilia 00

Necrophilia 00

Erotic Asphyxiation 00

Zoophilia 00

Sadism 00

Masochism 00

Pyromania 00

Recidivism 00

Erotophonophilia 00

DSM-IV 00

Jacob Wetterling 00

Concepts & Principles

Aberration 00

Continuous Transaction 00

Sexual Autonomy 00

Etiology 00

Ritualization 00

Sexual Psychopath Laws 00

Ligature 00

Void for Vagueness 00

Consent to Violence 00

Recurrent Urge 00

Exculpatory Witness 00

Chapter Four Select Court Cases	
Case	**Point of Law**
Lipham v. State 00	Res gestae determination of criminal offense
Draper Mortuary v. Thomas 00	Mortician duty of care to protect corpses from unwanted sexual touching
Robinson v. Maryland 00	Legal insanity analysis applied to necrophiliac
Braswell v. State 00	Legal distinction between accidental and purposeful death
Washington v. Metcalf 00	Circumstantial evidence applied to homicide
People v. Russo 00	Digital Web history used as evidence of paraphilic act
People v. Mitchell 00	Legal definition of "cruelty to animals"
Minnesota v. Bonygne 00	Vagueness renders bestiality law void
People v. Hathaway 00	Legal regulation of sex with a dead animal
New Hampshire v. Higgins 00	Prostitutes cannot be used for sexual experimentation
People v. Jovanovic 00	Consent to violent sexual act negates the criminality of the act
People v. Rundle 00	S/M related to lust murder and the charge of murder

Questions for Review

1. What is a paraphilia?

2. What is the leading medical authority on the subject of paraphilias?

3. How can a paraphilia violate the law?

4. Does sexual contact with a murder victim constitute the crime of necrophilia?

5. Is necrophilia a crime in all states? How about in all countries of the world?

6. What laws might apply, if any, in a case of erotic asphyxiation?

7. What are some of the terms or labels courts have used to describe sexual contact with animals?

8. What laws typically may apply in a case of sadomasochism?

9. How can the law of consent be complicated in a case of sadism or masochism?

10. What is the name of one notorious sadomasochistic killer?

1   People v. Hathaway, Superior Court of the State of Wisconsin, Douglas County. 2006. Case ID: 9881.

2   DeClue, Gregory, *Paraphilia NOS (nonconsenting) and Antisocial Personality Disorder.* 34 Journal of Psychiatry & Law 4, 495–514 (2006).

3   Am. Psychiatric Ass'n, Diagnostic and Statistical Manual of Mental Disorders (4th ed., 1994, Text Rev., 2000) 522–523.

4   Some of the more common paraphilias include exhibitionism, fetishism, frotteurism, pedophilia, sexual masochism, sexual sadism, transvestic fetishism, voyeurism, telephone scatologia (lewdness), necrophilia (corpses), partialism (exclusive focus on part of body), zoophilia (animals), coprophilia (feces), klismaphilia (enemas), and urophilia (urine).

5   Healy, James, *The Etiology of Paraphilia: A Dichotomous Model.* In Sex Crimes and Paraphilia, (Eric Hickey, ed., 2006).

6   "Whether any sexual behavior is considered atypical depends on the culture in which it exists." *Id.* at 58.

7   Craig, Leam A., Browne, Kevin D., Beech, Anthony, Stringer, Ian, *Psychosexual Characteristics of Sexual Offenders and the Relationship to Sexual Reconviction,* 12 Psychology, Crime & Law 3, 231-243 (2006).

8   The purpose of *DSM-IV* is to provide clear descriptions of diagnostic categories to enable clinicians and investigators to diagnose, communicate about, study, and treat people with various mental disorders. It is important to note that for clinical and research purposes a diagnostic category such as Pathological Gambling or Pedophilia does not imply that the condition meets legal or other nonmedical criteria for what constitutes mental disease, mental disorder, or mental disability. The clinical and scientific considerations involved in categorization of these conditions as mental disorders may not be wholly relevant to legal judgments, for example, that take into account such issues as individual responsibility, disability determination, and competency. Am. Psychiatric Ass'n, Diagnostic and Statistical Manual of Mental Disorders (4th ed., 1994, Text Rev., 2000).

9   Krafft-Ebing, Psychopathia Sexualis (Physicians and Surgeons Book Co.) (1906).

10 Freud, Sigmund, The Complete Introductory Lectures on Psychoanalysis (Norton Books) (1966).

11 Kinsey, Alfred, Sexual Behavior in the Human Male (University Press) (1998).

12 Masters, W., Johnson, V. and Kolodny, R., Human Sexuality (Little, Brown) (1982).

13 Michel Foucault, The History of Sexuality (Robert Hurley trans., 1978). Foucault, M., Khalfa, J., & Murphy, J., The History of Madness (Routledge) (2006).

14 Group for the Advancement of Psychiatry, Committee on Psychiatry and Law, Psychiatry and Sex Psychopath Legislation: The 30s to the 80s, 844-45 (1977).

15 *Id.* at 942.

16 *Id.*

17 Meaghan Kelly, *Lock Them Up—And Throw Away the Key: The Preventive Detention of Sex Offenders in the United States and Germany,* 39 Geo. J. Int'l L. 551 (2003).

18 *Id.* at 560.

19 John Q. La Fond, *Can Therapeutic Jurisprudence Be Normatively Neutral? Sexual Predator Laws: Their Impact on Participants and Policy,* 41 Ariz. L. Rev. 375, 410–11 (1999).

20 Kansas v. Hendricks, 521 U.S. 346 (1997).

21 *Id.*

22 Bruce J. Winick, A Therapeutic Jurisprudence Analysis of Sex Offender Registration and Community Notification Laws, in Protecting Society from Sexually Dangerous Offenders: Law, Justice, and Therapy (2003).

23 This requirement is pursuant to the Violent Crime Control and Law Enforcement Crimes Against Children, 42 U.S.C.A. § 14071 (2006).

24 The Violent Crime Control and Law Enforcement Act, H.R. 3355, Pub.L. 103-322, was an act of Congress dealing with crime and law enforcement that became law in 1994. It is the largest crime bill in the history of the U.S. at 356 pages and provided for 200,000 new police officers and $9.7 billion in funding for prisons.

[25] Sex Offender Registration and Notification Act § 118(a), 42 U.S.C.A. § 16918(a). In accordance with the proposed National Guidelines, the notification requirement "involves making information about released sex offenders more broadly available to the public. The means of public notification currently include sex offender web sites in all 50 states, the District of Columbia, and some territories, and may involve other forms of notice as well. NATIONAL GUIDELINES FOR SEX OFFENDER REGISTRATION AND NOTIFICATION, 72 Fed. Reg. at 30,211 (2005). The Department of Justice believes that the availability of such information helps members of the public take commonsense measures for the protection of themselves and their families, such as declining the offer of a convicted child molester to watch their children or head a youth group, or reporting to the authorities approaches to children or other suspicious activities by such a sex offender. Here as well, the effect is salutary in relation to the sex offenders themselves, since knowledge by those around them of their sex offense histories reduces the likelihood that they will be presented with opportunities to reoffend. NATIONAL GUIDELINES FOR SEX OFFENDER REGISTRATION AND NOTIFICATION, 72 Fed. Reg. at 30,210–11 (2005).

[26] The Pam Lychner Sexual Offender Tracking and Identification Act of 1996, 42, U.S.C. § 14072 (1997).

[27] The General Provisions of Title I of the Commerce, Justice, and State, the Judiciary, and Related Agencies Appropriations Act (CJSA), Section 15.

[28] Tewksbury, R., & Jennings, W. G., *Assessing the Impact of Sex Offender Registration and Community Notification on Sex Offending Trajectories.* 37 CRIM. JUST. & BEH. 5, 570–582 (2010). Letourneau, E. J., Bandyopadhyay, D., Armstrong, K. S., & Sinha, D., *Do Sex Offender Registration and Notification Requirements Deter Juvenile Sex Crimes?.* 37 CRIM. JUST. & BEH. 5, 553-569 (2010). Tewksbury, R., & Levenson, J., *Stress Experiences of Family Members of Registered Sex Offenders.* 27 BEHAV. SCI. & L. 4, 611-626 (2009). Jill S. Levenson and Leo P. Cotter, *The Effect of Megan's Law on Sex Offender Reintegration,* 21 J. CONTEMP. CRIM. JUST. 49 (2005).

[29] In addition, the field of psychiatry notes numerous sexual activities that are not paraphilias, but rather are "paraphilia-related." These "paraphilia-related" acts are thought to have greater social legitimacy and not contain the stigma applied to paraphilias. Paraphilia-related disorders may be categorized pursuant to the following three criteria:
A. Over a period of at least 6 months, recurrent, intense, sexually arousing fantasies, sexual urges, or behaviors involving culturally normative aspects of sexual expression that increase in frequency or intensity so as to substantially interfere with the expression of the capacity for reciprocal, affectionate sexual activity.
B. These sexual fantasies, urges, or activities cause clinically significant distress or impairment in social, occupational, or other important areas of functioning.
C. These sexual fantasies, urges, or activities do not occur exclusively during an episode of another primary Axis I psychiatric condition (e.g., mania/hypomania), psychoactive substance abuse (e.g., alcohol, cocaine, amphetamine), or a general medical condition.
Kafka, Martin, *The Paraphilia-Related Disorders: A Proposal for a Unified Classification of Nonparaphilic Hypersexuality Disorders.* 8 SEX. ADD. & COMPUL. 227-239 (2001).

[30] See generally Patrick A. Langan et al., U.S. Dep't of Justice, Office of Justice Programs, *Recidivism of Sex Offenders Released From Prison in 1994* (2003), www.ojp.usdoj.gov/bjs/pub/pdf/rsorp94.pdf.

[31] See generally Rhiana Kohl et al., Urb. Inst. Just. Pol. Ctr., *Massachusetts Recidivism Study: A Closer Look At Releases and Returns to Prison* (2008), http://www.urban.org/UploadedPDF/411657 massachusetts recidivism.pdf.

[32] See generally Patrick A. Langan et al., U.S. Dep't of Justice, Office of Justice Programs, *Recidivism of Sex Offenders Released From Prison in 1994* (2003), www.ojp.usdoj.gov/bjs/pub/pdf/rsorp94.pdf.

[33] R. Karl Hanson & Monique T. Bussiere, *Predicting Relapse: A Meta-Analysis of Sexual Offender Recidivism Studies,* 66 J. CONSULTING & CLINICAL PSYCHOL. 348, 357 (1998). A later meta-analysis breaks down the studies according to these different recidivism criteria: "The recidivism criterion was arrest in 25 studies, reconviction in 24 studies, and reincarceration in 3 studies." R. Karl Hanson & Kelly E. Morton-Bourgon, *The Characteristics of Persistent Sexual Offenders: A Meta-Analysis of Recidivism Studies,* 73 J. CONSUL. & CLIN. PSYCHOL. 1154, 1155 (2005).

[34] AM. PSYCHIATRIC ASS'N, DIAGNOSTIC AND STATISTICAL MANUAL OF MENTAL DISORDERS (4th ed., 1994, Text Rev., 2000). Also known as *DSM-IV.*

[35] HICKEY, E.W., SERIAL MURDERERS AND THEIR VICTIMS (4th ed.) (Wadsworth) (2006).

[36] *Id.*

[37] Heasman, Ainslie and Jones, Elizabeth, *Necrophilia.* In SEX CRIMES AND PARAPHILIA 277 (Eric Hickey, ed., 2006).

38   Rosman, J. P., & Resnick, P. J., *Sexual Attraction to Corpses: A Psychiatric Review of Necrophilia.* 17 Bull. Amer. Acad. of Psychi. & L. 2, 153–163 (1989).

39   Heasman, Ainslie, & Jones, Elizabeth, *Necrophilia.* In Sex Crimes and Paraphilia 273 (Eric Hickey, ed., 2006).

40   Ark. Code Ann. § 5-60-101. Abuse of a Corpse. (1975).
     (a) A person commits abuse of a corpse if, except as authorized by law, he or she knowingly:
     (1) Disinters, removes, dissects, or mutilates a corpse; or
     (2) Physically mistreats a corpse in a manner offensive to a person of reasonable sensibilities.
     (b) Abuse of a corpse is a Class D felony.

41   Troyer, John, *Abuse of a Corpse: A Brief History and Re-Theorization of Necrophilia Laws in the USA.* 13 Mortality 2, 132-152 (2008).

42   http://www.huliq.com/34426/us-states-lack-laws-explicitly-outlawing-necrophilia. Retrieved July 30, 2010.

43   Mass. Gen. Laws Ann. § 272-35 (1978).

44   *Id.*

45   Miss. Code Ann. § 97-29-59 (1984).

46   Doyle v. Nevada, 921 P.2d 901 (1996).

47   Nev. Rev. Stat. Ann. § 201.450 (2010).

48   *Id.*

49   Lipham v. State, 364 S.E.2d 840 (1988).

50   *Id.*

51   Gibson v. Jackson, 443 F. Supp. 239 (M.D. Ga. 1977).

52   Ga. Code Ann. § 16-6-1(a) (1976).

53   *Id.*

54   Lipham v. State, 364 S.E.2d 840, 893 (1988).

55   Stein, M. L., Schlesinger, L. B., & Pinizzotto, A. J., *Necrophilia and Sexual Homicide.* 55 J. For. Sci. 2, 443–446 (2010).

56   Tingle, J., *Understanding the Legal Duty of Care in the Course of Negligence,* 11 British J. Nurs. 16, 1065 (2002).

57   Draper Mortuary v. Thomas, 135 Cal. App. 3d 533 (1982).

58   *Id.*

59   Troyer, John, *Abuse of a Corpse: A Brief History and Re-Theorization of Necrophilia Laws in the USA.* 13 Mortality 2, 132–152 (2008).

60   Robinson v. Maryland, 238 A.2d 875 (1968).

61   *Id.*

62   Robinson v. Maryland, 238 A.2d 875, 893 (1968).

63   State v. Ryan, 899 P.2d 825 (1995).

64   Bader, M.J., Arousal: The Secret Logic of Sexual Fantasies (St. Martin's Griffin) (2003).

65   Price, M., Kafka, M., Commons, M., Gutheil, T., & Simpson, W., *Telephone Scatologia Comorbidity with other Paraphilias and Paraphilia-related Disorders.* 25 Int'l. J.L. & Psychi. 37-49 (2002).

66   De Silva, W.P., *ABC of Sexual Health: Sexual Variations,* 318 British Medical Journal 7184, 654–656 (1999). In Sex Crimes and Paraphilia 186 (Eric Hickey, ed., 2006).

67   Am. Psychiatric Ass'n, Diagnostic and Statistical Manual of Mental Disorders 529 (4th ed., 1994, Text Rev., 2000). Also known as *DSM-IV.*

68 Lee, J., Pattison, P., Jackson, H., & Ward, T., *The General, Common, and Specific Features of Psychopathology for Different Types of Paraphilias,* 28 Crim. Just. & Beh. 227-256 (2001).

69 Hickey, Eric, Sex Crimes and Paraphilia (Prentice-Hall) (2006).

70 De Silva, W.P., *ABC of Sexual Health: Sexual Variations,* 318 British Medical Journal 7184, 654–656 (1999). In Sex Crimes and Paraphilia 186 (Eric Hickey, ed., 2006).

71 Hickey, E. W., Serial Murderers and their Victims (4th ed.) (Wadsworth) (2006).

72 Turvey, B., An Objective Overview of Autoerotic Fatalities (1995). www.corpus-delicti.com/auto.html.

73 Todd v. AIG Life Ins. Co., 47 F.3d 1448, 1450 (5th Cir. 1995).

74 Klotter, John, Criminal Law 93-95 (7th ed.) (Anderson Publishing Co.) (1994).

75 Model Penal Code § 210.5 Causing or Aiding Lethal Self Destruction (2003).

76 *Id.*

77 Buzash, George, *The "Rough Sex" Defense,* 80 J. Crim. L. & Crim. 557 (1989).

78 Hanna, Cheryl, *Sex Is Not a Sport: Consent and Violence in Criminal Law,* 42 B.C. L. Rev. 239 (2001).

79 Tennessee v. Braswell, 2008 Tenn. Crim. App. LEXIS 43 (2008).

80 *Id.*

81 *Id.* at LEXIS 48.

82 *Id.*

83 *Id.*

84 Tenn. Code Ann. § 39-13-210 (1997).

85 Tenn. Code Ann. § 39-11-302(b) (1997).

86 Tennessee v. Braswell, 2008 Tenn. Crim. App. LEXIS 43 (2008).

87 *Id.*

88 Washington v. Metcalf, 2009 Wash. Crim. App. LEXIS 1687 (2009).

89 *Id.*

90 *Id.* at LEXIS 1693.

91 *Id.*

92 *Id.* at LEXIS 1699.

93 Brown, S., Treating Sex Offenders: An Introduction to Sex Offender Treatment Programs (Willan) (2005).

94 Russo v. State, 228 S.W.3d 779 (2007).

95 *Id.*

96 *Id.* at 785.

97 *Id.* at 789.

98 *Id.*

99 Tennessee v. Braswell, 2008 Tenn. Crim. App. LEXIS 43 (2008).

100 Nickchen, Katherine, & Jeanne Johnson, *Zoophilia and Bestiality.* In Sex Crimes and Paraphilia (Eric Hickey, ed., 2006).

101 Seligman, L., and Hardenburg, S. A., *Assessment and Treatment of Paraphilias,* 78 J. Couns. & Dev. 107–113 (2000).

102 Wiederman, M., *Paraphilia and Fetishism,* 11 Fam. J. 315–321 (2003).

103 Hensley, Christopher, Tallichet, Suzanne E., & Dutkiewicz, Erik L., *Childhood Bestiality: A Potential Precursor to Adult Interpersonal Violence,* 25 J. of Interp. Viol. 3, 557–567 (2010).

104 Fudge, E., *Monstrous Acts: Bestiality in Early Modern England,* History Today 20–25 (2000).

105 10 U.S.C.A. § 925.

106 Wilcox, D. T., Foss, C. M., & Donathy, M. L., *A Case Study of a Male Sex Offender with Zoosexual Interests and Behaviours,* 11 J. Sex. Agg. 3, 305–317 (2005).

107 Beetz, A. M., *Bestiality/Zoophilia: A Scarcely Investigated Phenomenon Between Crime, Paraphilia, and Love,* 4 J. For. Psychi. Prac. 2, 1–36 (2004).

108 Nickchen, Katherine, & Jeanne Johnson, *Zoophilia and Bestiality.* In Sex Crimes and Paraphilia (Eric Hickey, ed., 2006).

109 Schmalleger, F., Hall, Daniel E., & Dlatowski, J. J., Criminal Law Today 373 (4th edition) (Pearson/Prentice Hall) (2010).

110 Otto, Stephen K., *State Animal Protection Laws—The Next Generation,* 11 Anim. L. Rev. 131 (2005).

111 La. Rev. Stat. Ann. § 14:89(A)(1) (1972).

112 7 U.S.C. § 213 (1966).

113 Richard D. Reynnells, Basil R. Eastwood, U.S. Dep't of Agric., ANIMAL WELFARE ISSUES COMPENDIUM (1997), available at http://www.nal.usda.gov/awic/pubs/97issues.htm.

114 9 C.F.R. § 2.30 et seq. (2005); See also 7 U.S.C. § 2131 et seq. (2009). Report of the Committee on Legal Issues Pertaining to Animals of the Association of the Bar of the City of New York Regarding Its Recommendation to Amend the Animal Welfare Act, 9 Animal L. 345, 347 (2003).

115 Mariann Sullivan, *The Animal Welfare Act—What's That?,* 79 N.Y. ST. B.J. 17, 18 (2007).

116 Saturday, Jan 31, 2004, Marion County, Florida. Case ID: 2206. Classification: Bestiality. Found at Pet Abuse.com, http://www.pet-abuse.com/cases/2206/FL/US/.

117 Florida Anti-Bestiality Law Proposal Fails Again. Huffington Post, July 7, 2010. Found at http://www.huffingtonpost.com/2010/05/07/florida-anti-bestiality-l_n_568042.html.

118 Fla. Stat. Ann. § 828.12 (1971).

119 Saturday, Jan 31, 2004, Marion County, Florida. Case ID: 2206. Classification: Bestiality. Found at Pet Abuse.com, http://www.pet-abuse.com/cases/2206/FL/US/.

120 *Id.*

121 Miss. Code Ann. § 97-29-59 (1942).

122 Kan. Stat. Ann. § 21-3506 (2006).

123 Minnesota v. Bonygne, 450 N.W.2d 331 (1989).

124 Minn. Stat. Ann. § 609.294 (1988).

125 Minnesota v. Bonygne, 450 N.W.2d 331, 340 (1989).

126 Superior, Wisconsin, Douglas County Court Records. October 11, 2006. Found at Pet Abuse.com, http://www.pet-abuse.com/cases/9881/WI/US/.

127 *Id.*

128 Wis. Stat. Ann. § 944.17 (1998).

129 *Id.*

130 Superior, Wisconsin, Douglas County Court Records. October 11, 2006. Case ID: 9881. Classification: Bestiality. Found at Pet Abuse.com, http://www.pet-abuse.com/cases/9881/WI/US/.

131 *Id.*

132 *Id.*

[133] *Id.*

[134] People v. Haynes, 760 N.W.2d 283 (Mich. App. 2008).

[135] STROLLER, R.J., PAIN & PASSION: A PSYCHOANALYST EXPLORES THE WORLD OF S & M (Plenum Press) (1991).

[136] KRAFFT-EBING, PSYCHOPATHIA SEXUALIS 109 (Physicians and Surgeons Book Co.) (1906).

[137] FROMM, E., THE ANATOMY OF HUMAN DESTRUCTIVENESS (Penguin Books) (1977).

[138] Paclebar, Anne Marie, Furtado, Catherine, and McDonald-Witt, Melissa, *Sadomasochism: Practices, Behaviors, and Culture in American Society,* in SEX CRIMES AND PARAPHILIA 215 (Eric Hickey, ed., 2006).

[139] *Id.* at 219.

[140] *Id.* at 223.

[141] Commonwealth v. Appleby, 450 N.E.2d 1070 (1983).

[142] N.Y. LAWS § 235.20(5) (1981).

[143] CAL. STAT. §§ 314-318.6 (2000).

[144] OHIO REV. CODE ANN. § 2907.01(P) (1988).

[145] New Hampshire v. Higgins, 821 A.2d 964 (2002).

[146] *Id.* at 977.

[147] N.H. REV. STAT. ANN. § 632-A:2 (1996).

[148] N.H. REV. STAT. ANN. § 633:2 (1996).

[149] N.H. REV. STAT. ANN. § 631:4 (1996).

[150] N.H. REV. STAT. ANN. § 651:2, II-g (1996).

[151] New Hampshire v. Higgins, 821 A.2d 964, 979 (2002).

[152] *Id.* at 984.

[153] Yost, M. R., *Development and Validation of the Attitudes about Sadomasochism Scale,* 47 J. SEX RES. 1, 79-91 (2010).

[154] People v. Jovanovic, 700 N.Y.S.2d 156 (N.Y. App. Div. 1999).

[155] *Id.* at 167.

[156] People v. Jovanovic, 700 N.Y.S.2d 156 (N.Y. App. Div. 1999).

[157] *Id.* at 172.

[158] Money, J., *Forensic Sexology: Paraphilic Serial Rape (Biastophilia) and Lust Murder (Erotophonophilia),* 44 AMER. J. PSYCHO. 1, 26–36 (1990).

[159] CATHERINE PURCELL & BRUCE ARRIGO, THE PSYCHOLOGY OF LUST MURDER: PARAPHILIA, SEXUAL KILLING, AND SERIAL HOMICIDE (Elsevier/Academic Press) (2006).

[160] Senjo, Scott, *The Psychology of Lust Murder: Paraphilia, Sexual Killing, and Serial Homicide* by Catherine E. Purcell and Bruce A. Arrigo. San Diego, CA: Elsevier/Academic Press, 2006. 192 pp. 14 J. SEX. AGG. 3, 281–287 (2008).

[161] People v. Rundle, 180 P.3d 224 (2008).

[162] *Id.* at 229.

[163] *Id.* at 233.

[164] People v. Gacy, 468 N.E.2d 1171 (1984).

[165] Bhugra, D., Popelyuk, D., & McMullen, I., *Paraphilias Across Cultures: Contexts and Controversies,* 47 J. SEX RES. 2/3, 242–256 (2010).

[166] DSM-IV, pps. 522-523 (1994).

167 Senjo, Scott, *Sex Crimes: Patterns and Behaviors,* by Stephen T. Holmes and Ronald M. Holmes. Thousand Oaks, CA: Sage Publications, 2nd ed., 2002. 289 pp., 10 Journal of Criminal Justice and Popular Culture 2 (2002), http://www.albany.edu/scj/jcjpc/vol10is2/senjo.pdf.

168 Florida Anti-Bestiality Law Proposal Fails Again. Huffington Post, July 7, 2010. Found at http://www.huffingtonpost.com/2010/05/07/florida-anti-bestiality-l_n_568042.html.

169 Kansas v. Hendricks, 521 U.S. 346 (1997).

170 *Id.*

171 The Violent Crime Control and Law Enforcement Act, H.R. 3355, Pub.L. 103-322, was an act of Congress dealing with crime and law enforcement that became law in 1994. It is the largest crime bill in the history of the U.S. at 356 pages and provided for 200,000 new police officers and $9.7 billion in funding for prisons.

Chapter Seven

Digital Sex Crimes: Sexting,

Cellphone Porn, Computer Exhibitionism,

Internet Enticement of Minors

"Society is at war with the criminal classes, and courts have uniformly
held that in waging this warfare the forces of prevention and detection
may use traps, decoys, and deception to obtain evidence of the
commission of crime."

Sorrells v. United States
United States Supreme Court,
287 U.S. 435 (1932)[1]

Legal Background

This final chapter examines the digital revolution, sexual deviancy, and the legal regulations in place when digital sex becomes an offense of the law. No other realm of sexual deviancy has been so impacted as digital sex crimes as a result of the advent of computer and network technology. Prostitutes, escorts, and call girls can get off the streets, consumers of illegal porn no longer have to walk into an adult bookstore, and underworld predators can coordinate and share sexual interests with like-minded individuals in relative anonymity. Pornography itself has experienced a stunning transformation due to computers and chip technology.

Technological advancements don't initially seek to embellish people's sex lives, but rather do so as a byproduct. Throughout history, new technologies—like a computer—have always been useful for the betterment of one's quality of life. As examples, automobiles, heavy machinery, and computers have all assisted directly to modernize society and increase standards of living. Another thing is also true of new technology. Not only is it useful for society, it is also always capitalized on by criminal populations. Meaning, any new technology will tend to result in new crime, or at least the same crime, but done with a new technological tool.[2]

In the past, a new technology, such as the automobile, was a vast improvement over the horse and buggy. Automobiles were first used in a helpful manner. In no time, however, cars were used to facilitate an episode of deviance such as the facilitation of a bank robbery and means of a getaway. New technology will also be appropriated for sexual deviance. Cars quickly became useful to pick up prostitutes, engage in voyeurism, or become the stage for persons to engage in premarital sex, and teenagers to engage in underage sex.

This historical analogy is directly applicable to digital technology today. Computers, wireless transmission, e-mail, and the Internet were first adopted for socially useful and legal purposes. Quickly, however, these new technologies were seized on for sex-related activities, among many other uses. The Internet, in particular, is a primary repository for activities related to sex, love, fantasy, relationships, and romance.

Historical Trend in the Use of New Technologies:

1. Creation of a New Technology
2. Use of New Technology for a Legitimate Intended Purpose
3. Use of New Technology in a Socially Deviant Manner
4. Harm Is Caused
5. Creation of Law to Address the Harm

Digital computers using transistors and diodes were first created around 1945 for military, engineering, and math calculations. Personal computers (PCs) were originally thought to be unpopular for the mass market. But IBM took a risk to build and market this machine called a "computer" around 1970. Their idea paid off as consumers enjoyed the idea of a mechanism that could store a lot of complicated and useful programs into a single memory.[3] For the PC, the rest is history.

Then came networking technologies such as the TCP/IP common language and data transmission methods. Networks created the unique ability for two or more people to access a single or more files. Computer networks were first widely used around 1969 with ARPANet (also the name of the federal agency that helped build the first network), and were constructed for military purposes in the Cold War era.[4]

ARPANet worked in conjunction with the Stanford Research Institute and with help from UCLA, RAND, MIT, and other research entities, created the methods of packet switching, TCP/IP language, and digital transmission. This infrastructure of networks gave rise to the Internet as we know it today.[5] Technologies were developed to allow local networks to connect to each other and create a single global network. We know of this single global network as the World Wide Web today, first becoming public in 1992.

The Internet consists of a mass of computer systems that are all accessible from remote locations. The computer systems are connected by data highways and a multitude of computer networks. The process of connecting a standalone PC to the Internet is straightforward. A user with a PC makes a connection with another computer through standard cable or telephone lines. When computers communicate there can be immense amounts of data transferred simultaneously. An entire book can be sent across the globe in a few seconds, as can financial data, digitalized audio and video, and computer software. The speed and amount of information that can be transmitted through the Internet are multiplying at geometric proportions with the advent of new physical transport mechanisms, such as fiber optics, high-capacity copper wires, and high-bandwidth satellite transmissions that afford the potential for dramatically greater capacity than is available today.[6] This medium of communication is a medium that brings with it not only an immense potential for productivity, but also a wide range of novel problems and unique twists on old ones.

As soon as networks were invented, so were network break-ins. Shortly thereafter, the first laws that legally sanctioned network intrusions were created in 1978 in Arizona and Florida.[7] Following the states, the federal government first addressed illegal computing activity in 1984 with the CFAA (Computer Fraud and Abuse Act).[8] This statute was aimed at hacking and other illegal breaking and entering activities of hackers into the password-protected accounts and websites of unsuspecting parties. Today, networking and computing devices continue to get smaller, faster, more powerful, and best of all, cheaper. Digital computing represents one of the most revolutionary global changes since the automobile in 1920.

The silicon computer chip is what made the PC possible and it is what makes all other digital computing devices so handy to use. Digital cameras can take more enticing pictures, camcorders can make instant videos from any location, cellphones transmit a picture of one's nude body immediately, and scanners can make an old photograph a digital image and ready for

Regulating web pages to protect the public from viewing unsolicited pornography has proven to be a formidable legal challenge.

© Tumanyan, 2011. Used under license from Shutterstock, Inc.

upload and worldwide circulation.[9] Central to these examples is the technology of the computer and network. With standalone PCs and networks, sex is bought and sold in quantities beyond comprehension.[10] With this capability is the foremost concern of protecting children from harm since children are growing up using computers and developing a reliance on computing resources at a young age.

Regulating the Internet. Since it came online for public use in 1992, the global computer network known as the Internet has become a tool pointed at both ends. The choices made about its original structure—that is be a free space for the public—have been responsible for many of the headaches experienced in the legal community with regulation. Some of the original reasons behind the construction of the Internet have made it maddeningly difficult to regulate.[11] However, the reasons that make regulation complicated are the same reasons why the Internet is so important.

It did not take law enforcement and government long to see that the Internet could result in the accidental exposure of sex-related content to adults who do not want to see it, and more importantly, to minors who may accidentally—or purposefully—see it. It is common knowledge that most Internet users are young persons, specifically, ages 12–24 who flock to MySpace and Facebook social networking websites and invite strangers to communicate socially with them.[12]

Early on, government authorities and the public were alerted by one of the first studies on the prevalence of sex-related content on the Internet. In 1995, an undergraduate student named Martin Rimm published an article in the *Georgetown Law Journal* titled "Marketing Pornography on the Information Superhighway: A Survey of 917,410 Images, Descriptions, Short Stories and Animations Downloaded 8.5 Million Times by Consumers in over 2000 Cities in Forty Countries, Provinces and Territories."[13] Though his data collection has been critiqued, he found that 70 percent of all Internet imagery at the time was pornographic. The study painted the picture of a young Internet overrun by pornography; it even inspired an infamous sensationalized cover story in *Time* magazine and sparked a congressional bill complete with comments from U.S. Senators on the Senate floor.

Since Rimm's study, Congress, law enforcement officials, and the public have tried to protect children from both adult content and also from online predators. Controlling content has been much more legally cumbersome than controlling solicitation attempts. Regulating minors amid Internet communication is like trying to regulate whom children can speak with on the street or playground.

The government has tried to regulate the Internet, and the state attempting to control erotic materials through blocking technology is nothing new.[14] The current medium is simply a changeover from radio, television, and telephone to the Internet. When it comes to radio and broadcast television, the Supreme Court allows for a wide breadth of government regulation of speech (e.g., indecent speech) because of the ease with which those medias are central to the public. The Federal Communications Commission (FCC) has the legal authority to police the airwaves. The FCC can legally restrict the broadcast of "indecent" materials over radio and television frequencies to protect children from exposure to age-inappropriate subject matter.[15]

As one famous example, in 1973 a New York radio station owned by the Pacifica Foundation aired comedian George Carlin's infamous "Filthy Words" monologue as part of a radio program devoted to societal attitudes toward speech and language; it was an educational program. A man named John Douglas, who belonged to a national organization devoted to morality in the media, complained to the FCC that he heard the program while driving in his car with his young son. The FCC conducted an investigation and found that the monologue was "patently offensive" (though not obscene) and placed a reprimand in Pacifica's file.[16] The case made its way to the Supreme Court and the Court held that the First Amendment does not prohibit the government from regulating non-obscene indecent speech on the airwaves because of the pervasive nature of broadcasting and its accessibility by young children.[17]

For broadcast television regulation, the FCC requires that content that may be indecent can only be shown, if at all, late at night when children are less likely to be watching TV. Generally, cable operators may decline to carry indecent programming on "leased access" or commercial channels, but not with respect to community access channels used by local governments and community groups. Telephone services, on the other hand, provide the user with significantly more control over the receipt of content than the television or radio audience has over what it sees or hears. For this reason, the law subjects common telephone carriers to significantly less regulation than that governing broadcast or cable television. Motion pictures are regulated in the form of a ratings system. The Motion Picture Association of America movie ratings are a form of self-regulation and are not legally mandated by the FCC. The G, PG, PG-13, R, and NC-17 ratings are standards that give theaters, media, parents, and moviegoers advance notice of a movie's content.[18]

Internet regulation, however, is an entirely different story. Regulation of the telephone dial-a-porn industry is arguably the most analogous framework to use for the proposal to regulate the Internet. Courts often suggest that the Internet is most like this industry in terms of intrusiveness into the lives of its users. A customer must proactively make a phone call to access a recorded dial-a-porn message. This is much like Internet contact, where a user must similarly proactively initiate contact with a particular website; it is not like a minor could see or hear sex-related content on a website just by walking through a shopping mall.

In any event, good reason exists to regulate the Internet. On the Internet, no type of "virtual" shopkeeper exists to keep an eye on exactly who is looking at what. Internet service providers (ISPs) probably represent the most logical virtual shopkeeper/police officer. These companies facilitate access to myriad websites on behalf of their subscribers and could monitor (and even control) the sites and materials that their subscribers visit.[19] While Congress has used the PATRIOT Act[20] to engage ISPs in the role of police officer for terrorism, Congress has not done so concerning indecent material on the Internet.

One reason for this is because adults derive significant free speech benefits from an open, diverse marketplace of ideas and information on the Internet. When Congress has attempted to regulate adult content on the Internet, a heavily litigated environment ensues. There have been two major attempts to protect children's interests on the Internet, both of which have failed. The Communication Decency Act (CDA) of 1996[21] and the Child Online Protection Act (COPA) of 1997[22] dealt with the protection of children from exposure to obscene materials. Both of these laws mandated governmental control of the Internet and both were found unconstitutional. These and other cases on the subject of regulating speech/expression/porn are discussed in chapter 5 on the law of pornography.

With the inherent difficulty of government regulation of the Internet, a policy of self-regulation has proven to be effective. For example, many adult-content website companies and systems operators have taken steps to limit the access of minors to their websites while still being able to market their products to willing adults. A number of companies use age verification services that charge users a fee to access individual websites that have contracted with the service.

Filtering software also is used for self-regulation.[23] ISPs and third-party organizations provide filtering software that allows the user to block access to graphics as well as specific files and programs if they wish. Since the First Amendment generally protects Internet-based indecent speech and violent content, filtering technology would enable the user to filter out such material from their Internet access. Government mandates for filtering software, such as in public libraries, however, are a different story.[24]

Free speech advocates have noted the shortcomings of filtering technology and decry government mandates for filtering software. If filters worked as intended, there may not be constitutional issues with government-mandated filtering software. But since current filtering techniques are imperfect and arguably do more harm than good, government-mandated filtering requirements are failed legislation despite being upheld by the courts. Because current filtering implementations are both overbroad, blocking content that has legitimate educational value, and underinclusive, failing to block all sexually explicit content, Congress cannot mandate them without violating the First Amendment.[25]

Some Internet search engines have taken measures to reduce the amount of objectionable material encountered. There are also attempts, within the industry of ISPs to rate Web pages to allow Internet users to filter content. The Platform for Internet Content Selection (PICS), for example, is an assemblage of industry standards worldwide designed to establish a labeling system for the Internet that gives the Internet user the power to filter objectionable materials.[26]

A Digital Sexual Revolution. While self-regulation, including regulation by parents and teachers, continues, so will advances in the technology itself. Digital technology continues to spawn numerous subsystems. E-mail and e-mail variations, an infinite number of chatrooms and chat channels, an equally infinite number of BBSs (electronic Bulletin Board Systems) such as Craigslist, and an infinite number of personal blogs (Web logs of an individual's editorialized perspective on a particular topic) are all digital systems enjoyed by millions of legitimate computer users, but also by those with criminal intentions.

In many ways, network and computing technologies have created an entire new world of sex-related activities. Where many people were afraid to explore sex with someone else, or to walk into an adult bookstore, they can now do it online. Casey notes that Internet pornography is so prolific, it is not only available, it is unavoidable.[27] In 2005, Internet users viewed over 15 billion pages of adult content.[28] As network technology has improved, the easy availability of pornography has exponentially increased as the use of Web-enabled mobile phones and hand-held gaming devices permit the user to surf the Web unfiltered on any wireless signal.

It is guaranteed that new technologies will eventually be employed for use in some kind of illegal sexual activity. Government regulation is an ongoing effort.

Cellphone technology falls squarely within the parameters of this argument. Handheld mobile telephones with a wireless cell became an instant hit with corporate and other businesspersons by allowing spontaneous, rapid communications. Cellphones, unpredictably, also became an instant hit with teenagers, providing them with a fun way to chat with friends and otherwise gain a sense of independence and maturity often sought by persons in their late teens. The law has struggled to comprehend the culture of sexting and in New York, a 16-year-old is facing up to seven years in prison for forwarding a nude photo to his consenting girlfriend. It is not just high school kids who are being charged in sexting cases. Four middle-schoolers were arrested in Alabama for exchanging nude photos.[29]

Not as playful or innocent, Internet solicitation cases are another example of a new technology adapted for a seriously deviant act. Hiding behind the secretive veil of the Internet, adults have found the Internet the perfect anonymous tool to engage in conversations with minors. In many cases, the adult lies about his or her age, thus making the chat scandalous in many respects. When the conversation turns sexual, the law comes in to play and many persons have been arrested and convicted for sexual enticement of a minor over the Internet.

So widespread has become the solicitation, the federal government has made funding available to the states for the creation of task forces to manage these Internet-based cases.[30] Officers assigned to these task forces pose undercover in a virtual environment and simply wait for the "fish to jump in to the boat." Officers typically pose as a young girl, flirt with older men, and direct the conversation to a meeting for purposes of sexual contact. Since the law focuses on the enticement, mere asking is enough for a conviction. These cases have become well known through the MSNBC television series "To Catch a Predator."

The FBI saw a 2,062 percent increase over the last decade in open cases initiated through its Innocent Images National Initiative.[31] The FBI Initiative combats all aspects of computer-based attacks on children, including catching sexual predators online. Access to the Internet has increased tremendously over the last decade. As a result, the Initiative has expanded to twenty-eight FBI field offices and has "secured nearly 3,000 convictions."[32]

The evidence gathered for enticement cases is incontrovertible and is a main reason why law enforcement is drawn to these cases. Everything the offender types is used as evidence in court and there is no room to question the veracity of who did what, or who saw what. That said, the law of entrapment applies to enticement cases. Since many people enjoy chatting on-line and have no intention of getting involved romantically, when undercover officers initiate conversation that produces an emotional response in the chat partner that would never have manifested were it not for the officer's gestures, the law of entrapment applies. A successful defense in entrapment cases results in the dismissal of the case and the alleged offender being set free.

Cellphones have become an instant hit with prostitutes, escorts, and call girls who no lon-ger have to remain by the phone in a hotel room where the police could monitor activity. Now, prostitutes can travel freely, communicate with clients at will, and devise strategies to elude the detection of enforcement operations. For cellphones with an Internet browser and active account, the phones can be used for a variety of pornography-related activities and crimes, not to mention simply aiding in the furtherance of the business of distributing illegal pornography. Last, but not least, cellphones have become a tool for social rituals never imagined by their original creators. Sending nude or partly nude pictures (sexting) to close friends by high school teenagers is another way that new technology has been employed for a socially—and sexu-ally—deviant manner.

New digital technologies are created within other, new technologies. For example, the over $12 billion-a-year commercial pornography industry is now being matched by free porn sites such as YouPorn, a variation on the theme of the popular YouTube.[33] As its name suggests, YouPorn lets users upload and watch a virtually unlimited selection of sex videos for free. The user-generated clips on YouPorn—like those on YouTube—range from the grainiest amateur footage to the slickest professional product. The response to this new Internet "innovation" was astonishing. Just nine months after going live in September 2006, YouPorn was on pace to log about 15 million unique visitors. Today, YouPorn is the No. 1 digital adult sex site in the world.[34]

In all of the contexts of sex and porn, digital technology greatly facilitates speed and in-stantaneous production as well as possessing tremendous storage capacity. Prior to 1980, taking pictures of nude models and producing a pornographic magazine was cumbersome, labor intensive, expensive, and a lot of time passed before the magazine could hit the shelves. In 1970, the names Hugh Hefner (*Playboy* magazine) and Larry Flint (*Hustler* magazine) were relatively well known because there were so few porn magazines of wide circulation. With the digital technology of the 1990s, the average person can enter the world of amateur pornography in a single afternoon. As a result, today, the number of widely circulated magazines and websites related to sex number in the thousands. As the result of digital technology, the entire pornography industry has changed and morphed into a multi-billion-dollar business.[35]

Sexting

S exting represents the overbreadth of the law of minors and pornography and the faulty symbolism of most statutes pertaining to child pornography. Prior to cellular and other wireless data transmission technologies, the law took offense at any relationship between minors and nudity or sexuality no matter who was involved, adult or minor.[36] While the protection that was targeted toward teenage and pre-pubescent children is obviously necessary, the same ardent application of the law to late teens and other young adults is not as obvious. We do not exactly picture a teenager when it comes to the subject of a child pornographer.

Throughout U.S. history, legislators seemed to never question the propriety of laws that would punish a mature 17-year-old person who possessed a nude image of another teenager, and the penalties were harsh. With the advent of handheld technology and cellphones, the fundamental policy that sets the age at 18 and over has been discredited. Cellphones with built-in cameras allow for the instant taking and sending of a nude picture of oneself or another. The very first chance to apply child pornography laws to late teens revealed the glaring misapplication of the laws. Obviously, a 16- or 17-year-old who takes, sends, or receives a nude image of someone of the same age is not the sexual deviant the law sought to deter throughout the history of U.S. child porn laws. As a result of this new crime and inapplicability of old laws, numerous states have had to rewrite their laws so that sexting is a minor offense rather than a serious felony.[37] Four states passed new sexting laws in 2009, and at least fifteen other states have introduced sexting legislation since 2009.[38]

These states recognize the advent of the digital intersection between nudity, cellphones, teenagers, and the notoriously bad judgment of teenagers. In most cases, these episodes do not involve an excessive indulgence in blatant pornography or even hardcore porn. While sexting promotes either directly or indirectly a voyeuristic look at nudity, so long as the minors involved can maintain a balanced perspective by talking about it with understanding adults, the practice of exchanging nude pictures may represent more good than harm. It would be hard to find fault with an occasional look at nudity coupled with an education on human sexuality and safe sex. Relatively responsible parenting will go a long way toward ensuring that sexting does not become harmful or promote lurid values.

In the meantime, punitive criminal justice action has been taken against sexters and the arrests and convictions are all legal and constitutional. In Pennsylvania, three teenage girls between the ages of 14 and 17 engaged in "high tech flirting" and were charged with disseminating child pornography when they sexted their boyfriends. The boys who received the photos were charged with possession of child pornography. An Indiana teen faced felony obscenity charges for sending a picture of his genitals to female classmates. In Spotsylvania, Virginia, the prosecutor brought charges against two high school students in the county's first sexting case involving multiple girls, ranging in age from 12 to 16. In another state case, prosecutors contemplated bringing child pornography charges against a boy for forwarding a sext from his then 14-year-old girlfriend. In California, four 15-year-old boys were cited for "possession of harmful matter depicting a person under 18" and for sexual exploitation of a minor after posting nude and seminude pictures of their classmates on the Internet. In Georgia, a tenth-grade boy sent a naked image of himself to a 16-year-old girl. The photo was then forwarded to four other students, one of whom was 14 years old. The boy was arrested at school and charged with misdemeanor furnishing of obscene material to a minor.[39]

In sum, sexting cases have run into a serious problem as old child porn laws have been applied to innocent teenage sexting. Sexting was originally governed by traditional, nondigital obscenity laws including the Ferber and Osbourne Supreme Court decisions discussed in chapter 5. These cases explicitly outlaw pornographic images of minors and entertain serious felony sentencing. As with a lot of laws that were created for face-to-face settings, child pornography laws do not fit well with modern sexting cases and the fifty states are modifying their criminal codes to respond to sexting in a way that makes the law fit the crime. Local school districts have the freedom to enact regulations as well and have the authority to limit the use of cellphones, computers and other technological devices while students are on school premises. Of course, parental supervision is another avenue for the regulation of sexting practices and is recommended in lieu of police enforcement.

Without parental supervision, cellphones are inseparable from the lifestyle of a teenager today. The law is determined to prevent minors from viewing pornography.

© JHDT Stock Images LLC, 2011. Used under license from Shutterstock, Inc.

Definition of the Offense

Sexting is the act of sending sexually explicit messages or photographs, primarily between mobile phones via text message functions. The term is a portmanteau of sex and texting, where the latter is meant in the wide sense of sending a text possibly with sex-based images included. Sexting that involves teenagers sending sexually explicit photographs of themselves to their peers has led to a legal gray area due to the strict anti-child pornography laws in the U.S.[40]

Elements of the Offense

The elements to the crime of sexting that must be proven beyond a reasonable doubt are:

1. Knowingly and intentionally
2. Use of an electronic communication device
3. To transmit or receive
4. Any obscene material or child pornography[41]

Sample Statute

The State of Vermont Sexting Statute reads as follows:

Vermont Revised Statute § 13-2802B (2009).

    (a) (1) No minor shall knowingly and voluntarily and without threat or coercion use a computer or electronic communication device to transmit an indecent visual depiction of himself or herself to another person.

           (2) No person shall possess a visual depiction transmitted to the person in violation of subdivision (1) of this subsection. It shall not be a violation of this subdivision if the person took reasonable steps, whether successful or not, to destroy or eliminate the visual depiction.

    (b) Penalties; minors.

           (1) Except as provided in subdivision (3) of this subsection, a minor who violates subsection (a) of this section shall be adjudicated delinquent. An action brought under this subdivision (1) shall be filed in family court and treated as a juvenile proceeding pursuant to chapter 52 of Title 33, and may be referred to the juvenile diversion program of the district in which the action is filed.

           (2) A minor who violates subsection (a) of this section and who has not previously been adjudicated in violation of that section shall not be prosecuted under chapter 64 of this title (sexual exploitation of children), and shall not be subject to the requirements of subchapter 3 of chapter 167 of this title (sex offender registration).

           (3) A minor who violates subsection (a) of this section who has previously been adjudicated in violation of that section may be adjudicated in family court as under subdivision (b)(1) of this section or prosecuted in district court under chapter 64 of this title (sexual exploitation of children), but shall not be subject to the requirements of subchapter 3 of chapter 167 of this title (sex offender registration).

           (4) Notwithstanding any other provision of law, the records of a minor who is adjudicated delinquent under this section shall be expunged when the minor reaches 18 years of age.[42]

Arguments Made By The Prosecution

Anyone involved with a nude, partially nude, or provocatively dressed minor is subject to a degree of legal scrutiny. That includes both the model for the picture, creator, sender, and receiver of the image. The state need only locate the image for there to be enough evidence to proceed with the case. Technology-based tools such as a traceroute, bitstream imaging, and DataArrest allow for a search of cell phones and other handhelds and the proficient extraction of the digital evidence for the case.

Arguments Made By The Defense

If the image in question involves a partly nude minor, the defense does not have much to go on. It would be difficult to imagine a scenario where the image resulted by an accident or mistake (both would be valid defenses). The most effective thing that the defense can do is seek to plea the case down to a reduced charge. The strategy of a charge reduction can eliminate the application of a felony statute and the corresponding loss of rights that follows a convicted felon. In addition, a charge reduction can avoid the required placement onto the sex offender registry for someone who may only be a high school student.

Variations of the Law of Sexting

A. High School Romance and Felony Sexting

Laws drafted by older generations do not fully comprehend the culture of digital technology and teenage romance of newer generations. Asking a boyfriend or girlfriend to send via text message a sexually revealing photo is part of the romantic environment of the digital generation. Teenagers expect such requests for nude or seminude images and do not think of them as indecent, "wrong," patently offensive, or prurient. It is highly unlikely that newer generations of teenagers even know what "prurient" is.

In *State v. Canal,* two high school sweethearts had been spending time together in the same social group for about one year. In a phone call between them one evening, the teenage female requested on three separate occasions of the teenage male a picture of his penis to be sent via text message. He complied with her request, and also sent a second picture of his face along with the words "I love you" which he apparently meant sincerely.[43]

The female received the two texts, viewed them and deleted them, or so she thought. In actuality, she did not complete the delete function and the images remained on her phone. Her mother routinely searched her daughter's phone and e-mail account and found the two pictures, one of which was of the male's penis. The mother was alarmed and told the girl's father. The father told the police and the boy was arrested.

Since the boy was 18 and the girl was 14, the boy was charged with the distribution of obscene material to a minor, a felony offense. The boy was convicted at trial and appealed. On appeal, he tried to argue that he could not be found guilty of the distribution of obscene material to a minor because the material was not obscene. At trial, however, the case went to the jury and the jury was instructed to decide on their community standards via the Miller ruling whether or not they thought the image of the boy's penis was obscene. Jury instruction number eighteen defined "obscene material" as

> any material depicting or describing the genitals, sex acts, masturbation, excretory functions or sadomasochistic abuse which the average person, taking the material as a whole and applying contemporary community standards with respect to what is suitable material for minors, would find appeals to the prurient interest and is patently offensive; and the material, taken as a whole, lacks serious literary, scientific, political, or artistic value.[44]

The jury found that the photo of the penis was obscene and the appeals court found no error and upheld the conviction of the boy for felony distribution of obscene material.[45] The court stated:

> Canal's sole contention regarding the sufficiency of the evidence is that the material he sent to C.E. was not obscene. Applying the jury instructions as given and reviewing the evidence in the light most favorable to the State, the question we must resolve is whether, under this record, a rational juror could find Canal guilty beyond a reasonable doubt of knowingly disseminating obscene material to a minor. Canal took one photograph of his face and one photograph of his erect penis. He e-mailed the photographs to C.E. separately. He attached a text message to the photograph of his face that said, 'I love you.'
>
> Although Canal argued to the jury the material he sent C.E. only appealed to a natural interest in sex, under the instructions given the jury could find, by applying its own contemporary community standards with respect to what is suitable material for minors, that the material appealed to the prurient interest, was patently offensive, and lacked serious literary, scientific, political, or artistic value. On a sufficiency-of-the-evidence review, our task is not to refind the facts. Moreover, on this record we cannot conclude, as a matter of law, the materials Canal sent to C.E were not obscene. Therefore, even though another jury in a different community may have found this material not to be obscene, the evidence in this record was sufficient for this jury to determine, under its own community standards, that the material Canal sent to C.E. was obscene.[46]

B. Sexted Images Forwarded Without Consent

In most cases, the practices of sexting are limited to a single sender and a single, trusted receiver. Sometimes, multiple recipients are intended, but in those cases, the nudity is often discreet or merely suggestive. For more public displays, teens will simply post an image of themselves to their MySpace and/or Facebook account for the world to see. In the arena of tween romance, the recipient of a sexted picture is implicitly or explicitly trusted to not forward the image to anyone else or else be subject to a serious breach of social norms and etiquette.

Rules are often broken, however, and since the advent of sexting, quite a few cases have emerged where sweethearts have gotten into a romantic quarrel and one of the parties has retaliated by forwarding a trusted sexting picture to thousands of others who became shocked at the revelations. In response to the betrayal and forwarding of an image without consent, some parties have considered a civil cause of action known as IIED (Intentional Infliction of Emotional Distress).

In an IIED action, the aggrieved plaintiff must prove four elements: (1) the defendant's conduct was either intentional or reckless; (2) the defendant's conduct was outrageous and extreme; (3) there was a causal connection between the defendant's conduct and the emotional distress suffered by the plaintiff; and (4) the emotional distress suffered by the plaintiff was severe.[47] As defined by the Restatement (Second) of Torts, a plaintiff will prevail in an IIED if the defendant's conduct is so outrageous in character, and so extreme in degree, as to go beyond all possible bounds of decency, and to be regarded as atrocious, and utterly intolerable in a civilized community.[48] Generally, the case is one in which the recitation of the facts to an average member of the community would arouse his resentment against the actor, and lead him to exclaim, "Outrageous!"[49] However, the Restatement provides that liability does not "extend to mere insults, indignities, threats, annoyances, petty oppressions, or other trivialities."[50]

To date, there have been no sexting cases where courts have ruled on an IIED claim for the forwarding of sexted messages without consent. A nonsexting case, however, will illustrate the points of law required for a successful IIED case. In *Davidson v. City of Westminster,* two police officers were sued under an IIED statute when the plaintiff was assaulted by a stranger, and the officers did nothing to help, even though they witnessed the entire ordeal in a stakeout.[51] At trial, the plaintiff lost and was not able to clearly make out all four prongs of the IIED law as outlined above. The plaintiff appealed but the appeals court affirmed the dismissal of the case.

While the plaintiff may have prevailed under some other legal theory, and the department may have taken administrative action against the officers, the court held for the officers because there was no direct, inherent duty for the officers to come to the aid of this one individual, the plaintiff. The court stated:

> The defendant [police officers] owed no duty of care. No special relationship arose between defendants and the assailant as the visual identification of assailant from a distance created only a minimal connection. There was no special relationship between plaintiff and defendants. Defendants did not create the peril, nor was plaintiff relying on defendants for protection. The [trial] court rejected imposing a duty on police officers to warn potential victims or the general public as against public policy. The [trial] court rejected plaintiff's claim for intentional infliction of emotional distress because defendant's conduct was not so outrageous that it gave rise to a cause of action, nor had they intended to cause injury to plaintiff. The trial court's dismissal of plaintiff assault victim's claim was affirmed.[52]

Indeed, other legal theories may apply to sexted images forwarded without consent. Prosser's elaborates on the tort of privacy. His four-fold privacy torts (intrusion upon seclusion, public disclosure of private facts, false light privacy, and appropriation) are applicable, but equally tenuous when it comes to sexts forwarded. The tort of intrusion upon seclusion addresses harmful information gathering, but not the subsequent disclosure of its fruits. It would only apply if the information was uncovered in a secretive way from a place within which the plaintiff had a reasonable expectation of privacy, such as a home, hotel room, a tanning booth, or a shopping bag. Privacy tort encompasses the activities of high-tech Peeping Toms, as it covers "unwarranted sensory intrusions like eavesdropping, wiretapping, and visual or photographic spying." However, if the reluctantly photographed (and subject of the forwarded image) was not in seclusion, but rather was a willing and consenting party, no court would hold that such a person had a reasonable expectation of privacy, regardless of one's own expectation of "audience."

Appropriation, another possible legal remedy for forwarded sexts, is uniquely property focused and does not involve a false statement or a shameful disclosure. Instead, it focuses on the unpermitted commercial use of a person's identity and its ensuing dignitary harms. Hence it would only apply if the plaintiff's information or image were used without his consent for the defendant's commercial purposes. For example, Facebook has recently launched a platform called Social Ads that allows advertisers to use pictures of Facebook members in advertisements without their prior consent.

Intentional infliction of emotional distress is ineffectual or a privacy tort are options depending on the facts of the case surrounding forwarded sexts. According to the Restatement, "one who by extreme and outrageous conduct intentionally or recklessly causes severe emotional distress" will be liable for its emotional or physical manifestations. Most courts have held that actionable conduct must exceed all reasonable and socially tolerable bounds of decency. This has set a high bar for the tort.

C. Privacy Rights of Stored Phone Numbers, Pictures, or Videos

Nearly immediately after their appearance on the mass market, pagers, cellphones, and other handheld devices came to the attention of law enforcement as tools for the furtherance of criminal activity. Indeed, the short history of these digital devices indicates their value as a repository of evidence of criminal activity and especially of networks of criminal syndicates.

Data stored in a cellphone is a privacy right and not accessible to anyone but the owner of the phone and anyone whom the owner consents to have such information. Dialed numbers do not enjoy such a privacy right, but that is the subject of a different legal search.[53] The obvious exception to this right of privacy is in a situation where probable cause exists that evidence of a crime may be found in the phone. For example, if a student complains to a principal that someone sent an obscene text, the principal may convey the circumstances to a police officer. The officer would trace the text to its origins in a type of reverse look-up. If the sender of the unwanted text is located, his or her phone immediately becomes subject to a search pursuant to the law of search and seizure as governed by the Fourth Amendment to the U.S. Constitution. Searches incident to an arrest are legal pursuant to the Supreme Court case of *Chimel v. California.*[54]

Chimel allows for a lawful search of phone numbers, text messages, and videos stored in the phone and no search warrant is required if it is incident to a lawful arrest (or there happen to be exigent circumstances). This legal procedure allows the police to retrieve criminal evidence quickly so that the suspect does not have time to delete the valuable information.

In *U.S. v. Fierros-Alvarez,* the defendant was subject to an arrest while in his parked vehicle. The offender was suspected of engaging in a variety of crimes and the arresting officer immediately seized his phone and searched it later in the evening. The officer found further incriminating evidence in the phone and additional charges were filed. The offender was facing an uphill battle and asked for a suppression hearing to suppress the information gathered from the phone. At the hearing, the defendant argued that the search of the phone was illegal and he tried to use the exclusionary rule to suppress the use of the evidence found in the phone. The attempt to exclude the phone data seemed like a stretch and the presiding judge had no problem holding that the search of the phone was lawful and the evidence retrieved from the phone was admissible in an imminent trial on the multiple charges. The judge stated:

> The government argues the ... issue presented by the facts of this case preclude an expectation of privacy in the recent call directory as well as the phonebook directory. The defendant's only rejoinder is that a phone book directory may disclose more information than that revealed in a pen register. The defendant, however, has not shown that the phone book directory in his cellular telephone discloses more than the addressing information, the telephone number and the subscriber's name, on the same numbers

appearing in the recent calls directory. See *United States v. Forrester,* 512 F.3d at 509; *United States v. Perrine,* 518 F.3d at 1204. On the record as it stands, the court must conclude that the defendant has not carried his burden of proving a reasonable expectation of privacy in the addressing information retrieved from the recent calls directory and in the names and numbers taken from the phonebook directory. Thus, the court denies the defendant's motion for lack of standing.[55]

Additional Court Cases: Sexting

Miller v. Skumanick

605 F.Supp.2d 634 (2009)

CASE SUMMARY

PROCEDURAL POSTURE: Plaintiffs, parents, sued defendant district attorney on behalf of their minor children and alleged retaliation in violation of the First Amendment rights to free expression and to be free from compelled expression, and retaliation for the parents' exercise of their Fourteenth Amendment right as parents to direct their children's upbringing. The parents moved for a temporary restraining order (TRO) and to compel production of photographs.

OVERVIEW: At issue was the practice of sexting. According to the parents, this was the practice of teenagers sending or posting sexually suggestive text messages and images, including nude or seminude photographs, via cellular telephones or over the Internet. The parents sought an order from the court enjoining the district attorney from initiating criminal charges for two photographs, or for any other photographs of the girls unless the images depicted sexual activity. After determining that abstention was inappropriate because there were no underlying state proceedings, the court balanced the four TRO factors and determined that issuance of a TRO was appropriate under the circumstances. Regarding one factor, the minor plaintiffs claimed that they would be compelled to write an essay that explained what they did wrong. Because they contended that they in no way violated the law, they further claimed that being compelled to describe their behavior as wrong on threat of a felony conviction forced them to express a belief they did not hold and thus violated their right to be free of compelled speech. Thus, the parents and the children asserted constitutionally protected activity.

OUTCOME: The court granted the parents' motion for a temporary restraining order. The district attorney was enjoined from pressing charges against the children. The parents' motion to compel was denied.[56]

Cellphone Pornography

Innocent text messaging and photo sharing are incompatible with traditional laws that make child pornography a serious felony offense.

Partly related to sexting, but including the commercial aspect of the porn trade, picture taking with a cellphone that has a camera (cameraphone) has created a new dimension for pornography sales. Nudity and/or sexuality can be shot quickly and easily, sometimes with consent and sometimes not, and the images can be sent, stored, embellished, and circulated swiftly. Photography celebrates and often beautifies what is being done in the picture and imbues the subjects with a sense of value and legitimacy. This reality is especially troubling to those uncomfortable with sexual expression and particularly disturbing to those who oppose minors who take photos of themselves during legal sex (those minors over the age of consent). Not only do censorers of pornography not want photography to lend importance to sexuality, a legitimate fear exists that the photos may circulate among cellphones and eventually all over the Internet, thus legitimizing sexual relations between minors when they are not yet ready to divest their innocence and purity through sexual expression.

Cellphone technology has resulted in the creation of a device easily placed in one's pocket, but having high-powered capabilities at a relatively small expense. The result is that cellphones are used in many intimate settings such as bedrooms, bathrooms, and locker rooms. Cellphones not only have a built-in camera, but also a video function where streams of video can be taken and transmitted instantly. For those with an account, cellphones also have Internet browsing capabilities and mobile TV to watch television programming on the phone.

A unique culture has cropped up from the advent of cellphones with camera and video. People use cameraphones for purposes beyond those where they would ordinarily use a stand-alone camera. A cameraphone is there all the time, and photos are effectively cost free to take, so users employ them in a multitude of settings. A few examples include snapping a photo of a refrigerator to remember later at the grocery store what they have at home or photographing meals as part of a diet program.[57]

Researchers are just beginning to study usage patterns for cameraphones. Much of the available research today focuses on Japan and other Asian countries, where cameraphone use is more intense than in the U.S. Cameraphone users often employ the devices for ad hoc diaries of their life and sex is a part of many persons' lives. They take pictures any time something strikes their fancy and use them to construct "intimate virtual co-presence" among close friends.

As discussed in previous chapters, where a cellphone is used to take nude photos of adults who are consenting to non-obscene imagery, the law does not have a problem. The trouble area, of course, is when cellphones are used secretly or semisecretly without consent, or pictures are circulated beyond the user's phone, or where a minor is involved.

Cellphone photos and videos are not the only sex-related demon emanating from this advanced technology. The law also keeps a close eye on pornographic text messages without a photo. Adults or minors who text indecent or profane messages to a minor can be held criminally liable. In the state of Georgia, an adult sent several texts to a 14-year-old stating he wanted to engage in sexual contact with the minor. He was charged with electronically furnishing obscene materials to a minor, distributing harmful materials to a minor, and engaging in obscene telephone contact with a minor in violation of the Georgia Criminal Code.[58]

To date, only a few states, notably Florida[59] and Georgia,[60] have drafted laws specifically pertaining to the offense of cellphone pornography. Both statutes in those states prohibit a person over the age of 17 from engaging in obscene phone contact with a minor. Phone contact is obscene when it "involves any aural matter containing explicit verbal descriptions or narrative accounts of sexually explicit nudity, sexual conduct, sexual excitement, or sadomasochistic abuse which is intended to arouse or satisfy the sexual desire of either the child or the person."[61] A person convicted under this statute has committed "a misdemeanor of a high and aggravated nature," punishable by a fine of up to $5,000, incarceration up to twelve months, or both. The conduct prohibited is considered a "dangerous sexual offense," and a conviction requires registration as a sexual offender.[62]

Definition of the Offense

The definition of cellphone pornography is roughly consistent with the definition of pornography used in a nondigital medium. Cellphone pornography may be defined as the use of a cellphone to produce and transmit an image that visually depicts sexual activity of oneself or another.[63]

Elements of the Offense

The elements to the crime of cellphone pornography that must be proven beyond a reasonable doubt are:

1. Intentionally and knowingly
2. Use of a cellphone or similar digital communication device
3. To produce and/or transmit
4. Unlawful sexual imagery
5. Of oneself or another[64]

Sample Statute

A state of Michigan pornography statute related to electronic production reads as follows:

> Michigan Compiled Laws Annotated 750.145c(m) (2010). [A]ny depiction, whether made or produced by electronic, mechanical, or other means, including a developed or undeveloped photograph, picture, film, slide, video, electronic visual image, computer diskette, computer or computer-generated image, or picture, or sound recording which is of a child or appears to include a child engaging in a listed sexual act; a book, magazine, computer, computer storage device, or other visual or print or printable medium containing such a photograph, picture, film, slide, video, electronic visual image, computer, or computer-generated image, or picture, or sound recording; or any reproduction, copy, or print of such a photograph, picture, film, slide, video, electronic visual image, book, magazine, computer, or computer-generated image, or picture, other visual or print or printable medium, or sound recording is defined by the Michigan Code as "child sexually abusive material."[65]

Arguments Made By The Prosecution

The prosecutorial strategy in cellphone porn cases mirrors that of the state's role in other pornography cases. The first legal question concerns the propriety of the pictures. If the pictures fail the Miller Test and lack any social or artistic value, the images are illegal. In addition, any picture related to minors and sexuality is also illegal. If the images are found to be illegal, the parties associated with the images can be held criminally liable.

Arguments Made By The Defense

The defense can always raise the suspicion that the evidence was retrieved illegally by the police in violation of the Fourth Amendment prohibition on illegal searches and seizures by government. Another defense strategy that is highly applicable to cases of digital evidence is the defense challenge as to the validity and reliability of the electromagnetic evidence. The point of attack in this strategy is to question the evidence-gathering tools: Were the tools part of the Best Practices suggested by various associations of digital examiners? If not, the defense can allege sloppy evidence retrieval techniques, and as a result, the evidence fails to prove the facts asserted.

Variations of the Law of Cellphone Porn

A. Privacy Rights to Cellphone Self-Portraits

In several states, it is legal for teenagers over the age of 14 to have premarital, consensual sex. Society does not seek to encourage it, but as a legal matter, it logically follows that they should be able to take pictures of themselves during sex; the picture taking would seem to be the lesser of the two controversies (having sex or taking nude pictures). In addition, it has been noted in numerous court cases that juveniles have numerous constitutional rights and are not wards of the state under the concept of parens patriae.

Despite the aspects of propriety for sex among late teens, and constitutional rights that imply the legality of picture taking of oneself, is it legal to use a cellphone to take pictures of oneself during sex, if the parties are both minors?

In *A.H. v. Florida*, a 16-year-old woman (A.H.) and her 17-year-old boyfriend (J.G.W.) engaged in premarital sex and took a few pictures of themselves while doing so. The couple did not send anyone any of the photos, but told one or two of their friends about doing so. Somehow, word circulated and got to the police. The local police obtained a search warrant and searched J.G.W.'s computer and found the images. Both were arrested and convicted under a strict child pornography law in the State of Florida.[66]

A.H. appealed and argued that the child pornography laws of the State of Florida apply to sick pedophiles, and since she is not one herself, she should not be subject to such laws.[67] A.H.'s argument is a strong one. The reason the laws against child porn are so stringent is to target a depraved group of criminals. In addition, the child porn laws of Florida restrict housing and employment contexts of convicted offenders, can subject them to a state mental hospital *after* serving their entire sentence, and require they go up on the sex offender registry for a long time. Clearly, these laws were not targeted to a 16-year-old girl.

The appeals court however, was disturbed by any notion that sex by a minor should be given any credence whatsoever. The court seemed bothered by the independence of sexual expression by A.H. more than the existence of the photographs and even though the laws practically have no application to A.H., her conviction, and that of J.G.W.'s were upheld.[68] The court stated:

> Neither had a reasonable expectation that the other would not show the photos to a third party. Minors who are involved in a sexual relationship, unlike adults who may be involved in a mature committed relationship, have no reasonable expectation that their relationship will continue and that the photographs will not be shared with others intentionally or unintentionally … A number of teenagers want to let their friends know of their sexual prowess. Pictures are excellent evidence of an individual's exploits … It is not unreasonable to assume that the immature relationship between the co-defendants would eventually end. The relationship has neither the sanctity of law nor the stability of maturity or length.[69]

B. Fully Clothed but "Provocative": The Dost Factors

Cellphone porn has expanded the range of pornographic images that circulate in society and that has necessarily compelled the criminal justice system to continue its regulation of pornography. As noted in the introduction to this chapter, new technology results in new forms of criminality, especially in terms of sexual deviance. Cellphone porn has drawn more minors into the world of nudity, sexuality, and pornography and this, too, has necessitated a legal response such as the law as set forth in the U.S. Supreme Court cases of *New York v. Ferber*[70] and *Osborne v. Ohio*.[71] In the realm of minors and pornography taken with cellphones or digital cameras, the legal question boils down to "pornographic," bearing in mind there is no First Amendment protection in any type of case where a child is depicted pornographically.

New contexts of porn having emerged in recent years aided by digital technology. Sometimes a minor may not be nude at all. While fully clothed, the image can still be suggestive or "provocative" and, hence, illegal. This means the pose of the body, facial expression, hairstyle, clothing, etc., have a degree of sex appeal and are more or less sexualized. If a picture contains a fully clothed minor, shouldn't it always be legal? Could a picture of a minor ever be illegal if the person in the picture is fully clothed?

In *U.S. v. Dost*, the court sought to provide interpretation of federal law which prohibits the "lascivious exhibition of the genitals or pubic area" as found in 18 U.S.C. 2255(2)(E), the federal child pornography statute.[72] In the facts, the defendant had taken approximately 22 photos of minor children. While some of the pictures were obviously "pornographic" some of the others involved the subject fully clothed, but posed provocatively. The court had to decide if the pictures of a fully clothed minor were legal or illegal.

The court spelled out the six "Dost Factors" to determine whether an image (even an image of a fully clothed minor) constitutes a "lascivious exhibition of the genitals or pubic area." Of course, the picture need not involve all of these factors to be a "lascivious exhibition of the genitals or pubic area." The determination will have to be made based on the overall content of the visual depiction, taking into account the age of the minor.[73]

1. whether the focal point of the visual depiction is on the child's genitalia or pubic area;

2. whether the setting of the visual depiction is sexually suggestive, i.e., in a place or pose generally associated with sexual activity;

3. whether the child is depicted in an unnatural pose, or in inappropriate attire, considering the age of the child;

4. whether the child is fully or partially clothed, or nude;

5. whether the visual depiction suggests sexual coyness or a willingness to engage in sexual activity;

6. whether the visual depiction is intended or designed to elicit a sexual response in the viewer.[74]

The court elaborated, providing some context to the six Dost Factors and noted that a fully clothed subject can constitute illegal pornography.

Flirting and romantic gestures involves sending revealing images via text. Such activity can constitute the crime of the intentional distribution of illegal pornography.

> For example, consider a photograph depicting a young girl reclining or sitting on a bed, with a portion of her genitals exposed. Whether this visual depiction contains a "lascivious exhibition of the genitals" will depend on other aspects of the photograph. If, for example, she is dressed in a sexually seductive manner, with her open legs in the foreground, the photograph would most likely constitute a lascivious exhibition of the genitals. The combined effect of the setting, attire, pose, and emphasis on the genitals is designed to elicit a sexual response in the viewer, albeit perhaps not the "average viewer," but perhaps in the pedophile viewer. On the other hand, if the girl is wearing clothing appropriate for her age and is sitting in an ordinary way for her age, the visual depiction may not constitute a "lascivious exhibition" of the genitals, despite the fact that the genitals are visible.[75]

The court used the Dost Factors to affirm the conviction of the defendant and, in doing so, provided greater clarity around the law of minors, pictures, and cellphone pornography.[76] A picture of a fully clothed minor can be a federal offense.

C. Fully Nude but Legal

The 1994 case of *United States v. Knox* (below) held that a cellphone image could constitute the lascivious exhibition of the genitals" even if a minor is wearing clothes.[77] The Dost case (above), and the Dost Factors also provide for a finding of guilt even if the minor is fully clothed.[78] If the courts can become very uncomfortable with pictures of minors fully clothed, but posing provocatively/sexually for the camera lens, we can certainly imagine that the courts are not going to be very comfortable with nude pictures of minors, even if the pictures do not have a trace of sex appeal to them.

But while the courts may not legally approve of such imagery, there are far too many cases of family pictures or classic works of art that would be criminalized under such a blanket prohibition. Numerous contexts exist where young persons are captured in a picture with the family and may happen to be partly nude. Examples include innocent swim parties in the privacy of the backyard, or summer vacations and pictures of the family enjoying a trip to a cabin in the mountains.

Many courts believe in the protections of the First Amendment and are aware of the tinge of state control inherent in the chilling of speech when the speech is otherwise innocuous and socially acceptable. It is the duty of the courts to uphold constitutional rights and protect the principles of democracy such as free speech, including pictures, photographs, and digital images.

In the case of *U.S. v. Villard*, the accused transported across state lines what appeared to be a magazine that depicted sexual activity. An FBI agent stopped the defendant and, while on camera and taping the conversation, asked him about the content of the magazine. The transcripts of part of the conversation between the FBI agent (Feltman), and the accused (Villard) are found immediately below (the FBI agent is working undercover).

Feltman: Would you keep them books at home, or do you consider them too risque?

Villard: No. I don't keep them out where you can see them at home. But I keep them on a (unintelligible)

Feltman: I mean they have hard ones and I'm surprised that …

Villard: Just that one. That one, I don't keep them around the house with a hard on.

Feltman: What the Wonderboy one.

Villard: Yeah.

Feltman: Yeah. I mean some of the other pictures in there were …

Villard: No hard he's laying in the bed, just flopped up. I mean, it's you know, it's really not hard, there's no sexual activity going on.

Feltman: Yeah. Still, it's, huh, I think in some places just an erection will qualify as …

Villard: Yeah, I'm saying it's not erect really.

Feltman: Huh.

Villard: If he's standing up to make sure it's an erection wouldn't you.

Feltman: Uh huh.

Villard: And everything else is obviously, you know, innocent.

With no pictures or magazines available at all, and no other evidence other than the taped conversation above (a longer edition was used in court), Villard was indicted by a federal grand jury on charges of possessing child pornography in violation of 18 U.S.C. § 2252, the federal child pornography statute. Without seeing any pictures of any minors or anyone else, a jury convicted Villard and sentenced him to 121 months (10 years) in federal prison.[79]

Immediately after the conviction, Villard motioned the court for a judgment of acquittal (asked for the judge to overrule the jury verdict). The judge granted the motion, overruled the jury's decision, and aquitted Villard of the charges.[80]

The state appealed, but the appellate court upheld the dismissal of the case and the overruling of the jury decision. The appeals court reasoned:

> Whatever the exact parameters of "lascivious exhibition," we find it less readily discernable than the other, more concrete types of sexually explicit conduct listed in Section 2256 [of the statute]. The language of the statute makes clear that the depictions must consist of more than merely nudity; otherwise, inclusion of the term "lascivious" would be meaningless. The legislative history of the statute indicates, however, that an exhibition of the genitals need not meet the standard for obscenity in order to be considered lascivious. See *United States v. Dost,* 636 F. Supp. 828, 831 (S.D.Cal. 1986).[81]

> The district court determined that, absent the pictures themselves, the evidence presented in this case provided an insufficient basis for the jury to conclude beyond a reasonable doubt that the individual depicted was engaged in sexually explicit conduct—specifically, "lascivious exhibition of the genitals."[82]

> For the reasons discussed above, we will affirm the district court's judgment of acquittal.[83]

Additional Court Cases: Cellphone Porn

U.S. v. Knox

32 F.3d 733 (3d Cir. 1994)

CASE SUMMARY

PROCEDURAL POSTURE: The United States Supreme Court remanded for the court to reconsider its affirmance of the defendant's conviction for violating the Protection of Children against Sexual Exploitation Act, 18 U.S.C.S. § 2251 et seq., in light of the government's brief advancing the new argument that the appropriate inquiry under 18 U.S.C.S. § 2252(a) was whether the child acted or posed lasciviously.

OVERVIEW: The defendant was convicted of violating 18 U.S.C.S. §§ 2252(a), 2256(2)(E), arising from his possession of videotapes depicting minor females striking provocative poses while wearing abbreviated clothing. It was undisputed that the children were not nude and that their genitals and pubic areas were covered. The court originally affirmed the conviction. Responding to the defendant's petition for certiorari to the Supreme Court, the government changed its position and argued that while complete nudity was not required for a criminal exhibition, a criminal exhibition did require that the body parts be visible or discernible in some fashion and that the lasciviousness requirement applied to the actions of the child. On remand from the Supreme Court, the court considered and rejected the government's new argument. The court held that the phrase "lascivious exhibition" meant a display in order to attract attention to the genitals or pubic area of the children to stimulate the viewer sexually, and that lascivious intent on the part of the child subject was not required. The court held that its interpretation did not render the statute unconstitutionally overbroad or vague.

OUTCOME: The court affirmed the defendant's conviction, because the federal child pornography statute did not contain a requirement that the child subject's genitals or pubic area be fully or partially exposed or discernible, and the requirement of lasciviousness applied to the exhibition of the child's body rather any act, pose, or intent on the part of the child subject.[84]

Computer Exhibitionism

S tanford University professor Alvin Cooper notes, "Sex is an integral part of the Internet," such that 9 million individuals "log on daily for sexual pursuits."[85] Live strip shows, nude dancing, and various other sex-related performances may be seen for a fee on the Internet. One popular website, which has a market value of over $158 million, is the publicly traded Private Media Group. In addition to a plethora of pictures and adult videos available on the Internet, one of the many websites owned by Private Media Group, Privatelive.com, as well as several of its competitors, also offers live sex shows and interactive masturbation performances to its subscribers for a monthly fee or by the minute.[86] This type of live video streaming is dubbed as "the hottest ticket item among the pornicopia of online products available."[87]

Because Web users provide compensation for these types of sexual activities, local prosecutors could potentially target website owners and Internet performers for prosecution under pandering, pimping, and prostitution laws, while website subscribers, who purchase this type of service, would be like "johns" and may be prosecuted under solicitation statutes. Several of the states that outlaw prostitution provide very broad language in their prostitution statutes, where physical contact is not necessarily an element of the crime. For example, California's disorderly conduct statute describes "prostitution" as "any lewd act between persons for money or other consideration."[88] In Arizona, prostitution also occurs when a customer pays another to engage in sexual activities with a third person while the customer only views the sexual acts.[89] However, in New York (see *N.Y. v. Greene* below) a conviction for prostitution requires sexual contact with another [live] human being.[90] Prostitution statues vary by state, and evolve with community social mores.

In cases of providing sex for a fee, it is well established that "live theatrical performances" are protected by the First Amendment so long as they are free from the involvement of minors or obscenity of some form.[91] Exhibitionists on the Internet are like actors and actresses in motion pictures. Meaning, the Web consumer is not physically present where the sexual acts occur online and views the sexual performance through the lens of a computer monitor. Although the sexual performers may be giving live, "semiprivate" presentations, there is potentially a great distance separating the customer from the performer. When it comes to cases of a sex show for a fee, a court could reasonably rule that the live Web performances are identical to either a legal live sex show or legal adult film. So long as the live sex performance maintains some artistic value, such as including a storyline for the audience, these services are less likely to be illegal and found obscene since the Miller test for obscenity is a lack of any artistic value.[92]

Opponents of digital exhibitionism would encourage criminal liability of some kind such as with a prostitution law. A membership fee to view a live sex show could easily constitute solicitation. Some of these Web viewers pay up to $49.95 for a 20-minute show. As a result, so long as the Web performers engage in sexual acts either before or after the Web user agrees to pay for such services, that Web user's activities will likely violate prostitution statutes. It is unclear whether payment of a fee to gain access to view a performance already in progress, and not at the request of the Web user, would constitute solicitation. Opponents would probably view prostitution convictions of Web users and Internet performers as a means to reduce the exposure of indecent adult materials to minors who may inadvertently come across the material. Opponents may also advocate for a greater role of the criminal law in live sex shows by computer to decrease the amount of immoral behavior on the Internet. They would adopt a paternalistic view of the Internet and restrict "the adult population ... to only what is fit for children to view."[93]

Even if the Web performers' activities may constitute prostitution, several of these actors and performers are beyond the jurisdiction of American laws, because these sexual acts occur in foreign countries. For example, the live sex shows that occur on Private Media Group's website, Privatelive.com, occur in Barcelona, Spain. Although the actual sex act occurs outside the U.S., the American Web user who views or interacts with the sexual performer in Spain still may be guilty of solicitation of prostitution and could be prosecuted in the U.S.[94]

Sheer numbers alone, however, suggest support for computer exhibitionism.[95] Millions of users see these types of websites as part of a set of constitutional rights. In addition, many also see live sex shows on the Internet as providing entrepreneurial opportunities to women, many of whom have been successful. Twenty-eight-year-old Lori Michaels, the founder of Dreamy. com, is a "self-made millionaire" from the proceeds of her site, where users pay $9.95 per month for access.[96] Danni Ashe, a retired stripper, owns a website that generates over 5 million hits every day.[97]

Definition of the Offense

It is yet to be decided whether a person who provides consideration to gain access to an adult website and subsequently views a live sex show or directs an Internet performer to masturbate is engaging in criminal behavior. The types of criminal acts that could potentially be applied to the paying Web user include prostitution, solicitation of prostitution, pimping, pandering, placing or permitting placement of wife in a house of prostitution, keeping or residing in a house used for prostitution, and leasing an apartment with the knowledge that it will be used for prostitution.

Arguments Made By The Prosecution

State attempts to address computer sex-related exhibitionism are a tall order for many reasons. First, the state has to find evidence that the show, dance, performance, etc., fails the Miller Test and lacks any social or artistic value and, hence, is obscene and can be subject to criminal sanction. In cases where a minor is involved, the state has to determine, via the Dost Factors or other legal analysis, if the show, etc., is wrongfully "provocative." If so, the state secondly has the burden of establishing jurisdiction. Where are the parties located? And third, the state has to go find the accused parties, also a possible insurmountable obstacle.

Arguments Made By The Defense

The accused parties' best bet may be to actually elude discovery more than their defense can beat the case in court. Assuming a defense is prepared, the offenders can always argue the definition of obscenity and lewdness and allege that the exhibition was not intended to excite sexual arousal. The First Amendment is an important avenue the defense can go down as well as fighting issues pertaining to extradition and jurisdiction. The defense can also take advantage of amicus curiae briefs—supporting briefs filed by a voluminous number of other parties who do not want the Internet to be policed.

Variations of the Law of Computer Exhibitionism

A. Digital Zoning for Virtual Adult Entertainment

The social goal of the states and Congress in protecting children from harmful materials online cannot be achieved in a way that places impermissible burdens on free speech for adults. In the words of the Supreme Court, the Government may not "reduce the adult population ... to reading only what is fit for children."[98] As a result, Congress faces a dilemma: The legislature has not found a way to prevent children from viewing harmful materials online without infringing on an adult's ability to access protected speech. Ultimately, the problem comes down to a simple distinction—Congress has the ability to regulate some pornographic material even though it is constitutionally protected for adults because the standard for obscenity varies when applied to minors rather than adults. Digital zoning is one possible solution to the dilemma.[99]

The Internet is a global marketplace for ideas[100] Congress does not have jurisdiction to legislate over all the material that exists online, so it should not even try. The Internet provides a vast resource of material that anyone with a connection can access; it opens a user up to the global community, and to the different cultures, perspectives, and ideas. It is a medium that reaches the global community, whether one wants it to or not, and thus it is unlike any medium for the expression of ideas the world has known.

There are a number of approaches the government can take to limit minors' access to websites containing harmful materials, without interfering with adult access to constitutionally protected material. A zoning approach that allows the government to protect against this problem will regulate access by minors without any infringement on adult ability to access constitutionally protected material.

A zoning approach allows for the regulation of pornography in the virtual world to take the form of pornography regulation in the real world and place, for example, adult bookstores in specifically zoned areas of a city. Present forms of pornography regulation require those who want access to such materials to take affirmative steps to access such materials rather than confront them on accident.[102] Zoning regulation does this by keeping adult bookstores away from residential neighborhoods, and adult videos are reserved for a secluded section of the video store; strip clubs and bars exist only in certain parts of town. Real world zoning of activities and materials not fit for children is possible because age verification in the real world is relatively simple. To make zoning possible on the Internet, one must solve, or avoid, the age verification problems of Internet technology.[101]

While the age verification problem has led some commentators to conclude that zoning on the Internet is both economically infeasible and unworkable under current technology, there is one version of zoning that avoids the technological difficulties of verifying age on the Internet. By zoning harmful materials online into their own Internet domain, e.g., .net, .com, .edu, etc., the age verification problem can be avoided. This is because such a system could operate without the need to verify age online, but rather by verifying age the same way bars and adult bookstores verify age: by physically looking at an ID of the consumer who wants to look at a legal sex show online.

Zoning on the Internet can occur by placing all adult performances and other pornographic material on the Internet into one "area" of cyberspace.[102] It is possible to seclude pornography online the same way adult videos are secluded in their own section of the video store. This occurs by creating a separate domain name for all sex-related materials. Establishing a new domain for porn would require all websites containing such material to register under the new domain name, such as .xxx, .sex, and .obs (for obscene) as possible examples. This would ensure, at the very least, that no one, including minors, stumbles across illicit material online accidentally.

Nevertheless, even a separate domain in and of itself does not solve the problem of child access. There has to be some screening mechanism to ensure that minors do not have access to this domain. Otherwise, a child could go to the domain just as an adult could. In addition to the separate domain of .xxx, the access to the domain can be regulated. Access to the domain could be allowed in the same way access to strip clubs and adult bookstores is allowed: by making those who desire such access to take affirmative steps to gain access.

The system could work in the following manner: in the main, the .xxx domain would be inaccessible to all. To access the domain, an individual would have to purchase software that would enable access. By restricting the number of locations where this software would be available to purchase, the system would allow age verification to take place in the real world. To access the .xxx porn, an individual would be required to go to an adult bookstore or adult video store and purchase the software that would allow access to the .xxx domain. In such a transaction, the age verification problem is solved. Zoning online would allow for realistic age verification, which is the same mechanism that allows for age verification in the real world.[103] This zoning solution would take one aspect of the Internet and return it to the way it was before the Internet existed, at least with regard to access. By doing so, such a system would ensure that minors had no access to sex-related adult content online.

B. Digital Nuisance Abatement

Illegal sex shows, prostitution, and obscene imagery on the Internet, as noted, are difficult for the government to regulate. It should also be noted that obscene sex shows on the Internet are unpopular with federal prosecutors because the cases are difficult and consume valuable prosecutorial time and resources. Many federal prosecutors won't bother with an obscenity case unless a child is involved. Knowing this, systems operators of web-based adult entertainment exploit their opportunity. Pornographers and website operators know how to tone it down just enough (while still creating entertainment) so as not to produce obviously obscene entertainment that could result in a fine, jail time, and a loss of license. If federal prosecutors do investigate and prosecute a web-based obscenity case, it is often a long, drawn-out affair. Web-based obscenity cases are subject to a long trial by jury to allow for a detailed presentation of evidence to determine if the activity or material was a violation of community standards, admittedly a tough task in view of the amorphous Internet community. Additionally, in many cases, the defendant pornographer is often wealthy and able to conduct an elaborate court defense, all of which costs time and money for the federal prosecutorial effort to confront alleged illegal sex on the Internet.[104]

Since prosecutions are costly, defendants crafty, and jury trials uncertain, live sex shows and other forms of adult entertainment on the Internet may be managed differently, such as with nuisance abatement. Nuisance abatement laws have been used throughout the history of the U.S.[105] They were used widely for "new" social ills such as excess smoke, fumes, noise, water pollution, and even the loss of light and air that came with the industrial revolution in the late 19th century. Nuisance laws—even to this day—also regulate "moral nuisance" such as saloons, brothels, and dance halls, and also brick-and-mortar businesses that sell obscenity.[106]

A legal nuisance is "an unreasonable interference with a right common to the general public." Either the state or an individual can bring a public nuisance action if the individual can show a "special injury distinct from that suffered by the public at large." Courts use the nuisance remedy to address pervasive harms that seem minor at first, but that cause injury to the public when they persist for a long time.[107]

When it comes to the sale of obscene materials, many states allow public nuisance lawsuits against adult theaters and bookstores. Even under California law, the undisputed capital of the American pornography industry, "public nuisance laws may properly be employed to regulate the exhibition of obscene material to 'consenting adults.'" California's general nuisance statute, which applies to obscene material, states, "[a]nything which is injurious to health, including ... [that which] is indecent or offensive to the senses ... so as to interfere with the comfortable enjoyment of life or property ... is a nuisance." The broad language of the California law is a codification of the Common Law of nuisance.[108] One of the first applications of nuisance law on the Internet was a recent nuisance suit against Craigslist for facilitating prostitution.[109] Craigslist was able to prevail in court by using the "Good Samaritan" provision of the Communications Decency Act, but the case was a good example of using the legal theory of nuisance for Internet obscenity.

Another application of "Nuisance Abatement" and obscenity on the Internet concerns Internet sales of cigarettes to minors. In the case of *City of New York v. Smokes-Spirits.com, Inc.,* the City of New York discovered an internet-based cigarette sales website and also that minors were the customers at the site.[110] The City argued that the sale of cigarettes over the Internet was a "serious threat to public health, safety, and welfare, to the funding of health care, and to the economy of the state," and therefore, that common law public nuisance should apply.

The trial court dismissed the public nuisance claim, finding that "the number of cigarette sales over the Internet was 'small ... compared to brick and mortar sales' and that the City had not alleged a harm that 'endangers ... the public at large.'"

The City appealed the case and, based on the state's interest in protecting public health, the Second Circuit Court of Appeals reversed the trial court's dismissal and remanded the public nuisance question back to the state court for another hearing. The Second Circuit's willingness to let a public nuisance claim proceed based on the Internet sale of cigarettes suggests a future for nuisance in the legal landscape of the Internet.[111]

The ultimate goal of any nuisance suit against a website featuring obscene content would be injunctive relief. Injunctive relief is a court order and preludes any type of formal trial. An injunction against obscenity comes primarily in the form of an abatement injunction. An abatement injunction prohibits the distribution of materials that a court deems obscene in an abatement hearing. Such an injunction that comports with the Miller Test raises few constitutional issues and is a relatively more straightforward legal procedure.

With nuisance law, the state can target obscenity manufacturers online without the unpredictable enforcement of a jury trial with wealthy pornographers since nuisance is a civil injunction to desist. Nuisance law also offers procedural advantages to criminal law. Primarily, civil nuisance actions do not require proof beyond a reasonable doubt to get an injunction.

C. Cyberprostitution

As unusual as it may seem, computer technology has progressed to the point where two people sitting at their respective computer terminals can sexually stimulate one another with controls and devices attached to the USB port on the participants' computers. Hence, people can have sex with computers. They may live miles apart from each other, or just across the street. With the technology, it is as though one person is sexually touching the other, but uses a type of video game control handle to direct a tool that is on or around a person's genitals. While each persons' built-in computer camera shows the faces and bodies of each other, each person uses the "gaming controls" to stimulate the other to orgasm.[112] High-quality audio speakers and high-resolution monitors make the experience close to a real-life experience. If a fee or account is established for the participation in this activity, the term that can be used to describe the transaction is cyberprostitution.

Cyberprostitution may be defined as a virtual phenomenon that results in a sexual experience by at least one party who is not physically proximate to another and where the sexual transaction transpires in real-time through computer peripherals that communicate sensual audio, visual, and tactile communication. In cyberprostitution, at least one party remotely controls a computer peripheral that contacts the genitals of the other with physical apparatus like those that control a video game or Wii.[113] Since prostitution is a crime in most states, systems operators, ISPs, and the participants may be criminally liable for engaging in web-based prostitution.

Because of the difficulty of regulating the Internet, discussed in the Legal Background at the start of the chapter, the court system has not yet ruled on the legality of cyberprostitution. With the history of failures of policing vice on the Internet, it is not likely these kinds of cases will emerge in the near future. That said, the *N.Y. v. Greene* case is a good analogy for why a traditional prostitution statute is inapplicable to a case of cyberprostitution.

In *N.Y. v. Greene*, a female adult was paid by a male adult in a face-to-face setting to sexually stimulate herself to orgasm while the man watched.[114] The man was a voyeur and sought to engage in voyeurism. The parties were caught and both were charged and convicted under New York prostitution statute, Section 230.00 of the New York Penal Law, which states: "A person is guilty of prostitution when such person engages or agrees or offers to engage in sexual conduct with another person in return for a fee."[115] The female appealed, arguing that what she was charged with was inapplicable because the acts that she agreed to engage in would not, if performed by her, constitute "sexual conduct with another" as that phrase is used in section 230.00 of the Penal Law. Her main point was that she was not "with another person," did not touch anyone, and did not engage in sexual contact with anyone. The appeals court agreed with her and sided with the accused and reversed the decision of the trial court. The appellate court judge stated:

> It is clear that the Legislature did not intend section 230.00 of the Penal Law to proscribe commercial agreements to engage in any and all kinds of sexual conduct. Certainly, had the Legislature intended to proscribe the sale of all sexual conduct it could well have done so by excluding from section 230.00 the phrase 'with another person'. The inclusion of that phrase in section 230.00 connotes, at least, that the accused's agreement must, to be criminal, contemplate physical contact between the accused and one other person. Were section 230.00 intended to proscribe agreements by which only the accused "prostitute" was to engage in sexual conduct, while for example, the beneficiary was to act only as voyeur—that is, agreements to engage in sexual conduct for another person and without physical contact between them—it would have been necessary for the Legislature simply to proscribe all agreements to engage in sexual conduct for a fee.

More significantly, were the phrase 'sexual conduct with another person' to be interpreted as proscribing agreements calling for sexual conduct to be performed for another person, as well as with another person, section 230.00 of the Penal Law would surely intrude upon areas of behavior traditionally protected by the First Amendment to the United States Constitution.[116]

Additional Court Cases: Computer Exhibitionism

Voyeur Dorm, L.C. v. City of Tampa

265 F.3d 1232 (11th Cir. 2001)

CASE SUMMARY

PROCEDURAL POSTURE: The United States District Court for the Middle District of Florida, granted summary judgment in favor of defendant City of Tampa, on the ground that plaintiff entertainment company which offered adult entertainment over the internet, was an adult use facility in violation of Tampa's City Code, Tampa, Fla., Code § 27-523. The entertainment company appealed.

OVERVIEW: The issue before the appellate court was whether the Tampa, Florida Code § 27-523 applied to the activities that were alleged to have occurred in a residential neighborhood. The district agreed with Tampa's argument that the entertainment company was an adult use business pursuant to § 27-523 and therefore could not operate in a residential neighborhood. The entertainment company argued that it was not an adult use business, and that the code applied to locations or premises wherein adult entertainment was actually offered to the public. It further argued that because the public did not physically attend the location to enjoy adult entertainment, such location did not fall with the purview of the code. The court held that, since the offering occurred when the videotaped images were dispersed over the Internet and into the public eye for consumption, the code could not be applied to a location that did not offer adult entertainment to the public. The district court misapplied the code because it erroneously determined that the alleged activities constituted a public offering of adult entertainment as contemplated by § 27-523.

OUTCOME: The judgment of the district court was reversed.[117]

Internet Enticement of Minors

Internet chat channels and networks have become favorites for millions of people to communicate online. These chat channels were a precursor to the popular forms of digitized social networking we know of today. Many chat channels and Internet domains are for purposes of social contacts and also love, sex, and relationship exploration and formation. Numerous types of social chat occur on these sites daily and presumably most participants are interested in just that: chatting in a digital environment that is safe, anonymous, and invulnerable to physical threat. Most people engage in chat for personal enjoyment unrelated to sexual content. That is why these sites are so popular—almost everyone seeks to avoid the prospect of face-to-face exchanges that lead to role definition, confused expectations, and complicated emotional entanglements. In terms of sheer numbers, the actual number of face-to-face meetings that are a byproduct of original digital chat are extremely low.[118]

Enticement cases are an offshoot of Internet chat where the chat participants originally became acquainted by having conversations via the Internet. The original conversation could have begun in any number of contexts, such as talking about a mutually favorite local sports team or possibly a chatroom devoted to the topic of skateboarding and snowboarding. Most such discussion is between two or more adults and the law is typically not invoked. However, the media and law enforcement community have popularized sex-related Internet chat between an adult and a minor and strict laws have been created and are enforced aggressively today.[119]

The phenomena of adults who lurk around the Internet looking for strange things to do is now well established. Many of these Web wanderers look for minors to chat with. By 2002, an estimated 45 million children were expected to be online, giving cyber-stalking persons a huge pool of potential victims from which to choose.[120] As one federal prosecutor told a jury in a 1999 case involving a man accused of raping a 14-year-old girl after using Internet chatrooms to bait her to a motel, "[t]he Internet is a powerful tool that can be used for good, but it's also a powerful tool for predators looking to prey on young girls." Or, as a prosecutor in Orange County, California recently put it, the Internet "really is the promised land for child molesters."[121]

Not only have most of the fifty states passed laws prohibiting the use of the Internet to communicate with children in a sexual manner, Congress has also expanded the federal child sex crime law to ensure that the practice of Internet luring can be prosecuted.[122] In addition, the U.S. Departments of Justice[123] and Office of Homeland Security[124] have both established programs targeting Internet predation of children.

In sum, enticement cases represent a small minority of chat scenarios, ones where the participants are not two adults, and where the adult has an odd and medically unusual affection for minors. Even in such unusual scenarios, the adult often contains the interaction to merely chat, but in a smaller number of cases, the adult asks to meet the minor face-to-face for friendship with the latent possibility of having sexual contact and such a request is a serious affront to the law. Since the legal intent on the part of the adult offender is established in the request to meet the minor for sex, the request constitutes the illegal enticement of a minor and is prosecuted as such.

To catch online predators, law enforcement officials often go online and pose as youngsters. FBI agents, for instance, probe chatrooms "identified as popular meeting places for predators and their [young] victims." These undercover sting operations are so common today that Shari Steele, an attorney for the Electronic Frontier Foundation, recently remarked that "[t]he vast majority of 12- to 14-year-old girls hanging out in chatrooms with sexually explicit titles to them are most likely cops, and if pedophiles don't realize that, they're pretty stupid."[125]

Definition of the Offense

According to federal law, Title 18, U.S.C. 2422, **Internet enticement** may be defined as a form of coercion and enticement as follows:

> Knowingly persuading, inducing, enticing or coercing an individual to travel in interstate or foreign commerce with the purpose of engaging in prostitution or any criminal sexual activity, or attempting to do so, and imposes a maximum punishment of 10 years' imprisonment and/or a fine under Title 18.[126]

Elements of the Offense

The elements to the crime of Internet solicitation of a minor for sex that must be proven beyond a reasonable doubt are:

1. uses a computer or similar device;
2. to contact a person whom he knows or believes to be a minor;
3. to solicit, encourage, entice, or lure him or her;
4. for the purposes of engaging in sexual activity in violation of state laws[127]

Sample Statute

The state of Wisconsin statute on the Internet solicitation of a minor for sex reads as follows:

> Wisconsin Revised Statute § 948.075:

(1) Whoever uses a computerized communication system to communicate with an individual who the actor believes or has reason to believe has not attained the age of 16 years with intent to have sexual contact or sexual intercourse with the individual ... is guilty of a Class D felony.

(2) This section does not apply if, at the time of the communication, the actor reasonably believed that the age of the person to whom the communication was sent was no more than 24 months less than the age of the actor.[128]

Arguments Made By The Prosecution

The evidence in these cases is incontrovertible. The state will be in possession of word-for-word transcripts typed into the computer by the accused. That's one reason the state is interested in these cases—the evidence can be squeaky clean. In addition, the digital tools used to collect, store, and retrieve the transcripts have been shown to be reliable, if properly used, and hence the evidence is usually easily admitted into a court of law.

Arguments Made By The Defense

The defense has some room to work when it comes to enticement cases. First, if the conversation is not directly sex related (most of the time it is), the defense can argue that the chatting was merely for social purposes and not about sexuality. Second, even if the conversation involves the prospect of a physical meeting, there may be ambiguity about the purpose of the meeting. Possibly, the meeting is only for socializing. Third, the defense will want to examine the law in their jurisdiction because the statute may require an actual victim rather than an undercover officer posing as a victim. Lastly, the defense will want to examine the case for a possible entrapment scenario where the government might have been too aggressive in setting up the case.

Variations of the Law of Internet Enticement of Minors

A. Unscrupulous Vigilantism

Vigilante parties are not new across the horizon of criminal detection. Many private parties have taken it upon themselves to try and catch a criminal as a way to demonstrate their desire to maintain a safe and just world. The problem with vigilantes is that they often commit a crime in order to stop a crime. For example, they may break into homes to catch people, beat up a criminal to coerce information on other criminals, pay prostitutes to sleep with a crooked politician, and so forth.

Internet vigilantes have proliferated in proportion to the influx of Internet-based child pornography and the moral panic of enticement cases. Numerous private groups police the Internet, following 802.11 signals, eavesdropping on unsecured connections, and engaging in illegal firewall breaches (hacking) to lure someone who is thought to be trolling for a minor. Cyber vigilante groups engage in a quest for power in the same manner as an insecure child sex offender engages a minor in a quest for self-affirmation. Some of these groups include PedoWatch, Net Nanny, Predator Hunter, and their respective Cyber Posses. Paradoxically, many vigilantes practice the same type of enticement and predatory behavior employed by predatory sex offenders. In many cases, it is not possible to distinguish between the two groups.

In 2004, a major television network, MSNBC, began a reality television series produced by affiliate *Dateline NBC* titled "To Catch a Predator." The series showed the world of an undercover sting operation and was produced by Lynn Keller. In the series, an adult posed as a 14- or 15-year-old girl and enticed a 40-something male into a conversation. The posing party would carefully lure the 40-something into a conversation about sexual relations. The conversations may span several weeks, but before long, the posing adult would have succeeded in getting the predator to travel to a home with the idea of engaging in sexual contact with a 14- or 15-year-old female. Once the unsuspecting party was inside the home, a journalist-correspondent named Chris Hansen emerged from an adjacent room along with a camera crew where he titillated himself by shaming and humiliating the predator who was obviously a guilty party. Before the predator could leave, the local police were standing by to make an arrest for the crime of Internet enticement of a minor for sex.

The practices employed by the various entities involved in the show were unscrupulous and deceitful.[129] MSNBC wanted to use this show to arouse the general public and reinforce the public hatred for a group of sexual deviants. In so doing, MSNBC was able to boost its television ratings for purposes of profit maximization. To pull off its caper, MSNBC hired the services of a cyber vigilante group called Perverted Justice and paid them $100,000 for their work.

The job of Perverted Justice was to go online and ensnare unsuspecting, lonely men into a web of illegal chat and then have the offenders subject to shame and ridicule on the television show.[130] MSNBC was not interested in objective journalism. Rather, it was acting more in the capacity of the purveyor of a witch hunt. It was not reporting a story like a credible news show, but rather, *creating a story* by preying on the irrational fears of a gullible public.[131] As for Perverted Justice, they were being paid and therefore, like a prostitute, did anything to lure and entice suspects, or risk losing their lucrative contract.[132] Spin-offs of this reality show have been created such as "To Catch a Con Man," "To Catch an ID Thief," and "To Catch a Car Thief."

Most men who were caught in the MSNBC/Perverted Justice tryst pleaded guilty when faced with a criminal indictment so as to get away from the public attention as quickly as possible. Most offenders won't appeal their cases and address injustices because the social approbation is so biased, it dissuades any attempt to achieve justice. One suspect, however, stood up and defended himself against the actions of MSNBC and Perverted Justice. In the case of *State of California v. Wolin*, an oncologist named Maurice Wolin was chatting in a chatroom with a member of Perverted Justice who was posing as a minor.[133] Wolin told the pseudo-minor he didn't want to do anything sexual and was merely chatting. The "minor" then engaged in a series of aggressive taunts, dares, and challenges, doing anything to try and get Wolin to agree to meet—not for sex—just to meet face-to-face. The Perverted Justice decoy taunted Wolin and called him "just a chicken and a liar and a ditcher and a player." Eventually, Wolin agreed to a meeting where he was arrested by the police who worked with Perverted Justice.

Wolin hired a celebrity defense attorney and has successfully defended himself while also exposing the unscrupulous, devious, and unprincipled actions by both MSNBC and Perverted Justice. After a preliminary hearing, no trial date has been set and it appears that the case is heading for a dismissal.[134] The television show ceased filming new episodes in December 2007.

B. Social Gatherings as Predicate to a Criminal Act

The Internet has become the next generation's social meeting place. Persons young and old (mostly young) go to the Internet to chat and the subjects can range from knitting to hockey with a million more topics in between. In the case of *Illinois v. Patterson*, the accused (adult) engaged in chat with a "15-year-old minor" (actually a police officer), some of it sexual, but not all of it.[135] The court transcript of their IM conversation is as follows. The accused is Boysneeded and the police officer is Yacoo.

Boysneeded: having problems

Yacoo: yep

Boysneeded: lol

Yacoo: must be the rain

Boysneeded: yes not a good day but good for sex.

Boysneeded: would you like a blow job today?

Yacoo: ya it would be its cold and raining out

Yacoo: id love one

Boysneeded: so want me to cum to you

Boysneeded: are you home a lone

Yacoo: i do but im scard no my moms home

Boysneeded: oh

Yacoo: shes up stairs

Boysneeded: well if she is home i couldnt give a blow job then

Yacoo: if we ment [sic] some where

Boysneeded: where?

Boysneeded: then how would we do anything?

Yacoo: we could drive around and get to know each other then see

Boysneeded: I see so do youu [sic] want to do that ?

Boysneeded: so do you play around with any of you[sic] friends?

Yacoo: maybe we could meet at gurnee mills, no i havnt found a friend to do that with

Boysneeded: when do you want to meet..

Yacoo: whats good for you

Boysneeded: don't know need to get a shower and then a 30 min drive how will i find you?

Yacoo: you know where mcdonalds is

Boysneeded: don't know the area that is good a littel woried about this here about men going to meet young men and they get arrested.[136]

The accused (Boysneeded–Richard Patterson) traveled to the McDonald's for the meeting and was arrested and convicted at trial of attempted sexual abuse of a minor. On appeal, Patterson took the tack to argue about the insufficiency of the evidence. He stated that he chats with numerous people all the time and has met face-to-face with numerous people, many of whom he never intended to have sex with. He argues that he never intended to have sex with Yacoo and that it is no crime to meet someone for a social gathering. The appeals court did not believe the defendant and upheld his conviction and four-year prison sentence. The court stated:

> Defendant argues that he did nothing while at the McDonald's indicative of an intention to perform a sex act with a 15-year-old. Defendant argues that he did not make any overt sexual advances to anyone, did not expose or touch himself, did not approach any youths, and did not make any utterances of a sexual nature while at McDonald's. Defendant thus concludes that there was insufficient evidence from which to conclude that he had the intent to commit aggravated criminal sexual abuse. We disagree.
>
> The evidence in this case was sufficient to prove that defendant possessed the specific intent to commit the offense of aggravated criminal sexual abuse. Defendant offered to perform oral sex on Yacoo that day. Further, defendant arrived at the agreed-upon place, at the agreed-upon time, wearing the clothing he had informed Yacoo he would be wearing and driving the car he had informed Yacoo he would be driving. Additionally,

defendant sent a picture of himself to Yacoo to facilitate Yacoo's identification of defendant at their planned meeting. Last, when [officer] White approached defendant, defendant admitted that he was waiting for a 15-year-old boy named Rob. Viewing this evidence in the light most favorable to the prosecution results in the conclusion that the State provided sufficient evidence of defendant's intent and that the trier of fact could reasonably conclude, beyond a reasonable doubt, that defendant possessed the specific intent to commit aggravated criminal sexual abuse.[137]

Internet chat that involves minors and conversation about human sexuality can be legally scrutinized as unlawful sexual enticement.

C. Police Entrapment

Police officers have to deal with criminal offenders every day and are intimately familiar with numerous offending patterns and behaviors. In addition, in many cases, the officer has very good reason to suspect guilt and that is often why the officer pursues the case; officers will spend less time on suspects where culpability is questionable. Since experienced law enforcement personnel are aware of the tendencies of criminal behavior, they generally know what steps an offender will take to consummate a crime and, often but not always, just wait for the offender to walk into trouble. Or, the officer can subtly induce the offender, knowing most will take the bait.[138] An arrest can be made and trouble possibly averted.

Entrapment occurs when the officer induces an offender to commit a crime who otherwise would not have committed the crime. But, from the foregoing, most offenders are guilty and most officers know it, so why is there a law to prohibit officers from closing the deal? After all, to stand by idly could result in the offender getting away and maybe hurting someone in a future episode.[139]

The reason the law of entrapment exists, despite many offenders being guilty, is that many are not. Meaning, the criminal population is so full of mentally unstable individuals that many officers can easily draw a person into a crime when truly the person was not prone to commit a crime in the first place. Hence, the law of entrapment came about after a shocking number of cases where an innocent party was deceived into a crime by a savvy and experienced police officer.

Enticement cases bring entrapment into sharp relief.[140] Lonely, middle-aged men have joined droves of others in using the Internet to socialize with numerous other people. Depending on where they live, the Internet may be their only opportunity to have contact with the world. Officers have taken advantage of this vulnerable group and tapped into their loneliness and sexual proclivity to create cases of enticement that may have never been there otherwise. Officers will engage men in conversation, leading them to believe a sincere conversation and budding friendship is taking place. Once the officer knows the other person is beginning to feel attracted to the friendship, the conversation becomes friendlier and involves subtle flirtations. At that point, feelings of sexuality are likely, as is a gesture about meeting for romance and/or sex. Officers have become skilled in opening up the heart of lonely 40-year old men on the Internet, then arresting them.[141]

After this sophisticated—and often quite lengthy—process of manipulation and seduction, officers draw the individual away from the computer terminal and out into the real world. The government creates the conditions for a pursuit of a fantasy that, absent governmental contrivances with the powerful forces of sexuality and sexual fantasies, might never have been tapped into.

Priests, lawyers, cops, accountants, firefighters and other "professionals" have all been caught soliciting minors for sex on the Internet.[142] The pattern of entrapment in solicitation cases has been so pervasive that in many cases it seems like it is the officer who is the party preying on the Internet and the lonely middle-aged man who is doing what millions of other people are doing on the Internet, which is browsing around.

One of the most egregious cases of entrapment with enticement is *U.S. v. Poehlman,* a case that was thrown out due to police entrapment.[143] In the case, Mr. Poehlman was a military veteran, married with children. He was also a cross-dresser and when he disclosed this to his wife, she divorced him. Lonely and heartbroken, Poehlman sought solace and friendship in Internet chatrooms, just like millions of others.

In one room he met "Sharon" an undercover female police officer posing as a mother of three minor children. "Sharon" did everything possible in a series of e-mails to get Poehlman to express a sexual interest in "her three children." Poehlman, however, was interested in getting another wife, someone like "Sharon" but this time someone who would not divorce him for his cross-dressing; Poehlman had no interest in the three fabricated children. One of Poehlman's main e-mail messages reads as follows:

> I am retired Air Force after 16.8 years I took the early retirement, decided it was time to get out and work for a living again. I am extremely honest and straight forward type of guy I don't play head games and don't like to have them played against me. I tell you straight out and open that I am a in house tv, meaning I rather enjoy wearing hose and heels inside the house, not around small children of course but when mine are old enough to understand I will tell them that and the big foot fetish I have are about my only two major problems that need a open minded easy going woman, so as they say in the movies if you don't mind me wearing your hose and licking your toes then I am

open for anything [such as helping you in a partnership with me]. I also have a sense of humor. As far as your children are concerned I will treat them as my own (as I would treat my boys if I had them with me). I have huge family values and like kids and they seem to like me alright too. Well now you know all about me, if you are still interested then please write back, if not and I would understand why you didn't then I wish you all the best in finding the person you are looking for. If you wish to call my number is 904-581-5442, I am not home a lot due to work and school but there is an answering machine that only I listen to. Have a nice day.

Mark[144]

Seeing that Poehlman was a tough sell, the officer turned up the heat. The officer told Poehlman that he might be able to join her and her three children, but only if he would express an interest—a special type of interest—in her children. The officer continued to try and get Poehlman to start feeling sexual about her "three children." "Sharon" said she wanted a "special man teacher" for her children. To this Poehlman stated

Hi Sharon,

so happy to finnally learn your name, I am interested in being this special teasher, but in all honesty I really don't know exactly what you expect me to teach them other than proper morals and give support to them where it is needed.[146]

"Sharon" once again rebuffed Poehlman's interest in her, saying: "One thing I should make really clear though, is that there can't be anything between me and my sweethearts special teacher [Poehlman]."[145] The police officer meant that Poehlman was being solicited to have sex with her children and that any type of sincere partnership or marriage was not what Poehlman was being solicited for.

Poehlman and "Sharon" eventually made plans for him to travel to California from his Florida home. After arriving in California, Poehlman proceeded to a hotel room where he met "Sharon" in person. She offered him some pornographic magazines featuring children, which he accepted and examined. Sharon also showed Poehlman photos of her children: Karen, aged 7, Bonnie, aged 10, and Abby, aged 12. She then directed Poehlman to the adjoining room, where he was to meet the children, presumably to give them their first "lesson" (sex) under their mother's protective supervision. Upon entering the room, however, Poehlman was greeted by Naval Criminal Investigation Special Agents, FBI agents, and Los Angeles County sheriff's deputies.[147]

Poehlman never touched anyone, but was charged with attempted lewd acts with a minor in the State of California and convicted. He served one year in state prison. Two years after his release, he was arrested for the exact same offense (double jeopardy)—attempted lewd acts with "Sharon's" children. This time he was charged in federal court for crossing state lines for the purpose of engaging in sex acts with a minor. He was convicted again and sentenced to approximately 10 years in federal prison.[148] Desperate for relief from the injustices, Poehlman appealed, arguing double jeopardy and entrapment.[149]

The appeals court saw the flagrant injustice and dismissed the case. The court found that the government induced Poehlman and manipulated his desire for "Sharon" to make it appear that he had an interest in "Sharon's minor children." The court stated:

> At the initial stages of the e-mail correspondence, the only sexual relationship in which Poehlman expressed any interest was one with "Sharon." It was "Sharon" who first suggested that Poehlman develop an [implicitly sexual] relationship with her daughters, whose young ages, as well as their very existence, were invented by the government. It was also "Sharon" who, in the face of Poehlman's repeated expressions of desire for a relationship with her, made it clear that continuation of the correspondence between them was entirely contingent upon Poehlman's willingness to play the role [with "her" children] which she had in mind for him.[150]

> In their zeal to enforce the law ... government agents may not originate a criminal design, implant in an innocent person's mind the disposition to commit a criminal act, and then induce commission of the crime so that the government may prosecute. *Jacobson v. United States,* 503 U.S. 540, 548, 118 L. Ed. 2d 174, 112 S. Ct. 1535 (1992).[151]

Additional Court Cases: Internet Enticement of Minors

Indiana v. Kemp

753 N.E.2d 47 (2001)

CASE SUMMARY

PROCEDURAL POSTURE: The defendant was charged with attempted child molesting and child solicitation. The Clark Circuit Court (Indiana) dismissed the charges. The State appealed.

OVERVIEW: A police detective entered an Internet chatroom and posed as a 14-year-old girl. The defendant chatted with the detective in the Internet chatroom. The detective, still posing as the 14-year-old girl, made arrangements to meet the defendant for sex. The trial court determined that the offenses of attempted child molesting and child solicitation required that the victim be a child. The appellate court held that the facts alleged in the information did not reach the level of an overt act leading to the commission of child molesting and, therefore, did not constitute an attempt. At most, the allegations only reached the level of preparing or planning to commit an offense. The solicitation statute, Ind. Code § 35-42-4-6, required an urging toward the immediate commission of the crime. The appellate court found that any urging had been done by the detective and not the defendant.

OUTCOME: The judgment was affirmed.[152]

Chapter Seven Summary

Technological advances are designed for the betterment of any society. Motor vehicles, household appliances, and modern communication devices have increased the standards of living for millions of people. There is no doubt, however, that technological advances will eventually be adopted for criminal purposes, such as monetary theft or privacy invasion. Similarly, there is no doubt that new technologies will be used for licit and illicit sexual purposes. This chapter looked at how computers, computer networks, cellphones, and other technologies have been used in a sexually deviant manner and have run up against or violated the law.

The legal question about technological media and material harmful to a minor is not new. Radio and television, in particular, were immediately identified as having a potential to force innocent bystanders, adults and children alike, to listen to or see indecent material that they were not expecting to come across. As a result of this social harm, the government charged the FCC with the mandate to regulate the airwaves, define acceptable content, and sanction licensees and stations that violate content based rules and regulations. Motion pictures are also regulated for content, such as PG and R rated films, and telephone carriers also must abide by regulations, albeit less restrictive than those for television or radio. Next, the Internet has been subject to regulation. Once the Internet became public in 1992, it was filled with pornography and all sorts of love, sex, and relationship information. Instantly, lawmakers sought to regulate the Internet for the same reasons radio, television, and telephones were regulated. However, the features that make the Internet unique are the same features that work against subjecting it to a regulatory framework: It is too vast, changes too often, and users can hide out in too many places. Congress made two bona fide attempts to regulate age-inappropriate content on the Internet and both times—with the CDA and COPA—the U.S. Supreme Court ruled the laws unconstitutional. They were both underinclusive (not able to reach all objectionable content) and overinclusive (made important science, medical, and educational material illegal).[153]

Self regulation—especially by parents—is likely the best strategy for regulating the content on the Internet. Age verification devices, password-protected sites, and a special web-based page rating system assist are useful and effective self-regulation techniques. Filtering software is also used in self-regulation, but the filtering requirements spelled out in the CIPA have done more harm than good for users of the Internet in public libraries.[154]

The Internet is not the only digital medium highly prone to sex-related activity misused by minors. So is the modern cellphone with a large memory, camera, and videorecording device built in. Sexting cases represent the divide between legal conservatism and part of the culture of American teenagers today. Sexting may indeed represent flagrant involvement of minors with pornographic material. But if teenagers were so attracted to pornography, why is it only recently that so many have been involved with it? The answer lies mainly with the use and enjoyment of the cellphone by teen culture today. Nude images sent back and forth from one teenager to another are not so much an issue of pornography, but rather a matter of relating to one another and being silly, which is part of what being a teenager is about. Nudity or seminudity transmitted back and forth between teens who are "dating" has become part of the language of dating among teens and ritualized as a dating norm rather than viewed as a form of unacceptable sexual deviance.

The law of pornography among minors has trouble appreciating the changes that have taken place in the culture for American teens and many teenagers have been legally raked over the coals for doing nothing more than flirting with someone they have a crush on at school. Many teenagers have become convicted felony offenders, have a permanent criminal history, and a lifelong listing on the local sex offender registry for innocently flirting with a classmate. In Pennsylvania, three teenage girls between the ages of 14 and 17 were charged with disseminating child pornography when they sexted their boyfriends.[155] Such sentences may one day be challenged constitutionally as cruel and unusual punishment, since the sentence, in many cases, is out of proportion to the harm caused.

Many states have modified their criminal code to reflect the degree of innocence involved in sexting and many states can now prosecute sexting as a low-level misdemeanor with a conviction requiring no placement on the sex offender registry. In cases where sexting is flagrant and involves obscenity and more serious harm, traditional obscenity laws may apply. Since the realm of sexting can easily get out of control, and nude images have been circulated without the consent of the person whose picture was taken, this chapter also covered the civil law of emotional distress for cases where nude photos are sent to unsuspecting parties without anyone's consent.

Cellphone technology has advanced greatly and the prices of the devices are so reasonable, we might say that nearly everyone in mainstream society has a cellphone. As such, cellphones are found in very private settings and can be used secretly, silently, and swiftly. Cellphone pornography raises legal issues of consent, privacy, and obscenity. Since pictures of family members bathing or swimming in the backyard in a bathing suit are taken all the time, cellphone porn also asks important legal questions, such as what is pornography, what is a sexualized photo, and what it means to be sexually provocative. Ironically, courts have held that a nude photo of a minor can be legal, and conversely, a fully clothed picture of a minor can be illegal, depending on the context and the circumstances involved. Cellphone text messages, without a picture, are also scrutinized for pornographic content. An adult who texts a lewd message to a minor can be found guilty of distributing indecent material to a minor.

Live sex shows and prostitution-related activity are found around the Internet in various places. Presently, a live sex show and certain types of cyberprostitution are legal on the Internet. It remains undecided by the courts whether a person who pays a fee to gain access to an adult website to watch live-sex show, or directs an Internet performer to masturbate, is engaging in criminal behavior. Because the lack of physical human touching is inherent in Internet activity, the scenario of a Web user paying a fee to direct a "cyberprostitute" to masturbate does not presently constitute an act of prostitution.

Possibly the most popular digital technology ever created, the Internet is used by millions of people who have a computer, those who do not, even by those who are scarcely able to type on a keyboard. Medical information is one of the leading beneficial uses of the Internet, but as we have stressed throughout the chapter, new technology eventually finds a home with crime and the Internet is a good example of that. Dangerous sexual predators have a dark, but relatively safe haven in a virtual world where detection can often be impossible. There is no doubt about the threat of sexually depraved individuals who lurk the digital highways. Fortunately, many options exist for Internet users wary of criminals on the Internet. Strong filters exist, anonymous logins are possible, and the best solution is to avoid talking to strangers on the Internet.

Although a form of danger exists when it comes to sexually aggressive parties on the Internet, the overwhelming majority of sex-related Internet use is legal and probably enjoyed to some degree by Internet users. Nowdays, it is more unlikely that a person has not been on a dating or porn website than someone who has. The scenario of the "dangerous sexual predator" or "pedophile" has been blown out of proportion as society demands police officers do something about this hazily defined Internet phenomenon. The television series "To Catch A Predator" is a good example of the runaway moral panic behind the apprehension of supposed Internet predators.

Since a degree of threat from Internet predators is credible, the police have responded in kind. The Department of Justice provides funding to various states to establish an Internet Crimes Against Children effort where police officers pose undercover on the Internet to arrest and convict predators.[156] This effort, while seemingly reasonable by the standards of traditional police work, exemplifies the generational and cultural gap between traditional law enforcement and contemporary Internet use. Many Internet users seek only to socialize but the law enforcement effort overreacts and perceives only the worse. Many persons have been arrested and convicted for attempted sex with a minor when no such sex would have occurred. Undercover officers bring their own fury and misunderstanding to the cases and have engaged in unlawful entrapment in an effort to justify their crime fighting efforts. Police officers have induced and entrapped lonely, wayward men into relationships with minors when it is highly suspicious that such activity would have ever taken place without the inducement by the officer.[157] The role of appellate courts is to redress mistakes made by the police and lower courts and many appellate courts have dismissed cases where Internet users have been illegally entrapped by local law enforcement.

Key Terms

Digital Technology 00

Sexting 00

Cellphone Pornography 00

PICS 00

Computer Exhibitionism 00

Cyberprostitution 00

Craigslist 00

Privacy 00

Entrapment 00

Solicitation/Enticement 00

Digital Nuisance Abatement 00

Concepts & Principles

Regulating the Internet 00

Teenage Culture 00

Age Verification 00

The Dost Factors 00

Lascivious Exhibition 00

Social Chat 00

Vigilantism 00

Self-Photo 00

Virtual Zoning 00

IIED 00

Posing Undercover 00

Chapter Four Select Court Cases	
Case	**Point of Law**
State v. Canal 00	Sexting found to constitute illegal pornography trade
Davidson v. City of Westminster 00	Digital posting of nude images without consent can constitute a civil injury and the awarding of damages
U.S. v. Fierros-Alvarez 00	Privacy right to stored phone numbers
A.H. v. Florida 00	Nude photo of 17-year-old ruled felony child porn
U.S. v. Dost 00	Legal analysis of digital porn containing minors
U.S. v. Knox 00	Legal acceptability of nude photos of minors
U.S. v. Knox 00	Legal definition of "lascivious exhibition"
California v. Wolin 00	Illegal parameters of private vigilantism
Illinois v. Patterson 00	Digital chat between unrelated adult and minor presumed to be illegal
U.S. v. Poehlman 00	Illegality of police entrapment
Indiana v. Kemp 00	Undercover officer posing as 14-year-old is not a "victim" for purposes of enticement conviction

Questions for Review

1. How has digital technology facilitated sexual deviancy?

2. What makes sexting illegal and subject to criminal prosecution?

3. Why are child pornography laws inapplicable to sexting cases?

4. How can zoning laws apply to pornography websites?

5. Under what circumstances can an image of a fully nude minor be legal?

6. Under what circumstances can an image of a fully clothed minor be illegal?

7. Is cyberprostitution illegal?

8. When does Internet enticement become illegal?

9. How does police entrapment occur with Internet enticement cases?

10. Why is police entrapment illegal?

1 Sorrells v. United States, 287 U.S. 435 (1932, Roberts, J., dissenting)

2 Mitchell, K. J., Finkelhor, D., Jones, L. M., & Wolak, J., *Growth and Change in Undercover Online Child Exploitation Investigations,* 2000–2006, 20 Pol. & Soc. 4, 416–431 (2010).

3 Casey, Eoghan, Digital Evidence and Computer Crime: Forensic Science, Computers, and the Internet (2nd ed., Elsevier/Academic Press) (2004).

4 Alshathry, F., *A Framework to Integrate the Data of Interview Investigation and Digital Evidence.* Proceedings of the Conference on Digital Forensics, Security & Law, 25–32 (2010).

5 Casey, Eoghan, Digital Evidence and Computer Crime: Forensic Science, Computers, and the Internet (2nd ed., Elsevier/Academic Press) (2004).

6 Alshathry, F. (2010). A Framework to Integrate the Data of Interview Investigation and Digital Evidence. *Proceedings of the Conference on Digital Forensics, Security & Law,* 25–32.

7 Hollinger, Richard, & Lonn Lanza-Kaduce, *The Process of Criminalization: The Case of Computer Crime Laws,* 26 Criminology 1, 101–126 (1988).

8 *Id.*

9 Gogolin, Greg, *The Digital Crime Tsunami,* 7.1/2 Digital Investigation 3–8 (2010).

10 *Id.*

11 Drezner, D. W., *Weighing the Scales: The Internet's Effect on State–Society Relations,* 16 Brown Journal of World Affairs 2, 31–44 (2010).

12 *Id.*

13 Marty Rimm, *Marketing Pornography on the Information Superhighway: A Survey of 917,410 Images, Descriptions, Short Stories and Animations Downloaded 8.5 Million Times by Consumers in Over 2000 Cities in Forty Countries, Provinces and Territories,* 83 Geo. L.J. 1923 (1995).

14 Ronald J. Krotoszynski, Jr., *The Inevitable Wasteland: Why the Public Trustee Model of Broadcast Television Regulation Must Fail,* 95 Mich. L. Rev. 2101, 2103, 2105–08 (1997).

15 Anthony E. Varona, *Changing Channels and Bridging Divides: The Failure and Redemption of American Broadcast Television Regulation,* 6 Minn. J.L. Sci. & Tech. 1, 39–40 (2004).

16 Jeff Demas, *Seven Dirty Words: Did They Help Define Indecency?,* Comm & L., 43, (Sept. 1998).

17 FCC v. Pacifica Foundation, 438 U.S. 726 (1978).

18 Matthew J. McDonough, Note, *Moral Rights and the Movies: The Threat and Challenge of the Digital Domain,* 31 Suffolk U. L. Rev. 455, 464 (1997).

19 Douglas C. Sicker, *The End of Federalism in Telecommunications Regulations?* 3 Nw. J. Tech. & Intell. Prop. 130, 133–41 (2005).

20 Uniting and Strengthening America by Providing Appropriate Tools Required to Intercept and Obstruct Terrorism Act, Pub. L. No. 107–56, 115 Stat. 272 (2001) (USA PATRIOT Act, codified in scattered sections of the U.S.C.).

21 Telecommunications Act of 1996, Pub. L. No. 104-104, Title V, §§ 501-561, 110 Stat. 56, 133-43 (1996) (codified at 18 U.S.C. §§ 1462, 1465, 2422 (1996) and as scattered sections of 47 U.S.C.).

22 47 U.S.C. § 231 (2006).

23 Eneman, M., *Internet Service Provider (ISP) Filtering of Child-Abusive Material: A Critical Reflection of its Effectiveness,* 16 J. Sex. Agg. 2, 223–235 (2010).

24 See Children's Internet Protection Act (CIPA), 47 C.F.R. § 54.520 (2007).

25 Desai, Anuj C., *Filters and Federalism: Public Library Internet Access, Local Control, and the Federal Spending Power,* 7 U.Penn. J.Con.L. 3 (2004).

26 See, e.g., Cyber-Rights & Cyber-Liberties (UK) Report, Who Watches the Watchmen: Internet Content Rating Systems, and Privatised Censorship, Nov. 1997, http://www.cyber-rights.org/watchmen.htm (last visited Mar. 2, 2010). The second stage in content control began with the introduction of rating and filtering products that claim to permit users to block unwanted material from their personal systems. The most sophisticated and widely recognized of these systems is the Platform for Internet Content Selection (PICS), introduced by the World Wide Web Consortium.

27 CASEY, EOGHAN, DIGITAL EVIDENCE AND COMPUTER CRIME: FORENSIC SCIENCE, COMPUTERS, AND THE INTERNET (2nd ed., Elsevier/Academic Press) (2004).

28 Jerry Ropelato, INTERNET PORNOGRAPHY STATISTICS. http://internet-filter-review.toptenreviews.com/internet-pornography-statistics. html. Retrieved on June 15, 2010.

29 Susan L. Pollet, *Teens and Sex Offenses: Where Should the Law Draw the Lines?* 242 N.Y.L.J. 4 (2009).

30 The ICAC Task Force Program was created in 1998 to help state and local law enforcement agencies enhance their response to child pornography and enticement offenses on the Internet. The program is administered pursuant to the PROTECT Our Children Act of 2008. This law requires the Department of Justice to create and implement a National Strategy for Child Exploitation Prevention and Interdiction and establishes by statute the Internet Crimes Against Children (ICAC) Task Force Program. The PROTECT Our Children Act of 2008 is codified as 18 U.S.C. §§ 2258A–E; 42 U.S.C. §§ 17601, 17611–16.

31 In 1995, the FBI implemented a program called the Innocent Images Initiative composed of twenty-three task forces in fifty-six FBI field offices around the United States. The purpose of the Initiative is to investigate and eradicate online sexual exploitation of children and the production and distribution of child pornography. Three e-groups, groups of people communicating via the Internet, provided by the Internet service provider Yahoo! Inc., were found to be involved with posting, exchanging, and transmitting child pornography. One website, named "The Candyman," contained a welcome message for its e-group that stated, "This is a group for People who love kids." In March 2002, the Initiative implemented "Operation Candyman," which targeted the Candyman site as well as other similar sites and led to a number of arrests. See Jasmin J. Farhangian, *A Problem of 'Virtual' Proportions: The Difficulties Inherent in Tailoring Virtual Child Pornography Laws to Meet Constitutional Standards,* 12 J.L. & P ᴏʟʏ 241, 280 (2003).

32 Jasmin J. Farhangian, *A Problem of 'Virtual' Proportions: The Difficulties Inherent in Tailoring Virtual Child Pornography Laws to Meet Constitutional Standards,* 12 J.L. & P ᴏʟʏ 241, 280 (2003).

33 Claire Hoffman, Obscene Losses, Condé Nast Portfolio.com, Nov. 2007, http://www.portfolio.com/culture-lifestyle/culture-inc/arts/2007/10/15/YouPorn-Vivid-Entertainment-Profile (last visited Jan. 7, 2008).

34 *Id.*

35 Gorman, S., Monk-Turner, E., & Fish, J. N., Free Adult Internet Web Sites: How Prevalent Are Degrading Acts? 27 GENDER ISSUES 3/4, 131–145 (2010).

36 Osborne v. Ohio, 495 U.S. 103 (1990).

37 National Conference of State Legislatures, 2009 Legislation Related to "Sexting," http://www.ncsl.org/default. aspx?tabid=17756 (lasted visited Mar. 8, 2010); National Conference of State Legislatures, 2010 Legislation Related to "Sexting," http://www.ncsl.org/default.aspx?TabId=19696 (lasted visited March 30, 2010).

38 *Id.*

39 Robert D. Richards & Clay Calvert, *When Sex and Cell Phones Collide: Inside the Prosecution of a Teen Sexting Case,* 32 HASTINGS COMM. & E NT. L. J. 1 (2009).

40 http://en.wikipedia.org/wiki/Sexting. Retrieved July 10, 2010.

41 State v. Canal, 773 N.W.2d 528 (2009).

42 VT. S TAT. ANN. 13 § 2802b (2009).

43 State v. Canal, 773 N.W.2d 528 (2009).

44 *Id.* at 530.

45 *Id.* at 536.

46 *Id.*

47 Christensen v. Superior Court, 820 P.2d 181, 202 (Cal. 1991) (quoting Davidson v. City of Westminster, 32 Cal.3d 197, 209 (1982)) (setting forth the four elements of the tort of IIED as recognized in California).

48 Kircher, John J., *The Four Faces of Tort Law: Liability for Emotional Harm,* 90 Marq. L. R ev. 789, 806 (2007) (writing that "[a]ll states have recognized intentional infliction of emotional distress as an independent tort and have adopted Restatement (Second) of Torts section 46 in some form").

49 Calvert, Clay, *Sex, Cell Phones, Privacy, and the First Amendment: When Children Become Child Pornographers and the Lolita Effect Undermines the Law,* 18 Catholic University of America, Communications Conspectus 1 (2009).

50 Second Restatement of Torts, Section 46 (1965).

51 Davidson v. City of Westminster, 649 P.2d 894 (1982).

52 *Id.* at 917.

53 Smith v. Maryland, 442 U.S. 735 (1979).

54 Chimel v. California, 395 U.S. 752 (1969).

55 U.S. v. Fierros-Alvarez, 547 F.Supp.2d 1206 (2008).

56 Miller v. Skumanick, 605 F.Supp.2d 634 (2009).

57 Amanda Lenhart, Pew Internet & American Life Project, Teens and Mobile Phones Over the Past Five Years: Pew Internet Looks Back 3 (2009), http://www.pewinternet.org/<diff>/media//Files/Reports/2009/PIP %20Teens%20and%20Mobile%20 Phones%20Data%20Memo.pdf.

58 Ga. Code Ann. § 16-12-100.1 (1993).

59 Fla. Stat. Ann. § 827.071(3) (2005).

60 Amy Adler, *The Perverse Law of Child Pornography,* 101 Colum. L. R ev. 209 (2001).

61 Ga. Code Ann. § 16-12-100(b)(1) (2010).

62 Ga. Code Ann. § 16-12-100(b)(1) (2010). Fla. Stat. Ann. § 827.071(3) (2005).

63 LaRoy, Anna K., *Discovering Child Pornography: The Death of the Presumption of Innocence,* 6 Ave Mar. L. R ev. 559 (2008).

64 Shaw, Andrea Shepard, Casenote: *Constitutional Law—Freedom of Speech—Federal Ban on Pandering of Child Pornography Does Not Infringe Upon First Amendment Rights. United States v. Williams,* 128 S. Ct. 1830 (2008), 39 Cumberl. L. R ev. 581 (2008/2009).

65 Mich. Stat. Ann. § 750.145c(m) (2010).

66 Fla. Stat. Ann. § 827.071(3) (2005).

67 A.H. v. Florida, 949 So.2d 234 (2007).

68 Kimpel, Amy H., *Using Laws Designed to Protect as a Weapon: Prosecuting Minors Under Child Pornography Laws,* 34 N.Y.U. Rev. of L. & S oc. Ch. 299 (2010).

69 A.H. v. Florida, 949 So.2d 234, 245 (2007).

70 New York v. Ferber, 458 U.S. 747 (1982).

71 Osborne v. Ohio, 495 U.S. 103 (1990).

72 18 U.S.C. § 2255(2)(E) (1986).

73 U.S. v. Dost, 636 F.Supp. 828 (S.D. Cal. 1986).

74 *Id.*

75 *Id.* at 835.

76 *Id.* at 837.

77 U.S. v. Knox, 32 F.3d 733 (3d Cir. 1994).

[78] U.S. v. Dost, 636 F.Supp. 828 (S.D. Cal. 1986).

[79] U.S. v. Villard, 885 F.2d 117 (3d Cir. 1989).

[80] *Id.*

[81] *Id.* at 123.

[82] *Id.* at 127.

[83] *Id.* at 133.

[84] U.S. v. Knox, 32 F.3d 733 (3d Cir. 1994).

[85] Green, Matthew, *Sex on the Internet: A Legal Click or an Illicit Trick?* 38 Cal. West. L. Rev. 527 (2002).

[86] Raymond McCaffrey, Sex Sells: Millions Engage in Cybersex, The Colo. Springs Gazette Telegraph, Mar. 30, 1999, at A1.

[87] Green, Matthew, *Sex on the Internet: A Legal Click or an Illicit Trick?* 38 Cal. West. L. Rev. 527 (2002).

[88] Cal. Stat. § 314-318.6 (2009).

[89] Ariz. Rev. Stat. § 13-3201 (1998).

[90] N.Y. Laws § 230.00 (2001).

[91] Barnes v. Glen Theatre, Inc., 501 U.S. 560 (1991).

[92] Miller v. California, 413 U.S. 15 (1973).

[93] James Nahikian, Comment, *Learning to Love 'The Ultimate Peripheral'—Virtual Vices Like 'Cyberprostitution' Suggest a New Paradigm to Regulate Online Expression,* 14 J. Marshall J. Computer & Info. L. 779, 802 (1996).

[94] *Id.* at 387.

[95] Raymond McCaffrey, Sex Sells: Millions Engage in Cybersex, The Colo. Springs Gazette Telegraph, Mar. 30, 1999, at A1.

[96] Green, Matthew, *Sex on the Internet: A Legal Click or an Illicit Trick?* 38 Cal. West. L. Rev. 527 (2002).

[97] *Id.* at 541.

[98] Butler v. Michigan, 352 U.S. 380, 383 (1957). In Butler, the Court struck down a Michigan statute that prohibited making books that would be harmful to minors available to the general public. The Court found that the "legislation was not reasonably restricted to the evil with which it is said to deal."

[99] Casswell, Bryan-Low, Dangerous Mix: Internet Transforms Child Porn Into Lucrative Criminal Trade, The Wall St. J., Jan. 17, 2006 ("Child pornography web sites draw 'people who had never dreamed of indulging in the fantasy' by giving them the perception of anonymity.").

[100] Daniel Orr and Josephine Ferrigno Stack, *Childproofing on the World Wide Web: A Survey of Adult Webservers,* 41 Jurimetrics 465-75 (2001).

[101] Bryant Paul et al., *Government Regulation of Adult Businesses through Zoning and Anti-Nudity Ordinances: Debunking the Legal Myth of Secondary Effects,* 6 Comm. L. & Pol'y. 355, 256 (2001).

[102] *Id.*

[103] Stephanie Lasker, Comment, *Sex and the City: Zoning 'Pornography Peddlers and Live Nude Shows,'* 49 U.C.L.A. L. Rev. 1139, 1170 (2002).

[104] Declan McCullagh, House Bans "Morphed" Child Pornography, Cnet News.com, at http://news.com.com/2100-1023_3-939407.html (last visited Nov. 15, 2003).

[105] Doug Rendleman, *Civilizing Pornography: The Case for an Exclusive Obscenity Nuisance Statute,* 44 U. Chi. L. Rev. 509, 527-60 (1977).

[106] *Id.*

107 Am. Elec. Power Co., 582 F.3d at 328 (using the Restatement's definition of public nuisance even though "[i]t is true that the Restatement's definition of public nuisance—'an unreasonable interference with a right common to the general public'—is broad.").

108 Cal. Stat. § 3479 (West 1997).

109 Dart v. Craigslist, Inc., No. 09 C 1385, 2009 U.S. Dist. LEXIS 97596, at 12-28 (N.D. Ill. Oct. 20, 2009).

110 City of New York v. Smokes-Spirits.com, Inc., 911 N.E.2d 834 (N.Y. Ct. App. 2009)

111 *Id.*

112 James Nahikian, Comment, *Learning to Love 'The Ultimate Peripheral'—Virtual Vices Like 'Cyberprostitution' Suggest a New Paradigm to Regulate Online Expression,* 14 J. Marshall J. Computer & Info. L. 779, 802 (1996).

113 *Id.*

114 People v. Greene, 441 N.Y.S.2d 636 (1981).

115 *Id.*

116 *Id.*

117 Voyeur Dorm, L.C. v. City of Tampa, FL, 121 F. Supp. 2d 1373 (M.D. Fla. 2000).

118 M. Megan McCune, Comment, *Virtual Lollipops and Lost Puppies: How Far Can States Go to Protect Minors Through the Use of Internet Luring Laws,* 14 Commlaw Conspectus 503, 512–13 (2006).

119 Dru Stevenson, *Entrapment by Numbers,* 16 U. Fla. J.L. & Pub. Pol'y. 1, 67 (2005).

120 Ducat, L., Thomas, S., & Blood, W., *Sensationalising Sex Offenders and Sexual Recidivism: Impact of the Serious Sex Offender Monitoring Act 2005 on Media Reportage,* 44 Australian Psychologist 3, 156–165 (2009).

121 Dru Stevenson, *Entrapment by Numbers,* 16 U. Fla. J.L. & Pub. Pol'y. 1, 67 (2005).

122 18 U.S.C. § 2422(b) (2001). Section 2422(b) of Title 18 provides that if the individual who has been persuaded, induced, enticed, or coerced to engage in prostitution or other criminal sexual act is under the age of 18, then the penalty is 15 years imprisonment and/or a fine.

123 Internet Crimes Against Children Task Force Program, operated by the Department of Justice's Office of Juvenile Justice and Delinquency Prevention, at http://ojjdp.ncjrs.org/programs/ProgSummary.asp?pi=3.

124 See Information on "Operation Predator" program operated by the U.S. Immigration and Customs Enforcement division of the Department of Homeland Security, at http://www.ice.gov/graphics/predator/index.htm.

125 Douglas McCollam, The Shame Game, Columbia Journalism Review, Jan./Feb. 2007, http://cjrarchives.org/issues/2007/1/McCollam.asp.

126 18 U.S.C. § 2422 (2001).

127 Stanger, Julie Sorenson, *Salvaging States' Rights to Protect Children from Internet Predation: State Power to Regulate Internet Activity Under the Dormant Commerce Clause,* 2005 BYU L. Rev. 191 (2005).

128 Wis. Stat. Ann. § 948.075 (2004).

129 Douglas Lee, NBC 'Predator' Lawsuit: Journalism on Trial, First Amendment Center, March 4, 2008, http://www.firstamendmentcenter.org/commentary.aspx?id=19753.

130 Perverted Justice Convictions, http://www.perverted-justice.com/?con=full (last visited Feb. 17, 2009) (containing the full archives of convictions resulting from Perverted-Justice's online chats).

131 Marcus Baram, Turning the Tables on 'To Catch a Predator': Fired Producer Marsha Bartel Sues NBC for $1 Million, Claims Show Goes Too Far, ABC News, June 5, 2007, http://abcnews.go.com/US/Story?id=3235975&page=1.

132 Winters, Chris P., *Cultivating a Relationship That Works: Cyber-Vigilantism and the Public Versus Private Inquiry of Cyber-Predator Stings,* 57 Kan. L. Rev. 427 (2009).

133 John Simerman, TV Show on Trial along with Suspect, Contra Costa Times, Aug. 4, 2007, at A1.

[134] *Id.*

[135] Illinois v. Patterson, 734 N.E.2d 462 (2000).

[136] *Id.*

[137] *Id.* at 471.

[138] Paul H. Robinson, *Criminal Law Defenses: A Systematic Analysis,* 82 Colum. L. Rev. 199 (1982)

[139] *Id.*

[140] Dru Stevenson, *Entrapment and the Problem of Deterring Police Misconduct,* 37 Conn. L. Rev. 67, 97 (2004).

[141] *Id.*

[142] Senjo, Scott, Book Review, Criminal Justice Studies: A Critical Journal of Crime, Law and Society, Vol. 22, No. 1, 103–106 (reviewing Child Pornography: Crime, Computers, and Society by Ian O'Donnell and Claire Milner, 2007 (2009).

[143] U.S. v. Poehlman, 217 F.3d 692 (2000). Appellant's Excerpt of Record at Tab 5 (July 31, 1995).

[144] *Id.*

[145] *Id.* at 696.

[146] *Id.* at 697.

[147] *Id.* at 699.

[148] *Id.* at 700.

[149] Since the case was dismissed under the entrapment challenge, the issue of double jeopardy was not addressed.

[150] U.S. v. Poehlman, 217 F.3d 692, 700 (2000).

[151] *Id.*

[152] Indiana v. Kemp, 753 N.E.2d 47 (2001).

[153] Child Online Protection Act, 47 U.S.C. § 231 (1998). Communications Decency Act, 47 U.S.C. § 230 (1996).

[154] Children's Internet Protection Act (CIPA), 47 C.F.R. § 54.520 (2007).

[155] Calvert, Clay, *Sex, Cell Phones, Privacy, and the First Amendment: When Children Become Child Pornographers and the Lolita Effect Undermines the Law,* 18 Catholic University of America, Communications Conspectus 1 (2009).

[156] Internet Crimes Against Children Task Force Program, operated by the Department of Justice's Office of Juvenile Justice and Delinquency Prevention, at http://ojjdp.ncjrs.org/programs/ProgSummary.asp?pi=3.

[157] Dru Stevenson, *Entrapment and the Problem of Deterring Police Misconduct,* 37 Conn. L. Rev. 67, 97 (2004).